¡ARRIBA!

THE HEROIC LIFE OF ROBERTO CLEMENTE

EDITED BY

BILL NOWLIN AND GLEN SPARKS

ASSOCIATE EDITORS

LEN LEVIN AND CARL RIECHERS

SPANISH LANGUAGE EDITION TRANSLATED BY

TONY S. OLIVER DIAZ

Society for American Baseball Research, Inc.
Phoenix, AZ

"¡Arriba!": The Heroic Life of Roberto Clemente

Edited by Bill Nowlin and Glen Sparks
Associate editors Len Levin and Carl Riechers

Front cover design: The Clemente Museum / Rob Larson
Cover photograph: Les Banos
Design: David Peng

ISBN 978-1-970159-87-5 ebook
ISBN 978-1-970159-88-2 paperback
Library of Congress Control Number: 2022916985

Cronkite School at ASU
555 N. Central Ave. #416
Phoenix, AZ 85004
Phone: (602) 496-1460
Web: www.sabr.org
Facebook: Society for American Baseball Research
Twitter: @SABR

"The Great One," at PNC Park. Photograph courtesy of Michael Kane.

Photograph by Duane Rieder.

TABLE OF CONTENTS

Les Banos photograph courtesy of The Clemente Museum.

ROBERTO CLEMENTE

BY STEW THORNLEY

Roberto Clemente's greatness transcended the diamond. On it, he was electrifying with his penchant for bad-ball hitting, his strong throwing arm from right field, and the way he played with a reckless but controlled abandon. Off it, he was a role model to the people of his homeland and elsewhere. Helping others represented the way Clemente lived. It would also represent the way he died.

Jackie Robinson's breaking of the color barrier opened the way not just for African Americans in organized baseball but to many others whose skin color had excluded them. By the 1960s Clemente had emerged as one of the best of the players from Latin America.

Clemente came from Puerto Rico, which had established its own baseball history extending back to the late 1800s, at about the same time that the island became a possession of the United States.[1] Puerto Rico shares its love of baseball with many of the countries in and along the Caribbean Sea. Professional leagues formed and thrived in the winter in these areas, including Venezuela, Mexico, and the Dominican Republic.

Puerto Rico has produced many great players, such as Pedro "Perucho" Cepeda – because he was black, Perucho never got to play in the major leagues in the United States. His son Orlando did and eventually made the Hall of Fame.

The greatest Puerto Rican player, however, was Roberto Clemente.

Roberto Clemente Walker was born on August 18, 1934, to Melchor Clemente and Luisa Walker de Clemente in Carolina, which is slightly east of the Puerto Rican capital of San Juan. Roberto was the youngest of Luisa's seven children (three of whom were from a previous marriage).[2]

Melchor was a foreman overseeing sugar-cane cutters. He also used his truck to help a construction company deliver sand and gravel to building sites. Luisa was a laundress and worked in different jobs to assist the workers at the sugar-cane plantation. Roberto contributed to the family income by helping his dad load shovels into the construction trucks. He also earned money by doing various jobs for neighbors, such as carrying milk to the country store. Roberto used his money to buy a bike and to purchase rubber balls. He liked to squeeze the balls to strengthen his hands.[3] Many people commented on the size of young man's hands. He had strong hands, and it was clear at an early age that he had athletic ability.

Roberto had not just ability but a deep love of sports, especially baseball. He attended games in the winter and watched the star players from the United States mainland. One of his favorites was **Monte Irvin**. Irvin played for the Newark Eagles in the Negro National League in the summer and for the San Juan Senadores of the Puerto Rican League in the winter. Irvin remembers kids hanging around the stadium. "We'd give them our bags so they could take them in and get in for free," he said. Irvin didn't know Clemente was among the kids until Clemente told him years later, when both were in the major leagues. Clemente also told Irvin that he was impressed with his throwing arm. "I had the best arm in Puerto Rico," said Irvin. "He loved to see me throw. He found that he would practice and learn how to throw like I did."[4] Roberto began playing baseball himself. He wrote in his journal, "I loved the game so much that even though our playing field was muddy and we had many trees on it, I used to play many hours every day. The fences were about 150 feet away from home plate, and I used to hit many homers. One day I hit ten home runs in a game we started about 11 a.m. and finished about 6:30 p.m."[5]

When he was 14 years old Roberto joined a softball team organized by Roberto Marín, who became very influential in Clemente's life. Marín noticed Roberto's strong throwing arm and began using him at shortstop. He eventually moved him to the outfield. Regardless of the position he played, Roberto was sensational. "His name became known for his long hits to right field, and for his sensational catches," said Marín. "Everyone had their eyes on him."[6]

Roberto also participated in the high jump and javelin throw at Vizcarrondo High School in Carolina.[7] It was thought that he might even be good enough to represent Puerto Rico in the Olympics. Throwing the javelin strengthened his arm and helped him in other ways, according to one of his biographers, Bruce Markusen: "The footwork, release, and general dynamics employed in throwing the javelin coincided with the skills needed to throw a baseball properly. The more that Clemente threw the javelin, the better and stronger his throwing from the outfield became."[8]

Roberto said that throwing the javelin in high school was only part of the reason he developed a strong arm. "My mother has the same kind of an arm, even today at 74," in said in a 1964 interview. "She could throw a ball from second base to home plate with something on it. I got my arm from my mother."[9]

Although he had great all-around athletic ability, Roberto decided to focus on baseball, even though it meant forgoing any dreams of participating in the Olympics. He began playing for a strong amateur team, the Juncos Mules.

In 1952, Clemente took part in a tryout camp in Puerto Rico that was attended by scout **Al Campanis** of the Brooklyn Dodgers. Clemente impressed Campanis with his different skills, including his speed. The Dodgers did not sign Clemente then, but Campanis kept him in mind.

Also in 1952, Clemente caught the eye of Pedrín Zorrilla, who owned the Santurce Cangrejeros, or Crabbers, of the Puerto Rican League. The Juncos team was to play the Manatí Athenians in Manatí, where Zorrilla had a house on the beach. Roberto Marín advised Zorrilla to go to the game. Afterward, Zorrilla offered Clemente a contract to play with the Cangrejeros.

Clemente was barely 18 years old when he joined the Cangrejeros. As a young and developing player, he was brought along slowly by the team's manager, **Buzz Clarkson**. Clarkson had had an outstanding career in the Negro Leagues in the

United States and played many winters in Puerto Rico. Like many great black players, Clarkson's best years were behind him by the time he got his chance to play in the majors in 1952 at the age of 37. Two other such players were **Willard "Ese Hombre" Brown** and **Bob Thurman**, who were top hitters in the Negro Leagues. Both were outfielders (with Thurman also doing some pitching) on the Santurce team that Clemente joined in the winter of 1952-53.

"Clemente looked up to Bob Thurman," wrote Thomas Van Hyning. "Clemente pinch-hit for Thurman in a key situation and doubled off Caguas's Roberto Vargas to win the game, earning congratulations from Thurman."[10] Despite the big hit, Clemente did not play much his first winter in the Puerto Rican League.

He began playing more in 1953-54 and even played in the league's All-Star Game. (The star of the All-Star Game was **Henry Aaron** of the Caguas Criollos, who had four hits, including two home runs, and drove in five runs.) By midseason, Clemente's name was appearing along with Aaron's in the list of the Puerto Rican league leaders in batting average. Clemente finished the season with a .288 batting average, sixth best in the league.

The Brooklyn Dodgers had remembered Clemente from the tryout he had had in front of Al Campanis in 1952.[11] **Buzzie Bavasi**, the Dodgers' vice president, said that during the 1953-54 season a scout in Puerto Rico told him the Dodgers could sign Clemente.[12] Other major-league teams had noticed Clemente, too. One was the New York Giants, the Dodgers' great rivals. Brooklyn outbid the Giants and Clemente agreed to sign. The Milwaukee Braves also made an offer, one that was reportedly much more than the Dodgers', but Clemente stuck with his decision.[13] He knew that New York City had a large Puerto Rican population and looked forward to playing there.

On February 19, 1954, Clemente signed a contract with the Dodgers, who had to make a decision on what to do with him. The Dodgers had signed him for a reported salary of $5,000 as well as a bonus of $10,000.[14] Rules of the time required a team signing a player for a bonus and salary of more than $4,000 to keep him on the major league roster for two years or risk losing him in the offseason draft.[15] Many bonus players of this period were kept at the major-league level, pining on the bench for two years rather than developing in the minors. The Dodgers chose to have Clemente spend the 1954 season with the Montreal Royals in the International League, even though it meant they might lose him at the end of the season.

Buzzie Bavasi had the power to determine Clemente's fate. In 1955, Bavasi told Pittsburgh writer Les Biederman that the Dodgers' only purpose in signing Clemente was to keep him away from the Giants, even though they knew they would eventually lose him to another team.[16] Some writers said an informal quota system was in effect in the early years following the breaking of baseball's color barrier, but this is not supported by the facts.[17] In his biography of Clemente, Kal Wagenheim wrote that the Dodgers would never start all five of their black players in the same game. The box scores prove that is false. (There are other reasons to question the existence of a quota, although it is beyond the realm of this article to fully explore the issue.)[18]

In a 2005 e-mail message to the author, Bavasi wrote that while there was no quota system, race was the factor in the club's decision to have Clemente play in Montreal: "The concern had nothing to do with quotas, but the thought was too many minorities might be a problem with the white players. Not so, I said. Winning was the important thing. I agree with the [Dodgers'] board that we should get a player's opinion and I would be guided by the player's opinion. The board called in Jackie Robinson. Hell, now I felt great. Jackie was told the problem and after thinking about it awhile, he asked me who would be sent out if

Clemente took one of the spots. I said **George Shuba**. Jackie agreed that Shuba would be the one to go. Then he said Shuba was not among the best players on the club, but he was the most popular. With that he shocked me by saying, and I quote: 'If I were the GM, I would not bring Clemente to the club and send Shuba or any other white player down. If I did this, I would be setting our program back five years.'"[19]

So Clemente went to Montreal to play for manager **Max Macon**. Most accounts say the Dodgers were trying to "hide" Clemente in Montreal by playing him rarely, hoping that other teams wouldn't notice him and wouldn't draft him at the end of the season.

Several biographers, among them Phil Musick, Kal Wagenheim, and Bruce Markusen, provide examples to back up the contention that Clemente was hidden. However, a game-by-game check of Montreal's 1954 season indicates that many of the examples are incorrect.[20]

Wagenheim and Markusen go so far as to claim that Clemente did not play in the Royals' final 25 games of the season, another claim that is not correct. In fact, by the final part of the season, Clemente was playing regularly against left-handed starting pitchers.[21]

Montreal manager Max Macon, until his death in 1989, denied that he was under any orders to restrict Clemente's playing time. "The only orders I had were to win and draw big crowds," Macon said.[22]

It is true that Clemente, after an initial period when he was being platooned over the first 13 games of the season, played little over the first three months of the season. This was hardly unusual for a 19-year-old in his first season of organized baseball.

Also, for much of the year, the Royals had a full crop of reliable outfielders in **Dick Whitman**, **Gino Cimoli**, and **Jack Cassini**. In addition, the Dodgers sent **Sandy Amoros** down to Montreal early in the season, and Amoros hit well enough

for the Royals that he was recalled by Brooklyn in July. The crowded outfield situation didn't leave a lot of playing time for a newcomer like Clemente. He was often used as a late-inning defensive replacement for Cassini.

When he did play, he struggled. In early July his batting average was barely over .200. Part of that may be attributed to his infrequent playing time; it's hard for a batter to get in a groove and hit well when he doesn't play regularly. On the other hand, it's hard for a player to get regular playing time if he's not hitting well.

Macon said he didn't use Clemente much because he "swung wildly," especially at pitches that were outside of the strike zone: "If you had been in Montreal that year, you wouldn't have believed how ridiculous some pitchers made him look."[23] Clemente got more chances against left-handed pitchers. Macon was known for platooning, and Clemente often split time in the lineup with Whitman, a left-handed hitter.

Through June and July Clemente often went long stretches without seeing any action. Then, on July 25, he entered the first game of a doubleheader against the Havana Sugar Kings in the ninth inning. The game was tied and went into extra innings. With one out in the last of the 10th, Clemente hit a home run to win it for the Royals.

Macon rewarded him by starting him in the second game of the doubleheader, Clemente's first start in nearly three weeks. For the rest of the season Clemente started every game in which the opposition started a left-handed pitcher. He had a few more highlights during this time. Near the end of July, he came to bat in the top of the ninth inning of a scoreless game in Toronto. Clemente doubled and went on to score to put Montreal ahead. The Royals won the game, 2-0.

The next time the Royals were in Toronto, three weeks later, Clemente helped them win in a different way. Montreal had an 8-7 lead over the Maple Leafs in the bottom of the ninth. Toronto had a chance to tie the score, but Clemente threw out a runner at home plate to end the game.

Late in August he had two triples and a single at Richmond, although the Royals still lost the game. A week later he hit a home run to win the game for Montreal and give the Royals a sweep of a doubleheader against Syracuse.

Teammate Jack Cassini said, "You knew he was going to play in the big leagues. He had a great arm and he could run."[24] When Clemente began playing regularly against left-handers, the Royals rose in the standings and finished in second place. Clemente batted .257 in 87 games in his only season in the minors.

By the end of the 1954 season, it had become clear to Bavasi and the rest of the Brooklyn organization that other teams were interested in Clemente. However, Bavasi said he still wasn't ready to give up. The Pirates, by having the worst record in the majors in 1954, had the first pick in the November draft. If Bavasi could get the Pirates to draft a different player off the Montreal roster, Clemente would remain with the Dodgers organization. Each minor-league team could lose only one player.

Bavasi said he went to **Branch Rickey**, who had run the Dodgers before going to Pittsburgh. After Bavasi declined Rickey's offer to join him in Pittsburgh, Bavasi said, Rickey told him that, "Should I need help at anytime, all I had to do was pick up the phone." Bavasi said he used this offer to get Rickey to agree draft a different player, pitcher **John Rutherford**, off the Royals' roster. However, Bavasi was dismayed to learn two days later that the deal was off and that the Pirates were going to draft Clemente. "It seemed that [Dodgers owner] **Walter O'Malley** and Mr. Rickey got in another argument and it seems Walter called Mr. Rickey every name in the book," explained Bavasi. "Thus, we lost Roberto."[25]

When he was drafted by Pittsburgh, Clemente was in Puerto Rico playing for the Santurce Cangrejeros and on his way to his best-ever winter season. He again played with Bob Thurman, but the Santurce outfield had a new addition in 1954-55. It was **Willie Mays**, who had just led the New York Giants to the World Series championship and was named the National League's Most Valuable Player. An outfield of Clemente, Mays, and Thurman ranks as one of the best ever in the Puerto Rican League. By mid-season Santurce manager Herman Franks was calling Clemente "the best player in the league, except for Willie Mays."[26]

Clemente and Mays had been providing some real highlights. In late November, the Cangrejeros were behind by a run going into the ninth inning of a game against Caguas-Guayama. Clemente led off the ninth with a single, and Mays then hit a two-run homer to give Santurce a 7-6 win. Not long after that, the pair starred in another 7-6 win. Mays hit two home runs and Clemente one home run in an 11-inning win over Mayaguez.

Both players homered in the league's All-Star Game on December 12, leading their North team to a 7-5 win. By this time, Mays, Clemente, and Thurman were the top three players in the league in batting average, and Santurce moved into first place.[27]

While things were going well on the baseball diamond, there were other problems for Clemente. On New Year's Eve of 1954, one of his brothers, Luis, died of a brain tumor. Shortly before that, Clemente had been in a car accident that damaged some of his spinal discs. The back injury hampered him for the rest of his baseball career.[28]

Back on the field, Santurce finished first in the Puerto Rican League. The top three teams advanced to the playoffs, so the Cangrejeros had to win another series to capture the league title. They did that, defeating Caguas-Guayama four games to one. Clemente had four hits, including two doubles, and drove in four runs in the first game of the series, which Santurce won. Caguas-Guayama won the next game, but the Cangrejeros then won three in a row to finish the series. As

Les Banos photograph courtesy of The Clemente Museum.

champions of the Puerto Rican League, they advanced to the Caribbean Series.

The Caribbean Series was played in Caracas, Venezuela, in February of 1955. In addition to Santurce, teams from Cuba, Panama, and Venezuela participated. It was a double round-robin tournament. The team with the best record at the end would be the champion.

The Cangrejeros won their first two games and then faced Magallanes of Venezuela. The game went into extra innings. Clemente singled to open the last of the 11th inning, and Mays followed with a home run to win the game, 4-2.

One more win would clinch at least a tie for the title for Santurce. The Cangrejeros' fourth game was a rematch against Almendares of Cuba, a team they had defeated in their first game. Almendares opened up a 5-0 lead, but Santurce battled back to win. Clemente drove in two runs to help in the comeback.

Santurce played Carta Vieja of Panama with a chance for the championship. Clemente had a triple as the Cangrejeros scored three times in the top of the first. In the third, Clemente had another triple as Santurce scored four runs to take a 7-0 lead. Santurce won the game, 11-3, to wrap up the championship.

It was the second Caribbean Series title for Santurce in three years. Clemente had been a part of the team that had won the championship in 1953, but he did not play in the series. This time he was a key member of the team that won. Santurce shortstop **Don Zimmer**, who was voted the Most Valuable Player of the Caribbean Series, said, "It might have been the best winter club ever assembled."[29]

Soon afterward, Clemente was in training camp with the Pittsburgh Pirates, hoping to earn a spot in the major leagues. The Pirates had been keeping an eye on Clemente over the winter. Rickey said, "He can run, throw, and hit. He needs much polishing, though, because he is a rough diamond."[30]

The Pirates were loaded with outfielders when they began spring training in Florida in March of 1955. Clemente would have plenty of competition for a spot on the team. After the first week of training camp, Clemente earned some good words from Pirates manager **Fred Haney**. "The boy has the tools, there's no doubt about that. And he takes to instruction readily. Certainly I have been pleased with what I have seen," Haney said. "He has some faults, which were expected, but let's wait and see."[31]

Clemente's chances were helped when **Frank Thomas**, the Pirates' best outfielder, held out for more money and missed the first part of spring training. Thomas then got sick and missed more time. Clemente took advantage of this opportunity and made the team.[32]

Clemente's original number with the Pirates was 13, but early in the season he switched to 21, a number that became strongly associated with him. It is reported that Clemente chose the number because his full name, Roberto Clemente Walker, has 21 letters.[33]

Clemente didn't play in the first three regular season games. However, he was in the starting lineup, playing right field, for the first game of a doubleheader on Sunday, April 17, 1955, against the Brooklyn Dodgers at **Forbes Field** in Pittsburgh. Clemente came to the plate with two out in the bottom of the first inning for his first at-bat in the major leagues. He hit a ground ball toward the shortstop, **Pee Wee Reese**. Reese got his glove on the grounder, but he couldn't field it cleanly. Clemente had his first hit. He followed that by scoring his first run to give Pittsburgh a 1-0 lead. However, Brooklyn came back to win the game.

Clemente started the second game of the doubleheader, this time in center field and batting leadoff. He had a double, but the Pirates were unable to score and trailed the Dodgers, 3-0, going into the last of the eighth. Clemente got another hit, a single, as part of a two-run rally that closed the gap, but the Pirates still lost.

In Pittsburgh's next game, in New York against the Giants, Clemente hit an inside-the-park homer, but the Pirates lost again. At this point, their won-lost record was 0-6. Pittsburgh lost two more games before winning its first of the season. The Pirates went on to finish in last place in the National League for the fourth year in a row. However, Branch Rickey insisted that young players such as Clemente would help turn the team around.

Early in the 1955 season, the new players were leading the Pirates' offense. Clemente was leading the team in batting average over the first three weeks. On the base paths he was even more exciting. "When he starts moving around the bases he draws the 'Ohs' and 'Ahs' of the folks in the ball park," wrote Jack Hernon in *The Sporting News*.

Hernon added, "The fleet Puerto Rican was a stickout in the field."[34] Forbes Field, the home of the Pirates, was a classic ball park that had opened in 1909. The outfield fence was a brick wall. It was only 300 feet from home plate to the wall down the right-field line. But the wall jutted out and changed directions. Clemente learned the angles and how to play balls that caromed off the fence. He could corral long hits quickly and, with his great arm, opposing baserunners were careful on trying to take an extra base.

Less than a third of the way through the season, Clemente already had 10 assists, and he also made some outstanding catches. "The Pittsburgh fans have fallen in love with his spectacular fielding and his deadly right arm," wrote Les Biederman, a reporter who covered the Pirates.[35]

Clemente's rambunctious style in the field could be costly, though. In May, he made a nice catch in St. Louis, but he hurt his finger and ran into the wall. The injury caused him to miss a few games.

Clemente's hitting slumped as the season went along, in part because he still had trouble laying off pitches that were out of the strike zone. However, he became known as a good "bad-ball hitter," able to make good contact on bad pitches. Jack Cassini, who had played in the minors with Clemente the year before, said, "He could hit. He didn't need a strike. The best way to pitch him was right down the middle of the plate."[36]

Clemente played 124 games for the Pirates in 1955 and had a batting average of .255. He walked only 18 times. Drawing bases on balls would never become a strong point for him. While it wasn't a sensational rookie season, Clemente had earned a spot in the Pirates' outfield. More than that, his exciting style of play made the fans look forward to seeing more of him.

Clemente returned to Puerto Rico in the fall of 1955. It had been reported that he might not play winter ball in his homeland and instead would begin college and study engineering.[37] However, Clemente ended up back on the diamond, playing another season for Santurce.

Back on the mainland in 1956, Clemente had a new boss in Pittsburgh. **Bobby Bragan** had taken over as manager from Fred Haney. Bragan appeared to be well-liked by the players, although he quickly demonstrated his strictness. In the second game of the season, Clemente missed a signal for a bunt and Bragan fined him.[38] He also fined another player, **Dale Long**. Biographer Kal Wagenheim wrote, "This harsh action worked like a shot of adrenalin. The club was soon fighting for first place in the league. Dale Long hit eight home runs in as many games. Clemente moved his batting average up to .348, fourth best in the league."[39]

The Pirates were in first place in mid-June, but an eight-game losing streak dropped them to fifth and ended their pennant hopes. Even so, they avoided last place for the first time since 1951 and they were showcasing one of the major league's most exciting players. In the outfield, Clemente had 17 assists, a sign of his strong throwing arm. At the plate, his .311 batting average was third-best in the National League. Two of his biggest hits were game-winning home runs. On Saturday,

July 21, the Pirates trailed the Reds, 3-1, in the top of the ninth but had two runners on base as Clemente came to the plate. The Cincinnati pitcher was **Brooks Lawrence**, who had already won 13 games that season and hadn't yet lost. Clemente changed that, hitting a three-run homer, to give the Pirates a 4-3 win and spoil Lawrence's perfect record.

The following Wednesday, the Pirates were at home, playing the Chicago Cubs. Chicago led, 8-5, but Pittsburgh loaded the bases with no out. With Clemente due up, the Cubs brought in a new pitcher, **Jim Brosnan**. On Brosnan's first pitch, Clemente hit a long drive to left-center field. **Hank Foiles**, **Bill Virdon**, and **Dick Cole** raced around the bases toward home plate with the runs that would tie the game. Clemente also tore around the diamond. Manager Bobby Bragan was coaching at third base and held up his arms, giving Clemente the signal to stop at third. With no one out and good hitters coming up, Bragan figured they'd still get Clemente home with the winning run and didn't want to take the chance on him being thrown out at the plate. However, Clemente ignored his manager, kept running, and was safe at home. The inside-the-park grand-slam home run won the game for the Pirates.[40]

Bragan, who had fined Clemente earlier in the season for missing a sign, wasn't happy about Clemente deliberately disobeying this one. However, he decided not to fine him.[41]

Clemente's hits were the usual way for him to reach base because he rarely walked. He drew only 13 bases on balls in 1956, and at one point went 51 games without walking.[42] Branch Rickey wasn't concerned: "His value is in not taking bases on balls because he can hit the bad pitches. If I tried to teach him to wait for a good pitch, I'd simply make a bad hitter out of him. The cure would be worse than the disease. He'll cure his own ailments simply by experience."[43]

At the end of the season, Clemente headed home to play another season for Santurce in the Puerto Rican League. However, a couple of significant events took place between Christmas and New Year's Day. First, Santurce owner Pedrín Zorrilla sold the team. A few days later, the new owner of the Cangrejeros sold several players, including Clemente, to Caguas-Rio Piedras. The trade was extremely unpopular and even caused the Santurce manager, Monchile Concepcion, to resign.[44]

Clemente was leading the league in batting average and had gotten at least one hit in 18 consecutive games when he was traded. He continued his hitting streak, which reached 23 to set a new Puerto Rican League record. His streak was snapped when he was held hitless in a game by **Luis "Tite" Arroyo**, a longtime friend and teammate on the Pirates who was pitching for the San Juan Senadores in the winter.[45] Clemente finished with a batting average of .396.

His batting eye was certainly sharp, but Clemente's back was continuing to bother him, and he reported a day late to spring training in 1957 as a result. Bobby Bragan made light of the backache because Clemente had always played well even when he had some aches and pains. "The case history of Clemente is the worse he feels, the better he plays," reported *The Sporting News*, which quoted Bragan as saying, "I'd rather have a Clemente with some ailment than a Clemente who says he feels great with no aches or pains."[46]

Clemente's ability to play through pain and perform well may have contributed to charges that he wasn't really hurt. However, this time the back problems forced him to miss the first two games of the season. In all, Clemente played in only 111 games for Pittsburgh in 1957 and his batting average dropped to .253. The back problems lingered into the winter, and Clemente didn't play in the Puerto Rican League until mid-January of 1958.

The Pirates had finished tied for last in 1957, but they made a big jump in 1958 under manager **Danny Murtaugh**. Clemente, who was feeling better physically, helped them get off to a good start in their opening game. He had three hits, one of which tied the game in the eighth inning against Milwaukee. The Pirates eventually won in 14 innings.

Clemente continued to hit well. He had three hits again in a 4-3 win in Cincinnati on April 25. One was a double in the sixth inning when the Pirates were trailing, 1-0. Clemente eventually scored to tie the game. The next inning he broke the tie with a three-run homer.

Another game-winning home run came in Milwaukee on August 4. Clemente broke a 3-3 tie with two out in the top of the ninth with a home run off fellow Puerto Rican **Juan Pizarro**, who had also been a winter teammate.

A little over a month later, Clemente had an even more spectacular game, although he didn't hit any homers. He had three triples, tying a National League record, in a 4-1 win over Cincinnati on September 8.

Clemente batted .289 in 1958. From right field, he continued to terrorize opposing baserunners, finishing with 22 assists. Fans loved it when a ball was hit his way with runners on base, rising in anticipation of seeing him uncork a strong throw.

Led by Clemente, the Pirates climbed from last place all the way to second, eight games behind the Milwaukee Braves.

Clemente didn't play winter baseball in Puerto Rico in 1958-59. He wore a different uniform, for the United States Marine Reserves. He fulfilled a six-month military commitment at Parris Island, South Carolina, and Camp LeJeune, North Carolina. The rigorous training program helped Clemente physically. He added strength by gaining ten pounds and said his back troubles had disappeared. Clemente served as an infantryman in the Reserves until September 1964.[47]

When he reported to the Pirates in the spring of 1959, he complained of a sore right elbow. In May he made it worse when he hit the ground hard while making a diving catch. A few nights later, he had to be taken out of a game because he couldn't throw overhanded. He missed more than a month and continued to feel pain after he returned to the lineup.[48]

Clemente played in only 105 games and batted .296 as Pittsburgh dropped to fourth place. But he and the Pirates were primed for better things in 1960.

For the first time in several winters, Clemente played a full season in the Puerto Rican League in 1959-60. He was on a new team, having been traded to the San Juan Senadores, and he had a batting average of .330. Clemente and the Pirates hoped that he was ready for a big season back in Pittsburgh.

Another encouraging sign was that he was free of injuries. Feeling good and tuned up from his winter play, Clemente got off to a great start in 1960. In the Pirates' second game, at home against the Reds, he went three-for-three and drove in five runs as Pittsburgh won, 13-0. By the end of April, Clemente was batting .386. In 14 games, he had scored 12 runs, driven in 14, and hit three home runs. But he was just warming up. In Cincinnati, he had a home run and four RBIs on the first day of May. The 13-2 win was Pittsburgh's ninth straight and the team was in first place.

The Pirates cooled off a bit, but Clemente stayed hot. In May, he had 25 RBIs in 27 games, raising his season total to 39. He helped Pittsburgh regain the top spot in the National League standings and was named the league's Player of the Month by *The Sporting News*.

The Pirates battled for first with the San Francisco Giants and then the Milwaukee Braves. On the first Friday night in August, the Pirates were locked in a scoreless battle with the Giants at Forbes Field. **Vinegar Bend Mizell** was pitching for Pittsburgh and getting great help from his outfielders. Bill Virdon made a couple of good catches. Then Willie Mays led off the seventh inning for San Francisco with a long drive to right. Clemente chased the fly, reached out, and caught it, robbing Mays of an extra-base hit as he crashed into the outfield wall. He hurt his knee and also ended up with a gash in the chin that needed five stitches.[49]

Clemente stayed in the game the rest of the inning, but he was replaced by Gino Cimoli to start the eighth. Pittsburgh eventually won, 1-0, starting a four-game sweep of the Giants. Clemente missed the rest of the series as well as another three games.

He was out for a week. The day after he returned, he had a big game against the St. Louis Cardinals. St. Louis had beaten the Pirates the previous two nights and the Cardinals were in second place, only three games behind Pittsburgh. The Cardinals took the lead with a run in the top of the first inning. In the last of the first, Pittsburgh tied the game when Clemente singled home **Dick Groat**.

With the score still tied, Groat opened the third inning with a double, and Clemente followed with a homer. Clemente had another run-scoring single in the fourth as Pittsburgh won the game, 4-1. Clemente batted in all four of his team's runs.

The Pirates swept a doubleheader from the Cardinals the next day to open up a six-game lead. No one came close to them the rest of the way. Except for one day, the Pirates had been in first place since May 29.

Clemente finished the 1960 season with a .314 batting average and hit 16 home runs, more than doubling his previous high. He also made the National League All-Star team for the first time.

Pittsburgh's first pennant since 1927 put them in the World Series against the New York Yankees. Despite being outscored 46-17, the Pirates split the first six games to force a decisive seventh game.

New York came back from a 4-0 deficit to carry a 7-4 lead into the last of the eighth. The Pirates rallied, helped by a bad hop that turned a probable double-play grounder into a base hit. One run was in and Pittsburgh had runners at second and third with two out when Clemente came to bat against the Yankees' **Jim Coates**. Clemente swung and topped the ball toward first base. Coates couldn't get to it, and it was left to **Moose Skowron** to field it. Skowron had no chance of beating Clemente to the base, and Coates's pursuit of the ball left the bag uncovered. Clemente zipped safely across the base, his helmet flying off, while the two Yankees watched helplessly.

Clemente's hit drove in another run and the Pirates took a 9-7 lead when **Hal Smith** followed with a three-run homer. New York came back in the top of the ninth to tie the game, setting the stage for one of the most dramatic moments in Pittsburgh sports history--a Series-winning home run by **Bill Mazeroski** leading off the last of the ninth.

Clemente had had a hit in each of the seven games in helping the Pirates win the World Series.

Returning to his homeland following the 1960 season, Clemente skipped the first part of the Puerto Rican League season, but then joined the San Juan Senadores in the second half. Even after he became a star in the major leagues, Clemente continued playing winter ball well past the time that he needed to keep his batting eye sharp. He felt an obligation to the people of his homeland, who otherwise would not have a chance to see him play. Clemente is perhaps the most inspirational figure the island has ever known, and he took that responsibility seriously.

He frequently stood up for himself and his fellow Latin players, speaking out against injustices he saw. He approached this in the same manner in which he played--with a passion, sometimes an anger, which drove him on and off the field.

Much of his anger was justified. Although the game became more open to Latins after the breaking of the color barrier, certain attitudes and prejudices toward these players remained. Latin players were often accused of being lazy or faking an injury if they missed a game because they were hurt or ill. Clemente knew first-hand the feeling of being called a hypochondriac. He suffered through many ailments in his career and he burned when his manager or reporters didn't believe him when he said he was hurt.

One of Clemente's biographers, Kal Wagenheim, wrote, "The legend of his hypochondria became part of baseball's folklore. He claimed so many ills--and performed so well despite them--that his plaints evoked skepticism or laughter." Wagenheim also noted that Clemente had problems in the 1960s with Pirates manager Danny Murtaugh, who "reportedly accused him of feigning an injury and fined him for not playing."[50]

Beyond the injuries and claims of hypochondria, Clemente maintained that Latin players often did not receive the recognition they deserved. Once again, Clemente was an example of this. After helping the Pirates win the National League pennant, and then the World Series championship, Clemente finished eighth in the voting for the league's Most Valuable Player. Clemente thought he should have gotten more votes and finished higher in the balloting.

Each slight, whether at him or a fellow Latin, he took personally. He spoke out often, although some of the claims he made about being mistreated weren't always entirely correct.

Phil Musick, a reporter who covered the Pittsburgh Pirates during the final years of Clemente's career, said, "He was anything but perfect. He was vain, occasionally arrogant, often intolerant, unforgiving, and there were moments when I thought for sure he'd cornered the market on self-pity. Mostly, he acted as if the world had just declared all-out war on Roberto Clemente, when in fact it lavished him with an affection few men ever know."

However, Musick added, "I know that through all of his battles . . . there was about him an undeniable charisma. Perhaps that was his true essence--he won so much of your attention and affection that you demanded of him what no man can give, perfection."[51]

Clemente did eventually receive the respect he sought. Toward the end of his career, fans and reporters recognized his greatness on the field. More than that, they knew of his caring nature for all people.

Clemente said he rarely set goals, but that he did once: "After I failed to win the Most Valuable Player Award in 1960, I made up my mind I'd win the batting title in 1961 for the first time."[52]

Clemente did exactly that, leading the National League with a .351 batting average. He hit 23 home runs, scored 100 runs and drove in 89. He led National League outfielders with 27 assists and won a Gold Glove for his fielding excellence for the first time. Clemente would win a Gold Glove every year for the rest of his career.

In Puerto Rico, Clemente played winter ball less often. He skipped the 1962-63 season altogether. It was the first time he hadn't played in the Puerto Rican League other than the time he was in the Marine Reserves in 1958-59.

However, Clemente was back for a full season with San Juan in 1963-64. The Senadores finished third during the regular season but won the league playoffs and represented Puerto Rico in the International Series, which was played in Managua, Nicaragua. Author Thomas Van Hyning reports, "Clemente was a fan favorite and made a lot of fans in Nicaragua."[53] Clemente developed a fondness for the country and its people and would return again.

The race for the Puerto Rican batting title involved two National League stars—Clemente and Orlando Cepeda--and a young player on the verge of stardom in the American League, **Tony Oliva**. Back on the mainland in 1964, Oliva and Clemente led their respective leagues in batting average. Oliva, who credited his winter-league experience with helping his development as a hitter, had a .323 average in his first full season in the majors.[54] Clemente's .339 average was good for his second National League batting title.

The winter of 1964-65 was an eventful one for Clemente. He married Vera Cristina Zabala. He also began managing. In December of 1964, Clemente took over as manager of the San Juan Senadores. He still played, although less often. In his first game as manager, Clemente had two doubles off **Dennis McLain** of Mayaguez. "He drove in two runs with his second double and raced home on a wild throw, but twisted his left ankle slightly and left the game," reported Miguel J. Frau in *The Sporting News*.[55]

Clemente later suffered a more serious injury. He was mowing the lawn at his home when a rock flew out of the mower and hit him in the thigh. He missed some games as a player, but when the league's All-Star Game was played, Clemente felt obligated to make an appearance. He pinch-hit and singled, but he aggravated the injury. "I felt my thigh ligament pop and something like water draining inside my leg," he said. Clemente had partially severed a ligament in his thigh, and he had to have surgery.[56]

The injury, combined with a fever, left Clemente weak, and he got off to a slow start in 1965 with the Pirates. Under new manager **Harry Walker**, the team also began poorly, losing 24 of their first 33 games. A 12-game winning streak followed, lifting Pittsburgh in the standings. Clemente got hot over this stretch, hitting .458 during the winning streak. The Pirates never overcame their slow start and finished third. Clemente led the league in batting average for the second year in a row and the third time in his career.

No one knew, though, that he was on the verge of his best season ever.

In addition to his other skills, Clemente was increasing his walk total in the mid-1960s. Early in the 1966 season, the Pirates were in Chicago, trailing the Cubs by a run. Clemente came to bat with two out and no one on base in the ninth inning. Cubs reliever **Ted Abernathy** got two strikes on Clemente. The Pirates were on the verge of losing, but Clemente remained patient.

Abernathy's next three pitches were outside the strike zone, and Clemente laid off them. The count was full. Clemente stayed alive by fouling off the next eight pitches. Finally, Abernathy missed again and Clemente was on base with a walk. **Willie Stargell** followed with a double and Clemente came home with the tying run. Pittsburgh won the game in extra innings.

The win kept the Pirates in first place. They stayed in the pennant race all season, battling the San Francisco Giants and Los Angeles Dodgers. At the end of August the Pirates and Giants were tied for first. On September 2, Clemente hit a three-run homer off Chicago's **Ferguson Jenkins** that helped Pittsburgh beat the Cubs and take over sole possession of first place. It was the 2,000th hit of his career and his 23rd homer of the year, equaling his previous career high. In addition, it gave him 101 runs batted in, the first time he had ever reached 100 RBIs in a season.

He ended the season with career-highs in home runs (29) and RBIs (119). The Pirates finished third behind the Dodgers and Giants, but Clemente edged out Los Angeles' **Sandy Koufax** for the Most Valuable Player award.

Clemente had another outstanding season in 1967. He led the league with a .357 batting average for his third batting title in four years and his fourth overall. In addition to 209 hits, Clemente walked or was hit by a pitch more than 40 times, and he reached base at least 40 percent of the time for the first time in his career.

After having taken the previous winter off, Clemente played occasionally in the Puerto Rican League in 1967-68 and had a batting average of .382. Back on the mainland, things did not go well for him in 1968. The Pirates' opener was delayed two days because of the assassination of Martin Luther King. Clemente homered in the first game, but his batting average fell to .222 at the end of May. He said he was having trouble swinging the bat because he had injured his right shoulder in a fall at his home in Puerto Rico in

February of 1968. He added that he might retire from baseball if the shoulder didn't get better.[57]

He improved over the last part of the season and finished with a .291 batting average, his lowest since 1958. Clemente didn't play winter ball and rested his body. He felt good when spring training began in 1969, but then he hurt his left shoulder as he tried to make a diving catch and went back to Puerto Rico for treatment. Clemente returned in time for the start of the regular season, but for the second year in a row he got off to a slow start. In the latter half of May, after going hitless in the first game of a series in San Diego, his batting average had fallen to .225.

Clemente claimed something else happened--a strange and scary incident. He did not tell the story in public until a year later, but Clemente said he was kidnapped while in San Diego. According to Clemente, he was walking back to the hotel where the Pirates were staying after going out to eat. He said four men forced him into a car at gunpoint. They took him to an isolated area and took his wallet and his All-Star Game ring. "This is where I figure they are going to shoot me and throw me in the woods," he told Pittsburgh writer Bill Christine more than a year after the incident. "They already had the pistol inside my mouth." Two of the men spoke Spanish, and Clemente talked to one of them in Spanish. After that, the men returned Clemente's money and ring and brought him back to his hotel. They even gave Clemente back the bag of chicken he had purchased at the restaurant. He said he did not report the incident to the police.[58]

Despite the harrowing event, Clemente finished the series in San Diego by getting three hits against the Padres and raised his batting average above .300 by mid-June. For a while it looked like he might lead the league again. He didn't, but Clemente still finished the season with a batting average of .345. The Pirates didn't do as well, finishing third in the new East Division of the National League.

After a slow start in 1970, the Pirates caught fire as they moved from Forbes Field, where they had played since 1909, to **Three Rivers Stadium**. Pittsburgh and New York fought for first place through July, with Chicago staying close. The Pirates were hanging in without Clemente. He was hit in the wrist with a pitch on July 25 and, except for one pinch-running appearance, was out of the lineup for more than a week. He returned on August 8 and had a double and a home run against the Mets.

Later in August, Clemente had five hits in each of two straight games. The first one came on a Saturday in Los Angeles. Clemente already had four hits as he came to the plate in the top of the 16th inning. He singled, stole second, and later came scored the go-ahead run as the Pirates beat the Dodgers, 2-1. The next day, the Pirates won again, 11-0. Clemente had five of Pittsburgh's 23 hits in the game.

He had raised his average to .363, tops in the National League. However, he played little in September because of a bad back and did not win the batting title. The Pirates still won the National League East Division and advanced to the playoffs. Scoring only three runs in three games, however, they were swept by the Cincinnati Reds.

That winter, Clemente played for the last time in the Puerto Rican League. Although he played in only three games during the regular season, he appeared in one of the playoff series. In addition, he managed the San Juan Senadores in 1970-71. The Senadores' opening game that season was against Santurce, which was managed by **Frank Robinson**. Both Robinson and Clemente had been mentioned as possibilities to be the first black manager in the major leagues.

After he got off to a slow start with the Pirates in 1971, he said, "My biggest mistake was managing in Puerto Rico this past winter. I had more responsibilities and did not get my rest. The long bus trips out of town, I have to make them

Photograph by Duane Rieder.

because I am the manager. They take something out of me."59

Willie Stargell took the lead with Pittsburgh in 1971. He set a major league record by hitting 11 home runs in April and continued his great hitting throughout the year. Stargell finished with 48 home runs and 125 runs batted in.

Although Stargell had emerged as the team's star player, the team leader was still Clemente. He was receiving the recognition he had sought, and he was also showing he could continue playing with the same flair and hustle, even as he approached his 37th birthday. Clemente got off to a bad start, but he got hot in May and went on to finish the season with a .341 batting average. He was still outstanding in the field. In mid-June, Clemente preserved a shutout for **Steve Blass**, and a victory for the Pirates, on back-to-back plays. Pittsburgh held a 1-0 lead over Houston in the last of the eighth inning. The Astros had a runner on first with one out when **Cesar Cedeno** hit a soft liner to right field. Clemente hustled in and made a sliding catch of the ball before it could hit the turf. **Bob Watson** then hit a much harder drive toward the corner in right. Clemente raced toward the ball and made a twisting leap, grabbing the ball and robbing Watson of a two-run homer. Clemente crashed into the wall, bruising his ankle and elbow and cutting his knee. Astros manager Harry Walker, who had managed Clemente in Pittsburgh, said it was the greatest catch he ever made. Because of Clemente's catch, the Pirates maintained their lead and then padded it with two more runs in the ninth. Blass finished with a 3-0 win but said, "That shutout belongs to Clemente."60

The win gave the Pirates a 3 ½ game lead over the New York Mets and St. Louis Cardinals. Pittsburgh increased its lead to 9 ½ games at the All-Star break in July. The Pirates had several players in the All-Star game, including two starters — Willie Stargell in left field and **Dock Ellis**, who pitched. Clemente entered the game as a replacement for Willie Mays in the fourth inning.

Later in the game, he hit his first home run in an All-Star Game.

Pittsburgh went on to win the East Division and beat San Francisco in the league playoffs to make it back to the World Series, against the Baltimore Orioles. Clemente turned the event into a showcase for his greatness.

Baltimore took the first two games before the series shifted to Pittsburgh. Clemente drove in the first run of the third game with a fielder's choice. The Pirates added another run, but Baltimore came back on a home run by Frank Robinson to cut the lead to 2-1. Clemente led off the last of the seventh by grounding back to **Mike Cuellar**, who had briefly pitched for Clemente's San Juan team in the Puerto Rican League the previous winter.61 However, Clemente hustled down to first so hard that Cuellar hurried his throw and threw wildly. Clemente reached base on the error and, after Stargell walked, **Bob Robertson** hit a three-run homer. Pittsburgh won, 5-1.

The next game was the first night game in the history of the World Series. The Orioles got off to an early lead with three runs in the top of the first. Pittsburgh came back with two in the bottom of the inning, and the Pirates rallied again in the third. With one out, **Richie Hebner** singled. Clemente then hit a long drive to right. It cleared the fence and looked like a home run to put the Pirates ahead. However, the ball was ruled foul after the umpires had a long discussion. The ball was foul, and Clemente had to resume his at-bat. He couldn't come up with another long ball, but his single sent Hebner to second. One out later **Al Oliver** singled, scoring Hebner to tie the game. The score stayed at 3-3 until the Pirates pushed another run across in the seventh inning. Pittsburgh won the game, 4-3, and tied the World Series, 2-2.

The Pirates won again the next day as **Nelson Briles** held the Orioles to two hits. Clemente had a run-scoring single in the fifth inning to cap Pittsburgh's scoring as the Pirates won, 5-0.

The Series shifted back to Baltimore, but Pittsburgh had the lead. Just as he had done in the 1960 World Series, Clemente had at least one hit in each of the games. In the sixth game, with two out in the top of the first, he tripled off the fence in left-center field. However, Willie Stargell struck out, and Clemente was stranded at third.

By the time Clemente came up again in the third inning, the Pirates had a 1-0 lead. Clemente made the score 2-0 by hitting a home run to right field. The Orioles came back and tied the game in the seventh. In the last of the 10th inning, **Brooks Robinson** hit a sacrifice fly that scored Frank Robinson, giving Baltimore the win and extending the series to a seventh game.

Cuellar and Pittsburgh's Steve Blass were the starters in Game Seven, and both were sharp. Cuellar retired the first 11 Pittsburgh batters before Clemente came up with two out in the fourth. Cuellar threw him a high curve ball, and Clemente drove it over the left-center field fence. Clemente's second home run of the series gave Pittsburgh a 1-0 lead.

The Pirates got another run in the eighth inning, which they needed. In the bottom of the eighth, Baltimore got the first two runners on base. Blass was able to work out of the jam with only one run scoring, leaving Pittsburgh in the lead. Blass retired the Orioles in order in the last of the ninth. Clemente's homer had given the Pirates a lead they never gave up. Pittsburgh won the game, 2-1, and the Pirates were again champions of the world.

The Pirates had a number of pitchers who stood out, but when the voting was complete for the outstanding player of the World Series, the award went to Clemente. He had 12 hits, including two home runs, for a .414 batting average in the seven games.

There was no doubting his greatness nor his influence on the champion Pirates. Clemente had played in the All-Star Game, the World Series, had won the Most Valuable Player award, and had led the National League in batting average four times. He still had another milestone in his sights. "I would like to get 3,000 hits," he said in 1971.[62]

The Pirates had a rough start in 1972. They climbed in the standings and by the last half of June had taken over first place for good. Clemente was also doing well even though he had an intestinal virus that caused him to miss a few games. By the end of June, his batting average was .315, and he was making good progress toward the mark of 3,000 hits. On July 9, he got his 78th hit of the season, leaving him only 40 short. However, the virus returned, and Clemente left the Pirates to go back to Pittsburgh for treatment. He was out of the lineup for two weeks, then came back and got a big hit in a Pirates win on July 23.

Clemente missed another four weeks with strained tendons in both heels. Over a 40-game span between July 9 and August 22, he started only one game. Fortunately, the Pirates were still playing well and opened up a big lead in the National League East Division, but the illness and injuries had slowed Clemente in his drive toward 3,000 hits.

At the end of August he had 30 hits to go. He hit well in September and was within striking distance by the final week of the season. On Thursday night, September 28, he got his 2,999th hit off **Steve Carlton** of the Phillies. Because the game was in Philadelphia, he was taken out so he could get his 3,000th hit before the home fans.

Even this event would not happen without a bit of controversy as the Pirates opened a series against the New York Mets in Pittsburgh. Facing **Tom Seaver** in the first inning, Clemente hit a chopper up the middle. Second baseman **Ken Boswell** bobbled the ball, and Clemente reached first. Official scorer Luke Quay ruled the play an error. Seaver allowed only two hits, neither to Clemente, in winning his 20th game of the season. After the game, Clemente complained about the scoring decision and later made accusations that official scorers through the years had deprived him of two batting titles. Part of the outburst was a result of Clemente thinking (erroneously) that the scorer in the game was Charley Feeney, a local sportswriter who Clemente thought had deprived him of hits on borderline calls in the past.[63]

The next afternoon Clemente struck out in the first inning. The game was scoreless when he came up again, leading off the fourth. He hit a long fly toward left-center field. The ball hit the fence on one bounce, and Clemente cruised into second with a double, the 3,000th hit of his career. The Pittsburgh fans stood and applauded Clemente, who raised his cap to show his appreciation. That hit started a three-run rally, and the Pirates won the game, 5-0. Bill Mazeroski pinch hit for Clemente in the fifth inning.

Clemente played in only one of Pittsburgh's final three games as he rested for the playoffs. The Pirates played Cincinnati and looked like they were on their way back to the World Series. Pittsburgh carried a 3-2 lead into the last of the ninth inning of the decisive fifth game. However, **Johnny Bench** tied the game with a home run, and the Reds scored the winning run on a wild pitch.

As usual, Clemente went back to Puerto Rico. Although he didn't play baseball, he managed a Puerto Rican team that went to the Amateur Baseball World Series in Nicaragua. The Puerto Rican team finished third in the tournament.[64]

Clemente was back home a few weeks later when the city of Managua was racked by a massive earthquake on December 23. He had gotten to know people during his visits to Nicaragua. He was concerned about the people there and wanted to help.

Clemente got busy organizing a committee to raise money and get other items, such as medicine and food, that could be sent to Nicaragua. Through Christmas, he worked on the relief efforts. He finally decided he would go on one of the cargo planes that were flying the supplies to the stricken area.

A little after 9 p.m. on New Year's Eve, as others in Puerto Rico were celebrating, the plane took off. Besides Clemente, four other people were on board. Almost immediately, the plane had problems, and the pilot tried to return to the San Juan airport. Before the plane could make it back, however, it crashed into the Atlantic Ocean about a mile from the coast.

The fate of the people on board was not immediately known. But it soon became clear. The five men on the plane, including Roberto Clemente, were dead.[65]

People, not just baseball fans, mourned the loss of Clemente, who left behind his wife, Vera, and three sons, Roberto, Jr., Luis Roberto, and Roberto Enrique.

Normally, a player cannot be inducted into the Baseball Hall of Fame until at least five years after he stopped playing. Because of the circumstances, an exception was made for Clemente. A special election was held, and he received enough votes to be elected. In the summer of 1973, Clemente became the first player from Latin America to be inducted into the Hall of Fame.

There were other honors. An award, established in 1971 to honor a player for his accomplishments on and off the field, was renamed the Roberto Clemente Award.

Clemente had dreamed of establishing a Sports City for young people in Puerto Rico. He had a vision for a place where young people could come and play as well as read and learn other skills they would need in life. Vera Clemente continued her husband's work, aided by son Luis, and while the project remains uncompleted, the Foundation that was established works to **support clinics, sports activities, and similar efforts.**

Although he is gone, all sorts of reminders of Clemente still exist. More than anything, Roberto Clemente left behind memories of how he played the game on the field and how he lived his life off it.

SOURCES

Retrosheet (http://retrosheet.org) provided game-by-game details of Clemente's performance. The information used was obtained free of charge from and is copyrighted by Retrosheet.

NOTES

1   Peter C. Bjarkman, *Baseball with a Latin Beat: A History of the Latin American Game* (Jefferson: North Carolina: McFarland & Company, Inc., Publishers, 1994), 262.

2   Kal Wagenheim, *Clemente!* (New York: Praeger Publishers, 1973), 15.

3   Bruce Markusen, *Roberto Clemente: The Great One* (Champaign, Illinois: Sports Publishing, Inc., 1998), 4.

4   Telephone interview with Monte Irvin, June 30, 2005.

5   "Roberto Hit Ten HRs in 'Day-Long' Slugfest," *The Sporting News*, July 6, 1960: 6.

6   Wagenheim, 24.

7   "Starred in Javelin, Jumps Before Turning to Diamond," *The Sporting News*, July 6, 1960: 6.

8   Markusen, 8.

9   Les Biederman, "Pride Pushes Clemente: 'I Can Hit With Best'," *The Sporting News*, March 28, 1964: 11.

10   Thomas E. Van Hyning, *The Santurce Crabbers: Sixty Seasons of Puerto Rican Winter League Baseball* (Jefferson, North Carolina: McFarland & Company, Inc., Publishers, 1999), 39.

11   Frank Graham, Jr., "Spanish-Speaking Al Campanis Lures Latin Talent for Dodgers," *The Sporting News*, January 12, 1955: 21.

12   E-mail correspondence with Buzzie Bavasi, June 3, 2005.

13   Santiago Llorens, *The Sporting News*, January 20, 1954: 23.

14   *The Sporting News*, March 3, 1954: 26.

15   The bonus rule in effect at that time is chronicled by Brent Kelley, *Baseball's Biggest Blunder: The Bonus Rule of 1953-1957* (Lanham, Maryland: The Scarecrow Press, Inc., 1997).

16   Les Biederman, "Dodgers Signed Clemente Just to Balk Giants," *The Sporting News*, May 25, 1955: 11.

17   Wagenheim, 35; Markusen, 33-34.

18   The claim that the Dodgers would not start five blacks in the same game was made by Wagenheim on page 35 of *Clemente!* Box scores of Brooklyn Dodgers games in 1954 from *The Sporting News* indicate four instances in which Jim Gilliam, Jackie Robinson, Don Newcombe, Sandy Amoros, and Roy Campanella were all in the starting lineup: July 17, August 24, September 6 (second game), and September 15.

19   E-mail correspondence with Buzzie Bavasi, June 3, 2005.

20   Phil Musick, *Who Was Roberto? A Biography of Roberto Clemente* (Garden City, New York: Doubleday & Co., 1974). See also Wagenheim and Markusen.

21   The game-by-game analysis of the 1954 season was done through box scores of Montreal Royals games, published in *The Sporting News* in 1954, and cross-checked by SABR member Neil Raymond from box scores in Montreal newspapers.

22   Musick, 89.

23   Musick, 89.

24   Telephone interview with Jack Cassini, June 20, 2005.

25   E-mail correspondence with Buzzie Bavasi, June 3, 2005.

26   "Jack Hernon, "Backward Buccos Refuse to Go Overboard on Rookie," *The Sporting News*, January 12, 1955: 18.

27   Pito Alvarez de la Vega. "Mays, Gomez & Co. on Top in Puerto Rico: Santurce Takes Over Lead from Caguas; Willie Ups Swatting Average to .423," *The Sporting News*, December 22, 1954: 24.

28   Wagenheim, 43.

29   Interview with Don Zimmer, July 2, 2005.

30   Jack Hernon, "Clemente a Gem — in Need of Polish," *The Sporting News*, February 9, 1955: 4.

31   Jack Hernon, "Haney's Sizeup on Bob Clemente 'Much to Learn'," *The Sporting News*, March 16, 1955: 30.

32   http://www.bioproj.sabr.org/bioproj.cfm?a=v&v=l&bid=1187&pid=14117 Frank Thomas biography by Bob Hurte; Jack Hernon. "Holdouts Thomas and Law Absent as Bucs Start Drills" *The Sporting News*, March 9, 1955: 33.

33   *The Sporting News*, March 16, 1955: 27; "Uniform Numbers Range from 1 to 81," *The Sporting News*, April 13, 1955, 28; Thomas E. Van Hyning. *Puerto Rico's Winter League: A History of Major League Baseball's Launching Pad* (Jefferson, North Carolina: McFarland & Company, Inc., Publishers, 1995), 53.

34   Jack Hernon, "Haney's Young Bucs Shaking off Buck Fever," *The Sporting News*, May 11, 1955: 11.

35   Les Biederman, "Clemente, Early Buc Ace, Says He's Better in Summer," *The Sporting News*, June 29, 1955, 26.

36   Telephone interview with Jack Cassini, June 20, 2005.

37   Les Biederman, "Clemente, Early Buc Ace, Says He's Better in Summer."

38   "Bragan Cracks Down Early, Fines Clemente, Long $25," *The Sporting News*, April 25, 1956: 21; Les Biederman, "Bear-Down Bragan Means Business, Buc Fans Learn," *The Sporting News*, May 2, 1956: 7.

39   Wagenheim, 67.

40   Irving Vaughan, "7-Run Cub 8th Isn't Enough! Pirates Win, 9 to 8, on Clemente Homer," *Chicago Tribune*, Thursday, July 26, 1956: 6, 1.

41 "Clemente Ignored Stop Sign on 'Slam,' But Escaped Fine," *The Sporting News*, August 8, 1956: 18.

42 Les Biederman, "Clemente in 50 Games Without Walk," *The Sporting News*, August 8, 1956: 18.

43 Oscar Ruhl. "Rickey Rates Clemente as Top Draft Dandy," *The Sporting News*, March 20, 1957: 15.

44 Pito Alvarez de la Vega, "New Owner Peddles Trio of Santurce's Stars to Flag Rival," *The Sporting News*, January 9, 1957: 21.

45 Pito Alvarez de la Vega, "Bilko Released in Economy Move; Clemente Sets 23-Game Hit Mark," *The Sporting News*, January 16, 1957: 21.

46 "Clemente, Best When Ailing, Reports Late With Backache," *The Sporting News*, March 13, 1957: 10.

47 "Clemente to Start Six-Month Marine Corps Hitch, Oct. 4," *The Sporting News*, September 24, 1958: 7; "Buc Flyhawk Now Marine Rookie," *The Sporting News*, November 19, 1958: 13; *The Sporting News*, January 21, 1959: 9.

48 "Clemente Put on Disabled List and Baker Released by Bucs," *The Sporting News*, June 3, 1959: 13.

49 Bob Stevens, "Little Things Add Up to Big Plunge for Snoozing Giants," *The Sporting News*, August 17, 1960: 13, 18.

50 Wagenheim, 106.

51 Musick, 14-15.

52 Les Biederman, "Clemente—The Player Who Can Do It All," *The Sporting News*, April 20, 1968: 11.

53 Thomas E. Van Hyning. *Puerto Rico's Winter League: A History of Major League Baseball's Launching Pad*, 66.

54 Interview with Tony Oliva, June 5, 2005.

55 Miguel J. Frau, "Puerto Rico: Senators Dip As Clemente Grabs Reins," *The Sporting News*, January 9, 1965: 27.

56 "Clemente May Have Trouble As Result of Thigh Injury," *The Sporting News*, February 13, 1965: 25.

57 Les Biederman, "Shoulder Sore; Clemente Says He May Retire," *The Sporting News*, August 24, 1968: 18.

58 "Clemente Reveals Close Call With Kidnapers," *The Sporting News*, August 22, 1970: 24.

59 "Clemente Laments Managing," *The Sporting News*, May 15, 1971: 14.

60 Charley Feeney, "Greatest Catch? This One by Roberto Will Do," *The Sporting News*, July 3, 1971: 7.

61 Phil Jackman, "Orioles Shrug Off Cuellar's Winter-Ball Woes," *The Sporting News*, December 26, 1970: 37.

62 Charley Feeney, "Clemente Sets 3,000 Hits As Wish on 37th Birthday," *The Sporting News*, August 28, 1971: 9.

63 Charley Feeney, "Roberto Collects 3000th Hit, Dedicates It to Pirate Fans," *The Sporting News*, October 14, 1972: 15.

64 "Veteran Cuban Team Captures Amateur Title; U. S. Runner-Up," *The Sporting News*, December 30, 1972: 46.

65 "Baseball Mourns Loss of Buc Star Clemente," *The Sporting News*, January 13, 1973: 42.

ROBERTO CLEMENTE AND THE LATINO BALLPLAYER EXPERIENCE

BY ZAC PETRILLO

About Roberto Clemente, Ozzie Guillén, the three-time All-Star shortstop, outspoken World Series-winning manager, and fellow Latin American, said, "He is the Jackie Robinson of Latin baseball. … He lived racism. He was a man who was happy to be not only Puerto Rican, but Latin American. He let people know that. And that is something that is very important for all of us."[1] Guillén, a native of Venezuela, captures what so many like him hold dear: Roberto Clemente, the man as much as the myth, emboldened all Latino ballplayers coming to America after him.

Clemente debuted almost exactly eight years to the day after Jackie Robinson first stepped on the field with the Brooklyn Dodgers. Between those dates, dozens of Black players signed with major-league baseball clubs and all but three teams were integrated. Clemente faced not only the still-present difficulties of being a Black man in a deeply segregated nation, he also was acclimating himself to a new environment, experiencing high expectations and off-base stereotypes.

"There was a largeness to Clemente's persona that transcended baseball," said historian Doris Kearns Goodwin.[2] Like Robinson, representation and acceptance by Anglo United States only tells part of the story and, at times, reduces the complexities of the man. Clemente was full of contradictions, often belying the tidy version of an exotic Latin star that people, especially the media, wanted him to be. As such, he confronted both similar and uncommon issues compared with players who came before him, but his charisma and dominant play allowed him to pave a path to better prepare the many Latino superstars who followed.

The first Latino major leaguer was Colombian second baseman and outfielder Lou Castro, who debuted with the Philadelphia Athletics in 1902 and played in 42 games. The 1930s saw a small boom in Latino talent signing with major-league clubs, mostly out of Cuba. In 1934 Miguel Angel Gonzalez became a coach with the St. Louis Cardinals and four years later became the first major-league manager from that island nation. However, this representation was almost exclusively relegated to Cuban-born players and entirely for those with light skin.

It took until 1949 (47 years after Castro's appearance) for a Black Latino player to take the field, when Minnie Miñoso pinch-hit for the Cleveland Indians against the St. Louis Browns. Miñoso played only nine games that season (16 mostly ineffectual at-bats) before being sent back to the minors, where he was kept until 1951. Feeling Miñoso wasn't ready for the big leagues, Cleveland's manager Lou Boudreau said, "He was a raw star in the beginning, but in only two years he was a seasoned ballplayer."[3] Still, speculation persists that the color of Miñoso's skin played a part in keeping him in the minors longer than needed. He tore through minor-league pitching and once called up for good in 1951, he hit the ground running, swatting 10 homers and batting .326. He finished second in Rookie of the Year voting and became the first Latino star. A slew of Latino ballplayers followed Miñoso to the big leagues through the 1950s, including Clemente. While tolerance grew, stereotyping didn't cease:

Clemente signed with the Dodgers in 1954, but the team had no intention of playing him; they wanted to avoid his talent landing with the crosstown rival New York Giants. Manipulating the international signing system is a practice that continues for Latino ballplayers decades later. In 1955, after being selected by the Pirates in the Rule 5 draft, Clemente told Pittsburgh broadcaster Sam Nover that a Fort Myers, Florida, newspaper said, "Puerto Rican hot dog arrives in town," upon his arrival at spring training.[4] Reporters routinely quoted Clemente with exaggerated phonetics. After Clemente smacked the game-winning hit off future Hall of Famer Hoyt Wilhelm in the 1961 All-Star Game, the Pittsburgh Post-Gazette headline read, "I GET HEET, I FEEL GOOD." In the article, Clemente is quoted: "I 'ope that Weelhelm peetch me outside, so I could hit to right, but he peetch me inside. ..."[5] Clemente complained, "I never talk like that; they just want to sell newspapers."[6] Sportswriters also regularly referred to Clemente by pejorative nicknames such as "the dusky flyer" or the "lashing Latin" or the "chocolate-colored islander."[7] Clemente's experiences were far from uncommon.

Pirates broadcaster Bob Prince leaned into Clemente's Hispanic roots by creating the "¡Arriba! ¡Arriba!" signature call each time the right fielder did something spectacular on the field. It was a friendly play-by-play that helped endear both Clemente and his culture to the Rust Belt town. Pittsburgh fans took to it, commonly yelling, "¡Arriba!" at Roberto when he came to the plate or was spotted in public. However, the adoration, while meaningful to Clemente, did little to allay the effects of "othering" him, as he continued to feel dislocated culturally from most of his teammates. In 1960 Clemente believed he had a legitimate case to win the National League MVP Award, but writers not only placed him eighth overall, but behind three of his Pittsburgh teammates. Clemente believed the slight was because he was perceived as different and he never got over it.

In his superb Clemente biography, author David Maraniss explains that well into the right fielder's time in Pittsburgh, he remained an outsider:

Roberto Clemente was indisputably an important member of the team, yet also in many ways alone. At the end of his sixth and finest season, he was still separated by culture, race, language, and group dynamics. He was the lone black player in the starting lineup and a Spanish-speaking Puerto Rican, while none of the sportswriters for the major dailies in New York or Pittsburgh were black or spoke Spanish. Life is defined by images, especially public life, and the Pirates image was that of a band of scrappy, happy-go-lucky, fearless, gin-playing, hard-drinking, crewcut, tobacco-chewing white guys. Where was the place in that picture for the proud, regal, seemingly diffident Roberto Clemente?[8]

After a game, a New York Giants broadcaster commented to Clemente that he "reminds [him]

Les Banos photograph courtesy of The Clemente Museum.

of another rookie outfielder who could run, throw and get those clutch hits. Young fellow of ours name of Willie Mays." Clemente replied, "Nonetheless, I play like Roberto Clemente."[9] His "eccentric" tendencies remained a point of discussion, if also ridicule, in the press.

Sportswriters frustrated Clemente throughout his career. He never felt they saw his perspective and the constant stereotyping made him mad. On top of that, he was in a segregated country that told him where he could sleep and eat and even sit on a bus. Even though the word infuriated him, Clemente told author Roger Kahn he was a "double nigger,"[10] expressing his feeling of ostracization from both White and Black culture in the United States. "I am black and Puerto Rican," Clemente said. "I have to behave well. Perhaps I have more responsibility than others."[11]

Writing about Minnie Miñoso, Latin baseball historian Adrian Burgos Jr. said, "[Miñoso] presents a quandary for many about where to place a black Latino within U.S. categories of identity: Is he black? Just Latino? Can he really be both?"[12] Miñoso's Cleveland teammate Harry Simpson, an African American from Georgia, accused him of "not being Black."[13] Vic Power, a Black Puerto Rican like Clemente, shared Clemente's penchant for refusing to fit the mold of what Americans demanded of Latino ballplayers. He was gregarious, spoke out about injustice, and openly dated White women, a flagrant violation of 1950s racial sensibilities.[14] In the early 1950s Power was outstanding in the minor leagues for the New York Yankees, the only New York team yet to integrate, but he was held back. Yankees general manager George Weiss said that "the first Negro to appear in a Yankee uniform must be worth having been waited for" and that Power was not the "right kind of Negro."[15] Power was traded to Philadelphia without ever playing for the Yankees.

In 1969 Clemente said to the press, "The farther away you writers stay, the better I like it.

… Because you're trying to create a bad image of me. … You do it because I'm black and Puerto Rican, but I'm proud to be Puerto Rican."[16] Clemente developed a reputation as a hypochondriac who exaggerated his injuries. "Sometimes when I wake up in the morning," he once said, "I hurt so much I pray that I am still sleeping."[17] Clemente suffered from headaches, stomachaches, malaria, insomnia, tonsillitis, a hematoma in his right thigh, bone chips in his right elbow, a strained right instep, sore shoulders, and various pulled muscles. He freely talked about every ailment.[18] His fellow countryman Power ribbed him for making up illnesses. He took the jabs in stride, but when the press teased him with the same barbs, he got incensed.[19]

The constant moans fueled stereotypes that Latino players were complainers and whiners, and didn't take the game as seriously as their White counterparts. The perception only further galvanized Clemente to fight for his, and other Black Latino ballplayers', rightful place in the game.

A deeply prideful man, Clemente's stance against the media might've proved impactful toward getting fans to see him not only as a smiling construct, but as a human being. Instead, Clemente brought excitement to the ballpark and his connection with the fans was the one thing that never wavered. "He was our Jackie Robinson," said Clemente's friend and fellow Puerto Rican Luis Mayoral. "He was on a crusade to show the American public what a Hispanic man, a black Hispanic man, was capable of."[20]

Clemente spoke out, often in Spanish, against the racial prejudices he faced in the segregated United States. He was especially vocal about the injustice of being separated from teammates during spring training in Florida, including Black team members being unable to attend a Pirates Welcome Luncheon commemorating the team's 1960 World Series win. The only Black people allowed in were the waitstaff.[21] He was fond of Martin Luther King Jr., even welcoming King for an afternoon at his farm in Puerto Rico. "Sometimes you have to understand there are bigger things than you, bigger things than the game," said Carlos Delgado, a Black Puerto Rican whose path to major-league baseball was shaped by Clemente. "As an athlete, you have a platform with a lot of followers. You can push positive things; you can push movements and support movements."[22]

Early in Clemente's career, Black players were forced to stay on the bus after games while White players ate inside at roadside restaurants. The Black players had meals brought to them to eat on the bus once the others were finished. Clemente was so roiled by this process that he threatened to fight any Black player who tried to eat the meal. He pushed the Pirates to make better accommodations for Black players, which they eventually did, providing a separate means of transportation for them to get food.[23] "I hope that we can continue the conversation, that we can tell future generations: 'Look, this is Roberto Clemente. These are the values and integrity we want representing us,'" Delgado said.[24] On September 1, 1971, Clemente was part of history when Pirates manager Danny Murtaugh penciled him into the third spot in the first ever all-Black starting lineup.

When Clemente first reached the US mainland, he roomed with Bob Friend, a pitcher who took him under his wing. The pair watched *The Lone Ranger* television show together which, along with other Westerns, helped Clemente pick up English. It's a story told over and over for Latinos first coming to America. For example, when Miguel Tejada was assigned to the Medford A's, alone and thousands of miles from the only home he knew in the Dominican Republic, he relied on Disney cartoons to help him pick up English so he could connect with his new community.[25]

In the time since Clemente played his last game, the major leagues have seen an explosion of talent from Latin American countries, with every team putting enormous resources into international scouting. By the 1990s, Latin Americans replaced African Americans as the second most prevalent demographic in the majors. In 2017 nearly 30 percent of all players identified as Latino.[26] Clemente's wife, Vera, continued her husband's efforts to help Latin American talent by overseeing the Roberto Clemente Foundation as well as baseball clinics, including a "Sports City" complex in San Juan. Some successful major-league players who have gone through the system are Benito Santiago, Ruben Sierra, Juan Gonzalez, Carlos Baerga, both Alomar brothers, and Ivan Rodriguez.[27]

As detailed in Marcos Bretón and José Luis Villegas's book about the journey of a Latino ballplayer, *Away Games*, this explosion "didn't happen by accident."[28] With the advent of free agency in the mid-1970s, major-league teams scrambled to find talent as cheaply as possible. Felipe Alou, the major leagues' first Dominican-born manager, said, "It's like they throw a net in the ocean, hoping that maybe they'll get a big fish. The problem is, if they don't get a big fish, they'll throw all the smaller ones back."[29] For every player who makes it to the big leagues, several more become undocumented men in a country not their own, forced into blue-collar jobs such as construction or must go back to the impoverished villages they came from.

In 1989 Puerto Rican-born players, as American citizens, became a part of the annual amateur draft, affording them much higher bonuses than players procured from other Latin countries. Just as manipulation surrounded Clemente's signing, the process of scouting and signing international players has become fierce and detrimental to the many young men involved. In 2022 *The Athletic* dove into problems that persist around scouting of players from Latin American countries. Signing rules developed in 2017 limited the pool of money teams can allocate to talent. As a result, teams zero in on specific players, sometimes as young as 12 years old, so they may lock them up once they reach the allowable signing age. The report notes that use of performance-enhancing drugs is prevalent, especially among older players who have not yet secured a contract from big-league teams and risk falling behind if they don't stand out.[30]

While baseball fans have come a long way in accepting Latin American players as an asset to the game, stereotypes still remain. In 2017 ESPN sports analyst Doug Gottlieb openly accused Dominican ballplayer Adrián Beltré, who continued to play at a Hall of Fame level well into his 30s, of using performance enhancing drugs. Gottlieb cited the fact that eight of the 13 players named in the Biogenesis PED scandal were Dominican.[31] "Beltré's from the Dominican Republic," Gottlieb said. "Beltré (has) also been as or more productive into his mid- and now late-30s as he was in his 20s."[32]

Gottlieb, like so many Americans, didn't see Beltré as a human being who might operate independent of other Latinos, but instead as a stereotype who must represent the worst. It's this exact type of thinking that Clemente largely broke down. After Clemente died, Puerto Rican writer Elliott Castro observed, "That night on which Roberto Clemente left us physically, his immortality began."[33] Yet what made Clemente so important was that he was every bit a mortal.

Clemente's son Roberto Jr. recalled a story that encapsulates his father's legacy, "Once, when I was in Pittsburgh, I stopped to help an old lady change a tire. She said, 'Thankyou, young man, where are you from?' And I said Puerto Rico. And she said, 'Puerto Rico! Why that's where Roberto Clemente was from. He was a great man.'"[34] Clemente helped kids all around the world, but especially in Latin America, to understand they too could dream big. And dreaming big didn't mean being perfect, it meant being themselves – battles with the press, headaches, tonsillitis, and all.

NOTES

1   George Diaz, "Clemente 30 Years After His Tragic Death, the Influence of Baseball's First Hispanic Superstar Is Stronger Than Ever," *Orlando Sentinel*, March 31, 2002.

2   MLB, "MLB remembers the legacy of Roberto Clemente," YouTube, https://www.youtube.com/watch?v=KhWgUGbnko, December 17, 2017.

3   Lew Freedman, *African American Pioneers of Baseball: A Biographical Encyclopedia* (Westport, Connecticut: Greenwood Press, 2007), 286.

4   David Maraniss, *Clemente: The Passion and Grace of Baseball's Last Hero* (e-book edition) (New York: Simon & Schuster, 2013), 358.

5   Maraniss, 774-775.

6   Adrian Burgos, Jr., "Left Out: Afro-Latinos, Black Baseball, and the Revision of Baseball's Racial History," *Social Text*, Vol. 98, Spring 2009: 47.

7   Steve Wulf, "December 31: ¡Arriba Roberto!," *Sports Illustrated*, December 28, 1992.

8   Maraniss, 527-529.

9   Wulf.

10   Burgos, 47.

11   Burgos, 47.

12   Burgos, 45.

13   Burgos, 45.

14   Burgos, 46.

15   Burgos, 45.

16   Julio Ricardo Valera. "Time to Retire Roberto Clemente's Number 21," ESPN.com, July 11, 2017.

17   Wulf.

18   Wulf.

19   Maraniss, 705-707.

20   Wulf.

21   Maraniss, 741-742.

22   Jorge Castillo, "Remembering Roberto Clemente as a Black Man Who Fought Against Racial Injustice," *Los Angeles Times*, September 8, 2020.

23   Maraniss, 736.

24   Castillo.

25   Alex Coffey, "Has Anybody Heard from Miguel Tejada Lately? Well, Yes, as It Turns Out," *The Athletic*, June 22, 2020.

26   Federico Anzel, "MLB Demographics: The Rise of Latinos in Major League Baseball," Visme Visual Learning Center, https://visme.co/blog/mlb-demographics/, 2018.

27   "Roberto Clemente Day Official in Puerto Rico," *Washington Post*, August 18, 1993.

28   Marcos Bretón and José Luis Villegas, *Away Games: The Life and Times of a Latin Baseball Player* (Albuquerque: University of New Mexico Press, 2001), 39.

29   Bretón and Villegas, 40.

30   Marian Torres and Ken Rosenthal, "'A failed system': A Corrupt Process Exploits Dominican Baseball Prospects. Is an International Draft Really the Answer?," *The Athletic*, January 20, 2022.

31   Marissa Payne, "Doug Gottlieb Accuses Adrian Beltre of Using PEDS, Partly Because He's Dominican," *Washington Post*, August 1, 2017.

32   Payne.

33   Maraniss, 1782.

34   Wulf.

ROBERTO CLEMENTE'S YEAR IN THE DODGERS ORGANIZATION

BY JOE LEISEK

This article focuses on Roberto Clemente's season in the Brooklyn Dodgers organization — his first in a major-league organization. The subject of the Dodgers "hiding" Clemente from other major-league clubs has been researched and debated by baseball scholars and writers.[1] This article does not break any new ground on that topic; rather, the goal is to provide a glimpse into Clemente's season, from signing a contract with the Dodgers in February to being selected by the Pirates in the minor-league draft in November — nine important months in Clemente's career and life.

Ashort article in the *Montreal Star* on February 25, 1954, announced the signing of a young outfielder to the Montreal Royals, one of two Triple-A affiliates of the Brooklyn Dodgers.

The headline read: "Royals Sign Bonus Boy Clemente." Just below was a drop head that referred to the signee as a "Cuban Outfielder."

And finally, the body text: "Outfielder Roberto Clemente, a Negro bonus player from Puerto Rico, has been signed by the Royals, [general manager] Guy Moreau announced today."[2]

In those few lightly fact-checked column inches, 19-year-old Roberto Clemente was introduced to the city where he would play his first season under contract with a major-league baseball club. He was a Royal; the youngest player on a roster that during the 1954 season boasted more than two dozen players who had or would have major-league experience.

Just a short time before, the young Clemente had a breakout season with the Cangrejeros de Santurce in the Liga de Béisbol Profesional de Puerto Rico (now Liga de Béisbol Profesional Roberto Clemente). Scouted by several major-league teams, he was offered a salary of $5,000 and a signing bonus of $10,000 by the Dodgers — the largest bonus paid by the club since Jackie Robinson in 1945. On February 19 Clemente's father, Melchor, accepted the offer on behalf of his son, and both signed the contract.[3] Clemente was sent to Montreal for spring training.

Clemente biographer Bruce Markusen wrote about the contract's potential ramifications:

> On the surface, the move made sense, given Clemente's still raw and unrefined talents, but it created a future problem for the Dodgers. Under the rules in place in 1954, any player receiving a bonus of $4,000 or more who was assigned to the minor leagues would then be subject to a special draft at season's end. Under the new rule, which would eventually become known as Rule 5, such a player could be taken by another major league franchise at the cost of only $4,000. Al Campanis, working as a winter league manager at the time, warned Dodgers vice president Buzzie Bavasi that he was taking a huge gamble by not putting Clemente on the major league roster for the entirety of the 1954 season.[4]

The Dodgers' top affiliate, the Royals were part of the International League, which featured eight teams in 1954: the Royals, Buffalo Bisons, Havana Sugar Kings, Ottawa A's, Richmond Virginians, Rochester Red Wings, Syracuse Chiefs, and Toronto Maple Leafs.

The Royals played in Delorimier Stadium, located east of downtown Montreal. The steel and concrete ballpark featured bleachers in right and left fields with a capacity of around 20,000. Its rectangular shape created dimensions that favored left-handed hitters: 341 feet down the left-field line, 441 feet in center field, and 293 feet down the right-field line, with a 12-foot-high wall surrounding the outfield.[5]

Among Clemente's teammates was pitcher Joe Carbonaro, from San Jose, California, who was back from serving in the Korean War and trying to resurrect his baseball career. In a story by Canadian baseball historian Kevin Glew, Carbonaro fondly recalled playing in Montreal with the Royals.

"It was a very colourful town," he said. "We had good players there. Clemente was there, Tommy Lasorda, Sandy Amoros, Gino Cimoli – all the guys that made it to the majors later on. Ed Roebuck, Ken Lehman, Chico Fernandez, they were all good ballplayers. It was a good time."

Carbonaro recalls living in an apartment above a grocery store on Belanger Street with his wife.

"It was like being in Little France because the papers were in French and the people spoke French," he said. "I went to church there and the church was done in French. It was a whole different experience."[6]

Another of Clemente's teammates in Montreal was Joe Black, who was the National League's Rookie of the Year in 1952 with the Dodgers but was sent down after the 1953 season. "The thing that amazed me," Black said as he remembered Clemente, "is that sometimes one of his legs would be up in the air (while he was hitting), and the ball would still go out of the ballpark. He was just strong."[7]

In a phone interview with the author in 2021, Carbonaro provided further details about what it was like to have Clemente as a teammate.

"(Clemente) had a lot of the ability – he was very athletic, a good runner, had a good arm, and hit well," he recalled. "They used him primarily against left-handed pitching. Back then, you might see one left-hander a week compared to right-handers. At first, he was very easy to strike out with the slow stuff, because he looked for a fastball all the time. But he turned out to be a better hitter than I thought he would be."

Carbonaro remembered a game in Toronto against the first-place Maple Leafs, when Clemente was angry about being removed from the lineup before an at-bat because Toronto brought in a righty reliever. When he walked back to the dugout, he expressed his frustration.

"There was some metal piping along the box seats next to the dugout," Carbonaro said, "and he hit that pipe with his bat so hard that people jumped out of their seats." He added: "He didn't understand why he couldn't play every day. He was so strong and yet so raw."

Clemente with Montreal. Courtesy of The Clemente Museum.

Always the pitcher, Carbonaro added: "You didn't want to pitch outside in batting practice to Clemente – he'd hit it right back through the box!"

Carbonaro described Clemente as quiet most of the time. "He was a little overwhelmed," Carbonaro said, adding that Clemente's closest friends on the roster were outfielder Sandy Amoros and shortstop Chico Fernandez, both Cuban; Black; and third baseman Bob Wilson.

"Amoros and Clemente were the quiet guys," Carbonaro remembered. "They may have felt strange being in this country and not speaking English or French, but they both did okay."

"When we were on the road, in New York and Virginia, these guys ate and stayed together," Carbonaro said. "They couldn't eat or stay with us. In Montreal, Toronto, Ottawa, and in Havana, this wasn't a problem."[8]

In June the *Montreal Star*, reporting on a game in Richmond, added this to a short column after the game story: "Amoros, Fernandez, and Clemente, Royals colored players, stop at Slaughter's Hotel, a negro establishment."[9]

Slaughter's Hotel and Cafe, on North Second Street in Richmond's Jackson Ward, was part of what was known as the "Harlem of the South." Slaughter's was across the street from the Hippodrome Theater. The National Park Service notes that many performers who played at the theater – including Cab Calloway, Ella Fitzgerald, Nat King Cole, and Duke Ellington – also stayed at Slaughter's.[10]

In spring training, Clemente showed a glimpse of what was to come. On April 2, his first game with the Royals, he hit an inside-the-park home run and two singles to lead Montreal to a 12-2 win over a team of ex-servicemen.

The next day, local beat writer Lloyd McGowan praised Clemente: "Roberto Clemente, new bonus outfielder for the Royals, is a more spectacular player than Sandy Amoros. ... Clemente is a right-handed batter, a flash in the field with a bullet peg. ..."[11]

McGowan was skeptical of Clemente's hitting prospects, however: "But he is only 18 years old and might not murder International League pitching, exactly."[12] Clemente was 19, not 18, and four games into the season he led the Royals in hitting with a .500 average (4-for-8).

The day after the season opener, *Star* reporter Baz O'Meara made sure readers knew Clemente's potential: "(The Royals) seem to have a new star coming up in Roberto Clemente the Puerto Rican outfielder. He had three singles, bunted in smart style, caught on with the fans, was complimented by (manager Max) Macon."[13]

Clemente announced his arrival loudly and clearly in a doubleheader sweep against the Sugar Kings in Montreal, with a game-winning 10th-inning home run in the opener and two hits in the nightcap. The *Star* featured Clemente prominently in the next day's sports pages:

> The man getting on the tram outside the park was Harry Simmons of the International League office.
>
> The Royals had won two games from the Havana Sugar Kings, 7-6 and 4-1. Homeward bound, the 4,252 customers were satisfied, chatty, and cheerful.
>
> "They have a new idol, a new star," Harry Simmons said. "Roberto Clemente."
>
> No truer words were spoken on the weekend. Clemente's clout over the left-field wall yesterday, his first homer of the campaign, won the opening game Hollywood style in the tenth inning.
>
> Clemente is a player with potential greatness. He is what they call "showboat" in diamond dialect. But yesterday he delivered in very surprising style, indeed.
>
> At the start of the season Max Macon said that he didn't expect Clemente to prove much help to the club. He was too young and inexperienced, the manager had said.

It was noted, though, that yesterday Macon sent (Clemente) back into the second game. He smashed a double on his first try in that event. The rain-defying throng hooted derisively when they walked him intentionally on his next trip.[14]

In his SABR biography of Clemente, Stew Thornley captured the rest of the young star's season:

For the rest of the season Clemente started every game in which the opposition started a left-handed pitcher. He had a few more highlights during this time. Near the end of July, he came to bat in the top of the ninth inning of a scoreless game in Toronto. Clemente doubled and went on to score to put Montreal ahead. The Royals won the game, 2-0.

The next time the Royals were in Toronto, three weeks later, Clemente helped them win in a different way. Montreal had an 8-7 lead over the Maple Leafs in the bottom of the ninth. Toronto had a chance to tie the score, but Clemente threw out a runner at home plate to end the game.

Late in August he had two triples and a single at Richmond, although the Royals still lost the game. A week later he hit a home run to win the game for Montreal and give the Royals a sweep of a double-header against Syracuse.

Teammate Jack Cassini said, "You knew he was going to play in the big leagues. He had a great arm and he could run." When Clemente began playing regularly against left-handers, the Royals rose in the standings and finished in second place. Clemente batted .257 in 87 games in his only season in the minors.[15]

By the end of the season, Thornley writes, it was clear that other teams were interested in Clemente. Bavasi hoped that a gentleman's agreement with Pirates general manager Branch Rickey, who ran the Dodgers before coming to Pittsburgh, would keep Clemente with Brooklyn. However, Rickey and Dodgers owner Walter O'Malley got into an argument, and the agreement was off.[16]

In an article written for the National Baseball Hall of Fame website, Bruce Markusen reported that Rickey traveled to Puerto Rico and personally scouted Clemente, who had returned home after the Royals' season to play for the Santurce Cangrejeros. Not only was Rickey impressed with Clemente on the field: "He also took time to talk to him during his scouting trip. Rickey found the young prospect polite and respectful."[17]

Clemente's career as a Dodger ended on November 22, when the Pirates made him the first selection in the minor-league draft. The *Montreal Star* reported: "The Royals lost two of their most promising young baseball players to Major League clubs in the draft session in New York today. Roberto Clemente, Puerto Rican outfielder who batted .257, was claimed by the Pittsburgh Pirates and Glenn Gorbous, a Canadian, goes to the Cincinnati Reds."[18]

Under the rules of the draft, Clemente cost the Pirates just $4,000. Markusen called it "some of the best money the Pirates ever spent in the long history of their franchise."[19]

SOURCES

In addition to the sources cited in the Notes, the author accessed a file provided by the National Baseball Hall of Fame Library as well as Retrosheet.org, and Baseball-Reference.com.

ROBERTO CLEMENTE, 1954 MONTREAL ROYALS, INTERNATIONAL LEAGUE, AAA

HITTING

G	PA	AB	R	H	2B	HR	RBI	SB	BB	SO	BA	SLG	OBP	OPS	TB
87	155	148	27	38	5	2	12	1	6	17	.257	.372	.326	.657	55

FIELDING

CH	PO	A	E	Fld
83	81	1	1	.988

NOTES

1   In his biography *Who Was Clemente?*, Phil Musick titled his fifth chapter, "Hidden in Montreal," While Bruce Markusen's *Roberto Clemente: The Great One* uses the same three words for the title of his second chapter. Stew Thornley, in Clemente's SABR biography, uses the same three words in his title. See Phil Musick, *Who Was Clemente?* (Garden City, New York: Associated Features Books, 1974) and Bruce Markusen *Roberto Clemente: The Great One* (Champaign, Illinois: Sports Publishing, 1998). See also Stew Thornley, Clemente's Entry into Organized Baseball: Hidden in Montreal? https://sabr.org/journal/article/clementes-entry-into-organized-baseball-hidden-in-montreal/.

2   "Royals Sign Bonus Boy Clemente," *Montreal Star*, February 25, 1954: 54.

3   David Maraniss, *Clemente: The Passion and Grace of Baseball's Last Hero* (New York: Simon & Schuster Paperbacks 2007), 37.

4   Bruce Markusen, "Clemente's Lone Minor League Season Put Him on a Path to Pittsburgh,"https://baseballhall.org/discover/baseball-history/clementes-lone-minor-league-season-put-him-on-a-path-to-pittsburgh, accessed February 20, 2022.

5   William Brown, *Baseball's Fabulous Montreal Royals* (Montreal: Robert Davies Publishing 1996), 28.

6   Kevin Glew, 1954 Montreal Royals Team Photo ... Joe Carbonaro, https://cooperstownersincanada.com/2014/10/04/1954-montreal-royals-team-photo-joe-carbonaro/, accessed February 21, 2022.

7   Glew.

8   Author interview with Joe Carbonaro, October 12, 2021.

9   "Macon's Royals Register," *Montreal Star*, June 2, 1954: 36.

10   National Park Service, "The Hippodrome Theater and W.L. Taylor Mansion," https://www.nps.gov/places/the-hippodrome-theater-and-w-l-taylor-mansion.htm, accessed February 27, 2022.

11   Lloyd McGowan, "The Batter's Box," *Montreal Star*, April 3, 1954: 26.

12   McGowan, "The Batter's Box."

13   Baz O'Meara, "The Passing Sport Show," *Montreal Star*, April 30, 1954: 34.

14   Lloyd McGowan, "Clemente's 'Arrival' Pleasant Surprise for Macon, Royals," *Montreal Star*, July 26, 1954: 28.

15   Stew Thornley, "Roberto Clemente," SABR BioProject, https://sabr.org/bioproj/person/roberto-clemente/, accessed February 21, 2022.

16   Thornley.

17   Markusen, "Clemente's Lone Minor League Season Put Him on a Path to Pittsburgh."

18   "Royals' Clemente Gets 'Pirate' Call," *Montreal Star*, November 22, 1954: 34.

19   Markusen.

ROBERTO CLEMENTE'S PUERTO RICO WINTER LEAGUE CAREER (PART I)

BY THOMAS E. VAN HYNING

In 1952 Pedrín Zorrilla, a native of Manatí, one of Puerto Rico's 78 municipalities and the owner of the Santurce Crabbers, a team in the Puerto Rico Winter League (PRWL), received a tip from Roberto Marín, a salesman for Sello Rojo Rice Company. Marín had discovered 14-year-old Roberto Clemente four years earlier, hitting empty tomato cans with sticks — hitting them a long distance.[1] Clemente played on Marín's softball team prior to suiting up with the Juncos Mules, an amateur team in Puerto Rico's Double-A League. Zorrilla watched Clemente in an exhibition game for Juncos, at Manatí. He was impressed with Clemente's skills and offered him a $40-a-week contract and a $400 signing bonus for the 1952-53 PRWL season.[2] Zorrilla liked Clemente's solid upbringing, as a Baptist, and his support of the ideals of Luis Muñoz Marín, Puerto Rico's first elected governor in 1948. Muñoz ran on the Partido Popular Democrático's mantra of *Pan, Tierra, Libertad* (Bread, Land, Liberty) as a US Commonwealth.[3]

This essay focuses on Clemente's 4½ winter seasons with Santurce, his late-December 1956 sale to the Caguas Criollos, and his brief tenure with Caguas, 1956-57 and 1957-1958. It showcases his fine play in the memorable February 1955 Caribbean Series in Caracas, Venezuela, alongside Santurce teammate Willie Mays, and his all-star performance in center field for Caguas in the February 1958 Caribbean Series in San Juan. Part II covers his seasons with the San Juan Senators, who acquired him via a trade with Caguas before the 1959-60 season.

A 1952-53 ROOKIE SEASON WITH LINKS TO TED WILLIAMS AND JACKIE ROBINSON

An 18-year-old Clemente wore uniform number 39 for the 1952-53 Crabbers, a mostly veteran club dotted with some big-league prospects. Player-manager Buzz Clarkson defended shortstop and third base, part-time; a crowded outfield included spot starter Bob Thurman in right field, Billy Bruton in center field, and Willard Brown in left and

Jim "Junior" Gilliam and Roberto Clemente with Santurce.
Photograph courtesy of Jorge Fidel López Vélez.

center field, with left fielder Alfonso Gerard and Johnny Davis (pitcher-left fielder) in the mix. Island baseball fans bestowed colorful nicknames on players: *Ese Hombre* (The Man) was Willard Brown's sobriquet; Thurman was *El Múcaro* (The Owl) for his fine night vision displayed at Sixto Escobar Stadium, home of the Crabbers and archrival San Juan Senators; *El Gaucho* became Johnny Davis's moniker – his mannerisms were like Argentine cowboys. Rubén Gómez was *El Divino Loco* (Divine Crazy) for the way he drove his sports car to away games. Billy Hunter, Santurce's shortstop, recalled, "Clemente was just a kid. I don't think he got much playing time."[4]

Clemente looked up to 35-year-old Thurman for his elegance, professionalism, and calm demeanor. Both homered in an October 11 preseason game against a visiting team from the Dominican Republic, in Clemente's first appearance wearing Crabbers flannels.[5] A regular-season highlight was being summoned to pinch-hit for Thurman against Caguas left-handed pitcher Roberto Vargas, a.k.a. the "Joe Page of Puerto Rico," in a game tied 2-2. Clemente doubled down the left-field line to give the Crabbers a 4-2 win on November 30, 1952.[6]

Some of Clemente's 77 at-bats in the 72-game season came against the San Juan Senators, who featured a rotation of Harvey Haddix, Cot Deal, Diómedes Olivo, and Don Liddle. Haddix later joked around with Clemente as a Pittsburgh Pirates teammate but did not recall facing him in

Puerto Rico. "I remember Willard Brown, from that [Santurce] team," said Haddix,[7] – the first professional pitcher Clemente faced – after he replaced left fielder Gerard, on Tuesday, October 21, 1952.[8] Haddix retired Clemente en route to a 4-0 shutout. Clemente's 18 hits during the season included three doubles and a triple; he scored five runs and drove in five.[9] Santurce's most consistent hitter was second baseman Jim Gilliam. When Gilliam played in 1952 for the Montreal Royals of the International League, he contacted Bobo Holloman,[10] who pitched for Syracuse, and put him in touch with Zorrilla, who signed the pitcher. Each PRWL team was allowed eight "imports," normally stateside players. Quality imports could make the difference between winning a title or not qualifying for the postseason.

Clemente's first outfield start was at Escobar Stadium against the visiting Mayagüez Indians on October 22. From left field, he watched Ted Williams throw out the first pitch from the mound, next to Zorrilla and starting pitcher Holloman. Williams was available for the occasion during a break from doing joint maneuvers between Vieques and Roosevelt Roads Naval Station in Ceiba.[11]

Holloman (15-5) and Rubén Gómez (13-9) accounted for two-thirds of Santurce's wins in the team's second-place (42-30) finish, three games behind San Juan. Santurce beat the Ponce Lions in three straight semifinal series contests before defeating San Juan, four games to two, in the finals. Clemente sat on the bench throughout these playoffs but met Jackie Robinson prior to Game Five of the final, when Robinson was in San Juan, and attended this February 14 contest.[12]

Santurce team officials left Clemente off the February 1953 Caribbean Series 22-player roster for the Havana round-robin event. Clemente was replaced by Caguas star Vic Power. "Roberto was still in high school [then]," recalled Power. "I was 25 and had been in the PRWL six seasons."[13] Santurce overwhelmed its opponents – the Havana

Reds, Caracas Lions, and Panamá's Chesterfield Smokers – in winning all six games, scoring 50 runs and committing two errors.[14]

FIRST-TO-WORST (1953-54)

Guigo Otero Suro, Zorrilla's right-hand man with Santurce, tried to sign Ernie Banks and Ted Williams for the 1953-54 Crabbers. The Chicago Cubs did not allow Banks to play winter ball.[15] Guigo attended the 1953 All-Star Game in Cincinnati and saw Williams throw out the first pitch before both took the same flight out of Cincinnati. Guigo asked Williams – back from his tour of duty in Korea – if he would consider playing for Santurce (1953-54) to stay sharp. "Williams asked me if there were good golf courses and fishing in Puerto Rico," said Otero Suro. "I said yes to both ... spoke with Fred Corcoran, Williams's agent, by phone, in Pittsburgh. ... Later that summer, a Pittsburgh radio station announced that Williams might play winter ball with Santurce!"[16] The price tag for signing Williams would be $30,000, an unheard-of sum in the PRWL. Williams hit .407 with Boston (37-for-91) during August-September 1953 and did not sign a Santurce contract.

So Clemente earned the left-field job and appeared in 66 of Santurce's 80 games. He batted a respectable .292 with 2 home runs and 27 RBIs.[17] Santurce (32-48) finished fifth of five teams, 14 games behind first-place Caguas (46-34), which featured 19-year-old Hank Aaron. The Crabbers hit 20 homers in 80 games.[18] Aaron and teammate Jim Rivera tied for the league lead with nine home runs apiece.[19] Tom Lasorda (7-6, 3.60 ERA) and Rubén Gómez (5-6, 2.86) were Santurce's best hurlers. Lasorda noted that "Clemente had a great attitude and was not hesitant to seek out the veterans' advice."[20]

Mickey Owen, the Caguas player-manager, wanted Clemente in his Caguas outfield. Owen's left fielder, Juan "Tetelo" Vargas, was 47 years old, with Luis Olmo in reserve. "Aaron and Clemente would have been something else," mused Owen. "We had the veteran Olmo as trade bait for Clemente, but a deal [with Santurce] couldn't be worked out."[21] After Caguas emerged as playoff champion, the team's management considered adding Clemente to its February 1954 Caribbean Series roster when Aaron departed to the States. Instead, the Criollos added Mayagüez's Carlos Bernier. Owen vouched for Clemente but was overruled by Caguas's owner and GM.[22]

Caguas (4-2 W-L) won the four-team event at Escobar Stadium. First baseman Vic Power and a San Juan reinforcement, second baseman Jack Cassini, produced for Caguas, as did series MVP Jim Rivera. Cassini, Clemente's teammate with the 1954 Montreal Royals, opined that "Clemente had the makings of a future big-league star, as a 19-year-old, with Santurce."[23] Coincidentally, Clemente began wearing number 21 in the PRWL in 1953-54, as a gesture to honor his parents, Melchor Clemente and Luisa Walker.[24] Roberto Clemente Walker has 21 letters; it is a common practice in Puerto Rico to list paternal and maternal surnames.

ONE OF THE BEST WINTER LEAGUE TEAMS EVER ASSEMBLED (1954-55)

Don Zimmer was in a reflective mood as a Boston Red Sox coach when the author asked him about the talent on the 1954-55 Santurce Crabbers team, one with power, speed, defense, and three solid starters, Sam Jones (league MVP, pitching triple crown: 14 wins, 1.77 ERA, 171 strikeouts),[25] 13-game winner Rubén Gómez, and Bill Greason. "Without a doubt, it was probably the best Winter League baseball club ever assembled. I mean, we had guys like Buzz Clarkson, myself, Ronnie Samford, George Crowe, Valmy Thomas, and Harry Chiti catching. We had Mays, Thurman, and Clemente in the outfield. I mean, you're talking about a big-league ballclub. Not

only that, but Herman Franks was an outstanding manager. We could have beaten National League clubs."[26]

Clemente cracked a three-run homer on Opening Day, October 17, against San Juan and continued his torrid hitting throughout a 72-game season, one which 47-25 Santurce won by five games over Caguas (42-30) and by nine over San Juan (38-34). Left-handed pitcher Pete Burnside recalled that Clemente and Mays were "younger stars trying to outdo each other on the field in a friendly rivalry."[27] There were some similarities – Clemente started to use the basket catch, similar to Mays and Olmo, a reserve. (Clemente, Mays, and Olmo were the only outfield trio on a Winter League team to all use the basket catch.)

Throughout the season, Franks would convene Clemente for an 11 A.M. practice at Escobar Stadium, along with Mays, Olmo, and 17-year-old Orlando Cepeda, who worked out with the team prior to joining them a year later. Cepeda told historian Jorge Colón Delgado that Mays taught Roberto how to more effectively field grounders and release the ball more quickly. "I stood near the mound, from where Franks hit them to the outfield. ... Those incoming throws from Clemente and Mays burned my glove hand," Cepeda remembered."[28] Clemente benefited immensely from these practices, per Cepeda and Burnside. Franks put in a good word for Clemente to Branch Rickey Jr. of the Pittsburgh Pirates before the November 22, 1954, Rule 5 draft. (Clemente was the first pick of the draft.)[29]

Clemente impressed the Pirates brass by slugging two homers in the League All-Star Game, at Mayagüez on December 12. One was a solo shot off Caguas's Roberto Vargas in the third; Ponce's Dave Cole gave up his two-run shot in the fifth inning. (Caguas-Ponce-Mayagüez players comprised the "South" team, while San Juan-Santurce was the "North" squad.) Mays' inside-the-park homer in the first started the scoring in the North's 7-5 win, with Rubén Gómez the victor.[30]

Willie Mays, Roberto Clemente, Buster Clarkson, Bob Thurman, and George Crowe on a winter league dream team. Courtesy of Jorge Colón Delgado.

Through 50 games, Mays was hitting .404, with Clemente following at .378. Thurman, third in the race, was hitting .366.[31] Bill Greason had fond memories of Clemente: "I called Roberto 'hermano' [brother]. We were real close; he was a very fine young man, dedicated and determined. Wouldn't say too much, just come to the clubhouse and speak to some of the guys, get his uniform on, field infield grounders, then go to the outfield. He had a fine disposition.[32]

Thurman and the author took part in a radio sports talk and call-in show, Foro Deportivo, in Ponce, two days before the first induction ceremony (October 20, 1991) of the Puerto Rico Professional Baseball Hall of Fame. Thurman and Clemente were two of 10 inductees. One caller asked Thurman about Clemente's throwing arm, noting that he played left field for Santurce in 1954-55. Thurman,

a right fielder and pitcher, responded, "strong and accurate."[33]

Thurman was proud of his role as a mentor to Clemente, who respected all Negro Leaguers on the 1954-55 club.[34]

Clemente's .344 batting average was fourth best, behind Mays, but his league-leading 65 runs scored eclipsed Mays' 63.[35] Clemente had a good final series vs. Caguas, won by Santurce, four games to one. His four hits and four RBIs propelled Santurce to a 10-3 Game One win on February 3. Zimmer got the headlines with three home runs and 10 RBIs in five games.[36]

The February 1955 Caribbean Series in Caracas, Venezuela, resulted in Santurce's third title in five years – after winning the 1951 and 1953 events. Zimmer earned MVP laurels with a .385 average, three homers, and four RBIs. Here are Clemente highlights from the 1955 series:

Action photograph at Caguas in the 1956-57 season. Courtesy of Jorge Colón Delgado.

February 12 – First-inning homer off Ramón Monzant knotted the score, 1-1; Mays' walk-off homer in the 11th, with Clemente on first, won it, over Magallanes (Venezuela), 4-2

February 13 – Two RBIs, in a 7-6 win versus Almendares (Cuba)

February 14 – Two triples in an 11-3 win over Carta Vieja (Panamá).[37]

Clemente's eight runs scored were tops in the Series. He went 7-for-26, with a double, two triples, one home run, three RBIs, and a .577 slugging percentage.[38] Collectively, Santurce had a .290 batting average and .500 slugging percentage. Clemente, after Pittsburgh won the 1971 World Series, was asked if he had ever played on such a powerful team. His response was, "Yes, when the Santurce Crabbers won the [1955] Caribbean Series."[39]

CAGUAS UPENDS SANTURCE (1955-56)

Clemente mostly played center field, flanked by Gerard in left and Thurman in right. His 85 hits in 278 at-bats gave him a .306 average; his seven homers were the most he ever hit in a PRWL season.[40]

Clemente met Carl Hubbell at Sixto Escobar Stadium after the latter arrived in Puerto Rico on January 9, 1956, to get a closer look at Gómez, Steve Ridzik, and Al Worthington. (Hubbell was the New York Giants farm director.) "I introduced Roberto [Clemente] to Hubbell," noted Gómez. "Hubbell got to watch some of our games – he thought Roberto would eventually become a very good major league hitter."[41]

Owen, now managing Ponce, opined that Clemente had "improved offensively and defensively" since 1953-54. "He just had one season

[1954] in the minors, and 1955 Pittsburgh," said Owen. "He was on his way. ..."[42] Santurce (43-29) faced Caguas (38-34) in the finals, and lost it, four games to two.[43]

CLEMENTE FLIRTS WITH .400 AND IS SOLD TO CAGUAS (1956-57)

By late December of 1956, Clemente sported a .431 average (56-for-130), with Santurce.[44] Zorrilla publicly announced his team was for sale[45] and transferred team ownership to Ramón N. Cuevas, who in turn sold Clemente, Juan Pizarro, and Samford to Caguas, for $30,000 in cash on December 30 to liquidate Santurce's debt. Cuevas announced this to Santurce players, prior to a doubleheader that day in Mayagüez.

Rubén Gómez was so livid he took off his uniform, stormed out of the clubhouse, and drove home. "I replaced Roberto in center field in January," recalled Gómez. "We still won the [regular season] pennant without three key players."[46] Eighteen-year-old Marcial "Canenita" Allen, a Crabbers batboy and Clemente confidante, tearfully recalled Clemente's reaction years later. "Roberto told me to grab the stuff," said Allen. "'You're coming to Caguas with me.' He was a brother and a friend."[47]

Ted Norbert took over managing duties for Santurce from Ramón "Monchile" Concepción. The Crabbers (43-29) won their third straight pennant but lost to second-place Mayagüez (41-31), managed by Owen, in the finals.

Prior to his sale to Caguas, Clemente got two hits off Caguas's Sandy Koufax, in the young left-hander's last PRWL start on December 16, a 2-0, seven-inning shutout of Santurce, in the second game of a twin bill.[48]

With Caguas, Clemente went 33-for-95, a fine .347 average, but it dropped his league-leading final mark to .396, with 89 hits in 225 at-bats, still the best league batting average of the 1950s.[49]

Clemente joined Caguas in the midst of an 18-game hitting streak and extended it to 23 after game one of a January 5, 1957, doubleheader with San Juan, breaking Francisco "Pancho" Coímbre's standard of 22 straight in 1943-44. Luis Arroyo, aka Tite, put an end to it when he collared Clemente in game two of the twin bill. Tom Lasorda took the loss. "I was [Clemente's] teammate with Santurce and Caguas," recalled Lasorda. "What a great competitor."[50]

Caguas (39-33) and San Juan (39-33) tied for third, necessitating a one-game tiebreaker at Yldefonso Solá Morales Stadium, the Criollos' home. San Juan skipper Ralph Houk gave the ball to Tite Arroyo on one day of rest. Juan Pizarro took the mound for Caguas. Arroyo prevailed, 4-1, but all eyes were on Clemente, who entered the day hitting .398. He needed a 2-for-4 game on January 28 to reach .400 but fell short with one hit in four at-bats.[51]

When postseason awards were announced for 1956-57, José "Ronquito" García of Mayagüez garnered the MVP.[52] He finished second in batting average, but propelled Owen's club to a berth in the 1957 Caribbean Series. García remembered Clemente getting three or four hits whenever he would have two or three in a game. "Give Roberto credit for the batting title," said García. "We won the [PRWL] championship, and that's why the writers voted me the MVP."[53]

ABBREVIATED 1957-58 SEASON AND 1958 CARIBBEAN SERIES

The 1957-58 Caguas-Rio Piedras Criollos waited until January 12, 1958, to see Clemente in action. The club had added Rio Piedras to the team's name in 1956-57 to expand the franchise's marketing base. Clemente's debut came at Ponce's Paquito Montaner Stadium.[54] In nine games, he went 8-for-32.[55] Teammate Canenita Allen won Rookie-of-the-Year laurels. The 33-31 Criollos tied San Juan for second, three games behind

Santurce. Caguas bested San Juan three games to one in the semis before sweeping Santurce.

Clemente pulverized Santurce pitching in the league finals, with nine hits in 17 at-bats, a .529 average. On January 31, at home, he doubled and hit two singles off Greason, in game two, a 5-0 shutout by Roberto Vargas. Rubén Gómez was in center field for Santurce, with Clemente in center for Caguas.[56]

Caguas-Rio Piedras hosted the February 1958 Caribbean Series at Sixto Escobar Stadium. Juan Pizarro fanned 17 Carta Vieja Yankees on Opening Night, an all-time Caribbean Series record.[57] "I threw hard," said Pizarro. "It was an honor to represent Puerto Rico, with Clemente and Vic Power playing behind me."[58]

Clemente hit Caguas's only series homer,[59] off Marianao's Bob Shaw, in game three on February 10, an eventual 5-4 win for Cuba. Caguas and Marianao faced off in the February 13 finale. Ninth-inning singles by Solly Drake and Minnie Miñoso, preceded an error and Ray Noble sacrifice fly to give Marianao a 2-0 win.[60]

Marianao became the first team to win back-to-back Caribbean Series. Caguas duplicated this 60 years later (2017 and 2018).[61] Total attendance was 57,355, including 13,269 on Opening Night, and standing room 16,000 on the closing night.[62] Escobar's seating capacity was roughly 13,500.

Clemente distinguished himself by being voted center fielder on the Series All-Star Team, with a .391 average (9-for-23) and .609 slugging percentage. Vic Power, an all-star at third, had a .458 average. Pizarro fanned 29 in 16⅔ innings.[63]

CLEMENTE'S CARIBBEAN SERIES LEGACY

In 12 Caribbean Series games, Clemente went 16-for-49 for a .327 average, with one double, three triples, two homers, and six RBIs. He scored 14 runs. His .592 slugging percentage ranks fourth all-time, in Phase I, 1949-1960 of the Caribbean Series, for players with at least 45 at-bats.[64]

TABLE I: TOP 10 CARIBBEAN SERIES SLG, 45+ AT-BATS, PHASE I

Player	Country	AB	TB	SLG
Wilmer Fields	PR-Venezuela	57	38	.667
Willard Brown	PR	67	42	.627
Jim Gilliam	PR	47	29	.617
Roberto Clemente	PR	49	29	.592
Héctor Rodríguez	Cuba	83	49	.590
Bob Thurman	PR	63	37	.587
Orlando Cepeda	PR	45	26	.578
Pedro Formental	Cuba	60	34	.567
Héctor López	Panamá	97	51	.526
Luis R. Olmo	PR	76	37	.487

Note: Puerto Rico is abbreviated PR.
Source: Tony Piña Campora.

Clemente was posthumously inducted into the Caribbean Series Hall of Fame (aka the Caribbean Baseball Hall of Fame) in 2015.[65]

Overall, with Caguas and Santurce, Clemente played six winter seasons and posted a .325 batting average, 358 hits in 1,102 at-bats, with 55 doubles, 13 triples, 17 homers, 129 RBIs, and a .445 slugging percentage. He scored 173 runs and stole nine bases.[66]

ACKNOWLEDGMENTS

Grateful acknowledgment to Marcial "Canenita" Allen, Pete Burnside, Jack Cassini, José Crescioni Benítez, José "Ronquito" García, Rubén Gómez, Bill Greason, Harvey Haddix, Billy Hunter, Tom Lasorda, Luis R. Mayoral, Guigo Otero Suro, Mickey Owen, Tony Piña Campora, Juan "Terín" Pizarro, Vic Power, Steve Ridzik, Bob Thurman, and Don Zimmer, for phone/in-person interviews and emails. Jorge Colón Delgado provided Clemente's PRWL stats. Stew Thornley wrote Clemente's SABR bio.

SOURCES

Maraniss, David. Clemente: The Passion and Grace of Baseball's Last Hero (New York: Simon & Schuster, 2006).

Costas, Rafael. Enciclopedia Béisbol Ponce Leones (Santo Domingo, Dominican Republic: Editora Corripio, 1989).

NOTES

1   Hal Wagenheim, *Clemente!* (New York: Praeger Publishers, 1973), 23.

2   Luis Rodríguez Mayoral, *Roberto Clemente aún escucha las ovaciones* (Hato Rey, Puerto Rico: Ramallo Brothers Printing, 1987), 11.

3   Rodríguez Mayoral phone interview with Thomas Van Hyning, September 2, 2021. Muñoz Marín served four terms as governor (1948-1964). Rodríguez Mayoral confirmed that Clemente actively supported the PPD his adult life.

4   Billy Hunter phone interview with Thomas Van Hyning, May 11, 1991. All other phone and in-person interviews cited were with the subject and the author.

5   Jorge Colón Delgado, *Pedrín Zorrilla: El Cangrejo Mayor* (Colombia: OP Gráficas, 2011), 309.

6   El Mundo, December 17, 1954; Thomas E. Van Hyning, *Puerto Rico's Winter League* (Jefferson, North Carolina: McFarland & Company, 1995), 49.

7   Harvey Haddix phone interview, July 28, 1991.

8   Colón Delgado, *Pedrín Zorrilla: El Cangrejo Mayor*, 309.

9   https://www.beisbol101.com/roberto-clemente-3/.

10 https://sabr.org/bioproj/person/bobo-holloman/.

11 Williams, a Marine Corps aviator in World War II, had been called back to service during the Korean War. Colón Delgado, *Pedrín Zorrilla: El Cangrejo Mayor*, 309.

12 Thomas E. Van Hyning, *The Santurce Crabbers: Sixty Seasons of Puerto Rican Winter League Baseball* (Jefferson, North Carolina: McFarland & Company, 1999), 42.

13 Vic Power in-person interview, December 28, 1991.

14 Jorge S. Figueredo, *Cuban Baseball: A Statistical History, 1878-1961* (Jefferson, North Carolina: McFarland & Company, 2003), 372.

15 Guigo Otero Suro in-person interview, November 20, 1997.

16 Otero Suro in-person interview, November 20, 1997.

17 https://www.beisbol101.com/roberto-clemente-3/.

18 Van Hyning, *The Santurce Crabbers*, 43.

19 José A. Crescioni Benítez, *El Béisbol Profesional Boricua* (San Juan, Puerto Rico: Aurora Comunicación Integral, September 1997), 85.

20 Tom Lasorda in-person interview, Vero Beach, Florida, March 1993.

21 Mickey Owen phone interview, March 5, 1992.

22 Owen phone interview.

23 Jack Cassini phone interview, April 2, 1993.

24 Luis Rodríguez Mayoral, *Mas Allá de un Sueño* (Hato Rey, Puerto Rico: Ramallo Brothers Printing, 1981), 19.

25 https://www.beisbol101.com/sam-jones-2/. Accessed September 7, 2021.

26 Don Zimmer in-person interview, Winter Haven, Florida, March 1992.

27 Van Hyning, *The Santurce Crabbers*, 66.

28 Colón Delgado, *Pedrín Zorrilla: El Cangrejo Mayor*, 360.

29 Hy Turkin, "'Good Prospects Fewer' – Only 13 in Majors' Draft," *The Sporting News*, December 1, 1954: 4. On February 19, 1954, the Brooklyn Dodgers signed Clemente for a $10,000 bonus.

30 Víctor Navarro, *Los Juegos de Estrellas* (Aguadilla, Puerto Rico: Navarro's Publishing Services, 1992), 18-19.

31 *The Sporting News*, January 5, 1955: 23.

32 Bill Greason phone interview, March 25, 1991.

33 Bob Thurman, Foro Deportivo, Ponce, Puerto Rico, October 18, 1991.

34 Bob Thurman in-person interview, Ponce, Puerto Rico, October 19, 1991.

35 Crescioni Benítez, *El Béisbol Profesional Boricua*, 89.

36 Pito Alvarez de la Vega, "Zimmer's 3 HRs Pace Santurce to Puerto Rico Title," *The Sporting News*, February 16, 1955: 28.

37 *The Sporting News*, February 23, 1955: 28, 30.

38 Colón Delgado, *La Maquinaria Perfecta*, 170.

39 Colón Delgado, *La Maquinaria Perfecta*, 189.

40 https://www.beisbol101.com/roberto-clemente-3/. Accessed September 5, 2021.

41 Rubén Gómez in-person interview, Hato Rey, Puerto Rico, November 30, 1992.

42 Mickey Owen phone interview, March 5, 1992.

43 *The Sporting News*, February 15, 1956: 34.

44 José Crescioni Benítez work papers.

45 Jorge Colón Delgado, *Los Indios de Mayagüez* (Mayagüez, Puerto Rico: EASM Publishing Co. LLC), 142.

46 Rubén Gómez in-person interview, Hato Rey, Puerto Rico, November 30, 1992. Gómez was allowed to drive to away games in his Corvette.

47 Marcial "Canenita" Allen in-person interview, Hato Rey, Puerto Rico, December 15, 1991.

48 *The Sporting News*, December 26, 1956: 20.

49 José Crescioni Benítez work papers.

50 Tom Lasorda in-person interview, Vero Beach, Florida, March 1993.

51 El Mundo, January 29, 1957.

52 Héctor Barea, *Libro oficial béisbol profesional de Puerto Rico* (Guaynabo, Puerto Rico: Art Printing, 1981), 48.

53 José "Ronquito" García in-person interview, San Juan, Puerto Rico, December 1, 1993.

54 El Mundo, January 13, 1958.

55 https://www.beisbol101.com/roberto-clemente-3/. Accessed September 6, 2021.

56 Pito Alvarez de la Vega, "Clemente Paces Caguas Team to Sweep of Finals," *The Sporting News*, February 12, 1958: 24.

57 *The Sporting News*, February 19, 1958: 30.

58 Juan "Terín" Pizarro in-person interview, Santurce, Puerto Rico, February 10, 1982.

59 https://www.baseball-reference.com/bullpen/1958_Caribbean_Series. Accessed September 6, 2021.

60 *The Sporting News*, February 19, 1958: 30.

61 Thomas E. Van Hyning, "Caguas Criollos: Five Caribbean Series Crowns and Cooperstown Connections," *Baseball Research Journal* (Phoenix: SABR, 2018), 16.

62 *The Sporting News*, February 19, 1958: 30.

63 Tony Piña Campora work papers, Santo Domingo, Dominican Republic.

64 Thomas E. Van Hyning, https://www.beisbol101.com/jim-gilliam-baltimore-elite-giants-aguadilla-almendares-minors-and-santurce-part-i/. Accessed September 6, 2021.

65 Tony Piña Campora work papers, Santo Domingo, Dominican Republic.

66 https://www.beisbol101.com/roberto-clemente-3/. Accessed September 6, 2021.

ROBERTO CLEMENTE'S PUERTO RICO WINTER LEAGUE CAREER (PART II)

BY THOMAS E. VAN HYNING

In August 1959, Clemente was traded from Caguas of the Puerto Rico Winter League to San Juan, with Canenita Allen and José "Palillo" Santiago for minor-league outfielders Herminio Cortés, Rafael Sálamo, and $30,000.[1] Cortés played for York and Sálamo with Sioux City in the low minors. Allen insisted he was an "insurance policy" in case Clemente rested that winter.[2] Caguas coveted Cortés; he led the 1958-59 San Juan Senators in batting average (.291) and homers (10).[3] José M. Rivera, president of the San Juan club, officially accepted this trade via an August 15, 1959, letter to league President Carlos García de la Noceda.[4] A month later, Clemente signed his San Juan contract for $800 per month plus $200 per month for expenses.[5]

DEVOTED SAN JUAN SENATORS AND MONTE IRVIN FAN

Clemente idolized Monte Irvin, San Juan's superstar in 1945-47. He traveled from Carolina to Sixto Escobar Stadium by public transportation to see Irvin play. After 1945-46 early season games, Clemente waited for Irvin to come out of the ballpark so he could have a close glimpse of his favorite ballplayer.[6] As the season progressed, Clemente made an impression on Irvin outside the ballpark before San Juan games. Irvin told MLB.com's Tom Singer, "There'd be youngsters hanging around, and we'd let kids carry our bags to get in the park for free. Roberto and Orlando Cepeda, they were always there together. ... Clemente always told me he developed a throwing arm like mine because he'd always admired the way I threw the ball."[7]

Clemente once told Freddie Thon Jr. that he was "a big fan of my dad (Freddie Thon Sr.) and Monte Irvin, and always rooted for San Juan."[8] (Thon Sr. was San Juan's right fielder in 1945-47 and a starting pitcher in 1940-42, during Irvin's first two seasons with the Senators.) After a Clemente season with Pittsburgh, he would bring in a large amount of suits, pants, and shirts for cleaning at Freddie Thon Cleaners, located in Hato Rey, Puerto Rico, before expanding to other locations.[9]

SPLENDID 1959-60 SEASON

A 25-year-old Clemente wore number 21 for the 1959-60 Senators, managed by Nino Escalera. They became close friends and developed a bond, which lasted until Clemente's untimely passing.[10] "Roberto and I were PRWL rivals in the 1950s but this changed when I managed him [1959-60] and was his San Juan teammate," noted Escalera. "We thought alike when it came to baseball strategy and looked out for each other. ... He was a younger brother to me."[11] (Palillo Santiago gave the author a ride to Escalera's home and indicated that the 1959-60 San Juan team chemistry was outstanding.)[12]

Clemente's .330 batting average in the 1959-60 season trailed Caguas's Vic Power (.347) and Mayagüez's Ramón Conde (.336). Power remembered Clemente playing with a bad back. "Even though he played hurt, Roberto toiled with pride and was a winner," said Power. "Because of his bad back I wasn't sure Roberto was going to be the superstar he became from 1960 on, but (I) felt he would always give his best effort."[13]

Clemente's hustle was evident; his six triples trailed Escalera's league-leading seven, and surpassed the five hit by Mayagüez's Ray Barker and San Juan teammate Carlos Bernier.[14] San Juan games were broadcast on the radio in English and Spanish thanks to businessman Bob Leith Sr. Phil Rizzuto broadcast the games in English, while Luis Olmo did Spanish transmissions – the first time in Puerto Rico's baseball history that radio broadcasts were carried in both languages.[15] "It didn't take Phil long to realize this was a hotbed of baseball down here," said Leith. "Olmo did a great job, too, with the Spanish version."[16] Olmo added, "I enjoyed covering Roberto's exploits from the booth. He was a more complete player than he was with Santurce, mid-1950s."[17]

San Juan (41-23) edged Caguas (39-24) for the pennant and upended Mayagüez in a six-game semifinal series. Caguas bested Santurce and

Clemente with San Juan 1959.
Courtesy of Thomas Van Hyning.

then knocked off San Juan, five games to one, to qualify for the February 1960 Caribbean Series in Panamá.

A 1960-61 TITLE AND INTER-AMERICAN SERIES IN CARACAS, VENEZUELA

Bob Leith Sr., San Juan's new owner, forgot to send player contracts out by the deadline. All San Juan players were technically free agents, which drew the attention of the press and radio stations. Clemente, via Pittsburgh, came through like a true pro. Leith remembered their phone conversation. "Forget about it," said Clemente. "I'll sign for the same amount I made last year, $1,000 per month."[18] The contract was signed by all parties on December 15, 1960.[19]

Clemente was everybody's hero in Puerto Rico after Pittsburgh won the 1960 World Series. He took the first half (32 games) off, before playing the second half, one where San Juan (23-9) qualified for the finals after a 16-16 first-half.[20] The Senators and Caguas Criollos again faced off in a best-of-nine final. San Juan emerged victorious, winning five games and losing three.

In 29 games, Clemente went 31-for-109, a .284 batting average. Canenita Allen played right field in the first half. Luis Arroyo, Clemente's friend, won 10 games and league MVP honors. Lefty hurler Jim Archer noticed Clemente's leadership qualities. "Clemente drove us to win that second half," Archer declared. "He was a superstar and set a positive example for all."[21] Horace Clarke, a San Juan utility infielder, remembered Clemente being "nice to all the young San Juan players."[22]

Luman Harris, a Baltimore Orioles coach, managed San Juan. Lee MacPhail Jr., Baltimore's GM/president, agreed to send Orioles prospects to San Juan, including Jerry Adair, Jack Fisher, and Wes Stock.[23] Leith's friendship with Rizzuto brought him in contact with MacPhail. Leith recalled how Brooks Robinson interrupted a meeting in Baltimore between Leith and MacPhail and tried to pass as a rookie. Robinson played in Colombia and Cuba from the mid- to late 1950s and enjoyed it.

In Game One of the finals, on February 1, 1961, Clemente, in right field, witnessed a 536-foot homer hit by Frank Howard off Jack Fisher at Sixto Escobar Stadium, which was shared by the Senators and Santurce. Howard's homer was the second longest in PRWL history, after one estimated at 600 feet by Josh Gibson for Santurce on March 1, 1942.[24]

San Juan, reinforced by Orlando Cepeda and Juan Pizarro from Santurce, traveled to Caracas for a four-team Inter-American Series, arranged due to the political situation in Cuba. Clemente

solved a tense situation when San Juan's stateside imports wanted more money to play in Venezuela. "Clemente told me, 'Bob, let me handle this,'" said Leith. "So he closed the door to our dressing room and reminded [the imports] that their contract said they get the same salary for playing in the Inter-American Series as they got in Puerto Rico. … If anyone refused to honor their contract, he would be the first one to call [Commissioner] Ford Frick." Leith called this 10-minute episode the shortest strike in baseball history. No one argued with Clemente.[25]

San Juan was blanked twice by Bob Gibson of the Valencia Industrialists, series champs from Venezuela. The second was a 1-0 gem.[26] Leith recalled Clemente's reaction to seeing Gibson warming up before his first start versus San Juan. "Clemente says to me, 'We're in trouble.' I say, 'Why?' 'You see that pitcher warming up [per Clemente]? Well, he throws aspirins!'"[27]

MEL STEINER RHUBARB, 1961-62

On October 23, 1961, Clemente, Orlando Cepeda, and Luis Arroyo were welcomed to the Governor's Mansion (La Fortaleza) and recognized by Governor Luis Muñoz Marín for 1961 major-league accomplishments, including Clemente's batting title.[28] San Juan was languishing in fifth, at 23-33, in the 80-game season. Senators fans clamored for the 1961 National League batting champ to play. Canenita Allen did his best, but Clemente's return helped San Juan win 18 of 24 contests to tie Arecibo for fourth. Clemente went 18-for-66, a .273 batting average.[29]

The one-game playoff was at Sixto Escobar Stadium on January 23, 1962, the final regular-season game there. (New Hiram Bithorn Stadium opened in 1962-63.) Clemente played some center field for San Juan. Prior to the one-game playoff, Arecibo beat San Juan thanks to a bases-loaded double by rookie Art López, who felt he "had a future in baseball" after this double – which Clemente could not catch – with key implications for his career.[30]

Arecibo's Phil Niekro was removed early in the tiebreaker by skipper Luis Olmo. Clemente batted against Claude Raymond with the bases loaded in the second inning of a game tied, 3-3. Germán Rivera, Arecibo's shortstop, recalled: "Roberto bounced one up the middle on a 3-and-2 pitch. We got the force and there was a close play at first base and umpire Mel Steiner called him out. Nino and Napoleón Reyes [San Juan's manager] came up to Steiner and there were punches thrown. I intervened and tried to break up the fight."[31] In the mêlée, Steiner suffered torn ligaments in his left arm and a shoulder sprain. Escalera claimed Steiner had his hand up with the "out" sign before the ball reached first base. "I was willing to go back on the field when Steiner sarcastically told Reyes, our Cuban manager, to go back to Cuba. I told Reyes he should not take this and then it happened – Reyes bumped Steiner with his huge belly. ..."[32]

Arecibo won the game. According to Clemente's version, made public several days later, Tommie Aaron did not tag him or have his foot on the base. "Steiner's angle was not a good one. I argued the call, but my teammate Chico Ruiz grabbed me to keep Steiner from giving me the heave. If I had said something vulgar or even hit Steiner, he would have thumbed me out of the game."[33]

A hearing was held, attended by game umpires Doug Harvey, Paul Pryor, and Steiner, and Clemente, Escalera, and Reyes. Escalera was fined $50 and suspended for the first 10 games of the 1962-63 season. Reyes got a $100 fine and a three-week suspension to start 1962-63. Clemente was exonerated.[34] He managed the Rio Piedras Cardinals (Goya) Double-A amateur team in February 1963 due to his friendship with team official Caguitas Colón and compiled a 4-2 won-loss month.[35]

BATTING CHASE WITH TONY OLIVA (1963-64) AND NICARAGUA INTER-AMERICAN SERIES

Clemente's .345 average (61-for-177) trailed Arecibo's Tony Oliva (.365) and Ponce's Walt Bond (.349).[36] Arecibo's Art López (.337) and San Juan's Jerry McNertney (.333) finished fourth and fifth. San Juan, 15-22 on December 4, 1963,[37] won 20 of its final 33 games. Les Moss replaced Joe Buzas and piloted the club to the title. San Juan had a Chicago White Sox flavor with catcher McNertney, infielders Don Buford, Deacon Jones, and Marv Staehle, and pitchers Joel Horlen and Fritz Ackley. Palillo Santiago opined that a good chemistry developed between these White Sox prospects, Clemente, and others, beyond a typical "working agreement" between Chicago and San Juan.[38] McNertney saw a hitter in batting practice driving bullets into the outfield of Hiram Bithorn Stadium. He asked one teammate about the hitter, who was wearing uniform number 21. (McNertney had just replaced John Bateman on the roster.) "Clemente played every winter game hard – to win," recalled McNertney. "He played 150-plus big-league games, plus spring training. It had to be tough for him even though it was in front of his home fans. To see him come there and work so hard was very impressive.[39]

Staehle noticed that San Juan fans lit matches one night during a postseason game. He looked over to Cocó Laboy, playing third, and asked him what was going on. Laboy replied, "A funeral. We're burying them and they're holding a funeral."[40] Staehle asserted that Clemente never forgot where he came from. "His people were first, and he played because of that. He didn't need to play; he loved the people over there and that's why he played. I speak proudly that I was a teammate of his."[41]

Clemente made $700 a month in 1963-64, plus $200 a month for expenses.[42] His highest PRWL salary was $1,000 a month, according to Table I, and $500 per month (1969-70) was his top compensation for travel, food, and related expenses.[43]

Third-place San Juan (35-35) disposed of second-place Ponce (36-34) four games to two in the semifinals and then beat fourth-place Mayagüez, in a five-game final.[44] Palillo Santiago recalled Clemente's best 1963-64 catch.

"In the finals against Mayagüez, I had a one-run lead with two outs in the ninth. Boog Powell was at the plate. I threw him a fastball. It was 420 feet to dead center in Mayagüez and quite dark. The lights weren't too bright in that part of the stadium. Powell got hold of it, but Clemente was playing in center. He turned around, slid into the fence. It must have been dead quiet for five minutes, when he caught the ball with his back facing the infield. The game was over."[45]

The Senators traveled to Managua, Nicaragua, for the February 1964 Inter-American Series. San Juan reinforced itself with Cepeda, Pizarro, José Pagán, Horace Clarke, and Conde, but split six games, losing twice to Cinco Estrellas (5-1 record), one of two Nicaraguan teams.

Clemente went 7-for-19 (.368 batting average) with three RBIs.[46] He also lost a fly ball in the sun during one game and raced away from a native reptile in another when a fan in the bleachers threw a huge iguana toward Clemente, in right, and he bolted to the dugout. Palillo Santiago affirmed that Nicaraguan soldiers bearing rifles were stationed in the dugout for some games. Clemente, though, was a fan favorite and made a lot of friends. "What an irony," noted Santiago. "This experience is transformed into a mission to help the people of Nicaragua and history tells us what Roberto Clemente did for that country."[47] Art López, who reinforced Cinco Estrellas, scored the winning run in the final game versus San Juan on a sacrifice fly by Leo Posada. "We did the little things to win," said López. "I admired Clemente but felt vindicated after finding out the Puerto Rico sportswriters left me off the final All-Star Team in the PRWL. … Should have been on it with Clemente and Oliva."[48]

TABLE I: ROBERTO CLEMENTE'S SALARIES AND PER DIEM IN PUERTO RICO

Season	Team	Salary	Per Diem	Total
1952-53	Santurce	$40 / week	None	$40 / week
1953-54	Santurce	$110 / bi-monthly	None	$110 / bi-monthly
1954-55	Santurce	$275 / bi-monthly	None	$275 / bi-monthly
1955-56	Santurce	$1,000 / month	None	$1,000 / month
1956-57	Santurce-Caguas	$1,000 / month	None	$1,000 / month
1957-58	Caguas	$1,000 / month	$250 / month	$1,250 / month
1959-60	San Juan	$800 / month	$200 / month	$1,000 / month
1960-61	San Juan	$800 / month	$200 / month	$1,000 / month
1961-62	San Juan	$700 / month	$200 / month	$900 / month
1963-64	San Juan	$700 / month	$200 / month	$900 / month
1964-65	San Juan	$1,000 / month	$300 / month	$1,300 / month
1967-68	San Juan	$800 / month	$400 / month	$1,200 / month
1969-70	San Juan	$1,000 / month	$500 / month	$1,500 / month
1970-71	San Juan	$1,000 / month	$300 / month	$1,300 / month

Source: Jorge Fidel López Vélez, Roberto Clemente: "El astro boricua" (Colombia: Editorial Nomos S.A., 2019).

PLAYER-MANAGER (1964-65)

San Juan (34-36) finished fourth under Cal Ermer, and player-manager Clemente. Ermer noted that San Juan's brass wanted Clemente to manage so he would play on an everyday basis. He attended Clemente's November 14, 1964, wedding, and liked him a lot. "Roberto had just started playing and we lost a tough doubleheader," said Ermer. "The owners asked me to resign, but I told them, 'I didn't come here to resign, so put it in the paper and fire me.' Clemente was always hustling and played hard just like in the States. The first game he managed, he got hurt."[49]

Ermer was fired on December 21, 1964, by GM Pepe Seda.[50] As manager, Clemente was 9-12.[51] He played in 14 games and hit .385 (15-for-39), with three doubles, two triples, two homers, seven RBIs, and a .718 slugging percentage.[52] His managerial debut against Mayagüez and star pitcher Dennis McLain featured two doubles and a pair of RBIs, but he twisted his left ankle on the second double and took himself out of the lineup for a few games. His first managerial win came on December 27 in game two of a twin bill against Arecibo. "I'm only doing this [managing] until they get someone else," stated Clemente.[53]

A night was held in Clemente's honor on December 30 when Ponce visited San Juan. He received trophies from the Senators' board of directors and three Santurce fans. Ponce owner Yuyo González presented him with a plaque.[54]

Don Buford led San Juan regulars in hitting and developed a fine rapport with Clemente. Suffering from a bad knee, Buford accompanied Clemente on visits to a chiropractor. Buford remembered how managing responsibilities caused a little added pressure on Clemente, but he was very loose, in a sense, and did not interfere with his players. "A typical Clemente pep talk was, 'You guys know how to play; stay fundamentally sound and we'll be OK,'" said Buford. "It

Roberto Clemente as San Juan Senators manager 1970-71 season. Courtesy of Jorge Colón Delgado.

wasn't like Clemente had the San Juan players do additional things."[55]

Clemente inserted Canenita Allen in right while he recuperated from a lawn-mowing accident at his home after a sharp rock hit him on the thigh. Clemente felt better by January 6 and suited up for the Latin American team in the all-star game, and singled as a pinch-hitter for skipper Olmo, but his upper thigh ligament had been partially severed and was held together by a thin strand. After treatment, Clemente told a reporter, "The doctor told me that it will take some time for the injury to heal. Rest for now. ..."[56]

In the semifinals, Santurce (41-28) upended San Juan in six games. Marv Staehle, now with Santurce, conversed with Clemente and recalled that Roberto and coach José "Pantalones" Santiago were focused, personable, and friendly.[57] Rubén Gómez won the final game in relief when

Tony Pérez drilled a three-run homer in the 10th. "I played against Roberto in Puerto Rico and the National League, and with him on [National League] All-Star teams, said Pérez. "That [1964-65] playoff homer for Santurce was special – Roberto was in the other dugout."[58]

Tommie Sisk blanked Santurce in Game Two after refusing a $1,500 offer by Águilas Cibaeñas (Dominican Republic club) to pitch in a Caracas four-team tournament. He was impressed by Clemente's courage, leadership ability, and playing skills. (Sisk's locker was next to Clemente's his six years in Pittsburgh.) "Bobby was very proud of being a Puerto Rican. He never did anything dishonorable to his country. We were very good friends. … He was the best ballplayer I ever saw. I was in Puerto Rico to work on certain things and don't ever remember being as tired from playing the game on a year-round basis."[59]

A TWO-YEAR SABBATICAL (1965-67)

Clemente had two pinch-hit at-bats for the 1965-66 Senators and did not play in 1966-67. Joe Hoerner, Clemente's San Juan teammate in 1963-65, said the fifth-place Senators (31-39 in 1965-66) missed Roberto's presence in the 1965-66 season. "We had Sam Bowens in right, Jesús Alou in center and Danny Cater in left. The White Sox sent Duane Josephson and Tommy John to our club."[60]

(The author attended a Clemente baseball clinic at Hiram Bithorn Stadium in late 1966. Clemente illustrated hitting techniques and baserunning tips, and shared stories. Participants kept a certain distance from him when he took batting practice. The author's father (Sam, economic adviser to the governor with FOMENTO) mentioned a 1966 Clemente visit to La Fortaleza, the governor's mansion, related to him by island Governor Roberto Sánchez Vilella. Clemente was particularly interested in Puerto Rico's vibrant economy.[61] "Clemente was very intelligent," recalled Sam J. Van Hyning. "Sánchez Vilella said that Clemente, then in his early 30s, covered technical topics and asked probing questions."[62]

Sam and the author saw Clemente play a spring-training game for Pittsburgh vs. the New York Yankees at Bithorn Stadium on April 2, 1967. Juan Pizarro started for Pittsburgh, giving this game a Santurce-San Juan flavor.)

DON ZIMMER REUNION (1967-68)

In 1967-68, Clemente joined the Senators after Don Zimmer replaced Preston Gómez as San Juan's skipper. Archrival Santurce, managed by Earl Weaver, had a working agreement with the Baltimore Orioles. Santurce (47-22) won the regular season over Caguas (43-27), San Juan (36-34), Ponce (34-36), Arecibo (28-41), and Mayagüez (21-49). Zimmer was fired by GM Tuto Saavedra on December 15, 1967, and replaced by coach Pantalones Santiago.[63] Zimmer enjoyed living at the La Rada Hotel in the Condado section of Santurce and managing future Hall of Famers Johnny Bench and Clemente. "I appreciated Roberto," reminisced Zimmer. "We were [Santurce] teammates in the mid-1950s. The San Juan-Santurce rivalry was like the Red Sox-Yankees."[64] Clemente's debut on December 3, 1967, was a four-hit effort, including a homer, vs. Arecibo.[65] A week later, Pat Dobson fanned 21 Arecibo hitters to set a league nine-inning mark.[66] Bench caught, and Clemente saw very little action in right.

Prior to a Caguas-San Juan contest at Bithorn Stadium, Pirates GM Joe L. Brown made a surprise visit to the visitors' clubhouse. Brown introduced himself and told Caguas's Art López about a potential incentive to join the Bucs organization at the Triple-A level in 1968. Per López, Brown said, "If you have a good year at Columbus, we split the Rule 5 Draft amount – half of $25,000 or $50,000 – if you are selected by another team."[67] López replied, "I appreciate you and Roberto

[Clemente], but I'm going to Japan." Brown shook López's hand and left, but López "was forever grateful to him and Roberto – who must have put in a good word for me – for their kindness."[68]

Clemente's .382 batting average (26-for-68) and .629 slugging percentage[69] placed him on the league all-star team, along with four teammates, Bench, Tony González, Lee May, and Tony Taylor, who spoke for his Cuban countrymen when he called Roberto "The Great One."[70] May emphasized that Clemente helped him in his baseball thinking. "I would try to apply some of Roberto's ideas to my game," he said. Clemente's hospitality during the holidays made an impact on May as well. "They showed us a good time and I'll always be thankful to Roberto and his wife [Vera]."[71] Ted Savage, a Caguas outfielder, remembered Clemente as "the kind of guy who would take you home and feed you – a baseball player's baseball player."[72]

Caguas, managed by Nino Escalera, topped San Juan, four games to one, in the semifinals. Escalera managed Clemente in the January 1 all-star game, on the native team.[73] From February 8 to 15, Clemente was in Caracas, for a weeklong exhibition series. The 18-player Puerto Rico contingent comprised 16 Puerto Ricans and two US Virgin Islanders (Joe Christopher and Elrod Hendricks), natives for PRWL purposes.[74]

COT DEAL MANAGES CLEMENTE (1969-70) AND SPECIAL WINTER MEETING

Clemente rested during the 1968-69 winter, while Sparky Anderson managed San Juan. Pedrín Zorrilla was introduced as San Juan's 1969-70 GM at a March 13, 1969, press conference.[75] Zorrilla signed Cot Deal, who played against Clemente in 1952-54, to manage the Senators. Deal cherished managing Clemente. "Roberto made a statement to a friend from Puerto Rico, stating, 'I've never played for a manager that I enjoyed playing for

more.'"[76] San Juan (33-36) missed the postseason by one game. In 38 games, Clemente, was 40-for-135, a .296 batting average. Teammate Thurman Munson batted .333.[77] Clemente told Munson, "If you hit under .280, it should be considered a bad season."[78]

The December 13-14 annual winter meeting of the Major League Baseball Players Association Executive Board was held at the Sheraton Hotel in the Condado. Clemente represented Pittsburgh as the Pirates player rep – the first Latino/Caribbean native to be one. He showed his support for Curt Flood, a special guest.[79] Luis R. Mayoral noted that Clemente "was an intellectual – could have had a track and field scholarship (javelin) at the University of Puerto Rico, Mayaguez Campus; had the know-how to do front-office work for a big-league club ... but never had it in him to be a long-term manager."[80]

CLEMENTE TAKES SAN JUAN'S REINS (1970-71)

"San Juan owner Mario 'Mayito' Nevárez asked Clemente to manage San Juan as a favor," affirmed Mayoral.[81] Nino Escalera was at home in July 1970 when Clemente called him from Pittsburgh, and asked his old friend to join San Juan as a coach, adding, "Escalera could have the position for 1971-72."[82] Clemente's other coach was Clemente "Sungo" Carrera. During a preseason team workout, Escalera, complaining of severe back pains, was unable to do his coaching. Clemente gave Escalera a massage, one which completely solved this back problem the rest of Escalera's life.[83]

Clemente and Frank Robinson, Santurce's skipper, took their lineup cards to home plate just before the October 22, 1970, season opener at Bithorn Stadium. Bacardí Rum was the team's corporate sponsor. Nearly 20,000 paying fans (full seating capacity was 19,979) were in the stands when a power failure delayed the game's start for two hours. By the time San Juan's Ken Brett threw the opening pitch, the crowd had swelled to roughly 25,000 rabid souls.[84]

Brett commented on Clemente: "We loved him. There were times he would get frustrated because we didn't play at the level he expected us to play. I'll never forget the time he decided to play to prove his points. He was a hero down there; the people went crazy and it helped attendance."[85] Brett (8-3, 3.00 ERA) was Clemente's ace. Brett and Jim Lonborg (2-3, 4.93) were encouraged to pitch for San Juan by Palillo Santiago (5-1, 3.35). "Lonborg [and Brett] thought this was a good idea and so did Boston," noted Santiago. "We shared some good times. … Lonborg wasn't completely recovered from his (skiing) injury, but began showing signs of improvement."[86]

Clemente counted on Pittsburgh prospects Dave Cash, Al Oliver, and Manny Sanguillén. All played well for Clemente, but Cash and Oliver returned to the States before the postseason. Shortstop Freddie Patek hit exceptionally well (.338, 136 at-bats) when Clemente informed Patek on December 2, 1970, that Pittsburgh had traded him to the Kansas City Royals.[87] Patek returned to the States. Ken Singleton was Clemente's most consistent hitter, with a .300 batting average, 6 home runs, and 38 RBIs.[88] Singleton appreciated Clemente's advice and hospitality.[89] He elaborated: "Roberto Clemente was a true professional who gave me valuable advice on baseball and life within it. I'll never forget his views on discipline, concentration, dedication, and setting high goals, and by season's end, I would be pleasantly surprised by my accomplishments."[90]

The January 6, 1971, all-star game pitted Clemente's natives against Frank Robinson's imports. Special guest Marvin Miller threw out the first pitch. The natives prevailed 4-1, giving Clemente a 1-0 managing record in these contests.[91] On January 16 Clemente doubled off Mayagüez's Juan Veintidós for his final PRWL regular-season hit and only one in 1970-71, in four at-bats.[92]

Second-place San Juan (37-30) faced off against third-place (37-32) Santurce in the semifinals, won by the Crabbers, four games to two. Clemente's clutch two-run pinch-hit single helped San Juan win Game Three, on January 22.[93] Game Five featured Clemente hitting third, on January 25. Juan Pizarro faced San Juan's Jim Colborn. Santurce led 1-0 in the top of the fourth, when Clemente and Sanguillén singled, putting runners on first and third. Singleton flied to Reggie Jackson, the league home-run champion, in right. Jackson's best throw of the season nailed Clemente at home, and kept San Juan from a big rally.[94] Santurce won, 2-1.

Ken Brett, voted the left-handed pitcher on the final 1970-71 league all-star team, felt Clemente's managing inexperience showed in terms of running a game. "He was a wonderful man and a great player, but as far as running a game, he didn't do a great job. He had a very short temper at times about the way we played, because, let's face it, he took it very seriously. It was *his* team, and he was going to get credit or the blame for how the team played. As a result of our lackluster play at times, he got very mad at us and the guys would put towels over their faces and kind of laugh a bit – not at him [but] as a reaction to what was happening."[95]

Frank Robinson watched Clemente's growth as a major leaguer from the mid-1950s to the early 1970s. "I really can't judge him as a manager," Robinson said. "But with some more experience [he] would have made an outstanding major-league manager."[96]

Coincidentally, Santurce Crabbers fans rooted for Frank Robinson and the 1971 Baltimore Orioles in their World Series versus Pittsburgh. Puerto Rico's baseball aficionados identified with their Winter League team, when following a big-league club. Santurce's working agreement with Baltimore, 1966 to 1972, was the impetus behind Crabbers fans cheering for Baltimore. Conversely, San Juan Senators fans of the early 1970s closely followed Pittsburgh, due to Clemente and various Pirates who reinforced the Senators in that era. Historian Jorge Colón Delgado confirmed this: "Our fans [then] closely followed their favorite Winter League teams," noted Colón Delgado. "Now, they follow MLB teams, with players from Puerto Rico on their roster."[97]

With San Juan, Clemente played nine winter seasons, posting a .323 batting average (263 hits in 815 at-bats), 45 doubles, 12 triples, 18 homers, 139 RBIs, and a .466 slugging percentage. He scored 129 runs and stole 23 bases.[98] Clemente's lifetime .324 PRWL batting average (621-for-1,917) is fourth-best, behind Willard Brown (.350), Francisco "Pancho" Coímbre (.337), and Pedro "Perucho" Cepeda (.325).[99] Clemente's regular-season managing record with San Juan was 46-42, plus 4-8 in the postseason, or 50-50 overall.

BILL VIRDON AND JON MATLACK REMEMBER CLEMENTE FROM 1971-72

Bill Virdon managed the 39-30 Senators to a pennant and final series appearance versus Ponce. Virdon's respect for Clemente never wavered: "I saw him quite often in Puerto Rico," said Virdon. "Roberto would come to some of our games. He was an exceptional human being – very articulate, very sharp, very smart. I can't say enough about Roberto as a teammate, someone who I coached and managed."[100]

Jon Matlack, his wife, other San Juan imports, e.g., Bob Johnson, Bruce Kison, Milt May, Rennie Stennett, and Richie Zisk, were invited to Clemente's Trujillo Alto home. Matlack had "vivid memories of the 1971-72 PRWL season and visit to the Clemente home."[101]

1972 AMATEUR WORLD SERIES AND PRWL NAME CHANGE

Clemente managed Puerto Rico to a 9-6 record (sixth-place tie) in the 16-team XX Amateur World Series hosted by Managua, Nicaragua, November 15-December 5, 1972. Dennis Martínez, a 17-year-old hurler with Bronze Medal Nicaragua, noted: "Roberto Clemente has served as an inspiration to me since my days as an amateur baseball player in Nicaragua. He is the reason why I devote so much time and energy to charitable work for youth."[102]

On May 18, 2012, the PRWL officially changed its name to Roberto Clemente Professional Baseball League (Liga de Béisbol Profesional Roberto Clemente).[103] Circling back to Clemente's October 20, 1991, induction into the Puerto Rico Professional Baseball Hall of Fame, his widow, Vera, told the author: "Roberto played just as hard in Puerto Rico as in the majors. He felt very strongly about pleasing the local fans and did not want to let them down." [104]

ACKNOWLEDGMENTS

Grateful acknowledgment to Marcial "Canenita" Allen, Jim Archer, Luis "Tite" Arroyo, Ken Brett, Don Buford, Orlando Cepeda, Horace Clarke, Vera Clemente, José Crescioni Benítez, Cot Deal, Cal Ermer, Nino Escalera, Rubén Gómez, Bob Leith Sr., Art López, Jorge Fidel López Vélez, Jerry McNertney, Lee MacPhail Jr., Dennis Martínez, Jon Matlack, Lee May, Luis R. Mayoral, Luis R. Olmo, Tony Pérez, Juan "Terín" Pizarro, Vic Power, Raúl Ramos, Germán Rivera, Frank Robinson, José "Palillo" Santiago, Ted Savage, Ken Singleton, Tommie Sisk, Marv Staehle, Tony Taylor, Freddie Thon Jr., Bill Virdon and Don Zimmer, for phone/in-person interviews, text messages, Facebook messenger, and emails. Jorge Colón Delgado—Official Historian, Roberto Clemente Professional Baseball League—provided Clemente's PRWL stats and uncovered his final PRWL regular-season hit. Stew Thornley wrote Clemente's SABR bio.

NOTES

1 José "Palillo" Santiago in-person interview with Tom Van Hyning, San Juan, Puerto Rico, December 30, 1992. All in-person interviews, letters, emails, Facebook messenger and phone calls cited are between the subjects and the author.

2 Marcial "Canenita" Allen in-person interview, Hato Rey, Puerto Rico, December 15, 1991.

3 Roberto Inclán, Senadores de San Juan, 1938-39 al 1982-83 (San Juan, Puerto Rico: San Juan Baseball Club, 1983), 25.

4 Jorge Fidel López Vélez, Roberto Clemente: "El astro boricua" (Colombia: Editorial Nomos S.A., 2019), 102.

5 López Vélez, Roberto Clemente: "El astro boricua" (Colombia: Editorial Nomos S.A., 2019), 104-106.

6 Luis Rodríguez Mayoral, Roberto Clemente aún escucha las ovaciones (Hato Rey, Puerto Rico: Ramallo Brothers Printing, 1987), 64.

7 Bill Ladson, "Monte Irvin Was Close to Breaking Color Barrier," mlb.com, April 29, 2020, https://www.mlb.com/news/a-look-at-monte-irvin. Accessed September 19, 2021.

8 Freddie Thon Jr. via Facebook messenger, September 19, 2021.

9 Thon Jr. via Facebook messenger, September 19, 2021. Thon Cleaners was originally a partnership between Hiram Bithorn and Thon Sr. The latter bought out Virginia Bithorn after her husband died. The company once had a dozen vans and drivers who could do pickups at customers' homes.

10 Tony Oliver, Nino Escalera SABR biography, https://sabr.org/bioproj/person/nino-escalera/. Accessed September 9, 2021.

11 Nino Escalera in-person interview, San Juan, Puerto Rico, December 30, 1992.

12 José "Palillo" Santiago conversation, en route to Escalera's home, December 30, 1992.

13 Vic Power in-person interview, Guaynabo, Puerto Rico, December 28, 1991.

14 José A. Crescioni Benítez, El Béisbol Profesional Boricua (San Juan, Puerto Rico: Aurora Comunicación Integral, September 1997), 99.

15 The Sporting News, October 21, 1959: 26.

16 Bob Leith Sr. in-person interview, San Juan, Puerto Rico, December 28, 1992.

17 Luis R. Olmo in-person interview, Santurce, Puerto Rico, December 1, 1993.

18 Leith in-person interview, San Juan, Puerto Rico, December 28, 1992. Leith mentioned a $1,500 figure, but the actual signed contract was for $1,000, including expenses.

19 López Vélez, Roberto Clemente: "El astro boricua" (Colombia: Editorial Nomos S.A., 2019), 112-114.

20 Inclán, 27.

21 Jim Archer phone interview, October 27, 1992.

22 Horace Clarke phone interview, February 1, 1993.

23 Lee MacPhail Jr. letter, February 2, 2011. MacPhail was a high-school and Swarthmore College classmate of the author's mother, Paula S. Van Hyning, and remembered her.

24 El Mundo, March 3, 1942; Thomas E. Van Hyning, The Santurce Crabbers: Sixty Seasons of Puerto Rican Winter League Baseball (Jefferson, North Carolina: McFarland & Company, 1999), 16. Freddie Thon Jr., father of Dickie Thon, witnessed this blast.

25 Bob Leith Sr. in-person interview, San Juan, Puerto Rico, December 28, 1992.

26 The Sporting News, February 22, 1961: 27.

27 Leith in-person interview, San Juan, Puerto Rico, December 28, 1992.

28 El Mundo, October 24, 1961.

29 https://www.beisbol101.com/roberto-clemente-3/. Accessed September 16, 2021.

30 Art López phone interview, April 15, 2021.

31 Germán Rivera in-person interview, San Juan, Puerto Rico, December 29, 1992.

32 Nino Escalera in-person interview, San Juan, Puerto Rico, December 30, 1992.

33 El Mundo, January 26, 1962.

34 San Juan Star, February 4, 1962.

35 Phone conversation with Jorge Fidel López Vélez, September 23, 2021.

36 José A. Crescioni Benítez, El Béisbol Profesional Boricua (San Juan, Puerto Rico: Aurora Comunicación Integral, September 1997), 107.

37 The Sporting News, December 14, 1963: 28.

38 José "Palillo" Santiago in-person interview, San Juan, Puerto Rico, December 30, 1992.

39 Jerry McNertney phone interview, November 14, 1991.

40 Marv Staehle phone interview, December 5, 1991.

41 Marv Staehle phone interview, December 5, 1991.

42 López Vélez, Roberto Clemente: "El astro boricua" (Colombia: Editorial Nomos S.A., 2019), 133-135.

43 López Vélez, Roberto Clemente: "El astro boricua," 176-178.

44 Inclán, Senadores de San Juan, 1938-39 al 1982-83, 32.

45 José "Palillo" Santiago speech inducting Roberto Clemente into the Puerto Rico Professional Baseball Hall of Fame, Ponce, Puerto Rico, October 20, 1991. Santiago was the master of ceremonies.

46 López Vélez, *Roberto Clemente: "El astro boricua,"* 142.

47 José "Palillo" Santiago conversation, en route to Nino Escalera's home, December 30, 1992.

48 Art López phone interview, March 25, 2021. López received an offer from a colonel in the Nicaraguan Armed Forces, who flew to San Juan; and had López flown to Managua, Nicaragua. Tony Oliva reinforced the 1963-64 Licey Tigers, in the Dominican Republic, after the PRWL season ended. López, Oliva, and others could make extra money in other winter leagues. Clemente never opted to do this, when San Juan was eliminated from contention.

49 Cal Ermer phone interview, June 17, 1992.

50 *The Sporting News*, January 9, 1965: 24.

51 López Vélez, *Roberto Clemente: "El astro boricua,"* 212.

52 https://www.beisbol101.com/roberto-clemente-3/. Accessed September 20, 2021.

53 *The Sporting News*, January 9, 1965: 27.

54 Thomas E. Van Hyning, *Puerto Rico's Winter League: A History of Major League Baseball's Launching Pad* (Jefferson, North Carolina: McFarland & Company, 1995), 67.

55 Don Buford in-person interview, Binghamton (New York) Municipal Stadium, April 1992.

56 Van Hyning, *Puerto Rico's Winter League: A History of Major League Baseball's Launching Pad*, 67.

57 Marv Staehle phone interview, December 5, 1991. San Juan-Santurce was an intense rivalry but players, coaches, and managers conversed with each other before and after the games.

58 Tony Pérez in-person interview, Lake City, Florida, March 1993.

59 Tommie Sisk phone interview, October 27, 1991.

60 Joe Hoerner phone interview, December 5, 1991.

61 FOMENTO was Puerto Rico's lead economic development agency. Its mission was to attract a variety of companies and industries to build Puerto Rico's economic base.

62 Sam J. Van Hyning Jr. conversation with the author, Hato Rey, Puerto Rico, December 1966. FOMENTO formulated "Operation Bootstrap" to transform the Island's economy from an agrarian to an industrial one. Puerto Rico's economy in the mid- to late 1960s, included good-paying jobs in the petrochemical industry, and numerous manufacturing plants benefiting from federal tax exemption.

63 *The Sporting News*, December 30, 1967: 47.

64 Don Zimmer in-person interview, Winter Haven, Florida, March 1992.

65 Miguel Frau, "Clemente Signals Return with a Four-Hit Barrage," *The Sporting News*, December 16, 1967: 47.

66 *The Sporting News*, December 23, 1967: 47.

67 Art López email, March 13, 2021. https://sabr.org/bioproj/person/art-lopez/. Accessed September 22, 2021.

68 Art López email, March 13, 2021. https://sabr.org/bioproj/person/art-lopez/. Accessed September 22, 2021.

69 https://www.beisbol101.com/roberto-clemente-3/. Accessed September 22, 2021.

70 Tony Taylor in-person interview, Cocoa Expo Stadium, Florida, March 1993.

71 Lee May in-person interview, Baseball City, Florida, March 1992.

72 Ted Savage phone interview, May 14, 1992.

73 Miguel Frau, "Cepeda, Clemente Go Native for Annual All-Star Contest," *The Sporting News*, January 6, 1968: 53.

74 López Vélez, *Roberto Clemente: "El astro boricua,"* 172-173.

75 Jorge Colón Delgado, *Pedrín Zorrilla: El Cangrejo Mayor* (Colombia: OP Gráficas, 2011), 445.

76 Ellis "Cot" Deal phone interview, October 28, 1991.

77 *Estadísticas de Béisbol Profesional*, Temporada 1969 (San Juan, Puerto Rico: Palo Viejo, October 1970), 22.

78 Jimmy Keenan and Frank Russo, Thurman Munson SABR biography, https://sabr.org/bioproj/person/thurman-munson/. Accessed September 23, 2021.

79 David Maraniss, *The Passion and Grace of Baseball's Last Hero* (New York: Simon & Schuster, 2006), 230-233.

80 Luis R. Mayoral phone interview, September 2, 2021.

81 Luis R. Mayoral phone interview, September 2, 2021.

82 Nino Escalera in-person interview, San Juan, Puerto Rico, December 30, 1992.

83 Raúl Ramos phone conversation, September 22, 2021.

84 Van Hyning, *The Santurce Crabbers: Sixty Seasons of Puerto Rican Winter* League Baseball, 114.

85 Ken Brett phone interview, October 28, 1991.

86 José "Palillo" Santiago in-person interview, San Juan, Puerto Rico, December 30, 1992.

87 Jeff Barto, Freddie Patek SABR biography, https://sabr.org/bioproj/person/freddie-patek/. Accessed September 23, 2021.

88 *Inclán*, Senadores de San Juan, 1938-39 al 1982-83, 36.

89 Ken Singleton written responses to the author's PRWL survey, November 1992.

90 Luis R. Mayoral, *Ken Singleton: buen pelotero, gran narrador y mejor persona*, October 3, 2021, https://www.beisbol101.com/ken-singleton-buen-pelotero-gran-narrador-y-mejor-persona/. Accessed October 7, 2021. Singleton received the 1982 Roberto Clemente Award, the one he cherishes the most, per this blog.

91 Van Hyning, *The Santurce Crabbers: Sixty Seasons of Puerto Rican Winter League Baseball*, 116.

92 https://www.beisbol101.com/roberto-clemente-3/. Accessed September 23, 2021.

93   Van Hyning, *The Santurce Crabbers: Sixty Seasons of Puerto Rican Winter League Baseball*, 117.

94   El Mundo, January 26, 1971.

95   Ken Brett phone interview, October 28, 1991.

96   Frank Robinson in-person interview, Camden Yards, Baltimore, August 4, 1993.

97   Jorge Colón Delgado phone conversation, October 5, 2021.

98   https://www.beisbol101.com/roberto-clemente-3/.   Accessed September 23, 2021.

99   https://www.beisbol101.com/lideres-de-todos-los-tiempos/. Accessed September 23, 2021.

100   Bill Virdon in-person interview, Bradenton, Florida, March 1993.

101   Luis R. Mayoral Facebook post, June 20, 2021.

102   XX Campeonato Mundial de Béisbol Amateur, Managua, Nicaragua (1972), January 21, 2017. https://deportescineyotros.com/2017/01/01/xx-campeonato-mundial-de-beisbol-amateur-managua-nicaragua-1972/. Accessed September 23, 2021; Dennis Martínez interview, West Palm Beach, Florida, March 1992. Cuba won Gold and the United States got Silver. Martínez was 1-1 with a 1.86 ERA in the 1972 Amateur World Series.   https://sabr.org/bioproj/person/dennis-martinez/. Accessed September 28, 2021.

103   https://www.primerahora.com/deportes/beisbol/notas/nace-la-liga-de-beisbol-profesional-roberto-clemente/. Accessed September 17, 2021.

104   Doña Vera viuda de Clemente in-person interview, Ponce, Puerto Rico, October 20, 1991.

"THE WRITERS ARE BAD": CLEMENTE AND THE PRESS

BY VINCE GUERRIERI

In what turned out to be the last book of his illustrious career, Jimmy Breslin wrote a biography of Branch Rickey, focusing on his signing of Jackie Robinson and integration of baseball.

Breslin was himself a former sportswriter, most notably covering the New York Mets' comically inept expansion season for the *New York Journal-American*, using it as fodder for a book, *Can't Anybody Here Play This Game?*[1] In the Rickey biography, Breslin noted how unwilling or unable baseball writers were to advocate for integration, just as hidebound as the owners who paid for their meals and travel. "The Baseball Writers Association of America organization was a fake and a fraud," Breslin wrote. "A shill as white as the Klan."[2] He noted that the BBWAA controlled press-box access, restricting it to daily newspapers – which perhaps not coincidentally, excluded the Black press, most of which were weekly newspapers.

It was into this world that Rickey brought Jackie Robinson in 1947, and it wasn't much changed eight years later – almost to the day – when Roberto Clemente made his major-league debut. In some ways, it might have been even worse. While Robinson was college-educated and one of the first African Americans to attend Officer Candidate School during World War II, Clemente was a native of Puerto Rico with no more than a high-school education. Spanish was his first language, and initially, when he started playing professional baseball, his only one.

And that contributed to a mutually antagonistic relationship between Clemente and the press. The writers were only too happy to document his struggles with English and the reputation he earned – unfairly – as a hypochondriac and malingerer. He in turn had no interest in building any kind of relationship with the people who refused to recognize his greatness. It was a relationship that had only started to warm at his untimely death.

"The fans are good to me," Clemente said in an Associated Press article in spring training in 1969. "Only the writers are bad."[3]

Clemente was initially signed by the Dodgers, and it's easy to wonder what his relationship with the press would have been like had he played his career in Brooklyn and then Los Angeles. "If he were playing in New York they'd be comparing him to DiMaggio," said his former manager Bobby Bragan. "I would say his greatness is limited only by the fact that he does not hit the long ball consistently, and by the fact that he is not playing in New York, or even Chicago or Los Angeles."[4]

But the Pirates found Clemente and claimed him in the Rule 5 draft, and he ended up in Pittsburgh, which was a pro sports wasteland at the time. The Steelers were the laughingstock of the NFL and the Pirates hadn't won a pennant since they were swept by the Murderers' Row Yankees in 1927. The Pirates of that era could be summed up with Branch Rickey's riposte to slugger Ralph Kiner during contract negotiations: "We finished in last place with you. We can finish in last place without you."

At the time, Pittsburgh had three daily newspapers, the Scripps-Howard *Press*, the Blocks' *Post-Gazette*, and the Hearst *Sun-Telegraph*, then in its death throes. Les Biederman, the beat reporter for the *Press*, quoted Clemente phonetically, using "ees" for "is" and "dese" and "dose." (Biederman also wrote for *The Sporting News*, so Clemente's struggles with the language were spread to a national audience.)

Clemente was presented as a complainer, a player with a variety of aches and pains. He famously once said in spring training, "My bad shoulder feels good, but my good shoulder feels bad." Some writers saw the humor in this, noting that the worse Clemente felt, the better he performed. *Los Angeles Times* columnist Jim Murray called Clemente "baseball's Oscar Levant," referring to the musician, actor, and all-around personality (ironically, himself a Pittsburgh native) who would complain about his various ailments, saying Clemente "had to have one foot in the

Mayo Clinic before he could make a shambles of National League pitching."[5]

But some writers saw more detrimental characteristics beyond the weariness of Clemente's well-worn complaints. "Clemente's a hypochondriac," said Jack Hernon, who covered him for the *Post-Gazette*. "Always was. He can't hit in the clutch; it's a proven statistic. He's always making excuses for something."[6]

When Dick Stockton arrived at KDKA on his way to a national broadcasting career, he said Clemente was not a team player, a charge the outfielder found particularly distasteful – and he spelled out why in a spring-training tirade. "Did any ballplayer come up to you and say that I am not a team player? Who say that? The writers, right? Well I tell you one thing, the more I stay away from writers the better I am. You know why? Because they are trying to create a bad image for me. You know what they have against me? Because I am black and Puerto Rican." He bore a grudge against Stockton for the rest of his life, at one point saying, "He come in this clubhouse, I tell you, I kill him."[7]

Even positive press could lead to hurt feelings. Myron Cope, a celebrated magazine writer in the 1960s before going on to be the radio voice of the Steelers, wrote a profile on Clemente for *Sports Illustrated*, "Aches, Pains and Batting Titles." It was a largely complimentary piece, but Clemente didn't speak to Cope for several years afterward.

But while Clemente had a standoffish relationship with many of the reporters who covered baseball, he warmed quickly to Bob Prince, the Pirates' radio voice. Prince, known as "The Gunner," was an unabashed homer, willing to cheer on anyone wearing a Pirates uniform. Early in Clemente's career, a teammate, Lino Donoso, a well-traveled Cuban hurler whose brief major-league career coincided with Clemente's first two years in Pittsburgh, had taken to calling him *Arriba*, a Spanish word that literally means "upstairs" but has been

Clemente with reporters. Les Banos photograph courtesy of The Clemente Museum.

taken more figuratively to mean "lifting or upris- ing." Prince saw fit to yell *Arriba!* when Clemente came to bat or made a great play.[8]

Prince was not just a broadcaster. He became a friend and trusted adviser to many Pirates play- ers. One night in 1958, the Pirates were playing the Giants in what Prince called "a real beanball contest. It looked like we were going to have a terrible fight." Giants pitcher Ruben Gomez took a little chin music, and Orlando Cepeda, then a rookie, came out of the dugout carrying a bat to fight for his idol. Willie Mays tackled him and threw him to the ground. Prince said on the air, "This is a young Latin American player who's very excited and doesn't realize what he's doing. You must forgive him, because he didn't mean to do this." Apparently, Clemente heard about it, and the next day, he arranged a meeting with Prince and Cepeda, telling the Baby Bull in Spanish what Prince had said.[9]

Clemente himself relayed this story in 1971, at a dinner in Prince's honor in Puerto Rico. Prince was celebrating his 25th anniversary in broadcasting, and Clemente invited him to Puerto Rico, where he described him as "one of the best friends I have in the world" – indeed, Prince might have been the only person who could refer to Clemente as Bobby and not be upbraided for it – and bestowed on him one of his prized possessions: The silver bat he was presented in 1961 for the first of his four batting titles. The bat had special meaning to Clemente, who was determined to prove that he was a most valuable player after finishing eighth – below three of his Pirates teammates[10] – in MVP voting the year before. At the dinner, both Clemente and Prince were in tears.[11]

Clemente finally received his National League MVP Award in 1966, edging out runner-up Sandy Koufax, who had completed his final season in baseball. Koufax went 27-9 and won his second straight (and third overall) Cy Young Award as the Dodgers won the pennant.

It was the second straight year Koufax finished second in MVP voting.[12]

Clemente got a total of 218 points, 10 more than Koufax. By the rules of the day, each first- place vote was worth 14 points, each second-place vote was worth 9, 8 for third, and so on. Clemente appeared on all 20 ballots – the only player to do so[13] – but Koufax had received more first- place votes.[14]

Koufax himself was writing his own story, serialized in newspapers. He said Clemente "can hit any pitch any where at any time. He will hit pitchouts, he will hit brushback pitches. He will hit high, inside pitches deep to the opposite field, which would be ridiculous even if he didn't do it with both feet off the ground."[15]

After winning the World Series in 1960, The Pirates spent the rest of the decade spinning wheels, but a move from Forbes Field in the city's Oakland neighborhood to a new all-pur- pose facility on the North Shore, Three Rivers Stadium, seemed to revitalize their fortunes. In 1970 the Pirates won the first of three straight National League Eastern Division titles but were swept by the Cincinnati Reds in the National League Championship Series. The following year, the Pirates beat the San Francisco Giants and advanced to the World Series. The Pirates won in seven games – and Clemente hit safely in each of them, having done the same in the only other World Series he'd played in, in 1960.

"I feel that I would be considered to be a much better athlete if I were not a black Latin," he said during the 1971 World Series. "I play as good as anybody. Maybe I play as good as anybody who plays the game. But I am not loved."[16] His .414 average earned him World Series MVP – and the plaudits that he felt he didn't get enough of in his career to that point. "After 17 major-league seasons, 37-year-old Roberto Clemente is now an overnight sensation," wrote Jerry Izenberg.[17]

Clemente played for one more season, getting his 3,000th hit against the Mets. The Pirates lost a hard-fought NLCS to the Reds, and everyone went home for the offseason. Clemente died on a mission of mercy, on board a plane that crashed shortly after takeoff with supplies for Nicaraguan earthquake victims.

Even in death, Clemente was denied the recognition he thought he deserved. Joe Falls of the *Detroit Free Press* made it a point to write about how unhappy Clemente seemed to be – and how he lacked the charisma of Willie Mays (a comparison that always made Clemente bristle). "Remember the All-Star game of a year ago, how we all waited for the first appearance of Willie Mays in Tiger Stadium? I don't remember what Clemente did that night or even if he played."[18] (Clemente replaced Mays in the lineup and hit a home run off Mickey Lolich.)

Upon Clemente's death, an unprecedented special election was decreed by the Baseball Writers Association of America for the Baseball Hall of Fame.[19] Some sportswriters had a problem with this.

Bob Broeg wrote, "To steamroller Roberto into the Hall of Fame is really a disservice to the proud person who liked to feel he was best in life, not in death."[20]

Dick Young, who less than two years earlier had called Clemente "the best damn ballplayer in the World Series, maybe in the whole world," abstained.[21] He said Clemente's immediate election – a straight up-or-down vote with Clemente the only name on the ballot – was basically ... communist.

"Just take another look at the ballot," inveighed Young. "It is straight from beyond the Iron Curtain. Any man who has the temerity to vote no, and sign his name, will hear a knock on his door one night, and never again will be seen. Joe Stalin won more elections that way."[22]

Young suggested that the BBWAA could have waived the five-year waiting period and then put Clemente on the ballot with that year's other candidates.[23] Instead, Clemente was "railroaded in," preying on rank sentimentality, which offered him a chance to tee off on hoary clichés. "Anybody who says the presence of Roberto Clemente can be felt in the Pirates clubhouse is guilty of sentimental rot," Young wrote. "They do not think all the time of Roberto Clemente, these teammates of his. To do so would be unreal, and to suggest so is dishonest. It is three months now since Roberto died a hero's death in the shark-infested water of the Caribbean, and the time has tempered grief."[24]

Murray Chass of the *New York Times* – himself no stranger to Hall of Fame voting controversies – grew up in Pittsburgh's Squirrel Hill neighborhood, watching Clemente while a student at Taylor Allderdice High School and the University of Pittsburgh, and even covered him as one of those "New York writers" Clemente scorned. Chass said the ballot gave him pause as well, before voting yes. "I was reluctant to vote yes on this ballot because I was concerned that it might set an undesirable precedent. After debating with myself, however, I finally marked the yes box. I realized that if I didn't vote for Clemente then, I would never again have the opportunity."[25]

Of course, he was right. A total of 424 ballots were distributed, with 318 yes votes being the required 75 percent threshold. Clemente got 393. Young's abstention was one of two, and 29 writers voted against inducting Roberto Clemente into the Hall of Fame, most more concerned with process than with recognizing greatness.[26]

Courtesy of The Clemente Museum.

NOTES

1 The title was taken from a statement made in frustration by manager Casey Stengel.

2 Jimmy Breslin, *Branch Rickey* (New York: Viking, 2011), 106.

3 "Clemente Hits Press for Poor Coverage," *Wilkes-Barre* (Pennsylvania) *Times Leader*, March 31, 1969, 20.

4 Jim O'Brien, *Maz and the '60 Bucs* (Pittsburgh: Geyer Printing, 1993), 256.

5 Jim Murray, "Don't Cry for Clemente, Baseball's Oscar Levant," *Los Angeles Times*, September 18, 1966.

6 Phil Musick, *Who Was Roberto?* (New York: Doubleday, 1974), 137. Musick noted that Hernon, who died of cancer at the age of 48 in 1966, and Clemente didn't speak for the last year of Hernon's life for reasons known only to them.

7 Musick, *Who Was Roberto?*, 129.

8 Bruce Markusen, *Roberto Clemente: The Great One* (New York: Sports Publishing, 2001), 66.

9 Kal Wagenheim, *Clemente!* (New York: Praeger Publishing, 1973), 71.

10 Don Hoak was runner-up, and Vern Law was sixth in voting.

11 Wagenheim, 228-29.

12 The 1965 NL MVP was Williie Mays.

13 Clemente received eight first-place votes, 10 second-place votes, and two third-place votes.

14 Koufax received nine first-place votes. Clemente got eight. The Braves' Felipe Alou got two first-place votes, and Dick Allen of the Phillies got the remaining one.

15 Rafael Pont-Flores, "Puerto Rico Fans All Root for Roberto," *The Sporting News*, November 26, 1966, 26.

16 Wells Twombly, "Super Hero," *San Francisco Examiner*, January 3, 1973. Roberto Clemente File, Baseball Hall of Fame.

17 Quoted in O'Brien, *Maz and the '60 Bucs*, 256.

18 Joe Falls, "Clemente: Sad Ending for a Troubled Man," *Detroit Free Press*, January 2, 1973. Roberto Clemente file, National Baseball Hall of Fame.

19 The closest parallel is Lou Gehrig's election to the Hall of Fame. His career ended April 30, 1939, at the age of 36, and Gehrig was voted into the Hall of Fame on December 7, 1939. But at that point, there was no official five-year period between a player's retirement and his eligibility for induction.

20 Bob Broeg, "Instant Enshrinement Is a Disservice to Clemente," *St. Louis Post-Dispatch*, January 20, 1973: 2B.

21 Reprinted by Jim O'Brien, *Remembering Roberto* (Pittsburgh: Geyer Printing, 1994), 437.

22 Dick Young, "Wrong Way to Honor Clemente," *New York Daily News*, March 14, 1973. Clipping in Roberto Clemente file, Baseball Hall of Fame.

23 That year, Warren Spahn was the only player elected by the BBWAA. He was in his first year of eligibility, as were future inductees Whitey Ford and Robin Roberts. Other eventual Hall members who fell short of election that year included Bob Lemon, Duke Snider, and former Pirates slugger Ralph Kiner.

24 Young, "Wrong Way to Honor Clemente."

25 Jim O'Brien, *Remembering Roberto*, 432

26 "Clemente in Hall of Fame," *Cleveland Press*, March 20, 1973, part of the Press archives at Cleveland State University.

"ALL HE REQUIRED OF A BASEBALL WAS THAT IT BE IN THE PARK":

ROBERTO CLEMENTE'S OFFENSIVE SKILLS

BY MARK DAVIS

"In all due respect to Henry Aaron, Stan Musial and Willie Mays, the best hitter I ever played against was Roberto Clemente."

— Pete Rose, recipient of the 1976 Roberto Clemente Award[1]

Roberto Clemente's offensive accomplishments should leave zero doubt as to the merits of his special election to the Hall of Fame in 1973: a career batting average of .317; four National League batting titles (1961, 1964, 1965, and 1967); the 1966 National League Most Valuable Player Award (he batted .317 with 29 home runs and 119 RBIs); the 1971 World Series MVP; the 11th player to have 3,000 regular-season hits; and only the second player to hit in every game of two consecutive World Series appearances (1960 and 1971).

Despite these achievements, Clemente's offensive talent could be viewed as underappreciated by those who have cited his 240 regular-season home runs as a somewhat muted offensive record compared with other elite players of his era. He topped the 20-home-run mark just three times, for instance. Clemente for his part acknowledged this criticism throughout his career. "I can hit with anybody," he insisted. "I believe I'm as good a hitter as Willie Mays or Henry Aaron. My only drawback is lack of home run power."[2] (Aaron hit 755 home runs and Willie Mays hit 660.)

A closer examination of Clemente's offensive production reveals that he was arguably one of most intelligent hitters of his era. He demonstrated raw offensive power and was able to adjust his batting approach according to in-game circumstances. Simply put, Clemente could not only hit, but hit with power.

THE EARLY YEARS

Clemente's first playing experience occurred when he joined his local slow-pitch softball team in 1942, and taught himself the basics of hitting with a guava tree limb that served as his first bat.[3] He quickly fell in love with the game and spent hours on the neighborhood softball field, noting in his diary that he once hit 10 home runs during a marathon game.[4] Clemente next progressed to fast-pitch softball, where in 1952 his strong fielding skills and ability to consistently pull the ball led to an invitation to a tryout co-hosted by the Brooklyn Dodgers and the Santurce Cangrejeros at Sixto Escobar Stadium in San Juan, Puerto Rico.

Of the 72 players attending the tryout, Clemente was the only one to attract the interest of Dodgers scout Al Campanis. Impressed with his defensive abilities, Campanis invited Clemente to hit batting practice. Clemente did not disappoint. "The kid swings with both feet off the ground and hits line drives to right and sharp ground balls up the middle," marveled Campanis. "He was the greatest natural athlete I have ever seen as a free agent."[5] Campanis also rated Clemente's hitting power as "A+" in his scouting report.[6] Despite this strong interest, major-league rules dictated that Clemente could not sign with the Dodgers until his 18th birthday. However, the Dodgers' co-host, the Santurce Cangrejeros, wasted little time signing Clemente to a contract to play in the Puerto Rican Winter League.

Buster Clarkson, as the Cangrejeros' manager and Clemente's first skipper in professional baseball, recognized his raw offensive talent and made sure he was offered a similar amount of batting-practice pitches as his teammates.[7] Clemente credited Clarkson with helping him improve his batting stride toward the pitcher, thus increasing his offensive production. Of Clemente, Clarkson noted, "[His batting stance] had a few rough spots, but he never made the same mistake twice. He was baseball savvy."[8]

Clemente signed with the Dodgers a year later for a $10,000 salary and a $5,000 signing bonus. The Dodgers sent him to their International League affiliate in Montreal for the 1954 season,

which meant that he became eligible to be claimed by another organization via a supplemental draft at season's end.

Clemente saw limited playing time during the first half of his only season in Montreal. His manager, Max Macon, claimed this was due to Clemente's free-swinging nature at the plate. "If you had been in Montreal that year, you wouldn't have believed how ridiculous some pitchers made him look."[9] Despite limited playing time, Clemente showed flashes of offensive power. On July 25 he slammed a pinch-hit home run in the bottom of the 10th to win the first game of a doubleheader at home vs. the Havana Sugar Kings. The ball sailed over the 340-foot left-field fence and left the ballpark. "Clemente is a player with potential greatness," wrote one reporter. "His clout over the left field wall … won the opening game Hollywood style."[10]

FROM A YOUNG "BUC" TO "THE GREAT ONE": 1955-1972

After being claimed by the Pirates in the November 1954 supplemental draft, Clemente made his major-league debut the following spring. The 1955 season also showcased Clemente's unorthodox batting style, which was partly in response to a back injury sustained in an offseason car accident in Puerto Rico.[11] This approach at the plate quickly caught the attention of teammates and reporters. "He stood at the batting cage, his head rolling as he jerked his neck in a series of exercises. … The posture was awkward. The swing was sudden and appeared unpremeditated. … Only after the bat strikes the ball is it obvious that this is a good hitter."[12]

Clemente hit his first big-league home run on April 18, 1955, against the New York Giants. He hit the ball 450 feet to left-center field off the bullpen at the Polo Grounds (which was located in fair territory), and legged out an inside-the-park home run.[13] A few weeks later, on June 5, while facing the Cincinnati Reds at Pittsburgh's cavernous Forbes Field, Clemente hit a triple to dead center field that "must have traveled 450 feet in the air and would have been a homer in any National League park except Forbes Field and the Polo Grounds."[14]

Clemente's willingness to hit almost any pitch proved to be one of his strongest offensive abilities. He had only 18 walks in 501 plate appearances in 1955 and just 13 walks in 572 plate appearances in 1956. This led Clemente to develop a reputation that "he hit everything that didn't hit him first."[15] Indeed, opposing managers told reporters they instructed their pitchers to give intentional walks to Clemente, but on many occasions he would swing at the pitches for base hits.[16] Los Angeles Dodgers pitcher Don Sutton once remarked of Clemente, "Anything between the on-deck circles was a strike to him. I've seen him double on knock-down pitches."[17]

Interestingly, 2,154 (or 72 percent) of Clemente's 3,000 hits were singles. That high a percentage could be considered a misleading indicator of a lack of home-run power, as Clemente showed he could crush hits that didn't clear the outfield wall at Forbes Field. During a game against the Cincinnati Reds at Crosley Field on June 13, 1963, Clemente launched a pitch more than 400 feet; it was hit so hard to the wall that it quickly bounced to Reds' center fielder, Vada Pinson, who quickly relayed the ball back to the infield, "restricting Clemente to a laser single."[18]

On occasion, however, the baseball gods granted Clemente a trip around the bases for his line- drive efforts, such as on May 11, 1957, when Clemente scorched a hit over the head of Philadelphia Phillies center fielder Richie Ashburn. The ball rolled to the batting cage, which was stored in fair territory in deepest center field. When Ashburn finally got to the ball, Clemente was already at third base, and he scored easily for an inside-the-park home run.[19]

While Clemente is perhaps best known for hitting bullet line drives, he also hit monstrous home runs that left his fellow players speechless. In the first game of a doubleheader at Wrigley Field on May 17, 1959, Clemente hit a moon shot off Cubs pitcher Bob Anderson to deep right field, estimated at a minimum distance of 500 feet in negligible wind conditions. The Cubs hitting coach, baseball legend Roger Hornsby, remarked that it was the longest home run he had ever seen.[20]

Neither the daunting dimensions of Forbes Field nor the pressure of facing one of the National League's greatest pitchers intimidated Clemente. On May 31, 1964, he led off the bottom of the third inning by launching a pitch from Sandy Koufax that hit the light tower in left-center field, an estimated 450 feet from home plate. Koufax said the ball was still rising when it hit the tower, which suggests it would have gone even farther with no resistance.[21] Koufax later summarized his career facing Clemente as a sort of puzzle: "There is just no way you can develop a pitching pattern for him."[22]

Clemente also harnessed his power to carry the Pirates offense when necessary, such as on May 15, 1967, vs. the Cincinnati Reds. In one of his best run-producing games, Clemente had three home runs and a double and drove in all of Pittsburgh's runs in an 8-7 loss. "It was almost like Roberto Clemente playing the Reds all by himself and coming so close to wrecking them single-handedly," a sportswriter observed.[23] Clemente, much to his modest nature, downplayed his performance. "Yes, my biggest game, but not my best game," he said. "My best game is when I drive in the winning run. I don't count this one, we lost."[24]

When Clemente arrived in the big leagues, Willie Mays encouraged him to never be intimidated by pitchers. "Get mean when you go to bat," advised Mays. "And if they try to knock you down, act like it doesn't bother you. Get back up there and hit the ball. Show them."[25] Clemente made good use of this advice during a game at Dodger Stadium on June 4, 1967. After Clemente hit a home run in the fifth inning, Don Drysdale threw a "duster" at him in his next at-bat, sending him to the ground.[26] With the count 3-and-1, Clemente drove the next pitch an estimated 430 feet over the center-field wall. For his efforts, Clemente was greeted with a loud round of applause by the Dodgers faithful as he rounded the bases.[27]

Clemente's power production was so consistent that offnights at the plate attracted attention. In the All-Star Game in Anaheim on July 12, 1967, he struck out four times for only the second time in his career. Clemente's National League teammates were shocked by what they saw, prompting Atlanta Braves catcher Joe Torre to deadpan, "Did everybody take notes on how to pitch to Clemente?"[28]

Perhaps one of the most overlooked of Clemente's home runs came in the second game of a doubleheader on June 27, 1971, at Veterans Stadium in Philadelphia. He belted a pinch-hit homer off Joe Hoerner to become the first of only seven players to hit a home run to Veterans Stadium's upper decks in its 33-year history.[29] Clemente's feat was underappreciated at the time because of a newspaper strike in Pittsburgh but has since been validated by multiple witnesses, including the Phillies players.[30]

On September 30, 1972, Clemente became only the 11th player to reach 3,000 career hits. His landmark hit came at home off the Mets' Jon Matlack, a leadoff double in the fourth inning. Clemente dedicated the hit to Pirates fans, the people of Puerto Rico, and Roberto Marin, the Puerto Rican businessman who originally invited Clemente to play on his softball team and became so impressed with his performance that he recommended that the Brooklyn Dodgers sign Clemente.[31]

CLEMENTE'S APPROACH TO HITTING

Through the years baseball fans and historians have offered several possible reasons for why Clemente, a perennial challenger for the National League batting title, rarely set home-run records. Clemente, for his part, claimed it was due to the deep dimensions of Forbes Field: 365 feet in left field, 406 feet to left-center field, 457 feet to deep center field. "I would hit more homers if I were playing anywhere but in Pittsburgh," he said. "Forbes Field is the toughest park to hit home runs. If I played in Wrigley Field, I'd be a power hitter. I could hit 35 to 40 homers a year with my home games there."[32] Said longtime teammate Bill Mazeroski, "Don't let anybody kid you he can't hit for distance. When he wants to, he can power one as far as anybody in baseball. He's smart enough to go for line drives at Forbes Field. That's no park for home run hitters."[33]

Pirates manager Danny Murtaugh offered his own rationale for Clemente's offensive results. "I have always said that everybody expects too much of Roberto. He's batting in the third position and in my style of play his job is to set up runners as well as drive them in. If you were to take Roberto's runs set up, you'll come up with a tremendous plus in his favor. Everybody always mentions the RBIs, but nobody ever mentions the runs set up. That's equally important."[34]

A potential clue to the origin of Clemente's raw offensive power likely lies in the mechanics of his swing. According to Clemente biographer Bill Christine, "No kid on a sandlot will ever be taught to swing a bat like Roberto Clemente. The batter's box was never deep enough for him. He had reflexes which enabled him to wait until the last fraction of a second before whipping the bat around. His hands, those strong hands and powerful wrists, he kept them close to the midsection. He felt that there was no pitch that was impossible for him to attack."[35]

Generating power off his left foot, Clemente "would never swing the bat at the baseball, he would always throw the bat at the baseball."[36] His unique lunging motion meant that "Clemente made his charge at the pitchers like a mad man."[37] Interestingly, during his 1966 MVP season, Clemente's offensive numbers rose to career highs in home runs and RBIs, which he attributed in part to improved field conditions at his home ballpark that helped him enhance his swing. "For years, I have been pleading with somebody in charge at Forbes Field to put clay instead of sand in the batter's box," he said. "Suddenly, this year, they put clay in the batter's box. Now I have firm footing. Now I can get a toe-hold."[38]

Regardless of how he did it, Clemente demonstrated incredible offensive ability to hit virtually any pitch for power to any part of the ballpark. As Jim Murray of the *Los Angeles Times* noted, "They didn't make the pitch Roberto Clemente couldn't hit. All he required of a baseball was that it be in the park. He was the most destructive World Series player I ever saw outside of Ruth and Gehrig."[39]

The baseballs are signed by Bob Gibson, Steve Carlton, Ton Seaver, Ferguson Jenkins, Don Drysdale, and Sandy Koufax – each one a Hall of Fame pitcher against whom Clemente hit .300 or higher. Photograph by Duane Rieder.

ACKNOWLEDGMENTS

The author would like to thank David Speed and Bill Nowlin for their helpful feedback on an earlier draft of this article.

SOURCES

In addition to the sources cited in the Notes, the author consulted Baseball-Reference.com, Retrosheet.org, Newspapers.com, and Clemente's file at the National Baseball Hall of Fame.

NOTES

1   Associated Press, "Pete Rose Given Clemente Award," *Wilmington* (Ohio) *News Journal*, May 13, 1976: 16.

2   Associated Press, "Clemente Claims He's Best in Game," *Pittsburgh Post-Gazette*, April 21, 1964: 23.

3   Bruce Markusen, *Roberto Clemente: The Great One* (Champaign, Illinois: Sports Publishing, Inc., 2013), 22.

4   Markusen, 23.

5   Markusen, 26.

6   David Maraniss, *Clemente: The Passion and Grace of Baseball's Last Hero* (New York: Simon & Schuster, 2006), 27.

7   Bill Christine, "Roberto! A Self-Made Hitter," *New York Daily News*, April 3, 1973: 146.

8   Markusen, 29.

9   Stew Thornley, "Roberto Clemente's Entry into Organized Baseball: Was He Hidden in Montreal?" Accessed April 7, 2022, https://milkeespress.com/clemente1954.html.

10   Lloyd McGowan, "Rookie Roberto's homer, Lasorda Win, Revive Hopes," *Montreal Star*, July 26, 1954: 28.

11   Markusen, 52.

12   Jimmy Cannon, "Clemente Still Wonders: Who's Stranger in Field?," *Orlando Evening Star*, March 21, 1972: 30.

13   Les Biederman, "Roberto's Bat Softens Rivals for Buc Raids," *The Sporting News*, September 17, 1966: 6.

14   Les Biederman, "The Scoreboard," *Pittsburgh Press*, June 6, 1955: 22.

15   Jim Murray, "Roberto's Revenge," *Los Angeles Times*, July 1, 1964: 1.

16   Murray, "Roberto's Revenge."

17   Associated Press, "300-Win Hurlers History?" *Rome* (Georgia) *News-Tribune*, January 7, 1998: 3B.

18   Les Biederman, "Bailey in Fast Company," *Pittsburgh Press*, June 14, 1963: 28.

19   Les Biederman, "Phils Blast Friend Early, Turn Back Pirates, 7 to 2," *Pittsburgh Press*, May 12, 1957: 69.

20   Les Biederman, "Tape Measure Homer Belted by Clemente at Wrigley Field," *The Sporting News*, May 27, 1959: 10.

21   Sandy Koufax with Ed Linn, *Koufax* (New York: Viking Press, 1966), 220.

22   Frank Finch, "Bucs' Clemente Toughest NL Hitter," *Los Angeles Times*, June 24, 1965: 50.

23   Les Biederman. "Clemente's 'Biggest' Game Wasted," *Pittsburgh Press*, May 16, 1967: 34.

24   Biederman. "Clemente's 'Biggest' Game Wasted."

25   Biederman. "Clemente's 'Biggest' Game Wasted."

26   Charley Feeney, "Veale Gets 7th Victory with Help," *Pittsburgh Post-Gazette*, June 5, 1967: 34.

27   This Day in Baseball, "Roberto Clemente Hits 2 Home Runs off Don Drysdale," Accessed April 22, 2022, https://thisdayinbaseball.com/roberto-clemente-hits-2-home-runs-off-don-drysdale-accounting-for-all-of-pittsburghs-runs-in-a-4-1-victory-over-los-angeles-clementes-first-bomb-travels-400-feet-to-tie-the-s/.

28   Les Biederman. "Reds' Perez Lives Like a King, Plays Like One," *Pittsburgh Press*, July 12, 1967: 62.

29   Gene Collier, "Of Veterans: One Spit On, the Other Knocked Down," *Pittsburgh Post-Gazette*, September 26, 2003: B-2. This home run has often been misquoted as the "Liberty Bell Ringer" that hit the decorative Liberty Bell attached to the center-field upper deck at Veterans Stadium. Clemente researcher David Speed has noted that while the home run did not hit the bell, it was nonetheless an excellent example of Clemente's raw offensive power.

30   David Speed Facebook post: June 27, 2018, Accessed April 30, 2022, https://www.facebook.com/photo/?fbid=10215342221376250.

31   Charley Feeney, "Roberto Collects 3000th Hit, Dedicates It to Pirate Fans," *The Sporting News*, October 14, 1972: 15.

32   "Clemente Claims He's Best in Game."

33   Al Abrams, "Sidelights on Sports: Clemente Not Appreciated?," *Pittsburgh-Post Gazette*, February 26, 1965, 20.

34   Associated Press, "Clemente Sparks Late Rally, Pirates Win, 6-5," *Monessen Valley Independent* (Monessen, Pennsylvania), May 18, 1971: 9.

35   Bill Christine, "Roberto! A Self-Made Hitter."

36   Markusen, 168.

37   Les Biederman, "Clemente Sinks Feet in Clay to Mold Stout Swat Figures," *The Sporting News*, July 2, 1966: 8.

38   Biederman, "Clemente Sinks Feet in Clay to Mold Stout Swat Figures."

39   Jim Murray, "Clemente: You Had to See Him to Disbelieve Him," *Los Angeles Times*, January 3, 1973: 49.

"I WILL CATCH THE BLEEPING BALL." ROBERTO CLEMENTE'S DEFENSIVE SKILLS

BY MICHAEL MARSH

Roberto Clemente had gained many admirers of his defense as a right fielder for the Pittsburgh Pirates since his major-league debut in 1955. Clemente's strong right arm and an array of running catches, basket catches, sliding catches, and leaping catches amazed fans, teammates, and rivals. During the twilight of his career, however, Clemente surprised even longtime observers with one of the greatest catches in major-league history.

On the night of June 15, 1971, Clemente patrolled right field at Houston's Astrodome. Pirates pitcher Steve Blass held a 1-0 lead with one out in the bottom of the eighth inning. The Astros' Joe Morgan, a fast runner, stood at first base. Houston's Cesar Cedeno hit a line drive to short right field. Clemente slid and made the catch inches from the field to record the second out. Morgan stayed at first base.

The next batter, Bob Watson, nearly gave the Astros the lead. Watson drove a Blass pitch toward the right-field corner. Clemente knew the Astrodome had a unique rule: If the ball struck the wall above the home run line, Watson would get credit for a two-run home run.

Clemente bolted toward the wall. According to an article by Charley Feeney in *The Sporting News*, "Clemente, going full speed, raced toward the wall and, in one sudden move, makes a twisting leap for a one-handed grab, back to the plate, just before the ball would have hit above the yellow line on the wall, which is home run territory. When Clemente came down, his body hit the wall. He suffered a bruised left ankle and his left elbow also was swollen. Blood spilled from a gash on the left knee. Clemente slumped on both knees, back to the infield. The Houston fans stood up and cheered."[1]

Astros manager Harry Walker had managed the Pirates between 1965 and 1967. Walker said Clemente's catch was the best he had seen. "He never slowed up," Walker said. "I don't see how he could keep the ball in his glove."[2]

The Pirates won 3-0. After the game, Clemente told reporters: "I don't even think I could get the ball, but I had to try and I jump."[3]

Clemente did more than try during his 18 seasons. He became part of a quartet of outstanding right fielders in Pirates history, along with Paul Waner, Kiki Cuyler, and Dave Parker, and he earned a place among the greatest right fielders in major-league history. He won 12 Gold Gloves, sharing the record for the most such awards by outfielders with Willie Mays. Among right fielders who have played in the major leagues since 1901, Clemente ranks second in putouts with 4,459 and second in assists with 255. He participated in 40 double plays as a right fielder.

Many runners tested Clemente's arm and lost. Clemente record 266 assists as an outfielder. He led the National League in outfield assists five times. In 15 games, he recorded two outfield assists. He threw out runners at first base 22 times. Decades after Clemente's death in 1972, an article in *Inside Sports* magazine rated his arm the best in baseball history.[4]

Clemente's quest for fielding supremacy began in his hometown of Carolina, Puerto Rico.

According to Clemente biographer David Maraniss, Clemente's mother, Luisa, passed on her strength to him. Maraniss wrote: "Luisa was a dignified woman, correct and literate reading her Bible, always finely dressed and not bulky but she had muscular shoulders and arms with which she could lift the carcass of a freshly slaughtered cow from a wheelbarrow and butcher it into cuts of beef. (A powerful right arm was something she passed along to her youngest son. When people later asked about his awe-inspiring throws from right field, he would say, *You should see my mother.* At age eighty, she could still fling a baseball from the mound to home plate.)"[5]

Luisa Clemente recalled that her son began to prepare for a baseball career at an early age. "'I can remember when he was five years old. He used to buy rubber balls every time he had a chance.' Roberto constantly carried rubber balls in his hands; he squeezed them tightly, strengthening his hands and fingers. Roberto loved to bounce balls off the ceilings and walls of the family's large, five-bedroom home."[6]

During his preteen years, he befriended Monte Irvin. Irvin played outfield for the San Juan Senadores during winter baseball seasons on the island in the mid-1940s. Clemente admired Irvin's batting style and throwing arm.[7]

Clemente further developed his skills during his teenage years. At 14, he played shortstop for a youth team. Clemente threw well, but the coach of the team thought Clemente was too slow for the infield and put him and his arm in the outfield. At Julio C. Vizarrondo High School, Clemente excelled in baseball and track and field. He especially liked the javelin. Clemente's expertise in throwing the javelin aided him in playing baseball. "He may not have known it at the time, but the footwork, release, and general dynamics employed in throwing the javelin coincided with the skills needed to throw a baseball properly. The more that Clemente threw the javelin, the better and stronger his throwing from the outfield became."[8]

Clemente's efforts paid off in 1952, after he turned 17 years old. Clemente joined 71 other attendees at a tryout at the Santurce Cangrejeros's stadium. Brooklyn Dodgers scout Al Campanis watched the hopefuls. Clemente made two strong throws, including one that flew nearly 400 feet.[9] His batting and fielding impressed Campanis. The Dodgers eventually signed Clemente, who played for the team's Montreal affiliate in 1954. Brooklyn lost him to the Pirates in a supplemental draft after the season.

During the following winter, Clemente played for Santurce in the Puerto Rico winter league. Herman Franks managed the team. Clemente played left field. Willie Mays played center. Bob Thurman played right field.[10] Luis Olmo was a reserve outfielder. Clemente started using the basket catch during the season, encouraged by Franks and Olmo. "I miss fly ball many time 'cause I try to catch too high," Clemente told

United Press reporter John Carroll a few years later. "It make it more easy for me to throw too, after I make the catch." Mays had used the basket catch before Clemente, but Clemente denied that he imitated Mays.[11]

Clemente joined the Pirates in 1955. He paid dividends for the team quickly while on defense. On May 4 Pirates pitcher Bob Friend held a 5-3 lead over the visiting Milwaukee Braves with two outs in the ninth inning. The Braves' Hank Aaron singled to right field, driving in a run and cutting the deficit to one run. Andy Pafko advanced to third. Clemente fielded the ball, but his wild throw allowed Aaron to move up to second. Next Friend pitched to George Crowe. Crowe blasted a ball to deep right field. Clemente jumped in front of the fence and caught the ball above it. He had taken a home run from Crowe to end the game.[12]

Clemente spent some time in center field, but Pirates manager Fred Haney made right field his primary position. Another Clemente biographer, Bruce Markusen, stated the reason: "Although Clemente played center field adequately, he seemed more comfortable in right. More importantly, his supreme throwing ability mandated a move to right field, a position that required a strong arm to deter runners from advancing too frequently from first to third base."[13]

Markusen wrote that Clemente liked tracking balls in the spacious right field at Forbes Field and learned how to play caroms off the walls, which had wire screening and concrete that produced unpredictable bounces.[14]

Clemente employed three effective tactics in right field. He often picked up balls barehanded in order to execute a throw more quickly.[15] He learned how to make sliding catches. Markusen wrote: "As Clemente slid with his legs extended, he grabbed the ball with his glove, and then almost immediately jumped to his feet and flung the ball toward the infield. By executing this genuinely athletic play, Clemente often prevented runners from stretching base hits into doubles or triples."[16] Finally, Clemente occasionally threw behind runners who had strayed too far after they rounded first base and thus recorded assists.[17]

Pittsburgh fans enjoyed Clemente's play in the outfield. Markusen wrote: "With runners on base, any ball hit to right field became a source of anticipation for fans, who wondered if Clemente might unleash one of his patented powerful throws. Drives to the gap and bloopers to short right field often resulted in a furious chase by Clemente, who repeatedly ran out from underneath his poor-fitting cap. Even on routine plays, Clemente entertained fans with his delightfully unorthodox basket catch."[18]

One fan, Henry Peter Gribbin, detailed his memories of Clemente. "Watching Clemente was indeed a treat for baseball fans," Gribbin wrote, "when he was in Forbes Field's right field, he developed his own special style of play, which was scrutinized by countless youngsters, including myself. After watching him, I had visions of making basket catches below the knees, of racing to the ball hit to right and then firing a strike to the first baseman, hoping to nail a runner who made too wide a turn."[19]

Clemente expressed supreme confidence in his abilities. "I'm a better outfielder than anyone you can name," he said. "I can go get a ball like Mays and I have a better arm."[20]

During the 1960 regular season, Clemente had 19 assists. He had spectacular plays on successive nights. On August 4 the Pirates defeated the visiting Dodgers 4-1. Clemente played a ball off the right-field wall and threw John Roseboro out at second base to end the game. After the game, Pittsburgh Press sportswriter Les Biederman called Clemente better at playing the bounces than Waner. "With all due apologies to Paul Waner, who had first claim on the right-field wall, Roberto Clemente plays that sector better than any outfielder who ever went out there," Biederman wrote.[21]

On the following day, Clemente made a catch similar to the one he would make in 1971 at the Astrodome. On August 5, 1960, the Pirates hosted the San Francisco Giants. Pirates pitcher Vinegar Bend Mizell held a 1-0 lead in the seventh inning. Mays stepped to the plate for the Giants and slammed a liner down the right-field line. "I must catch it. … I must catch it," Clemente told himself.[22] Clemente hit the right-center-field wall while he caught the ball. He fell to the ground with a bloody gash under his chin and knee bruises. The Pirates' doctor closed the gash with five stitches.[23] The Pirates won 1-0.

Danny Murtaugh, the Pirates manager, said it was the best catch he ever saw.[24] The catch was included in the book *Going, Going … Caught! Baseball's Great Outfield Catches as Described by Those Who Saw Them, 1887-1964.*[25]

Clemente's defense helped the Pirates upset the New York Yankees in the World Series that year. After the Pirates took a 3-2 lead in the Series, a reporter for the Associated Press wrote that Clemente's defense had boosted the Pirates. "Yet here was the player whose bullet throwing arm had stopped the Yankees from taking an extra base on hits to his territory, a feat that contributed mightily to Pittsburgh's three victories."[26]

Clemente notched another achievement in 1961. He won his first Gold Glove Award after he recorded a career-high 27 assists, 26 in right field. He supplanted Aaron, who had won the award the previous three years. That season, Aaron started 80 of 154 games in center field. Biederman wrote: "When Hank Aaron moved from right field to center for the Braves, Roberto Clemente moved front and center as the No. 1 right fielder. Clemente also has always felt miffed because Aaron was always voted the Rawlings Golden [sic] Glove as the best right fielder. Now he has full sway there."[27]

A sample of Clemente's fielding plays during the ensuing years demonstrate his prowess.

June 18, 1962: Cincinnati defeated host Pittsburgh 4-2. During the game, Clemente threw out Don Zimmer when the latter slid past second base.[28]

June 19, 1962: Cincinnati defeated host Pittsburgh 2-1. Clemente threw out Don Blasingame at first base when Blasingame tried to get back to the base after making a wide turn.[29]

August 27, 1965: Pittsburgh beat Houston 10-9 in 11 innings. As the Pirates' infielders charged to the plate in the eighth inning, Houston's Bob Lillis bunted near second base. Clemente, who had moved to shallow right field, ran into the infield, fielded the bunt and threw out Walt Bond at third base.[30]

September 6, 1965: Clemente helped Pittsburgh sweep Cincinnati 3-1 and 4-2. In the second game, he threw out Tony Perez trying to advance from first to third on Tommy Helms's single in the sixth inning.[31]

September 1, 1966: Clemente threw out Jim Barbieri, who was running from third base, at home plate on a bases-loaded hit by Willie Davis in the top of the 10th inning. Los Angeles beat host Pittsburgh 4-3 in 10 innings.[32]

July 8, 1967: The Pirates defeated the visiting Reds 6-1. The Reds' Lee May led off the top of the seventh inning with a triple off Tommie Sisk. After Sisk struck out Jim Coker, Jake Woods hit a pop fly to right field. Clemente pretended to prepare to catch the ball, freezing May at third base. Instead, Clemente let the ball fall in front of him, then threw out May at home plate.[33]

April 13, 1968: The visiting Pirates led San Francisco 2-0 in the bottom of the seventh inning at Candlestick Park. Clemente threw out Mays in the seventh inning as the latter tried to advance from first to third on Willie McCovey's single. The Pirates eventually won 2-1.[34]

September 20, 1969: Pirates pitcher Bob Moose no-hit the host New York Mets 4-0. The Mets nearly broke up the no-hitter with two out in the sixth inning. Mets third baseman Wayne

Garrett hit a fly to deep right field. Clemente went back to the fence and leaped to catch the ball.[35]

July 24, 1970: Pittsburgh beat Houston 11-0 during Roberto Clemente Night at the recently opened Three Rivers Stadium. Clemente dived to catch Joe Morgan's line drive in the third inning and slid to catch Denis Menke's fly ball in the seventh.[36]

Both Clemente's opponents and teammates praised his defense.

Perez recounted Clemente's 1965 throw against him years later. "I was on first base," Perez said. "He was playing right field. I see he's playing deep and [Tommy Helms] hit a bloop with one out. And I tried to get to third because he hit a bloop over the second baseman's head. I say I think I'm not even watching the third base coach. I say I've got to make it to third and I turn around and I say it's going to be easy. I'm running, I'm watching the third base coach Reggie Otero. Reggie said 'Slide! Slide!' I said, 'Slide?' I think you're not supposed to slide.' Before I slide, the guy got the ball and was waiting for me and I was out and I can't believe it. How he threw me out when he was playing deep, the ball was hit soft and I look at Reggie like that [Perez looked up], like asking 'How?' and he said, 'Come on kid, get out of here. It's Roberto Clemente out there.' I said 'Oh man.' I feel so bad about it. But it was great. I think that's when I knew Robert Clemente had a great arm."[37]

Ernie Banks compared Clemente to Willie Hoppe, the legendary carom billiards player: "Roberto, who plays a shallow right field, has been known to throw out batters at first base on drives hit on the ground. It's practically impossible to go from first to third on singles into his territory. He plays those caroms off the slanting wall in right field like a Willie Hoppe. A runner on third is seldom sent home on a short fly to our friend."[38]

Former Pirates pitcher Steve Blass said: "When Clemente was out in right field, there was nothing more a pitcher could want. I used

to kid the guys by saying, 'Bobby's playing and there is peace in right field.' I figured if the ball was hit to right and stayed in the ballpark, I had a chance. Some way, if it was humanly possible, and sometimes when it wasn't, he would get there. If they had a rally going, I knew he might make an impossible catch and double off a runner and the rally would die. With him, it was like having four outfielders."[39]

Two of Clemente's longtime teammates, second baseman Bill Mazeroski and left fielder Willie Stargell, had watched him for 17 and 11 seasons respectively. They provided in-depth analysis about Clemente's abilities.

Mazeroski said: "The fans may not realize it, but part of Clemente's skill at running fly balls down comes from an unusual knowledge. Baseball is more of a mental game than it often is credited with being, and players like Clemente aren't mechanical in their approach to it. For instance, he doesn't just play the hitter, he plays the hitter with the pitch. The majority of outfielders go right to a spot thinking of something like: 'Play this guy to pull just off the left side of the mound.' And there they stay. But say there are two strikes on a hitter, Clemente knows he won't be probably trying to pull as much, that he's more apt to punch the ball; so he adjusts his position."[40]

Stargell said: "First of all, he would make sure that he had good balance in throwing. Everything was [thrown] across the seams. And he knew how to throw the ball so that it could land in a certain spot and take one perfect hop to the infielder or the catcher so that it doesn't handcuff him." Stargell also mentioned a drill Clemente used to increase his accuracy. He placed a garbage can at third base. The opening faced him. Someone would hit a ball to him. Clemente fielded the ball and threw it into the can with one hop.[41]

Clemente's annual assist totals declined from 1961. He never recorded as many as 20 again. Biederman defended him after the 1964 season. He wrote: "Roberto Clemente was charged with

Roberto Clemente and Bill Virdon receiving Gold Gloves in 1962 from Rawlings employee Guy Palso. Courtesy of The Clemente Museum.

ten errors in right field but as one who saw Clemente in every inning, this correspondent believes Bobby is many times the victim of a scoring rule. Possibly half of Clemente's ten errors came when his lightning throws from the outfield hit a runner as he slid into a base. Clemente, who often led the league in assists, only had 13 in 1964. The runners simply don't take the chance on his fine arm anymore."[42]

Later in his career, physical ailments affected Clemente. Among other issues, he suffered from a bad back, bone chips in his elbow, and shoulder soreness.[43] He played only 108 games in 1970.

The following season, Clemente rebounded by playing in 132 games during the regular season. During the postseason, he helped spur the Pirates.

The Pirates upset the San Francisco Giants three games to one in the National League Championship series that season. Clemente's defense helped preserve the Pirates' 9-4 win in the second game. Pittsburgh led 4-2 in the sixth inning. San Francisco had loaded the bases. Mays batted with two outs. He hit a line drive that nearly fell between center field and right field. Clemente, who had moved to his right just before the blast, caught the ball to end the threat.[44]

Clemente also shined on defense while the Pirates beat the Baltimore Orioles in seven games to claim victory in the 1971 World Series. Clemente made two outstanding throws, one in Game Two and one in Game Six.

In Game Two, Clemente caught Frank Robinson's fly ball near the right-field line, then spun and threw a strike to Richie Hebner at third base. Clemente nearly caught Merv Rettenmund, who had tagged from second base. The host Orioles won 11-3.

Clemente talked about his arm after the game. "Ask the other players," he said. "They remember a few years ago when my arm was really strong. No one can compare with my arm when it feels right. I'm not bragging. That is a fact."[45]

In Game Six, the teams were tied, 2-2, in the bottom of the ninth inning. The Orioles' Mark Belanger stood at first base. Teammate Don Buford hit a ball that bounced off the right-field wall. Clemente fielded the ball at the warning track, turned clockwise, and threw to catcher Manny Sanguillen. The ball arrived with one bounce. Belanger held at third base. The throw helped preserve the tie, but the Orioles won 3-2 in 10 innings.

Despite Clemente's fielding exploits, he had some problems. During his rookie season, he disliked playing in Ebbets Field and the Polo Grounds because he couldn't figure out how the ball bounced off the walls at those fields.[46] In 1959 Clemente made 13 errors in 104 games in right field and recorded only 10 assists. Maraniss explained, "Most of Clemente's errors were on wild throws, often to third base. Some fans with seats in the third base boxes brought gloves to games with the specific hope of catching an errant heave from Roberto."[47] Clemente finished his career with a relatively low .973 fielding percentage and finished third all time with 131 errors in right field, in 2,433 games.

Yet, Clemente rose to the occasion throughout his career. His play on Watson's June 1971 drive exemplified that quality.

After the game, Clemente discussed his catch with Nellie King, a former Pirates pitcher who broadcast the team's games at the time. King recalled: "I'm sitting with him on the bus going back to the hotel, and I said, 'Roberto, I've seen a lot of good catches, but that's the greatest I've ever seen you make.' And he said, 'Nellie, I want to tell you something. If the ball is in the park and the game is on the line, I will catch the bleeping ball.' That's what he said."[48]

SOURCES

The author wishes to thank Bill Nowlin and the National Baseball Hall of Fame.

In addition to the sources cited in the Notes, the author consulted the following books, periodicals, and websites:

ARTICLES

"Runs Continue to Elude Astros," *Odessa* (Texas) *American*, June 16, 1971: 18.

Biederman, Les. "Roberto's Rifle Wing Amazes Fans, Shoots Down Cardinals," *The Sporting News*, July 1, 1967: 15.

Hano, Arnold. "Roberto Clemente – Baseball's Brightest Superstar," *Boys' Life*, March 1968, 24-25, 54; Vol. 58, No. 3.

Prato, Lou. "Why the Pirates Love the New Roberto Clemente," *Sport*, August 1967: 34-37, 81-82.

https://pittsburghquarterly.com/articles/roberto-clemente-in-retrospect/.

Preston, J.G. "Dave Parker's Remarkable 26 Assists in 1977 … and Roberto Clemente's 27 in 1961," https://prestonjg.wordpress.com/2015/08/08/dave-parkers-remarkable-26-assists-in-1977/.

WEBSITES

Newspapers.com

PaperoOfRecord.com

https://www.Baseball-Reference.com/

https://www.baseball-reference.com/bullpen/Roberto_Clemente%27s_%27Toolbox%27:_The_Arm#Pedr.C3.ADn_Zorrilla

Retrosheet.org

NOTES

1   Charley Feeney, "Greatest Catch? This One by Roberto Will Do," *The Sporting News*, July 3, 1971: 7.

2   Bruce Markusen, *Roberto Clemente: The Great One* (Champaign, Illinois: Sports Publishing, Inc., 1998), 222.

3   Darrell Mack, "Roberto Draws Dome Cheers," *Cleveland News-Herald*, June 16, 1971: 21.

4   Dennis Tuttle, "The Arms Race," *Inside Sports*, August 1997: 30-37.

5   David Maraniss, *Clemente: The Passion and Grace of Baseball's Last Hero* (New York: Simon & Schuster, 2006), 20.

6   Markusen, 4.

7   Markusen, 5.

8   Markusen, 8.

9   Markusen, 9.

10   Markusen, 36.

11   John Carroll, "Clemente Credits Willie Mays' 'Basket Catch' for 'No Drops, *Monongahela* (Pennsylvania) *Daily Republican*, May 7, 1957: 2.

12   "Pirates Stun Milwaukee Braves, 5-4 To Cop 4th Straight Victory," *Somerset* (Pennsylvania) *Daily American*, May 5, 1955: 7.

13   Markusen, 44.

14   Markusen, 44.

15   Markusen, 77.

16   Markusen, 191.

17   Markusen, 77.

18   Markusen, 65.

19   Henry Peter Gribbin, "Watching Roberto Clemente Was Always a Consummate Treat," *Pittsburgh Senior News*, July 28, 2016.

20   "Clemente Is Cassius Clay of Baseball," *Chicago Tribune*, April 21, 1964.

21   Lester J. Biederman, "Hodges Lights Fuse, Dodgers Then Blow Top at Umpires," *Pittsburgh Press*, August 5, 1960: 25.

22   Phil Musick, *Who Was Roberto?: A Biography of Roberto Clemente*, (Garden City, New York: Doubleday & Co., 1974), 147.

23   Lester J. Biederman, "Pirates Win 'Finest Game,'" *Pittsburgh Press*, August 6, 1960: 6.

24   Maraniss, 95.

25   Jason Aronoff, *Going, Going ... Caught! Baseball's Great Outfield Catches as Described by Those Who Saw Them, 1887-1964* (Jefferson, North Carolina: McFarland, 2009), 235.

26   Maraniss, 123.

27   Les Biederman, "Corsairs Look to Patch Up Holes in Leaking Flagship," *The Sporting News*, June 7, 1961: 13.

28   Les Biederman, "Brosnan's 2 Books Sell," *Pittsburgh Press*, June 20, 1962: 51.

29   Biederman, "Brosnan's 2 Books Sell."

30   Les Biederman, "Pirates Save Victory Streak with Six Run Rally in Ninth," *The Sporting News*, September 11, 1965: 6; Markusen, 142.

31   Earl Lawson, "National League Race Tightens," *Cincinnati Post and Times-Star*, September 7, 1965: 13.

32   "Pirates Miss Chance as Last Rally Fails," *Latrobe* (Pennsylvania) *Bulletin*, September 2, 1966: 12.

33   Jim Ferguson, "Bucs Bounce Arrigo in 6-1 Waltz," *Dayton Daily News*, July 9, 1967: 1D; Arnold Hano, "Roberto Clemente – Baseball's Brightest Superstar," *Boys' Life*, March 1968: 24-25, 54.

34   "Pirates' McBean Baffles Giants, 2-1," *Lancaster* (Pennsylvania) *Sunday News*, April 14, 1968: 40.

35   Phil Pepe, "Moose 0-Hitter Mortifies Mets, 6-0," *New York Daily News*, September 21, 1969: 112.

36   "Clemente Shines on His Night," *Pittsburgh Press*, July 25, 1970: 6.

37   Tony Perez interview. https://www.youtube.com/watch?v=ZkPf_ziVXwE.

38   Ernie Banks, "Clemente the Toughest in Banks' Opinion," *Chicago Tribune*, July 6, 1969: B1, B2.

39   Steve Blass, as told to Phil Musick, "A Teammate Remembers Roberto Clemente," *Sport*, April 1973: 58, 90-92.

40   Bill Mazeroski, as told to Phil Musick, "My 16 Years with Roberto Clemente," *Sport*, November 1971: 61, 63, 110, 111.

41   Markusen, 75-76.

42   Les Biederman, "Buccos Aren't Bragging Over Their No. 1 Butterfinger Niche," *The Sporting News*, November 14, 1964: 18.

43   Markusen, 255; C.R. Ways, "'Nobody Does Anything Better Than Me in Baseball,' Says Roberto Clemente," *New York Times*, April 9, 1972: VI 39.

44   Bill Christine, "Robby Snaps Out of It Just in Time," *Pittsburgh Press*, October 4, 1971: 38.

45   Maraniss, 248.

46   Les Biederman, "Clemente, Early Buc Ace, Says He's Better in Summer," *The Sporting News*, June 29, 1955: 26.

47   Maraniss, 90.

48   Markusen, 222.

ROBERTO CLEMENTE'S TWO-ASSIST GAMES

BY BILL NOWLIN

In the course of his career, Roberto Clemente played in 2,433 games and earned 266 assists.

He made any number of spectacular defensive plays. One often cited is the time that Clemente, playing right field, earned an assist on a bunt. The game was at Forbes Field in Pittsburgh on Friday night, August 27, 1965. The Houston Astros were in town and held a 4-3 lead in the top of the eighth, with runners on first and second and nobody out. With the Astros looking to add an insurance run, it was, journalist Phil Musick wrote, "an obvious sacrifice situation." Rusty Staub was on second and Walt Bond on first. Bob Lillis pinch-hit for Jim Gentile. Musick explains that the Pirates' counterstrategy was to have the third baseman rush in to field the anticipated bunt and have the shortstop run over to cover third. Here's what he said happened: Lillis "popped his sacrifice attempt into the air near second base. The runners held up briefly, and suddenly Clemente was skidding across the infield in pursuit of the ball. After recovering from the shock of discovering

Clemente in his midst, Houston's Walter Bonds [sic] streaked for third base. Clemente's throw preceded him to the base, and the humiliated Bonds [sic] was out."[1] Clemente was, Musick wrote, "the only outfielder ever known to play a bunt."[2]

In 15 of those games, Clemente had two assists in the same game. In 13 of them, the two assists were both outfield assists.

MAY 22, 1956
St. Louis Cardinals 6, Pirates 3
at Forbes Field.

In this game, Clemente had two assists but also made two errors. The errors were committed in the second and ninth innings. In the top of the eighth inning, Clemente moved from right field to play third base. Neither of his assists were outfield assists; both were fielding groundballs and throwing to first base, once in the eighth and once in the ninth. He made his ninth-inning error while fielding a sacrifice bunt.

JULY 14, 1956
Chicago Cubs 6, Pirates 2
(first game of doubleheader) at Wrigley Field.

The Cubs swept, 6-2 and 6-5 (in 10 innings). In the first game, Clemente played right field for the first six innings, then played second base in the seventh and eighth. His first assist came in the bottom of the fifth; he caught a fly ball to right and then cut down Ernie Banks, who had tagged up at second base, on a "rifle shot throw" to third.[3] Clemente's second assist was as a second baseman, a routine 4-3 grounder that ended the seventh inning.

APRIL 17, 1958
Milwaukee Braves 6, Pirates 1
at County Stadium

In the bottom of the third, Johnny Logan led off with a double. Del Crandall singled to right field but tried to take two bags on Clemente's throw to the plate intended to prevent Logan from scoring. Logan held up at third, but Crandall was out when catcher Hank Foiles quickly fired the ball to second base, 9-2-4.[4] After Eddie Mathews' three-run homer in the fifth, Hank Aaron singled to center. Frank Torre singled to right, but Aaron overran the bag at second base, making a turn toward third base, and was thrown out, 9-4.[5]

JULY 18, 1958
San Francisco Giants 5, Pirates 4
at Seals Stadium.

In the bottom of the third, with the Pirates ahead, 1-0, Stu Miller laid down a sacrifice with Valmy Thomas on first base. The ball was misplayed by Pirates third baseman Frank Thomas, whose throw to second sailed into right field. Clemente threw the ball to shortstop Dick Groat, who bobbled the ball, allowing Miller to reach second safely, but Groat quickly threw home and cut down Valmy Thomas at the plate.[6] The Giants built up a 5-1 lead and in the bottom of the fifth with two outs and a man on first, Orlando Cepeda singled to right. The runner ran to third. Clemente gunned the ball in and nipped Cepeda at second base.

AUGUST 10, 1961
St. Louis Cardinals 3, Pirates 2
at Forbes Field.

In the top of the fourth, with the game tied, 1-1, St. Louis's Ken Boyer on first and nobody out, Stan Musial flied out to right field. Clemente caught the ball and threw behind the runner to Dick Stuart at first base; before Boyer could get back to the bag, he was out. The very next inning, the score still the same and again a man on first and nobody out, Curt Flood hit a ball down the right-field line. Trying for a double, he was thrown out by Clemente, with a throw to shortstop Groat at second.[7]

SEPTEMBER 4, 1961
St. Louis Cardinals 9, Pirates 4
at Busch Stadium.

In the bottom of the third, Curt Flood singled with Ray Sadecki on first and no outs. Sadecki took third, but "when he suspected Bob Clemente would throw to third, he was caught in his thoughts trying to get back to first."[8] Flood was thrown out RF-2B-1B. Julian Javier singled and drove in Sadecki. Javier took second on a groundout, and was driven in by Musial's single. A double by Boyer and a walk to Charlie James loaded the bases. Alex Grammas singled, driving in two runs, but James was out at third base on Clemente's throw. For James, it was the second time in the game he was thrown out by an outfielder. In the second inning, center fielder Bill Virdon threw him out at second base as he tried to stretch his RBI single into a double.

MAY 3, 1962

San Francisco Giants 8, Pirates 4
at Candlestick Park.

In the bottom of the first inning, Orlando Cepeda singled to right field, but took too wide a turn at first base. Clemente threw behind him and, rather than there being runners on first and second, the inning was over. In the fourth, with runners on first and third and Willie Mays at the plate, the Giants broke a 2-2 tie on a wild pitch. Mays then singled to right field, driving in another run, but was thrown out, Clemente to Dick Stuart at first base to Bill Mazeroski at second.

MAY 17, 1964

Los Angeles Dodgers 3, Pirates 2
(first game of doubleheader)
at Dodger Stadium.

Clemente tripled, doubled, and singled in the game, "but it was his arm that captured the fans' fancy and left two baserunners for dead."[9] As the Dodgers scored their second run in the bottom of the second on a single to right field by Sandy Koufax, Dick Tracewski tried to go first to third, but Clemente's throw to third base got him as he "fell trying to scramble back to second base," the tag applied by shortstop Dick Schofield.[10] In the seventh inning, Ron Fairly led with a triple. With one out, he tagged and scored on a sacrifice fly to right – though Clemente's "sensational throw" to the plate nearly got him.[11] The very next batter, Willie Davis, grounded the ball into right field but was thrown out at second base "by a couple of lengths," Clemente to shortstop Schofield.[12]

MAY 13, 1965

Milwaukee Braves 5, Pirates 4
at Forbes Field.

The Braves got 19 hits to eight for Pittsburgh, but just edged the Pirates by one run. In the fourth inning, center fielder Bill Virdon got credit for a double play, catching a fly ball and then throwing out Denis Menke at the plate. Menke was hurt on the play and had to leave the game.[13] The Pirates held a 4-1 lead after five innings, but saw the Braves tie it in the sixth. With two outs and runners on first and third in the top of the eighth, Joe Torre singled to give the Braves a 5-4 lead, but when he tried to take second, Clemente's throw to Schofield got Torre for the third out. The very next inning, the ninth, the Braves angled for an insurance run. With one out and runners on first and third, Sandy Alomar flied out to right field. Clemente threw home to catcher Jim Pagliaroni, who tagged Phil Niekro trying to score on a sacrifice fly.

MAY 12, 1966

San Francisco Giants 3, Pirates 0
at Forbes Field.

Jesus Alou singled for the Giants in the top of the second inning. Hoping to put runners on second and third with nobody out, Alou aimed for two bags but was out when Clemente threw the ball behind him to first baseman Donn Clendenon, who then got Alou in a rundown, the ball going 9-3-4-6. The next batter, Ollie Brown, drove in Giants third baseman Jim Ray Hart from third and the Giants led, 1-0. Hart hit a solo homer leading off the fourth. Still nursing a 2-0 lead in the eighth, Willie Mays singled and Hart came to bat. He grounded out – to Clemente in right field, the play going RF to SS Gene Alley for a force out of Mays at second base.

JUNE 13, 1967

St. Louis Cardinals 7, Pirates 4
at Forbes Field.

In this game, Clemente cut down two runners, both at home plate, but also committed two errors. In the bottom of the first, with two outs, Orlando Cepeda was on first base, having just singled in the first run of the game. Tim McCarver singled to center, the ball played by Clemente, whose error enabled McCarver to scoot all the way to third base, though Clemente quickly recovered and fired the ball to home plate and got Cepeda. The Giants scored three more runs in the second inning, another Clemente assist resulting in a third out at the plate, this time it being Curt Flood, who tried to go first to home on Bobby Tolan's double to right.[14] Clemente committed his second error in the top of the third, allowing a sixth run to score and setting up the seventh.

JULY 7, 1967

Cincinnati Reds 6, Pirates 2
at Forbes Field.

In this game, Clemente the baserunner was a victim of an outfield assist himself. In the top of the second, Clemente recorded his first assist of the game, throwing out Lee May trying to score on Tommy Helms' fly ball.[15] With the score 1-1 in the bottom of the fourth, Clemente tried to give the Pirates a go-ahead run. Bill Mazeroski hit a fly ball to Vada Pinson in center field, but Pinson's 8-4-2 throw to the plate erased Clemente. The Reds led, 3-1, heading into the top of the seventh. With a walk and a single, they had runners on first and second with nobody out. Pinson grounded a single into right field, but Clemente fielded it and threw to second base quickly enough to force Helms there.

AUGUST 12, 1969

San Francisco Giants 6, Pirates 3
at Candlestick Park.

With two outs and a 3-0 lead in the bottom of the second, the Giants' Ron Hunt walked and stole second. Bobby Bonds singled to right field but Hunt was thrown out at home plate by Clemente. In the top of the fifth, San Francisco right fielder Ken Henderson threw out Bill Mazeroski at the plate. In the bottom of the eighth, with the Giants ahead 6-1, Hal Lanier was on first with two outs. Gaylord Perry singled off Pittsburgh's Bo Belinsky. Lanier tried to go to third, but was erased on

Clemente's throw to Richie Hebner at third base. There were also the plays that were never made, because opposing baserunners respected Clemente's instincts and his arm. Bill Mazeroski, who played for 17 years with Clemente on the Pirates, once said of his teammate, "He changes the game. In almost every one of our games, a runner is afraid to try to go from first to third on a single to right. In a year's time, that makes a hell of a difference in how many runs we give up."[16]

SEPTEMBER 14, 1971

Pittsburgh Pirates 4, Chicago Cubs 3
at Wrigley Field

Clemente earned two outfield assists in this game as well, remarkable in that after every one of the 13 previous occasions coming in a game the Pirates lost, Pittsburgh won this one, 4-3. Clemente played no role in the offense, going 0-for-4 and never getting the ball out of the infield. In the bottom of the fourth, the Cubs' Cleo James hit a two-out double but was thrown out at third base after Clemente's throw went 9-4-3. (First baseman Al Oliver applied the tag at third base.) The Pirates held a one-run lead (4-3) in the bottom of the seventh. Brock Davis reached on an error at third base. The next batter, Billy Williams, doubled into center field. Clemente fielded the ball and threw to second baseman Paul Popovich, who threw home and Davis was out.

JUNE 25, 1972

Pittsburgh Pirates 9, Chicago Cubs 2
at Wrigley Field.

Two months before Clemente turned 38 years old in August, he had another two-assist game, his 15th and final one. Despite the lopsided final score, the Cubs led 2-1 after seven full innings. In the bottom of the sixth, Clemente got credit for an outfield assist on a popup to second base. Ron Santo was on first base. Paul Popovich popped up to second baseman Dave Cash. Santo was out at second base, the play going Cash to Clemente to shortstop Gene Alley. Santo said he hadn't seen Cash catch the ball.[17]

After a Manny Sanguillen grand slam gave Pittsburgh a 5-2 lead in the top of the seventh, the Cubs' Jim Hickman hit a ball into right field, fielded by Clemente, who threw to shortstop Gene Alley in time to force out Billy Williams at second base. The *Tribune*'s Dozer wrote that Williams had been "decoyed into thinking it would be a catch" and only belatedly "turned on a burst of speed."[18] Clemente had "no chance" of catching the ball, "stopped 10 feet from where the ball landed, grabbed the ball on one hop and fired to Alley."[19]

THE PLAYERS THROWN OUT

The players thrown out by Clemente on outfield assists could have helped build an All-Star team. Eight of them are Hall of Famers. *Hank Aaron*, Jesus Alou, Ken Boyer, *Orlando Cepeda* (thrown out three times), Del Crandall, Brock Davis, Willie Davis, Curt Flood (thrown out twice), Tommy Helms, Ron Hunt, Charlie James, Cleo James, Lee May, *Willie Mays*, *Phil Niekro*, *Gaylord Perry*, Ray Sadecki, *Ron Santo*, Valmy Thomas, *Joe Torre*, Dick Tracewski, *Billy Williams*. (Those in the Hall of Fame are in italics.)

OUTFIELDERS WITH FOUR-ASSIST GAMES

Tom Ruane of Retrosheet notes that according to the last *Sporting News Record Book*, the record for outfield assists in a game is four, done by four players (five times) in the nineteenth century. Bill Crowley of the Buffalo Bisons accomplished it twice, both in the same season, on May 24, 1880, and August 27, 1880. He had 46 assists that year.

Harry Schafer of the Boston Red Stockings had been the first, on September 26, 1877. Mike Griffin had a four-outfield-assist game for the Brooklyn Grooms on July 17, 1893 and the Cincinnati Reds' Dusty Miller had one on May 30, 1895.

In the twentieth century, it was done six times: Ducky Holmes (Washington Senators, August 21, 1903), Fred Clarke (Pittsburgh Pirates, August 23, 1910), Lee Magee (New York Yankees, June 28, 1916), Happy Felsch (Chicago White Sox, August 14, 1919), Bob Meusel (New York Yankees, September 5, 1921), and Sam Langford (Cleveland Indians, May 1, 1928). As of this writing in 2022, it has been nearly 100 years since an outfielder recorded four assists in one game.

ACKNOWLEDGMENTS

Thanks to Dave Smith and Tom Ruane of Retroheet.org.

NOTES

1   Phil Musick, *Who Was Roberto?* (Garden City, New York: Associated Features/Doubleday, 1974), 289.

2   Musick, 288. Bruce Markusen described the play as well, saying that Bond was out by five feet. Bruce Markusen, *Roberto Clemente: The Great One* (Champaign, Illinois: Sports Publishing 1998), 142.

3   Irving Vaughan, "Cubs Beat Pirates, 6 to 2 in 9 Innings, 6 to 5 in 10," *Chicago Tribune*, July 15, 1956: A2.

4   Jack Hernon, "Mathews Swats 2 More HRs to Sink Bucs, 6-1," *Pittsburgh Post-Gazette*, April 18, 1958: 17.

5   "Sanford, Phils' Jinx, Faces Buhl Tonight," *Milwaukee Journal*, April 18, 1958: Part 2, 17.

6   Bob Stevens, "Late Pirate Rally Falls a Run Short," *San Francisco Chronicle*, July 19, 1958: 1H.

7   Jack Hernon, "Cards Nip Pirates for Eighth Straight, 3-2," *Pittsburgh Post-Gazette*, April 18, 1958: 16.

8   Jack Hernon, "White's 'Grand Slam' Sinks Pirates, 9-4," *Pittsburgh Post-Gazette*, September 5, 1961: 20.

9   Frank Finch, "Sandy Sizzles, 3-2; Podres Fizzles, 8-3," *Los Angeles Times*, May 18, 1964: B1, B4.

10   Finch.

11   Photo caption, "Just Barely for Fairly," *Los Angeles Times*, May 18, 1964: B1.

12   Finch.

13   Jack Hernon mistakenly wrote that it was Clemente, not Virdon, who threw out Menke at the plate. Had that been the case, it would have been Clemente's third outfield assist. "Braves' 19-Hit Attack Dumps Pirates, 5-4," *Pittsburgh Post-Gazette*, May 14, 1985: 24.

14   There had been another out at the plate earlier in the second inning, albeit not one involving Clemente. Mike Shannon was out on an unusual 4-2-5-4 play with second baseman Bill Mazeroski making the out at home plate.

15   A photograph of the play appeared on page 10 of the July 8 *Columbus Dispatch.*

16   Musick, 290.

17   Richard Dozer, "Pirates' Late Rallies Slam Door on Cubs 9-2," *Chicago Tribune*, June 26, 1972: C1, C6. The *Chicago Defender* said the ball was caught by center fielder Al Oliver, who had raced in, caught it, "did a bellyflop but hung onto the ball," and then flipped it to Clemente, who threw to Alley for the out. See Norman O. Unger, "Fergie on Bench, Brightens Day," *Chicago Defender*, June 26, 1972: 28. Retrosheet, however, has two separate scoresheets for the game, both in agreement with the *Tribune* account.

18   Dozer: C6.

19   Charles Feeney, "Sangy-Giusti Duo Clinches Sweep of Cubs," *Pittsburgh Post-Gazette*, June 26, 1972: 16, 18.

Clemente's Rawlings Gold Glove Award, 1962.
Photograph by Duane Rieder.

ROBERTO CLEMENTE IN ALL-STAR GAMES

BY MALCOLM ALLEN

As inadvisable as it would be to draw conclusions based on 34 plate appearances or 72 innings of defense spread out over more than a decade, it's safe to state that Roberto Clemente's All-Star Game performances only enhanced his legacy. The lifetime .317 hitter batted .323 in 15 midsummer exhibitions against his most skilled competitors and provided some memorable moments.

In 1960 the Los Angeles Dodgers visited Pittsburgh the weekend before All-Star Game rosters were announced. The Pirates hadn't won a pennant since 1927, but they'd moved atop the National League in May when Clemente earned Player of the Month honors by driving in 25 runs in 27 games. By the conclusion of the first half, the sixth-year right fielder ranked third in the majors with a .325 batting average. Before leaving Pittsburgh, Dodgers skipper Walter Alston – who also was to manage the NL All-Stars – remarked, "Clemente is the worst-looking good hitter in the game. I have some batters who swing like .400 hitters and wind up with .200, yet Clemente swings like a .200 batter and winds up close to .400."[1]

As it happened, Clemente was one of eight Pirates on the National League squad, five of whom were on the field when he made his All-Star Game debut on July 11 at Kansas City's Municipal Stadium, where the game time temperature was a muggy 100 degrees.[2] After replacing the Braves' Hank Aaron in the bottom of the seventh inning, Clemente flied out against Athletics lefty Bud Daley in his only at-bat and caught both balls hit his way in right field, including Harvey Kuenn's liner for the final out of the NL's 5-3 victory. There were two All-Star Games that year so, two days later at Yankee Stadium, Clemente replaced Aaron again, this time as an eighth-inning pinch-hitter. He was walked by the Tigers' Frank Lary and the NL won again, 6-0. After the regular season resumed, Clemente summed up his first All-Star experience: "It's rush, rush, rush. No time to rest. ... It tired me out."[3] But he was just getting started.

There were also two All-Star Games in 1961, played nearly three weeks apart. Clemente started both contests in right field after receiving 170 of the 233 votes cast by his fellow NL players, managers, and coaches. (Only the Milwaukee Braves' second baseman, Frank Bolling, received more support.)[4] Puerto Ricans were understandably proud to have two starters in the lineup for the first time on July 11 in San Francisco, as the Giants' Orlando Cepeda – the island's first All-Star Game starter, two years earlier – and Clemente batted fourth and fifth for the National League, respectively. Clemente carried a major-league-best .357 average into the contest on his way to his first career batting title.

Facing Whitey Ford his first time up, Clemente tripled off the right-center-field fence between two of the southpaw's Yankees teammates, Mickey Mantle and Roger Maris.[5] He scored the game's first run when Bill White of the Cardinals followed with a sacrifice fly. In the fourth inning, Clemente delivered a sacrifice fly of his own against the Senators' Dick Donovan to increase the NL's advantage to 2-0. The ball traveled nearly 400 feet to right-center, but Candlestick Park's notorious swirling winds kept it in play. "In any other park, I['d] have two home runs," Clemente lamented.[6]

Similar gusts knocked Giants reliever Stu Miller off the mound in the ninth inning, causing him to balk during the American League's game-tying rally. After the AL went ahead in the top of the 10th, San Francisco's Willie Mays doubled home Aaron to tie the contest in the bottom of the frame. After Cincinnati's Frank Robinson was hit by a pitch, Clemente faced Baltimore's Hoyt Wilhelm – who'd struck him out in the eighth – with runners at first and second and nobody out. Clemente swung and missed at one inside knuckleball before lifting the next pitch into right-center for a game-winning single. "Big thrill for me," he said. "My mother, father, [and] brothers were watching on TV and listening on radio in Puerto Rico."[7] The All-Star Game MVP award was not established until the following year, but had it existed, Clemente's 2-for-4, two-RBI performance with a run scored in the NL's 5-4 victory would likely have earned it. "What makes me feel most good is that the skipper [Pittsburgh's Danny Murtaugh] let me play the whole game," he said in the winning locker room, where he was photographed smiling with Mays and Aaron. "He [paid] me a big compliment."[8] In 1961's second All-Star Game, at Fenway Park on July 31, Clemente went 0-for-2 before giving way to Aaron in the bottom of the fourth of a game that ended tied, 1-1.

Clemente's peers elected him a starter again in 1962, the last year that baseball staged two All-Star Games. In the first, at D.C. Stadium in front of President John F. Kennedy on July 10, he delivered a two-strike double down the right-field line against Tigers righty Jim Bunning in the opening frame.[9] It would be the NL's only extra-base hit, and he also stroked two singles. The first was pulled to left against Twins ace Camilo Pascual in the fourth, an inning that ended with Minnesota catcher Earl Battey cutting down Clemente on an attempted steal of third base to complete a double play after Cepeda struck out. Before yielding right field to the Giants' Felipe Alou, Clemente legged out an infield safety against Pascual in the middle of the two-run sixth-inning rally that keyed the NL's 3-1 victory. Through 2022, his three-hit performance has been surpassed by only three players in All-Star competition. (Joe Medwick in 1937, Ted Williams in 1946, and Carl Yastrzemski in 1970 all had four hits.) On July 30 at Wrigley Field, Clemente played for a losing NL team for the first time, though the score was tied when he departed after playing three innings and going 0-for-2 against the Senators' Dave Stenhouse.

In 1963 Clemente finished second to Aaron in voting to start for the NL in right field. Aaron, who was leading the majors in home runs and RBIs, played the entire midsummer classic at

Cleveland Stadium on July 9, and Clemente replaced Mays in center for the bottom of the ninth inning with the NL on top, 5-3. He fielded Brooks Robinson's one-out single just before the game-ending double play.

Clemente regained his starting role for the July 7, 1964, All-Star Game at Shea Stadium. His mother was in attendance, and he entered the contest with the majors' best average (.345) and the NL lead in doubles (22).[10] Facing the Angels' Dean Chance, Clemente whiffed leading off the bottom of the first and grounded to shortstop his next time up. He stroked a two-out single against Pascual in the fifth, however, with the ball bouncing up after striking the second-base bag.[11] When Pittsburgh's Dick Groat followed with a double, Clemente raced home from first to increase the National League's lead to 3-1. The AL battled back to seize a short-lived lead after Clemente left the game in the top of the sixth, but the senior circuit prevailed on a three-run walk-off homer by his successor in right field, the Phillies' Johnny Callison.

In the summer of 1965, Clemente enjoyed a career-best 20-game hitting streak that ended against the Dodgers' Sandy Koufax on the final day of the first half. He was already a two-time batting champion and won his third title that year. When Clemente learned that he'd finished third behind Aaron and Callison in his peers' All-Star Game voting, he made it clear that he didn't intend to suit up as a reserve, saying, "I won't play."[12] Pittsburgh coach Harry Walker encouraged him to reconsider, and he relented after National League manager Gene Mauch of the Phillies told him, "It won't be a game without you. You belong there with the rest of the stars."[13] Before the July 13 contest at Metropolitan Stadium in Bloomington, Minnesota, Clemente and his fellow Puerto Rican Félix Mantilla were photographed alongside Juan Marichal of the Dominican Republic, Vic Davalillo from Venezuela, and Cubans Leo Cárdenas, Tony Oliva, Cookie Rojas, and Zoilo

Versalles – an image that foreshadowed baseball's changing demographics. In the top of the seventh, Clemente pinch-hit for his Pittsburgh teammate Willie Stargell against the Indians' Sam McDowell with the score tied and runners at the corners; he grounded into a force out just before the Cubs' Ron Santo delivered the eventual game-winning infield hit. Clemente played three innings in left field and finished 0-for-2 at the plate after grounding out in the ninth.

Midway through his 1966 MVP season, Clemente started another All-Star Game for the NL. By appearing in his 10th such contest, he surpassed Arky Vaughan for the most in Pirates' franchise history. The game was played on July 12 at Busch Stadium in St. Louis, where the Cardinals' Joe Torre – who caught the first seven innings – estimated that the on-field temperature was 115 degrees.[14] Batting second against Detroit's Denny McLain, Clemente flied out to center in his first trip. In the fourth inning, he followed Mays's leadoff safety with a single of his own against the Twins' Jim Kaat. After Clemente was erased on a force, the Nationals evened the contest, 1-1, on an infield hit by Santo. That score held until the National League prevailed in the bottom of the 10th. Clemente played the entire game in the oppressive heat and went 2-for-4, including a sixth-inning, opposite-field double off the Yankees' Mel Stottlemyre. "I never felt so tired and weary in my life," he said.[15]

Entering the 1967 All-Star Game, only Cepeda (.356) boasted a better batting average than Clemente's .352. Both made what proved to be their final All-Star starts on July 11 at Anaheim Stadium and played all 15 innings. After Clemente beat out an infield single against the Angels' Dean Chance in the top of the first, however, he struck out in four straight at-bats; against Chance, the White Sox' Gary Peters (looking), the Yankees' Al Downing and the A's Catfish Hunter. A heavy haze on a 92-degree afternoon and shadows resulting from the 4:15

first pitch contributed to an All-Star Game record 30 strikeouts – 11 on called third strikes.[16] "It was hard to see the breaking stuff at this time of day," Clemente remarked.[17] He finished 1-for-6 after grounding out against Hunter in the 14th, but the NL prevailed one inning later. Both his six putouts in right field and four strikeouts remain All-Star Game records as of 2022. (Clemente had only one other four-strikeout game, in Los Angeles against Don Drysdale on May 21, 1966.)

Before leaving for spring training 1968, Clemente injured his right shoulder in a fall at his home in Puerto Rico. He failed to reach double figures in outfield assists for the only time in 14 seasons from 1958 to 1971 and entered the All-Star break hitting just .245. "I don't want to alibi," he replied when asked about his shoulder. "It's not real good, see, I say something like that and it sounds like an alibi."[18] For the first time in nine years, he wasn't selected for the National League squad. Clemente batted .347 after the break, however, and led NL position players with 8.2 WAR in 1968.

When Clemente returned to the All-Star Game at Robert F. Kennedy Stadium in Washington in 1969, he was in the middle of earning NL Player of the Month honors for batting .418 in July. The game was played in damp, overcast conditions on July 23 after being rained out the previous night. Clemente replaced Aaron in right field in the bottom of the fifth and struck out against McDowell in his only plate appearance, "after he had tomahawked a couple of high, hard ones foul," reported the *Pittsburgh Press*.[19] On defense, Clemente made a valiant diving attempt to glove the Orioles' Boog Powell's sinking liner in the eighth inning but trapped the ball.[20] The National League won again, 9-3.

When the privilege of choosing starters for the All-Star Game returned to the fans in 1970, Aaron, Mays, and the Reds' Pete Rose received the most votes among NL outfielders on the ballot, although the majors' leading hitter – Rico Carty

of the Braves – bumped the latter from the lineup on the strength of a write-in campaign. "The hell with the All-Star Game," said Clemente, who entered the break batting .355. "The only way I would play is if the game were being played in Pittsburgh."[21] His neck had been bothering him for weeks and with the Pirates leading their division by 1½ games, he said, "I want to use those three days to rest."[22] NL President Chub Feeney called Pittsburgh GM Joe Brown, however. Clemente missed the workout the day before the contest to visit a chiropractor, but he was in uniform for the game at Riverfront Stadium in Cincinnati.[23] When the teams were introduced, he was one of only three National Leaguers to be audibly booed by the 51,838 in attendance. (Dick Allen of the Cardinals and Cubs manager Leo Durocher were the others.)[24]

Clemente did not see action until the bottom of the ninth. The NL, after trailing, 4-1, at the beginning of the inning, had pulled within one run and had runners at the corners when he pinch-hit for the Cardinals' Bob Gibson. Stottlemyre relieved for the American League and fell behind in the count 3-and-1 before Clemente fouled off a curve that would've probably been ball four.[25] The next pitch was another down-and-away breaking ball, and Clemente lined it to center with a one-handed swing for a game-tying sacrifice fly, drawing cheers from the fickle crowd.[26]

When the Tigers' Willie Horton lined a hit off the right-field fence with one out in the top of the 10th, "it appeared to everybody in the new ballpark that it would be an easy double."[27] But Clemente played the carom off the wall perfectly and fired a bullet to second base to hold Horton to a single. An NBC cameraman caught Richard Nixon smiling in the box seats after the strong throw, prompting broadcaster Tony Kubek to remark, "Roberto has gained the admiration of our president."[28] Horton was erased when the next batter grounded into a double play. After Clemente made the second out in the bottom of the 12th, the NL strung together three straight singles to win, 5-4, improving the senior circuit's record in All-Star Games that he appeared in to 11-1-1.

The National League lost the All-Star Game at Tiger Stadium on July 13, 1971, that featured a record 22 future Hall of Famers. Clemente was a reserve after batting .342 to help the Pirates build the majors' best first-half record. He replaced Mays in right field in the bottom of the fourth inning and struck out looking against Orioles ace Jim Palmer to end the top of the fifth. Clemente's eighth-inning plate appearance against Detroit's Mickey Lolich proved to be his last in All-Star competition, though there was no way for the 53,559 ticket-holders to know that. The count went to three balls and one strike as Lolich followed a pair of hard deliveries with two benders. On the fifth pitch, Clemente committed himself to swinging early but kept his hands back. Balanced on his left leg, he connected and drove the ball more than 450 feet into the right-field upper deck for his only All-Star Game homer.[29]

In 1972 fans elected Clemente an All-Star Game starter for the first time. His total of 1,091,623 votes ranked fifth in the majors overall, trailing only Johnny Bench, Torre, Aaron, and Allen.[30] After being sidelined for two weeks by an intestinal virus, he'd played in Pittsburgh's final game before the break but bruised his left knee sliding into second base in the eighth inning.[31] Nevertheless, he arrived in Atlanta intending to start in center field. "There's no other place to be than the All-Star Game," he said. "I have to be excited about playing center field. It's a compliment, especially when we have so many good centerfielders in our league."[32] Clemente, nearly 38, hoped to play three innings, but he was limping noticeably two hours before game time. When a doctor informed Murtaugh that Clemente risked aggravating his knee injury, the NL (and Pirates) manager had no choice but to scratch him from the lineup.[33]

Five months and six days later, Clemente died tragically. Stargell and pitcher Dave Giusti had commemorative patches on their left sleeves with his number 21 when they represented the Pirates at the 1973 All-Star Game in Kansas City. The 1974 contest was played at Three Rivers Stadium in Pittsburgh with Clemente's widow, Vera, and three sons in attendance.[34] When the All-Star Game returned to the same ballpark 20 years later, the unveiling of a 12-foot-high bronze statue of Roberto Clemente was part of the festivities.[35] In 1998 at Coors Field in Denver, Vera became the first female captain of an All-Star team.[36] The 2006 All-Star Game, at PNC Park in Pittsburgh, was paused after four innings so that Bud Selig could present her with the Commissioner's Historic Achievement Award.[37]

Roberto Clemente's All-Star Game legacy will never be forgotten. Since Vic Power and Luis Arroyo became Puerto Rico's first All-Stars in 1955, a total of 50 players from the island have earned selections through 2022, but none of them have been in uniform for more All-Star Games than Clemente.[38]

SOURCES

In addition to sources cited in the Notes, the author consulted www.Baseball-Reference.com and www.Retrosheet.org.

NOTES

1   Lester J. Biederman, "Bucs May Dominate NL All-Star Team with Eight Players," *Pittsburgh Press*, July 4, 1960: 30.

2   Lester J. Biederman, "The Scorecard," *Pittsburgh Press*, July 12, 1960: 28.

3   Harry Keck, "Bravos and Bards Bounce Off Bucs' Danny," *The Sporting News*, August 10, 1960: 7.

4   "Clemente, Burgess Named N.L. All-Stars," *Pittsburgh Press*, July 2, 1961: 54.

5   Jack Hernon, "Roberto Drives in Two Runs, Scores One for Nationals," *Pittsburgh Post-Gazette*, July 12, 1961: 20.

6   "Clemente Explains Game-Winning Hit," *Pittsburgh Post-Gazette*, July 12, 1961: 20.

7   Lester J. Biederman, "Clemente 'Misses' Two Homers but Still Comes Out a Hero," *Pittsburgh Press*, July 12, 1961: 47.

8   "Clemente Just Hoped to Move Mays Along," *Asbury Park* (New Jersey) *Evening Press*, July 12, 1961: 28.

9   Jack Hernon, "Pirates Spark NL Stars to 3-1 Win," *Pittsburgh Post-Gazette*, July 11, 1962: 18.

10 Al Abrams, "Sidelights on Sports," *Pittsburgh Post-Gazette*, July 8, 1964: 18.

11 Lester J. Biederman, "NL Win Upholds Alston's Faith in Callison," *Pittsburgh Press*, July 8, 1964: 54.

12 Les Biederman, "Hats Off...!" *The Sporting News*, July 24, 1965: 29.

13 Bill Christine, "Clemente Drills Phils, Snubs Stars," *Pittsburgh Press*, July 8, 1970: 61.

14 Lester J. Biederman, "Would You Believe 115 Degrees?" *Pittsburgh Press*, July 13, 1966: 71.

15 Biederman, "Would You Believe 115 Degrees?"

16 John Hall, "N.L. Wins a Real Swinger in 15th, 2-1," *Los Angeles Times*, July 12, 1967: B1.

17 "Richie Is All Smiles as Tony Arrives Late," *Camden* (New Jersey) *Courier-Post*, July 12, 1967: 46.

18 Charley Feeney, "Roamin' Around," *Pittsburgh Post-Gazette*, July 9, 1968: 17.

19 Vince Leonard, "NBC's Double Day of Delight," *Pittsburgh Press*, July 24, 1969: 50.

20 "Alou Makes Most of All-Star Chance," *Pittsburgh Press*, July 24, 1969: 32.

21 Bill Christine, "Clemente Drills Phils, Snubs Stars," *Pittsburgh Press*, July 8, 1970: 61.

22 "Clemente to Pass Up 'Star Game,'" *Pittsburgh Post-Gazette*, July 8, 1970: 18.

23 "Will Hodges Use Clemente Tonight?" *Pittsburgh Post-Gazette*, July 14, 1970: 16.

24 "Fans Swing to Clemente," *Pittsburgh Press*, July 15, 1970: 63.

25 "Fans Swing to Clemente."

26 "Rose 'Nationalizes' a Classic," *Camden Courier-Post*, July 15, 1970: 57.

27 Charley Feeney, "Nationals Keep 'Star Grip,' Win by 5-4 in 12," *Pittsburgh Post-Gazette*, July 15, 1970: 19.

28 Roy McHugh, "Roberto's Reverse," *Pittsburgh Press*, July 15, 1970: 63.

29 Joseph Durso, "Nationals Also Connect 3 Times – 6 Equals Record," *New York Times*, July 14, 1971: 23.

30 "All-Star Balloting," *Pittsburgh Press*, July 18, 1972: 30.

31 "Injured Knee Puts Clemente Out of Game," *Pittsburgh Post-Gazette*, July 26, 1972: 21.

32 Bob Smizik, "Clemente Center of Star Attention," *Pittsburgh Press*, July 25, 1972: 30.

33 Charley Feeney, "Playing Games," *Pittsburgh Post-Gazette*, July 27, 1972: 15.

34 Joe Grata, "All-Star Fan Recalls Past, Calls 'Shot,'" *Pittsburgh Press*, July 24, 1974: 2.

35 United Press International, "Statue Dedicated to Clemente," July 8, 1994, https://www.upi.com/Archives/1994/07/08/Statue-dedicated-to-Clemente/3985773640000/ (last accessed July 19, 2021).

36 Claire Smith, "Baseball Names Clemente's Widow Captain," *New York Times*, July 3, 1998: 3.

37 Robert Dvorchak, "Clemente All-Star Tribute Another Touching Moment," Pittsburgh Post-Gazette, July 13, 2006, https://www.post-gazette.com/sports/pirates-all-star-game/2006/07/13/Clemente-All-Star-tribute-another-touching-moment/stories/200607130453 (last accessed July 19, 2021).

38 Iván Rodríguez, like Clemente, saw action in 14 All-Star games. Clemente was in uniform for 15 All-Star Games over 12 different seasons, while Rodriguez made All-Star teams in 14 separate years.

"THE BEST DAMN PLAYER IN THE WORLD SERIES":

CLEMENTE, THE WORLD SERIES, AND THE MAKING OF A CAREER

BY ALEX KUKURA

In baseball, there is only one goal. Each season teams play 162 games, plus up to 15 more in the playoffs, to earn the right to play in the World Series.[1] The Series has an uncanny ability to be perfectly unpredictable, capable of turning both stars into legends and nobodies into heroes. One of the most fascinating aspects of the World Series is the effect it has on the people involved. Players, fans, and the press, understanding that a championship is the universal goal, place a considerable amount of stock in World Series performance. The Yankees, for example, are virtually synonymous with the phrase "27 rings," while Ted Williams is known not only as the last man to hit .400 and one of the greatest hitters ever, but also as possibly the greatest player to never play on a winning World Series team. Given this, it's evident that World Series performances, or lack thereof, play an important role in the narrative of a player's career.

Roberto Clemente, much like Williams, is omnipresent in conversations about the greatest players in baseball history. Throughout his career,

Clemente hit .317 and finished with exactly 3,000 hits. His presence in right field struck fear not only into batters, but also baserunners, as he was known to nail runners at third base or home plate from even the deepest of right-field corners. But perhaps more important than Clemente's on-field achievements were his actions off the field. Hailing from Puerto Rico, Clemente was an incredible ambassador of the game, especially for Latin Americans, and since 1971 his charitable actions have been recognized with a prestigious award given in his name.

Clemente was also a two-time World Series champion, winning with the Pittsburgh Pirates in 1960 and 1971. These two championships, separated by 11 years, tell two different stories, each one equally important to the story of Clemente. In 1960 a young Clemente, still adjusting to life in the United States and the major leagues, began to come into his own and was recognized as a fan favorite in Pittsburgh. In 1971 a 14-time All-Star Clemente, leader of one of the most diverse teams the game had ever seen, gained the national notoriety he had long craved. In these ways and more, the narratives of these two World Series are imperative to the fascinating story of Clemente's life.

1960

On September 25, 1960, the Pirates lost a baseball game, but that didn't stop 100,000 fans from welcoming the team back to Pittsburgh that night. Despite losing 4-2 to the Milwaukee Braves, the Pirates had clinched their first National League pennant since 1927.[2] The Bucs, as hometown fans called them, went on to finish the season with 95 wins, 59 losses, and one tie, good for first place in the National League and a trip to the World Series by a margin of seven games.

In the American League, the Yankees clinched their 10th pennant in 12 years and ended the season on a 15-game winning streak to finish with 97 wins, 57 losses, and one tie. The Yankees were led by the dominant batting lineup of Mickey Mantle, Roger Maris, Yogi Berra, and Moose Skowron, considered to be a second coming of the Yankees' Murderers' Row of old.[3] Despite this dominant lineup, the Yankees weren't the absolute favorites to win the pennant in 1960. J.G. Taylor Spink of *The Sporting News* predicted that they would finish third behind Cleveland and Chicago. The Pirates fared even worse and were predicted to finish fifth in the National League.[4] In fact, only three of the 266 writers who participated in *The Sporting News*'s preseason poll predicted a Yankees-Pirates matchup come October.[5]

Given that nearly three decades had passed since Pittsburgh's last World Series, the city was going crazy for their beloved Bucs. In addition to the throng who welcomed the team back to Pittsburgh in late September, more than 5,000 fans filled Schenley Park Plaza in front of Forbes Field on October 4 for a pep rally that the *Pittsburgh Post-Gazette* described as "the wackiest night in Pittsburgh's history ... a combination of the Mardi Gras, the Newport Jazz Festival, a honky-tonk carnival, and a page from the roaring twenties."[6] Elsewhere throughout the city, businesses hung banners encouraging the team, while men added a yellow stripe to their black derby hats to show their support.[7] Pirates fans had waited a long time for this moment, and they were going to make the most of it. Fans also recognized Clemente's performance in the 1960 season by naming him their favorite player, an award he cherished greatly.[8]

The local and national media, however, did not afford Clemente the same respect. Only one Pittsburgh newspaper, the *Courier*, featured Clemente prominently in the buildup to the Series, and Clemente was little more than a name in the lineup in most national coverage leading up to the Series. In an interview with Bill Nunn Jr. of the *Courier*, Pittsburgh's most prominent African American newspaper, Clemente predicted that the Pirates would win in six games.[9] That was all fans got to hear from their favorite player before the Series began.

On October 5, Pirates ace Vern Law gave up a single to Tony Kubek to open the 1960 World Series. In this first game, Clemente batted fifth rather than his usual third, as Pirates manager Danny Murtaugh had concerns about how he might perform against Yankees starter Art Ditmar.[10] Clemente made himself known to the Yankees and national media alike in the bottom of the first with an RBI single to center field that scored Bob Skinner and increased the Pirates lead to 3-1.[11] That was the only hit he recorded in the game, finishing 1-for-4 with a fly out to right, a fielder's choice grounder, and a foul out in the third, fifth, and seventh innings respectively. The Pirates won, 6-4, despite knocking only eight hits to the Yankees' 13.

For Game Two, it was Yankees skipper Casey Stengel's turn to make a change in the lineup. Berra was moved from catcher to left field, with Elston Howard taking over behind the plate. Clemente returned to his standard position of third in the lineup. Once again, he registered a hit during his first plate appearance in the bottom of the first with a single to right field but was stranded by Rocky Nelson's groundout in the next at-bat. He picked up a second hit in the third inning with a single past third baseman Gil McDougald but was once again stranded, by a Nelson fly out to center. Stranded baserunners were a pattern for the Pirates in this game, with 13 runners being left on base. Unsurprisingly, the Pirates lost, 16-3, despite 13 hits. Clemente had one of the hits, a single to center field in the top of the ninth. He had a .333/.333/.333 slash line through two games.

With the Series tied at one game apiece and heading to New York, the Pirates knew they needed just one win in New York to bring the action back to Pittsburgh. They didn't, however, find that win in Game Three. The Yankees drubbed the Pirates, 10-0, on Saturday, October 8, to take a 2-1 Series lead. Yankees ace Whitey Ford threw a shutout, giving up only four hits. Clemente had one of the hits, a single to center field in the bottom of the ninth. By that point, however, the crowd was more interested in catching glimpses of former presidents and world dignitaries taking a break from the United Nations General Assembly in New York to experience America's pastime.[12]

"Don't dump us in the grave yet," implored Pirates captain Don Hoak in his *Pittsburgh Post-Gazette* column on October 9. After all, although the Yankees had outscored the Pirates 30-9 through the first three games, they led the Series by only a single game. A Pirates win in Game Four would tie the Series. For this critical Game Four, the Pirates had their ace Law back on the mound, and he delivered. He got into some trouble early, but a midgame adjustment of how to pitch to Yankees shortstop Tony Kubek, who was hitting .500 through three games, helped turn the tide in Pittsburgh's favor.[13] Clemente extended his Series hitting streak to four games

with a single to right in the top of the sixth inning, while his biggest defensive contribution came in the seventh inning. With Law struggling to pitch through an ankle injury, Skowron hit a ground-rule double to deep right field. McDougald, next up, followed with a single to deep right, which Clemente fielded and gunned to home plate. Yankees third-base coach Frank Crosetti, knowing better than to send a runner on Clemente from any distance, held Skowron at third.[14] The Pirates won the game 3-2, evening the Series at two games apiece.

Going into the fifth game, the Pirates found themselves with the opportunity to head back to Pittsburgh with a Series lead, as good a prospect as any team could want. The Pirates faced Ditmar for the second time in the Series, and they lit him up once again. They jumped out to an 2-0 lead in the top of the second inning after an error by McDougald and a double by Bill Mazeroski. Clemente joined in on the scoring in the top of the third with an RBI single to left field that scored Dick Groat, his only hit in the game. Clemente also made the final putout of the game, catching a fly ball off the bat of Dale Long. He gave the ball to Pirates owner John Galbreath, who was expecting his grandson to be born within the next few days. Galbreath intended the ball to be his grandson's first gift.[15]

Pirate fever returned to Pittsburgh along with the team the night of October 10, drawing a crowd of 10,000 fans to the airport once again. Only these Pirates could manage to draw more attention than US Senator and presidential candidate John F. Kennedy, who arrived an hour and 45 minutes before the Pirates.[16] Kennedy, unlike most sportswriters, managed to work Clemente into his remarks later that night, telling a crowd of more than 6,000 supporters, "I'm not Roberto Clemente, I'm your Democratic presidential candidate."[17] The crowd roared its approval.

The Series resumed on October 12 at Forbes Field, where Pirates fans among the crowd of

38,580 hoped to see their team lift the trophy. Unfortunately for them, they would have to wait another day as Ford pitched his second shutout of the Series. The Pirates banged out seven hits, three more than they got off Ford in Game Three, but they still weren't enough for a run.[18] Clemente contributed two of the Pirates' seven hits, singles in the first and sixth innings, along with four put-outs in the field. With his two singles, Clemente extended his World Series hitting streak to six games and improved his batting average to .320, the best of any Pirate through six games.

The Series-deciding Game Seven came on Thursday, October 13, and throughout Pittsburgh children and adults alike were making excuses to skip school or work and follow the game.[19] Despite a bad loss the day before, Hoak reassured fans in his morning column, "by the time we reached the seventh inning yesterday, all of us were thinking about the seventh game. No point in crying over spilled blood."[20] This focus seems to have paid off, as the Pirates jumped out to an early 4-0 lead by the end of the second inning. Clemente's only contribution to this early start was a pop fly to second baseman Bobby Richardson in the bottom of the first. He grounded into a double play to end the third inning. Not the start to the day Pirates fans must have wanted from their favorite player.

Things got even worse for Pirates fans in the fifth inning, as Mantle and Berra combined to score four runs, giving the Yankees a 5-4 lead. This advantage was extended further to 7-4 in the eighth inning. The Pirates, no doubt recognizing that only six outs remained to save their season, regained the momentum in the eighth. A single by Groat scored Gino Cimoli and advanced Bill Virdon to second. Bob Skinner followed with a weak groundout to third but, importantly, advanced both Virdon and Groat. Rocky Nelson, next up, flied out to right, not quite deep enough to score Virdon from third.

Clemente stepped into the batter's box. Two out, runners on second and third, still hitless in the game. In perhaps the biggest moment of his career to this point, Clemente delivered a weak groundball between first and second. Virdon, who ran at the sound of contact, scored, while Clemente hustled to first for an RBI infield single.[21] In this biggest of moments, Clemente's speed and determination to give it all on every play kept the Pirates alive.

Hal Smith, next up in the Pirates order, homered on a 2-and-2 pitch, scoring himself, Groat, and Clemente, Clemente's first and only run of the Series. The Pirates took a 9-7 lead into the top of the ninth, but the Yankees had more left in the tank. Mantle and Berra once again combined to score two more runs, tying the game going into the bottom of the ninth. In the position that every baseball player dreams about, Mazeroski stepped to the plate in the bottom of the ninth of the seventh game of the World Series, the score tied. Mazeroski delivered. He teed off on a 1-and-0 pitch, sending it over Berra's head in deep left field and into the seats for a Series-winning home run. The Pirates had done it despite being outscored 55-27 in the seven games.

In typical fashion, Clemente helped Mazeroski navigate through the throng of fans who had stormed the field and make it into the clubhouse.[22] Unlike his teammates, however, Clemente left the joyful clubhouse early. Bill Nunn Jr., once again one of the few writers paying attention to Clemente in the moment, insisted that the player was happy but already focused on the future. He didn't want to stick around long; when the Pirates celebrated their pennant, all he did was stand in the corner. And so Clemente, while carrying the trophy awarded to him for being voted the Pirates fans' favorite, left the clubhouse celebration early but not alone. He was joined by Diomedes Antoni Olivo, the Pirates' Dominican batting-practice pitcher, and Bill Nunn Jr.

Once the trio had reached the parking lot, Clemente was joined by a crowd of fans eager to catch a glimpse of their favorite player.[23] He was,

Clemente congratulates teammate Hal Smith after his home run in Game Seven of the 1960 World Series. Courtesy of The Clemente Museum.

after all, the unsung hero of the Series. He was the only player to get a hit in all seven games and finished with a batting average of .310 through 29 at-bats. His fielding, too, was consistent, while his hustle had kept the Pirates alive in Game Seven. In a way, it seemed only right that Clemente marked the end of his first World Series in this manner. Rather than celebrate with the team, with which he still felt like an outcast as a Latin American and Spanish speaker, he celebrated with the fans, whom he credited as one of the primary reasons why he played. At this moment of his career, they were all he needed.

1971

The major leagues incorporated substantial changes between 1960 and 1971. Perhaps most significantly, following the expansion of the American and National leagues in 1969, each league split into two divisions, East and West. The winners of each division would play a best-of-five League Championship Series, whose winner would win the league pennant and a trip to the World Series.[24]

In the National League, the Pirates defeated the San Francisco Giants three games to one. Clemente, now cemented as a star in Pittsburgh, hit .333 with 4 RBIs in 18 at-bats in the four games. It was their first pennant since 1960, and more than 35,000 fans were on hand in new Three Rivers Stadium to storm the field and celebrate the victory.[25] The popularity of baseball, however, was declining nationwide, resulting in much less hype around the 1971 World Series.

Further dimming Pirates fans' spirits was their opponent, the Baltimore Orioles. The Orioles came into the World Series on a 14-game winning streak, including a sweep of the Oakland Athletics in the American League Championship Series. They were a pitching powerhouse, with three of their four starters finishing with a sub-3.00 ERA, while the fourth finished with 3.08. With the odds at 9-5 in favor of an Orioles victory, the consensus was that they would have few issues beating the Pirates.[26]

A crowd of 53,229 filled Memorial Stadium in Baltimore for Game One on Saturday, October 9. Clemente, as he had throughout 1960, batted third for the Pirates. He doubled to right field with two out in the top of the first but was stranded when Willie Stargell struck out. His double, however, extended Clemente's World Series hitting streak to eight games. Clemente singled in the top of the third to start 2-2 in the Series but ended the day 2-for-4 with a fly out in the fifth and a groundout in the eighth. Clemente was one of only two Pirates to get a hit off Orioles starter Dave McNally, who threw a complete game with nine strikeouts. (Dave Cash singled in the second.) Unsurprisingly, the Pirates lost, 5-3.

The Orioles' dominant pitching continued in Game Two, as Jim Palmer struck out 10 through eight innings. The Pirates managed three runs on eight hits, two of which Clemente contributed, a single to center field in the first and a double to right field in the third. He was left on base each time. Clemente also made one of his most memorable defensive plays of the Series in the bottom of the fifth. With Merv Rettenmund on second, Frank Robinson roped a ball to the deep right-field corner. Clemente caught the ball, turned, and fired a laser toward third base. The ball got to Richie Hebner just as Rettenmund reached the base. Rettenmund was called safe, but Hebner insisted that it was one of the best right-field-to-third-base throws he'd ever seen or fielded.[27] Despite not altering the outcome of the game, or even registering an out, the play has become an iconic example of the threat Clemente posed to baserunners from even the deepest of outfield corners.

After the loss, Clemente did something that would have been unthinkable in 1960. He decided to give a speech to his dejected teammates in the locker room. He reminded them that they were headed back to Pittsburgh, where they would be at an advantage. He later told reporters, "If I put my head down they'll say, 'Why try?' A man they trust, if he quits, everyone quits."[28] Then in Game Three the Pirates shut down the Orioles, 5-1. Clemente knocked in a run with a groundout in the top of the first, his first RBI of the series. He singled in the bottom of the fifth, extending his World Series hitting streak to double digits. He reached base again on a bad throw to first in the seventh, showing that even at age 37 he still hustled on every play. Years later, Orioles manager Earl Weaver said it was this play that changed the course of the Series in favor of the Pirates.[29]

Game Four made history as the first World Series game played at night.[30] With the opportunity to tie the Series in front of their home fans, the Pirates delivered. They rattled off 14 hits and scored four runs, enough to beat the Orioles, 4-3. Bruce Kison pitched 6⅓ innings of one-hit relief and got the win. Clemente went 3-for-4 with singles in the third, fifth, and eighth innings, along with a walk in the sixth. In the *New York Daily News*, Dick Young declared Clemente "the best damn ballplayer in the World Series, maybe in the world."[31] The Clemente that Pittsburgh had known and loved since before 1960, it seemed, was finally getting national attention.

McNally returned to the mound for the Orioles in Game Five, but even he couldn't stop the machine that Clemente had started with his speech after Game Two. Clemente extended his World Series hitting streak to 12 games with an RBI single in the fifth, lifting the Pirates to a 4-0 lead, which remained the final score. Afterward, Clemente let the national press know how he felt about their coverage of him. He insisted that he was misunderstood by the media, that he was not a problematic hypochondriac but rather one of the most consistent players in Pirates – and indeed baseball – history. Most emphatically, he reminded reporters that the performances they had seen in the first five games were how he played every single game of every single season.[32] He had always been Clemente; they had just never recognized it. Now he wanted the world to know it.

The Pirates took a 3-games-to-2 lead back to Baltimore for Game Six. Clemente hit a triple in the top of the first but was left on base once again. He followed this up with a solo home run in the third to give the Pirates a 2-0 lead. The Pirates squandered the lead in the bottom of the seventh, but Clemente prevented the Orioles from taking the lead in the ninth with another laser from right field to home plate, keeping Mark Belanger from scoring. Clemente came to the plate with a man on in the top of the 10th and was intentionally walked. The Pirates scored no runs that inning. In the bottom of the 10th, Brooks Robinson hit a walk-off sacrifice fly to deep center field to win the game, 3-2. Clemente and the Pirates were going to Game Seven once again.

Before Game Seven, Clemente found himself once again in a leadership role. As one of few World Series champions on the 1971 roster, he took it upon himself to reassure his teammates that they could win it all that night.[33] Things, however, did not start out well for the Pirates. They opened the game with 11 straight outs, including a Clemente groundout to shortstop to end the first inning. Pirates starter Steve Blass, meanwhile, was holding the Orioles at bay. Clemente batted in the top of the fourth with two out. This time he blasted a home run to deep left-center to give the Pirates a 1-0 lead. With his second home run of the Series, Clemente had collected a hit in all 14 of his World Series games. Jose Pagan doubled Stargell home in the top of the eighth to increase the lead to 2-0, and the Pirates held on for a 2-1 victory and the World Series championship.

Clemente finished the Series with a .414 batting average (12-for-29), with two home runs, a triple, and two doubles. In an interview after Game Seven, Clemente did something he might have considered unthinkable in 1960: He opened the interview in Spanish.[34] This was no longer the quiet Puerto Rican fan favorite sitting in the corner of the clubhouse after the 1960 Series. This was a 37-year-old 14-time All-Star, 1966 National League MVP, two-time World Series champion, and vocal leader of one of the most diverse teams baseball had ever seen. National sportswriters, whose recognition he had so long craved, had named him the most valuable player of the World Series. In this way, much as in 1960, he had achieved his goal. While he had played for the fans of Pittsburgh in 1960, in 1971 he wanted to play for all the world to see. He wanted the world to know how Clemente played baseball, day in and day out. The 1971 World Series, and his one-of-a-kind performance throughout, granted him his wish.

NOTES

1   The 162-game schedule began the year after Clemente's first World Series appearance, in 1961. Postseason play prior to the World Series was implemented in 1969.

2   "Pirates Lose, But So Do Cards and It's Over," *Pittsburgh Post-Gazette*, September 26, 1960: 1.

3   David Maraniss, *Clemente: The Passion and Grace of Baseball's Last Hero* (New York: Simon and Schuster, 2006), 105.

4   J.G. Taylor Spink, "Spink Sees All-Redskin Romp in Races," *The Sporting News*, April 13, 1960: 7.

5   Ed O'Neil, "Scribes Stubbed Toes in Tabbing '60 Flag Teams," *The Sporting News*, October 5, 1960: 13.

6   Al Gioia, "Bucco Fans Jam Park at Rally," *Pittsburgh Post-Gazette*, October 5, 1960: 1.

7   Maraniss, 109.

8   Bill Nunn Jr., "Change of Pace," *Pittsburgh Courier*, October 22, 1960: 18.

9   Bill Nunn Jr., "Clemente Goes on Record as Saying Pirates Will Win Series in Six Games," *Pittsburgh Courier*, October 1, 1960: 2.

10   Maraniss, 112.

11   All statistics, play-by-play, and box-score information was sourced from baseball-refrence.com.

12   Maraniss, 119.

13   Don Hoak, "Confidence Brought Us Big Victory Over Yankees," *Pittsburgh Post-Gazette*, October 10, 1960: 24.

14   Maraniss, 121.

15   Maraniss, 123.

16   Silas W. Pickering, "Team Gets Greeting of Heroes," *Pittsburgh Post-Gazette*, October 11, 1960: 1.

17   Harry Brooks, "'Let Nixon Visit and Tell 100,000 Jobless They Never Had It So Good' – J. Kennedy," *Pittsburgh Courier*, October 15, 1960: 3.

18   Jack Hernon, "Yankees Torpedo Buc Brig, 12-0, to Even Series," *Pittsburgh Post-Gazette*, October 13, 1960: 1.

19   Maraniss, 125.

20   Don Hoak, "Give 'Em Credit, They Beat Us," *Pittsburgh Post-Gazette*, October 13, 1960: 34.

21   Maraniss, 130.

22   Maraniss, 134.

23   Nunn, "Change of Pace."

24   "Postseason History: League Championship Series," MLB.com, accessed January 5, 2022, https://www.mlb.com/postseason/history/league-championship-series.

25   Charley Feeney, "Hebner, Oliver's HRs, Clemente Hit Bury Giants, 9-5," *Pittsburgh Post-Gazette*, October 7, 1971: 1.

26   Charley Feeney, "Birds 9-5 Favorites for Series," *Pittsburgh Post-Gazette*, October 7, 1971: 9.

27   Maraniss, 247.

28   Maraniss, 248.

29   Maraniss, 250.

30   Bill Francis, "A Classic Under the Lights," National Baseball Hall of Fame, accessed January 5, 2022, https://baseballhall.org/discover/a-classic-under-the-lights.

31   Dick Young, "Young Ideas," *New York Daily News*, October 14, 1971: 111.

32   Maraniss, 256.

33   Maraniss, 261.

34   Maraniss, 264.

ROBERTO CLEMENTE AND THE BIG GRAB

BY BENJAMIN SABIN

This story begins and ends with fried chicken. It also includes four armed men, an All-Star ring, an abduction, and a brush with the grim reaper. Oh yeah, and in the middle of it is the greatest Puerto Rican baseball player of all time, Roberto Clemente. So why isn't this story common knowledge among baseball fans? How do we not know the story's specifics like we know that Clemente has exactly 3,000 hits or that he has a lifetime .317 batting average? Because nobody is sure if the following events even took place. That's right, we have a mystery on our hands.

THE BIG GRAB

Time has a way of blurring the details. What one remembers about an incident the day after the occurrence may be very different from what they recall, say, a year later. And such may be the case with Roberto Clemente's alleged kidnapping that took place in 1969 but wasn't made public until Clemente sat down with *Pittsburgh Press* reporter Bill Christine on August 9, 1970. Also, the only

account we have to go on is Clemente's, so there is no one to corroborate or disprove his account.

We know that the supposed abduction took place in San Diego in 1969. The Pirates visited San Diego twice that season. The first three-game series took place May 20 to 22 at San Diego Stadium. Published reports list this series as the time of the incident. The second series the Pirates played in San Diego, from August 8 to 10, better matches certain details given by Clemente, except, of course, the date that he stated as the time of the incident.

So what is the story? It goes like this: It was a dark and stormy night ... just kidding. But it was dark out. It was just after midnight and Clemente was in the mood for a snack. Earlier, he'd been ejected by home-plate umpire Lee Weyer for arguing a called third strike in the fourth inning. (This is the main reason that, even though Clemente says the abduction happened during the May series, all signs point to the August series, because Clemente was ejected from only one game in both series and that was on August 8.)[1] After being ejected, he left the ballpark and went back to the El Cortez hotel (where the Pirates were staying) alone. But other sources state that the Pirates as well as Clemente may have been staying at the Town and Country Hotel, which is near the freeway that runs right past San Diego Stadium.[2]

When he got back to his hotel room, he called his wife to tell her he was going to retire. His shoulder had been hurting him and he'd been thrown out of the game. She told him to "finish the road trip, then if you come back to Pittsburgh and don't feel any better, it will be alright to quit."[3] Clemente said, "Okay, you're the boss. But if I don't feel any better when I get back to Pittsburgh then it's all over."[4]

Sometime after midnight, he grew hungry and decided to go out and get some food. He ran into Willie Stargell, who had just come out of a coffee shop with a bag of fried chicken. Stargell told Clemente that the chicken was good, and Clemente decided to get a bag for himself. Clemente purchased the chicken and started back to the hotel. It was then that he noticed a car following him. The car pulled up beside him and he was held at gunpoint by four men (although some accounts say three). He was forced into the back of the car and told to lie down on the floor. One of the assailants put a gun to Clemente's chin and told him, "We're going to teach you some manners."

The kidnappers took Clemente to a park, which was most likely Balboa Park.[5] He was told to get out of the car and strip, which he did except for his underwear. He was then forced over the hood of the car and held at gunpoint while the kidnappers went through his clothes. They took his wallet, along with $250 and the All-Star ring off his finger.[6]

Clemente was sure they were going to shoot him, saying "they already had the pistol inside my mouth."[7] But, he was able to talk his way out of the scary situation. He told them that he was a professional baseball player for the Padres because he thought that they might not know who the Pirates were. And upon finding Clemente's Player's Association card in his wallet, they believed that he indeed was a big-league ballplayer.

When the kidnappers found out that he was a major leaguer, their tone changed from threatening to nearly apologetic. Two of Clemente's abductors were Spanish-speaking, and after talking to the men, they returned his wallet, along with the money and his All-Star ring.[8] They even helped Clemente put his clothes back on and straightened his necktie for him.[9] They then drove him back to within three blocks of the Pirates' hotel and dropped him off.

But the bizarre events of that San Diego night aren't quite over yet. There is still one last little twist. Do you remember how I said that the story begins and ends with fried chicken? Well, I wasn't lying, because as Clemente walked away, he heard his abductors pull up behind him again. He thought that maybe they had changed their minds about letting him go, but that wasn't the case. One of his kidnappers said, "Here's your chicken," and handed the bag back to Clemente, who took it, waited for the car to speed away, and then tossed the snack across the street.[10] He went back to the hotel but didn't report the incident to the police.

A CRIME DIVULGED

The day after the alleged kidnapping, if we are to believe that it took place on August 8, 1969, the Pirates and Padres had a break in their three-game series. The game on the 8th was the first game of the series. The next day, Saturday the 9th, the NFL San Diego Chargers had priority for the use of San Diego Stadium, so a doubleheader was scheduled to be played on the 10th. This break in the schedule may explain why Clemente (and Stargell) were up so late tracking down food. Although I can't pretend to understand the late-night eating habits of young baseball players, this could be their normal activity whether there was a game the following day or not. But one thing did happen on the 9th; Clemente told a few people about the harrowing events from the previous night.

More than a year after the incident, on August 27, 1970, after the emergence of the Bill Christine article, the Pirates were in San Diego for the first time since the kidnapping became public knowledge. After a two-game series on the 25th and 26th, the 27th was a travel day for the Pirates as they headed north to San Francisco for a four-game series against the Giants. Before the Pirates left, though, the San Diego Police Department wanted to have a word with Clemente about the alleged kidnapping.

Clemente was questioned by San Diego police detective Hanly Pry on the 27th and he stated that before the Bill Christine article, which was published just two days after the one-year anniversary of the kidnapping, he had told only three other people about the incident. He said that the day after the kidnapping (August 9, 1969), he told teammate Jose Pagan, Pirates coach Bill Virdon, and umpire Lee Weyer (yes, the same umpire who had ejected him the previous day). It came to light that Clemente also divulged the incident to teammate Matty Alou and Pirates general manager Joe Brown.[11]

So why didn't Clemente tell anyone other than a handful of people about the incident? And why didn't he report it to the police? Clemente told Christine that "I haven't told this story to many people because I figured if any of the four robbers heard about it they might be looking for our ballplayers when we go out there again."[12] Another article quoted him as saying, "why should I report it? I am alive, no?"[13]

As to why he finally decided to make the incident public, Clemente said that he "forgot about the whole thing until somebody brought it up. Then I figure I better tell the story so it be printed right."[14]

And while the story may have been "printed right," the validity, or lack thereof, is in the confusing details given. Whatever the actual reality of the incident is, Clemente's biographer, David Maraniss, put it best in *Clemente: The Passion and Grace of Baseball's Last Hero*, stating that the abduction "fit perfectly into the mythology of Roberto Clemente as a man of the people, respected even by urban desperados."[15]

SOURCES

In addition to the sources cited in the Notes, the author also consulted Baseball-Reference.com. Thanks to George Skornickel and to Craig C. Britcher of the Heinz History Center.

NOTES

1   Associated Press, "Clemente's Kidnapping Confirmed," *Pottstown* (Pennsylvania) *Mercury*, August 28, 1970: 25.

2   Bill Christine, "Clemente Reveals Abduction," *Pittsburgh Press*, August 10, 1970: 25.

3   Christine.

4   Christine.

5   "Clemente's Kidnapping Confirmed."

6   "People," *Sports Illustrated*, August 24, 1970. https://vault.si.com/vault/1970/08/24/people.

7   "People."

8   "Clemente Reveals Close Call with Kidnapers," *The Sporting News*, August 22, 1970: 24.

9   "Clemente's Kidnapping Confirmed."

10 "Clemente's Kidnapping Confirmed."

11 "Clemente Reveals Close Call with Kidnapers."

12 RetroSimba, "The Night Roberto Clemente Was Snatched in San Diego," retrosimba.com, February 9, 2021. https://retrosimba.com/2021/02/09/the-night-roberto-clemente-was-snatched-in-san-diego/.

13 "Clemente Reveals Close Call with Kidnapers."

14 "Clemente Reveals Close Call with Kidnapers."

15 RetroSimba, "The Night Roberto Clemente Was Snatched in San Diego."

THE GREAT ONE:
ROBERTO CLEMENTE'S RACE TO 3,000 HITS

BY JUAN JOSE RODRIGUEZ

The Great One.

When looking at players' performances both on and off the field over the past several decades, few have surpassed the work of The Great One, Pittsburgh Pirates right fielder Roberto Clemente.

The first Latino player inducted into the National Baseball Hall of Fame, Clemente gained plenty of recognition for his stellar play over the course of his career, a stretch that began with his debut in major-league baseball in 1955 at the age of 20 and ended with his achievement of becoming the 11th major-league player to collect 3,000 hits. (As of 2022, Clemente and Honus Wagner were the only Pirates to reach that milestone.)

Clemente entered the 1972 season with 2,882 hits and needed just 118 to reach the vaunted mark. By all accounts, health permitting, Clemente should have had very little trouble eclipsing the 3,000-hit threshold in 1972. In his first 17 seasons (1955-1971), he averaged nearly 170 hits per season. And he never batted below .250 for a season in his career, only twice finishing below .280 and finishing sub-.300 in just five seasons.

Clemente had one other challenge. Because of a players' strike, the 1972 season started late, and the team played 155 games instead of the usual 162. But the Pittsburgh newspapers took it as a given that he'd reach the mark. In April the *Courier* wrote, "Clemente shows no signs of slowing down or losing his batting eye. In fact, his combined batting average over the past three seasons is a robust .346. ... He remains one of the most complete players who has ever played the game. Before the 1972 season comes to a close he will be the all-time Pirate leader in several offensive categories and will also reach the coveted 3,000 mark in career hits."[1]

In public utterances, Clemente himself played down the importance of getting 3,000 hits in 1972, but in private he let friends and teammates know he truly wanted it. He reportedly told Manny Sanguillen, "I have to get that hit this year. I might die."[2]

Clemente did not get off to a great start in 1972, managing just 12 hits in April to post a .255 batting average after the first month of play. He was averaging a hit per game, though. His month of May was decidedly better, as he nearly tripled his hit total in just double the at-bats. Clemente raised his per-month batting average by 110 points from April to May, batting .365 thanks to 35 hits in 96 at-bats. One of the major keys driving that surge: limiting the frequency of strikeouts. Clemente struck out six times in 47 at-bats in April 1972 and six times in May 1972, but in 96 at-bats, making May his only month with less than one strikeout per 10 at-bats.

Clemente's slugging percentage nearly doubled from April (.298) to May (.583), the latter his best slugging percentage in any month of the 1972 season. Additional evidence of Clemente's turnaround is clear in the trajectory of his batting average over the course of the season, as the .338 mark that he reached in the final week of May was the highest it climbed at any point in the season.

With 47 hits through May, Clemente was 71 shy of 3,000 with four months to go. He ultimately missed 53 games, however, and 46 of the 53 games that he missed came in June, July, and August – due in large part to an intestinal virus and strained tendons in both heels – compared to just one missed game in April and two in May.

In the 39 games in which Clemente did see the field during those three months, however, he totaled 41 hits for a .283 batting average. His slugging percentage reached a season-high .517 on July 5, at which point his OPS (on-base plus slugging) had climbed to .880, just a shade below its season-best .892 after Clemente's only four-hit game of the season on May 26.

Clemente added 22 hits in June. His total was 2,951 – 49 to go. In July, he played in only nine games, adding 10 more hits. In August, Clemente appeared in 12 games and hit safely nine times. He entered the final full month of the 1972

regular season with 88 base hits, leaving him 30 shy of 3,000.

Clemente started the month hitless but then added seven hits in the next six games. He stood 23 hits shy of 3,000 with 25 games remaining. He was hitless in the September 8 doubleheader, registering no plate appearances in the first game while in the second he walked twice – once intentionally – and had a sacrifice fly. In the game on the 9th, he entered only as a ninth-inning defensive replacement and did not bat once.

He singled on the 10th and subsequently got 12 hits in his next five games, including three-hit road games on September 12, 13, and 17. Now 3,000 seemed attainable, but he still needed 10 more hits with 15 games remaining.

Playing the Mets at Shea Stadium, he was, however, 0-for-4 on the 18th, 1-for-4 on the 19th, and 0-for-4 on the 20th.

There were just 12 games remaining on the 1972 regular-season schedule, and Clemente needed nine hits to reach 3,000. In the final game of the series against the Mets, on the 21st, Clemente singled twice – and the Pirates clinched the NL East, relieving any pressure on that account.

The Expos came to Pittsburgh for two games. Clemente came to the plate nine times (two walks, leaving seven official at-bats) but added only one hit. There were eight games remaining and his total was 2,994.

The Pirates traveled to Philadelphia for three games at Veterans Stadium. Clemente singled twice in the first game and twice more in the second game. On September 28 he singled again, in the top of the fourth, for base hit number 2,999. He never batted again in the game. When his turn in the order came up, manager Bill Virdon had Bob Robertson (another right-handed hitter, batting .193) pinch-hit for Clemente, despite the Pirates being down by just one run, 2-1. Robertson struck out. The move afforded Clemente the opportunity to get his 3,000th hit in front of the Pirates faithful.

Clemente hits #3,000. Les Banos photograph courtesy of The Clemente Museum.

The *Pittsburgh Press* reported, "It was Clemente's desire that Pittsburgh fans should be there when he sends forth his 3,000th hit."[3]

The team returned to Three Rivers Stadium for a weekend series against the Mets. Clemente came across as almost modest, saying that he was getting home late Thursday night and had a doctor's appointment on Friday but would likely play at least one of the next two games. Acknowledging that thousands would be waiting on every pitch, he said, "I'll probably play,"[4] and the home fans were indeed presented the opportunity to see hit number 3,000. In the first inning of the September 29 game, after a leadoff walk to left fielder Vic Davalillo, Clemente reached on a groundball to second that advanced Davalillo to second. It seemed that Clemente had just produced his 3,000th hit and had joined the exclusive club — and the scoreboard

even announced the play as a hit — only for the official ruling to be changed moments later to an error.[5] He went 0-for-4 in that game and the Mets won, 1-0.

On the morning of Saturday, September 30, the *Courier* acknowledged the possibility that Clemente might fall short, writing that he "would like to get the hit during the regular season even if it means waiting until next year."[6]

Such uncertainty was extinguished fairly soon thereafter. What did in fact result in being Clemente's 3,000th and final hit — a double against the New York Mets on September 30, 1972 — fittingly came in front of the home crowd. Despite compiling nearly 200 more at-bats on the road than at home over the course of his career, Clemente collected 56 more hits at home, with 8 more doubles and 27 more runs scored at home than away.

After a 4-6-3 double-play grounder off the bat of center fielder Rennie Stennett erased a leadoff single to right field by second baseman Chuck Goggin, Clemente struck out in his first trip to the plate to end the first inning against the Mets' left-handed starter Jon Matlack.

Matlack had previously faced Clemente six times, keeping him hitless and surrendering just one walk, but the Mets' young left-hander was not at all aware of Clemente's imminent feat.

"I was a 22-year-old rookie that had absolutely no clue this baseball icon was sitting on 2,999 when I went out to pitch that game," Matlack said. "None."[7]

Clemente's second trip to the plate came as the leadoff batter of the fourth inning as Matlack faced the heart of the Pirates' order with Clemente, first baseman Willie Stargell, and Zisk due up, batting third, fourth and fifth. Clemente started the inning with a line-drive double to left field. Play was halted and Clemente was presented with the milestone baseball.

One of the other batters to have reached 3,000 hits was Willie Mays, in his first season with the Mets after being traded in May from the San Francisco Giants. Though not in the game, the legendary Say Hey Kid walked out of the dugout and onto the field to surprise and congratulate Clemente.

After advancing to third base on a passed ball with Willie Stargell batting, Clemente scored two batters later on catcher Manny Sanguillen's single to left field.

Clemente was lifted for a pinch-hitter in the bottom of the fifth inning, and only entered the Pirates' October 3 win as a ninth-inning defensive replacement.

That leadoff double marked the final plate appearance of Clemente's career ... and, ultimately, of his life. He had played his final game for the Pirates.

For the month of September, Clemente notched exactly those 30 remaining hits he had needed – 10 of which were extra-base hits – in his final 90 at-bats, which amounted to a .333 batting average, .511 slugging percentage, and .890 OPS in that span. Another .333 clip appears in his multihit games for the month of September, in which he recorded two or more hits in nine of his 27 games for the month.

Clemente was the first player from Latin America to reach 3,000 career hits during the regular season, excluding the postseason. He lost his life on the final day of 1972 while attempting to bring relief supplies for earthquake victims in Nicaragua.

IN PERSPECTIVE

Clemente's feverish run to end the season catapulted him into a position alongside league leaders in overall player value by many sabermetric measures. Clemente finished the 1972 season 15th in wins above replacement (WAR) with 4.8, the only player older than 35 (age as of the midseason mark) during the 1972 season who compiled more than 4 WAR. Clemente also was one of just four position players 30 years old or older in 1972 who amassed at least one defensive win above replacement, joining Ron Hunt (31 years old, 1.5 dWAR), John Boccabella (31, 1.2), and Willie Davis (32, 1.5).

To put Clemente's final stretch in perspective, only eight players in the Live-Ball Era (since 1920) have ever tallied 30 or more hits in the final 90 plate appearances of their careers. Only two active players – Bryce Harper (30 hits, 86 at-bats) and Juan Soto (33 hits, 90 at-bats) – ended the 2021 season on such a strong run; they finished one-two for the National League Most Valuable Player Award. Of those eight who have retired, only outfielder Timo Perez (2007) has completed such a stretch in the nearly 50 years since Clemente did so in 1972; the other six – Ralph Shinners and Joe Evans (1925), Zack Wheat and Frank Snyder (1927), Joe Wood (1943), and Hillis Layne (1945) – all preceded Clemente in achieving this feat.

Hit #3,000 memorialized on the Three Rivers Stadium scoreboard. Les Banos photograph courtesy of The Clemente Museum.

Of the 32 players to reach 3,000 hits, only five have done so in fewer at-bats than Clemente's 9,454: Tris Speaker (8,263), Stan Musial (8,774), Tony Gwynn (8,874), Rod Carew (9,101), and Wade Boggs (9,151).

Clemente's portfolio of accolades throughout his 18-year career comprises quite the list. His extensive collection includes 4 batting titles, 12 Gold Glove Awards, and 15 All-Star selections, two World Series titles, and a selection as the National League Most Valuable Player in 1966. Clemente was recognized five years later as the World Series Most Valuable Player in 1971. His potent bat alongside his electric speed and defensive prowess in right field combined to form a truly era-changing star.

"Well, I said to myself, there's a boy who can do two things as well as any man who ever lived," scout Clyde Sukeforth said after discovering Clemente as a teenager while on a scouting trip of the Montreal Royals, a top minor-league affiliate of the Brooklyn Dodgers. When Sukeforth later followed general manager Branch Rickey from Brooklyn to Pittsburgh and likewise joined the Pirates, he played a vital role in recommending that the Pirates select Clemente from the Dodgers in the 1954 Rule 5 Draft. "Nobody could throw any better than that, and nobody could run any better than that."[8]

"I want to be remembered as a ballplayer who gave all he had to give," Clemente once said.[9]

Throughout his career, and throughout his life, The Great One did just that.

SOURCES

In addition to the sources cited in the Notes, the author consulted:

"Beyond Baseball: The Life of Roberto Clemente," Smithsonian Institution Traveling Exhibition Service," accessed November 22, 2021, http://www.robertoclemente.si.edu/english/virtual_legacy.htm.

"Roberto Clemente," Baseball-Reference.com, accessed October 17, 2021, https://www.baseball-reference.com/players/c/clemero01.shtml.

NOTES

1   Jess Peters Jr., "Jess' Sports Chest," *Pittsburgh Courier*, April 22, 1972: 11.

2   Phil Musick, *Who Was Roberto?* (Garden City, New York: Associated Features Books, 1974), 292-3.

3   Bob Smizik, "Clemente Set to Join the Club," *Pittsburgh Press*, September 29, 1972: 42. A large sports page cartoon by Bill Winstein, titled, "Arriba, Arriba," depicted Clemente connecting for the hit as a sculptor in the background chiseled his name onto a monument.

4   Smizik. To get rest for the National League Championship Series, he had already announced he would sit during the last two regular-season games.

5   Bruce Markusen, *Roberto Clemente: The Great One* (Champaign, Illinois: Sports Publishing, 1998), 295-6. The official scorer was Luke Quay and it was indeed a very difficult play to score, wrote Smizik in the Press, saying that most of the reporters in the pressbox agreed – though for his part Clemente said, "All my life they have been stealing hits from me. A close play? There was no play. There was no way he could have got me." Bob Smizik, "Scorer Makes No Hit with Clemente," *Pittsburgh Press*, September 30, 1972: 6.

6   Bill Nunn Jr., "Change of Pace," *Pittsburgh Courier*, September 30, 1972: 9.

7   Tyler Kepner, "Clemente's 3,000th Hit Was Muted Milestone in Ambivalent City," *New York Times*, June 11, 2011: 2.

8   "Roberto Clemente," National Baseball Hall of Fame, accessed November 27, 2021, https://baseballhall.org/hall-of-famers/clemente-roberto.

9   "ROBERTO CLEMENTE STATS," Baseball Almanac, accessed November 27, 2021, https://www.baseball-almanac.com/players/player.php?p=clemero01.

Clemente with the ball and bat used to hit #3,000.
Courtesy of The Clemente Museum.

"MOMEN" AND MONTE: THE LINKAGE BETWEEN ROBERTO CLEMENTE AND MONTE IRVIN

BY DUKE GOLDMAN

Roberto Clemente Walker was one of six baseball immortals inducted into Cooperstown's Hall of Fame on August 6, 1973. Along with Clemente, pitching greats Mickey Welch and Warren Spahn, both 300-game winners, longtime AL umpire Billy Evans, New York Giants first baseman George "Highpockets "Kelly, and New York Giants and Newark Eagles star outfielder Monford "Monte" Irvin" were all celebrated that day.

"The Great One" had 167 at-bats vs. Spahn, as their careers overlapped 11 seasons, from 1955 (Clemente's rookie season) through 1965. Clemente hit.407/.420/.605 for a 1.025 OPS (on-base plus slugging) against Spahn, with four home runs and only five walks and seven strikeouts – quite a success story.[1] In addition, both Spahn and Clemente wore uniform number 21.

In contrast, Monte Irvin and Roberto Clemente played against each other only in 1955 and 1956. The connection between Irvin and Clemente, though, went back 10 years further than the confrontations with Spahn – to 1945, when Roberto was an 11-year-old baseball fanatic and Monte was playing winter-league baseball for the San Juan Senadores. Both "Momen" and Monte were outstanding players who significantly impacted others – and Monte had an important formative influence on Roberto. In addition, there were several interesting parallels in the lives and careers of Monte Irvin and Roberto Clemente – two pioneers of major-league baseball's integration era.

MOMEN'S CHILDHOOD BASEBALL IDOL

As a child, Roberto Clemente was nicknamed Momen. When interviewed in the early 1970s, Roberto's older brother, Matino, initially said that "[W]e called him Momen from the time he was little. When he had grown up and become a star, no one could remember what the name meant."[2] Thirty years later, according to author David Maraniss, Matino maintained that "Momen" was short for momentito, in English "wait a minute," because Roberto would constantly say "momentito" whenever he was interrupted or was asked to do something.[3] Either way, "to his family and Puerto Rican friends, at school and on the ball fields, Momen was his nickname from then on."[4]

Roberto's father, Melchor, was a foreman for a sugar-processing company, which meant that the family was not as poor as many other families in Roberto's hometown of Carolina. But money was still not plentiful. Late in his tragically short life, Roberto described buying a secondhand bicycle for $27 with his own money — money made by waking up at 6 A.M. to deliver milk, earning a penny a day, for three years. As Roberto described it, he "grew up with people who really had to struggle to live"– and his father had said, "I want you to learn how to work and I want you to be a serious person."[5]

By age 11, Roberto Clemente traveled from Carolina, where he lived, to San Juan to see his favorite baseball team, the San Juan Senadores, play at Estadio Sixto Escobar. He may well have used his recently purchased bicycle, but he sometimes traveled by bus, with his dad giving him 25 cents –10 cents for the bus and 15 cents for admission to the ballpark.[6] Roberto was still looking for ways to avoid spending his dad's hard-earned money, so some days, rather than paying admission, he apparently watched the Senadores from a tree overlooking right field.[7] Wherever he was perched, Roberto's eyes were riveted to one particular ballplayer – versatile outfield star Monte Irvin of the Negro National League's Newark Eagles – and in the 1945-46 Puerto Rican Winter League season, primarily the second baseman for the Senadores.[8] Irvin started his Negro League career by playing third base and then became the center fielder for the Eagles,[9] but when he returned in 1945 to Puerto Rico, where he had previously played during the winters of 1940-41 and 1941-42, he discovered a set outfield of Felle Delgado, Luis Olmo, and Freddie Thon (Dickie Thon's grandfather). According to Irvin,

"(W)e needed a second baseman, and Olmo told me, '(Y)ou're fast, can hit, and have a great arm, so why not?'"[10]

Whether at second base or in the outfield, where Irvin did play a limited amount in 1945-46,[11] he displayed that great arm – and Roberto was watching. In his autobiography, Irvin recalled, "[W]hen I went to Puerto Rico and played winter ball, the crowd would just *oooh* and *aah* when I warmed up" (italics in original). Not only was Roberto watching, but when he was unable to be in attendance, Momen listened at night to radio broadcasts of the San Juan games while he threw a rubber ball against the wall. "Irvin was my first idol because he was not only a good hitter, but he had such a good arm," Clemente said.[12]

Monte Irvin was indeed a good, and perhaps a great, hitter. According to statistics reported by baseball-reference.com, Irvin led the Negro National League in batting with a .395 average in 1942 and a .369 mark in 1946.[13] He said that he came back from World War II service overseas "with three years of athletic rust and a bad case of war nerves, and I needed to work back into my pre-war playing condition. ... So, I said, 'I'll start to climb back slowly. ... And, in order to regain my old form, I went down to San Juan, Puerto Rico, and played ball that winter."[14] All he did was hit .368 for San Juan, barely losing the batting title to Ponce's Fernando Diaz Pedroso.[15] Yet Irvin won the Puerto Rico Winter League MVP award, and in the league championship series against Mayaguez, he smashed three home runs in a doubleheader sweep by the Senadores as they took the series, four games to two.[16] It is unknown whether Roberto attended these games, but it seems likely that in 1962, such performances led Clemente to praise Irvin to the *New Pittsburgh Courier's* Bill Nunn Jr., saying, "I think he had the best eye, best stance, and sharpest cut of any of the big leaguers who play winter ball in Puerto Rico. He also (fielded) real good and (threw) like a bullet."[17]

Throwing like a bullet is a description that clearly applied not only to Monte Irvin. After all, Roberto Clemente had 10 outfield assists in his first 55 major-league games for the 1955 Pittsburgh Pirates, and *The Sporting News* contributor and *Pittsburgh Press* sportswriter Les Biederman commented that "the Pittsburgh fans have fallen in love with his spectacular fielding and his deadly right arm."[18] While Clemente led the National League in outfield assists five times during his 18-year major-league career,[19] Irvin ranked in the top five in assists by a left fielder four times, the only four times he played more than half the league's games in the outfield.[20] And while Michael Humphrey's book *Wizardry* rates Roberto Clemente as the best defensive right fielder of all time by a substantial margin, it rates Monte Irvin as the 10th best defensive left fielder of all time despite his short, eight-season career in the formerly White major leagues and states that "Irvin may have been the best fielding left fielder before the Modern Era (1969-1992)."[21]

One element of youth competition that the two ballplayers had in common was that they each participated in track and field. In Irvin's case, he "threw the javelin, the shotput, and the discus" and set the state record for throwing the javelin with a heave of 192 feet 8 inches.[22] In Clemente's case, he threw the javelin 195 feet, but also jumped 6 feet in the high jump and 45 feet in the triple jump.[23] According to Clemente biographer Bruce Markusen, "Clemente's expertise in the javelin aided him in playing baseball. He may not have known it at the time, but the footwork, release and general dynamics employed in throwing the javelin coincided with the skills needed to throw the baseball properly.[24] According to David Maraniss, "[T]he javelin became an iconic symbol in the mythology of Clemente. It represented his heroic nature, since the javelin is associated with Olympian feats."[25]

It has been said by many that Monte Irvin was Roberto Clemente's boyhood hero. In the words of Clemente:

I used to watch Monte Irvin play. When I was a kid, I idolize him. I would never have enough nerve. I did not want to look at him straight in the face. That why when he pass I turn around and look at him.[26]

Monte Irvin elaborated further:

I first met Roberto Clemente in the early 1940s in Puerto Rico. I used to play down there. This is when I was in the old Negro Leagues. He was just a youngster. And one day I let him carry my bag in order to get into the stadium. So we became friendly. Used to give him a ball. ... I don't know ... might have given him a glove that I had but I never did see him play.[27]

It is not entirely clear how the relationship developed. In an interview Irvin gave to SABR member Stew Thornley in 2005, he made it clear that Clemente was one of many kids who wanted to get into the ballpark, but that he did not get to know a young Roberto at the time: "They wanted to get into the game, and I let them take my bag in, so they wouldn't have to pay. You know, kids hanging out outside the game, and we'd give them our bags so they could take them in and get in free."[28]

In contrast, Maraniss indicated that Irvin and Clemente developed a friendship when Clemente was a teen: "Just by being there, hanging around, as shy as he was, Clemente eventually struck up a friendship with Irvin. And Irvin made sure that his young fan got in to watch the game, even without a ticket."[29] And in his autobiography, Irvin stated, "[W]hen Clemente was a youngster ... he was a protégé of mine."[30]

There is no doubt, however, that upon becoming a major-league player, Clemente told Irvin about the impact Irvin made upon him as a teenager. The young professional let Irvin know that he admired his throwing arm and had modeled his throwing motion after it: "He told me he admired, not only the way I hit the ball, but also the way I threw the ball. He wanted to throw the way that I did and later, when he had one of the best throwing arms in baseball, I considered it a compliment."[31] Irvin clearly was proud of the "mentoring relationship" that he had with young Clemente, as he told Maraniss: "(Y)eah, I taught Roberto how to throw. ... [O]f course, he quickly surpassed me."[32]

THE DODGERS AND THE GIANTS — AND THE PIRATES AND THE CUBS

Both Clemente and Irvin had some history with each of the two New York National League teams. Irvin signed with the Brooklyn Dodgers' St. Paul farm team after the 1948 season, when the Negro National League folded. Newark Eagles owner Effa Manley objected to the signing because Dodgers general manager Branch Rickey refused to compensate her for Irvin's contract, so Rickey released Irvin.[33] Subsequently, Irvin was signed in 1949 by Horace Stoneham, the New York Giants owner, who paid $5,000 to the Eagles owners, past and present, for Irvin's contract.[34]

Clemente was also first signed by the Dodgers, who first spied Roberto at a tryout at Sixto Escobar Stadium on November 6, 1952. Dodgers scout Al Campanis characterized Clemente as follows: "Has All the Tools and Likes to Play. A Real Good Looking Prospect!"[35] It was the Giants, though, that first made an offer to Clemente after Pedrin Zorilla, the Santurce Cangrejeros owner,[36] for whom Roberto played in the Puerto Rico Winter League, touted Clemente to Stoneham. The Giants, however, refused to spend $4,000 on Clemente, so Zorilla, who had an informal relationship with the Dodgers, turned to Campanis.[37] The Dodgers' top farm team, the Montreal Royals, offered Clemente a $5,000 contract with a $10,000 signing bonus, and he signed on February 19, 1954.[38]

Roberto Clemente played sporadically for the Royals, in 1954, batting only 148 times with a

.257/.286/.357 slash line for a .657 OPS – hardly the performance of a future superstar.[39] It has been endlessly debated whether the Dodgers were nonetheless trying to hide Clemente by playing him infrequently. It is undisputed that Clyde Sukeforth, a former Dodgers scout and the first major-league manager (for one game) of Jackie Robinson, wanted Clemente for the Pittsburgh Pirates. Said Sukeforth: "I saw Clemente throwing from the outfield and I couldn't take my eyes off him."[40]

The Dodgers knew when they signed Clemente that they could potentially lose him to the minor-league draft after the 1954 season, because they paid him a bonus of more than $4,000, and a rule passed by the major-league owners in December of 1952 stated that any player who was given a bonus of that size by a minor-league club had to go through an unrestricted draft before he could be assigned to the parent major-league club.[41] The Dodgers, according to E.J. "Buzzie" Bavasi, signed Clemente just to make sure that the Giants did not get him: "[W]e didn't want the Giants to have Clemente and a fellow like Willie Mays in the same outfield."[42] In 1956, former Giants (and before that, Dodgers) manager Leo Durocher told Les Biederman that "[W]e knew the boy [Clemente] in high school. ... [W]hen the Dodgers heard we were after him, they got into the act."[43]

Perhaps the Dodgers also were aware that Clemente could complete an outstanding outfield featuring him in right field, Willie Mays in center, and Monte Irvin in left – three future Hall of Famers, all with outstanding throwing arms, not to mention other baseball talents. Though Irvin's career was about to take a downturn when Clemente signed in early 1954, he was coming off a stellar season, batting .329 with 21 home runs and 97 runs batted in only 444 at-bats.[44]

At the end of the 1954 season, the Pirates, who had finished last again in the National League, picked first in the minor-league draft and chose Clemente. In 1955, when Clemente was a rookie,

Irvin was sent to the minor-league Minneapolis Millers in late June.[45] Irvin starred for the Millers, hitting .352 with 14 home runs and 52 RBIs and figured prominently in their Junior World Series victory. As a result, like Clemente a season earlier, Irvin was drafted by the Chicago Cubs in the season-end minor-league draft.

MAJOR-LEAGUE OPPONENTS

Momen and Monte were opponents for two seasons – the first two of Clemente's stellar career and the last two of Irvin's truncated career in the National League. Neither was at his best. Clemente started out in 1955 at .255/.284/.382 for a 77 OPS+, albeit with some outstanding defense, as earlier noted. Irvin batted only 150 times for the Giants before being demoted to Minneapolis of the American Association, with a .253/337/.333 performance for a 79 OPS+ – a similar under-whelming offensive performance.[46]

In 1956 both rebounded. Clemente hit over .300 for the first of 13 times in his legendary career, ending up with a .311/.330/.431 slash line for a 106 OPS+, while Irvin, playing part-time for the Cubs (and mentoring Ernie Banks) ended up at .271/.346/.460 with a 116 OPS+, a decent career-ending result. More interesting, though, is that five of Clemente's 12 home runs combined in his first two seasons, were against Irvin's team, with Irvin missing the second half of the 1955 season's games against Clemente due to his demotion.[47]

Clemente's first major-league home run came on April 18, 1955, at the Polo Grounds in front of only 2,915 fans.[48] In this his third major-league contest, he hit an inside-the-park home run in the fifth inning off Don Liddle of the Giants, famed for giving up the 430-plus-foot shot by Cleveland's Vic Wertz that preceded "The Catch" by Willie Mays in Game One of the 1954 World Series. Clemente went 2-for-4 and drove in Pittsburgh's second run with a sacrifice fly. Irvin played as well,

going 1-for-4 with a double, a sacrifice fly, and two RBIs as Pittsburgh lost its sixth straight game to start the season, 12-3. In their first contest playing against each other, both got off to flying starts![49]

Clemente hit a 430-foot triple against the Giants on May 6, scoring the tying run in a three-run rally against Johnny Antonelli as the Pirates won their sixth game in a row, 3-2, with Irvin contributing two singles and a run scored to the losing cause.[50] Clemente's third career home run also came against the Giants, a leadoff hit in a 3-2 loss at Forbes Field on May 21, with Irvin only playing as a late-inning defensive replacement.[51]

In 1956 Roberto Clemente had by far his best statistics against Irvin's Chicago Cubs, with a .394/.400/.636 slash line,[52] and had two especially notable games against the Cubs. On June 6 at Wrigley Field, Clemente went 4-for-4 with a home run and three runs batted in in an 8-2 victory over the Cubs. Although Irvin typically played in left field that year, he shared the position with Jim King, and in this game King was playing in left field when Clemente launched his fifth-inning drive over the left-field fence. Irvin did provide a pinch-hit single to the losing cause.[53] In the other game, on July 25 at Forbes Field, Clemente performed a feat that had never been done before in major-league baseball – and has never been done since.[54] In the bottom of the ninth inning, with nobody out, the bases loaded, and the Pirates losing 8-5, Clemente faced relief pitcher Jim Brosnan, who had just been brought into the game. On the first pitch, a slider high and inside,

Clemente drove it against the light standard in left field. Jim King had backed up to make the catch but it was over his head. The ball bounced off the slanted side of the fencing and rolled along the cinder path to center field. Here came Hank Foiles, Bill Virdon, and then Dick Cole, heading home and making it easily. Then came Clemente into third. Bobby Bragan had his hands up – stretched to hold up his outfielder. The relay was coming in from Solly Drake. But around third came Clemente and down the home path. He made it just in front of the relay from Ernie Banks. He slid, missed the plate, then reached back to rest his hand on the rubber with the ninth run in a 9-8 victory as the crowd of 12,431 went goofy with excitement.[55]

In 2015 poet Martin Espada wrote about Clemente's home run and the reaction to it by manager Bragan and the various media commentators, including the pitcher who gave up the only inside-the-park, walk-off grand slam (ITPWOGS) in major-league history, Jim Brosnan. While discussing how Clemente disobeyed his manager and arguably made "a fundamental error – trying to score a run on a potentially close play with no one out," Espada argued that Brosnan's critique was not only an example of stereotyping – but it was also fundamentally wrong. For Brosnan, writing a scouting report on the Pirates for *Life* in advance of the 1960 World Series, the Clemente home run, which in his words "excited the fans, startled the manager, shocked me, and disgusted my club," was an example of Clemente's "Latin-American variety of showboating."[56] Instead, Espada argued that "to accomplish his unprecedented feat, Clemente had to make a number of split-second calculations involving the dimensions of the ballpark, the path traveled by the baseball after it struck the light standard, the position of the outfielders, the accuracy of the relay throws, his own speed around the bases, and his manager's gestures to halt, which he ignored because he knew that his instantaneous calculations were correct."[57]

Were Clemente still alive, he would undoubtedly say that his play in the 1971 World Series was his greatest thrill in baseball, not his unique ITPWOGS. But to the end of his long life, Monte Irvin would say that his greatest thrill in baseball was his straight steal of home in the first inning of the first game of the 1951 World Series against the New York Yankees.[58] Unlike Clemente's daring dash to home plate, Irvin's steal was given the green light by manager Durocher, coaching at third, and it occurred with two outs in the first inning, when Irvin noticed that Yankees pitcher Allie Reynolds was "taking a long time to deliver the ball. He was ducking his head and going into that long pumping motion before he let go of the ball."[59] Reynolds was clearly surprised, and threw high to catcher Yogi Berra, enabling Irvin to successfully complete the first straight steal of home in a World Series game in 30 years.[60]

In his autobiography, Irvin speculated that his steal "might have embarrassed the Yankees a little."[61] Clearly, based on his reaction, Jim Brosnan was more than a little embarrassed by Clemente's successful tour of the bases on July 25, 1956, which was his second career inside-the-park home run, both against Irvin's teams. Irvin's play, the sixth time he stole home in 1951, was different from Clemente's play in that it was both practiced and deliberate (and had been approved by his manager), but it was similar in that it was an arguably low-percentage, high-excitement, thrilling maneuver that worked. Could it be that Roberto listened to Irvin's steal of home when he was 16 years old, and later incorporated his own daring, groundbreaking play as a way to show his mentor what he had gleaned?

MOMEN AND MONTE — AS MENTORS... AND MEN

Roberto Clemente and Monte Irvin were men of different backgrounds and different temperaments. Irvin was more of a "go along to get along" individual. Although he did express himself openly about racism, he was a relatively quiet and cooperative teammate, and later assistant to Commissioner Bowie Kuhn, breaking ground as the first Black baseball executive in the formerly White major leagues. As a groundbreaking Black and Latin superstar, Clemente faced racism and language/cultural adaptation difficulties, and he spoke of them openly and loudly. Both were parts of significant moments in baseball's integration. Irvin was the first Black New York Giant in 1949 with Hank Thompson, and in the first all-Black outfield with Thompson and Willie Mays in the 1951 World Series. Clemente played in the first all-Latino outfield, with Puerto Rican Carlos Bernier and Cuban Ramon Mejias, during spring training of 1955,[62] and was part of the first all-Black starting nine for the Pirates in 1971.

Each man became celebrated for his humanity. This author, who has been researching Irvin's life and career for many years, has come across no one with anything bad to say about Irvin as a human being. In contrast, Clemente was often criticized – but by the end of his short and eventful life, he had become celebrated as a great humanitarian.

Despite different methods, both Momen and Monte were mentors. One of Irvin's first subjects was in fact Roberto himself. Whether or not Irvin truly was aware of young Roberto, he had a great impact on Roberto's baseball development. Later, Black pitcher Brooks Lawrence, as quoted by Jim Brosnan – yes, the very same man who critiqued Roberto's "showboat" style of play – said that "Monte was the Black player all the other Black players looked up to. Jackie Robinson was aloof to them, while Irvin was willing to help. So while they idolized Jackie, they loved Monte. Lawrence explained, 'I want my idols to talk to me.'"[63]

Roberto Clemente's life was replete with instances where he helped others – teammates and even sometimes opponents – to perform better, or just to be ready to compete. For example, in 1966 Matty Alou joined the Pirates and proceeded to win his first (and only) batting title. Clemente, speaking to Alou in Spanish, had exhorted him to hit to left and stationed himself at third base during batting practice to get Alou to hit to him. Pirates manager Harry Walker, in describing Clemente's principal role in Alou's transformation and success, said, "Clemente has his critics, but no man ever gave more of himself or worked more unselfishly for the good of the team than Roberto."[64] Longtime teammate Al Oliver not only called Clemente "my biggest booster,"[65] but also expressed that "he was the biggest inspiration of my career, and he was an inspiration to all the rest of the members of the team."[66] Even longtime opponent Bobby Bonds was helped by Clemente in 1972 when he noticed that Bonds was slowing down when fielding routine plays: "Clemente felt motivated to talk to Bonds in 1972. Clemente stressed to the young Bonds the importance of playing hard at all times."[67]

CONCLUSION – EPITAPHS

In Roberto Clemente's Hall of Fame player file, there is a typewritten document entitled "Epitaph." A handwritten notation says "Interview July 1971." Of course, Clemente did not know he would be dead in less than two years – although he had premonitions of an early death. In the document, Clemente stressed the importance of always playing hard, just as he underscored with Bobby Bonds. He also said, "I believe the kids must have idols. A country without idols is nothing. ... I do it for baseball [give out 2,000 autograph cards to kids] because baseball has given me a good life. ... I get mad, but I do not hate. I raise my voice when I speak. That is the way I am. But I do not hate."[68]

In the immediate aftermath of the plane crash that took Clemente's life, Commissioner Bowie Kuhn, among many others, spoke eloquently of Clemente's legacy: "Somehow Roberto transcended superstardom. ... (H)is marvelous playing skills rank him among the truly elite. ... *And what a wonderfully good man he was. Always concerned about others.* He had about him the touch of royalty" (emphasis added).[69] And at the Hall of Fame induction for both men on August 6, 1973, Kuhn spoke similarly about Irvin: "[N]ever ... has baseball produced a kinder, more decent, more beloved man, nor one who has meant more to me personally, than Monte Irvin.[70]

And what did Monte Irvin have to say about Clemente, near and at the end of Clemente's life? In his autobiography, he wrote, "[W]e used to communicate with each other often and he and I became real close until the day he died."[71] And when he heard Clemente express how much he idolized Irvin as a youngster, he said, "If I had anything to do with Roberto becoming a baseball player, or becoming involved with baseball … I think that my life in baseball is complete."[72]

According to Roberto Clemente's oldest son, Roberto Jr., Irvin certainly had quite a bit to do with his father's success: "(T)he man was a gem … and he did not know – Monte really did not know – how much he had to do with Dad and how much of an impact he had on Dad."[73] In living, and expressing, their concern for and continual efforts to help others, both Momen and Monte, each a baseball pioneer, lived lives that fulfilled Jackie Robinson's epitaph: "A Life Is Not Important Except in The Impact It Has on Other Lives."

NOTES

1 http://www.retrosheet.org pitcher-batter matchups, accessed March 28, 2022. Clemente far exceeded his .317 lifetime batting average against Spahn – noteworthy in that Spahn was far from an ordinary pitcher. His home run, walk, and strikeout totals against Spahn were more closely in line with his lifetime percentages.

2 Phil Musick, *Who Was Roberto? A Biography of Roberto Clemente* (Garden City, New York: Doubleday & Company, Inc. 1974), 59.

3 David Maraniss, *Clemente: The Passion and Grace of Baseball's Last Hero* (New York: Simon & Schuster, Advanced Reader's Edition 2006), 21.

4 Maraniss, 21.

5 Sam Nover, "A Conversation with Roberto Clemente," WIIC TV, October 8, 1972, www.youtube.com/watch?v= Pe-KQ15vWOA.

6 See Jake Crouse, "The HOFer Who Inspired a Young Clemente," www.mlb.com, February 24, 2022. https://www.mlb.com/news/roberto-clemente-inspired-by-negro-leaguer-monte-irvin, accessed March 29, 2022. (Clemente using a bicycle to "trek to San Juan to watch Puerto Rico's Winter League"); Maraniss, 25 ("Clemente sometimes had a quarter from his father. He used a dime for the bus and fifteen cents for a ticket" to get to San Juan.)

7 Maraniss, 25.

8 Thomas E. Van Hyning, *Puerto Rico's Winter League: A History of Major League Baseball's Launching Pad* (Jefferson, North Carolina: McFarland & Company, 1995), 89.

9 Monte Irvin, *Nice Guys Finish First: The Autobiography of Monte Irvin* (New York: Carroll & Graf Publishers, 1996), 42-43.

10 Van Hyning, 89-90.

11 Van Hyning, 89. ("Irvin also filled in at the other infield positions and saw limited duty in the outfield.")

12 Musick, 59.

13 Baseball-Reference.com, Monte Irvin page, accessed March 29, 2022.

14 Irvin, 117.

15 Irvin batted .3677 to Pedroso's .3684, but batted 155 times to Pedroso's 95. Van Hyning, 89.

16 Van Hyning, 89.

17 Bill Nunn, Jr., "CHANGE OF PACE: Scribes Now Rate Clemente as 'Best,'" *New Pittsburgh Courier*, February 24, 1962: 28.

18 Les Biederman, "Clemente, Early Buc Ace, Says He's Better in Summer," *The Sporting News*, June 29, 1955: 26. The number of 55 games comes from Retrosheet.org.

19 Nathalie Alonso, "Revisiting Roberto Clemente's Best Moments," www.mlb.com December 31, 2021, https://www.mlb.com/news/roberto-clemente-greatest-moments, accessed March 29, 2022. Clemente led right fielders in assists six times. Baseball-Reference.com Appearances on Leaderboards, Awards, and Honors.

20 Baseball-Reference.com, Appearances on Leaderboards, Awards, and Honors.

21 Michael Humphreys, *Wizardry: Baseball's All-Time Greatest Fielders Revealed* (New York: Oxford University Press, 2011), 42 (Clemente) and 207 (Irvin).

22 Irvin, 26-27.

23 Ira Miller, *Roberto Clemente* (New York: Grosset & Dunlap Publishers, 1973), 13.

24 Bruce Markusen, *Roberto Clemente: The Great One* (Champaign, Illinois: Sports Publishing Inc., 1998), 8.

25 Maraniss, 25.

26 *Roberto Clemente: A Touch of Royalty*, www.youtube.com/watch?v=oKIRDgmwg8w, accessed March 30, 2022.

27 *Roberto Clemente: A Video Tribute*, www.youtube.com/watch?v=PnyDAZZI7lpk, accessed March 30, 2022.

28 Email from Stew Thornley to author, February 10, 2022.

29 Maraniss, 25.

30 Irvin, 221.

31 Irvin, 221. The author has spent considerable time trying to parse the tenses and intentions of various statements of Irvin's and of authors either quoting or characterizing Roberto Clemente's early involvement with Monte Irvin to determine definitively if he knew who Roberto Clemente was in 1945 – concluding that it is likely that Irvin did not remember Clemente clearly after their early encounters.

32 Maraniss, 25.

33 See e.g. Irvin, 119-120. The full story is much more complicated but not relevant to this article.

34 Irvin, 123.

35 Maraniss, 26-27.

36 Clemente had been signed by Santurce in 1952.

37 "Giants Had First Chance at Clemente, Nixed Price," *The Sporting News*, November 26, 1966: 26. According to Markusen, Giants scouts noted that Clemente was an undisciplined hitter and Stoneham became concerned that Clemente would strike out too frequently. Markusen, 15.

38 Maraniss, 37.

39 Baseball-Reference.com, Roberto Clemente page, accessed March 30, 2022.

40 "Sukey First to Glimpse Clemente," *The Sporting News*, June 29, 1955: 26. It is worth mentioning that Sukeforth likely scouted Monte Irvin for the Dodgers in 1945 and perhaps earlier as a potential pioneering Black player for the Dodgers.

41 Brent Kelley, *Baseball's Biggest Blunder: The Bonus Rule of 1953-1957* (Lanham, Maryland: Scarecrow Press, Inc. 1997), 20.

42 *The Sporting News*, May 25, 1955: 11.

43 Les Biederman, "Hats Off ! Roberto Clemente," *The Sporting News*, June 20, 1956: 19.

44 Perhaps Bavasi in 1955 forgot that when the Royals signed Clemente, Mays had just missed most of the past two years in the military, and had yet to truly prove himself a superstar, although Irvin was about to turn 35 at the time of Clemente's signing and Mays certainly showed enormous potential in 1951.

45 Whitney Martin, "The Sports Trail," *Bedford* (Pennsylvania) *Gazette*, June 29, 1955: 4.

46 Baseball-Reference.com, Roberto Clemente and Monte Irvin pages.

47 Clemente Home Run Log, Compiled by Joseph A. Mercurio, Roberto Clemente player file at the National Baseball Hall of Fame. Clemente hit three of his five home runs against the Giants in 1955, but the third was hit after Irvin had been sent to Minneapolis.

48 Baseball Reference.com Game Logs for Roberto Clemente 1955, accessed March 30, 2022. It is noteworthy that the Giants drew very few fans in an early-season game in the year following their four-game World Series sweep of the Cleveland Indians, an indication that trouble was ahead for the Giants (and their fans) as a New York entity.

49 "Willie Hits Two Triples and Single," *Washington Post*, April 19, 1955: 27.

50 "Pirates 3 In 7th Upset Giants 3-2," *New York Times*, May 7, 1955: 11.

51 Baseball-Reference.com Game Logs for Roberto Clemente 1955.

52 Baseball-Reference.com Game Logs for Roberto Clemente 1956.

53 Baseball-Reference.com Game Logs for Roberto Clemente 1955.

54 It is certainly possible that Clemente's feat was performed in the Negro Leagues, whose league play between 1920 and 1948 has been recognized as major league.

55 *Pittsburgh Post-Gazette*, July 26, 1956, cited in Martin Espada's "The Greatest Home Run of All Time," *The Massachusetts Review*, Volume 56, Number 2, Summer 2015: 249-255. Note that Monte Irvin was not playing left field in that game.

56 Espada. Quotes from Brosnan cited by Espada appeared in *Life* magazine, October 5, 1960.

57 Espada.

58 Irvin, 164.

59 Irvin, 164. See https://sabr.org/gamesproj/game/october-4-1951-monte-irvin-steals-home-as-giants-take-game-1-over-yankees/.

60 Andrew Heckroth, "October 4, 1951: Monte Irvin Steals Home as Giants Take Game 1 over Yankees," Games Project, www.sabr.org accessed March 31, 2022.

61 Irvin, 163.

62 *The Sporting News*, March 23, 1955: 34. Note that the article incorrectly called it an all-Puerto Rican outfield.

63 Danny Peary, ed., *We Played the Game: 65 Players Remember Baseball's Greatest Era 1947-1964* (New York: Hyperion, 1994), 319.

64 Arthur Daley, "A Matter of Value," *New York Times*, December 16, 1966. Clipping in Clemente Hall of Fame player file.

65 "Memory of 'Great One' Inspires Bucs Still," *Philadelphia Inquirer*, April 7, 1973.

66 "What Clemente Meant to the Pirates," from unidentified newspaper 1973. Clipping in Clemente Hall of Fame player file.

67 Bruce Markusen. "#Card Corner: 1981 Fleer Bobby Bonds," www.baseballhall.org, accessed March 27, 2021.

68 Document entitled "Epitaph" in Clemente Hall of Fame player file.

69 Associated Press, "Baseball Respected Clemente as Greatest, 'Super Star,'" *Beaver Falls* (Pennsylvania) *News Tribune*, January 2, 1973.

70 *New York Times*, August 7, 1973.

71 Irvin, 221.

72 *Roberto Clemente: A Touch of Royalty*.

73 Crouse, "The HOFer Who Inspired a Young Clemente."

ROBERTO CLEMENTE AND CURT FLOOD:
RACE, LABOR, AND THE NATIONAL PASTIME

BY EMMANUEL MEHR

To place baseball on a pedestal as America's foundational pastime from time immemorial serves to maintain its culturally ordained immunity from negative aspects of American history. By studying individuals who fought for equality within the confines of a sport embedded within the national ethos, we illuminate the complexities of identity in baseball history. The stories of Roberto Clemente and Curt Flood provide powerful examples of this. Clemente became the trailblazer for Latin American players in major-league baseball during the same era that Flood emerged as the icon of and greatest champion for player labor rights.[1] Clemente was killed in a plane crash on December 31, 1972, a tragic ending to a life dedicated to humanitarianism, baseball, and social justice. Six months earlier, in June of 1972, Flood lost a monumental labor case before the US Supreme Court.[2] This chapter weaves together the stories of Clemente and Flood to explore how their lives intersected with the histories of race, labor, and baseball in the United States during the latter half of the twentieth century.

Three months before his death, Roberto Clemente graced the cover of *Baseball Digest*, America's authoritative and longest-running baseball magazine.[3] His image previewed a feature on the on-field successes of his 1971 World Series champion Pittsburgh Pirates.[4] However, much of his legacy extends beyond championships to the pursuit of equality for Latin American and African American ballplayers. As historian Adrian Burgos Jr. argues, Clemente and the original wave of Latin American major-leaguers worked to ameliorate the multifaceted "racial glass ceiling in baseball created by the slow pace of integration."[5] Identifying as both Latin American and Black, Clemente pushed for greater representation and accommodation, and he greatly contributed to shattering barriers of inequality.

Center fielder Curt Flood, himself African American, emerged as the best-known advocate of player rights in the early 1970s. In the lead-up to the 1972 *Flood v. Kuhn* Supreme Court case, Flood's name appeared on the February 1971 cover of *Baseball Digest*. The imageless headline read, "Curt Flood: An Angry Rebel." The article described him derisively as "in revolt against the baseball establishment."[6] Other media outlets made similar degrading claims, with one reporter writing, "Flood is so angry with everyone and everything, he turns you off."[7] Aware of baseball's place in American society, Flood noted in his memoir that "[t]o challenge the sanctity of [O]rganized [B]aseball was to question one of the primary myths of the American culture."[8] His main argument was that the reserve clause, which gave teams permanent and complete control over their players, enabled treatment of players as property rather than human beings.[9] The subject of Flood's ire was not just the baseball establishment, but also the exploitative nature of unbridled capitalism in America.

LABOR DISPUTES AND PLAYER ADVOCACY

Flood and Clemente shared a meeting room on December 13, 1969, at a gathering of the executive board of the Major League Baseball Players Association (MLBPA) in San Juan, Puerto Rico. Flood received the invitation specifically as an opportunity to convince the board that supporting his reserve-clause lawsuit would be worthwhile.[10] As he spoke, union members expressed their doubts. In his book on Flood's life, legal scholar Brad Snyder relies on oral histories to claim that Clemente intervened by placing himself firmly behind Flood's cause at the meeting and that this support proved pivotal in convincing the union.[11] This connection would certainly be significant, but it cannot be corroborated from sources other than Snyder's unpreserved interviews. Other scholars reconstruct the meeting without mentioning Clemente's contributions at all.[12] In Flood's own memoir, he also describes the meeting with no mention of Clemente.[13] Either way, the uneven impacts of economic inequalities upon historically marginalized groups likely connected their agendas at the meeting.

Baseball became a medium for broader advocacy, leading the 1972 *Flood v. Kuhn* case to become about much more than the antitrust exemption.[14] Flood understood the danger of granting baseball cultural immunity from criticism, writing that "[t]o diminish the established insanity in one area of life is to undermine it elsewhere as well. In due course, the quality of justice changes. Values alter."[15] He also made clear that he viewed the exemption as an outgrowth of exploitative labor relations connected to the history of American chattel slavery. Shortly after the San Juan meeting, Flood wrote to Commissioner Bowie K. Kuhn:

> After twelve years in the Major Leagues, I do not feel that I am a piece of property to be bought and sold irrespective of my wishes. I believe that any system which produces that result violates my basic rights as a citizen and is inconsistent with the laws of the United States and of the several States.[16]

Looking back on this in his memoir, Flood wrote that "[t]he hypocrisies of the baseball industry could not possibly have been sustained unless they were symptoms of a wider affliction."[17] Race relations and labor relations both received great popular attention in the 1970s, and *Flood v. Kuhn* must be viewed within this context.[18] His awareness of broad national implications is clear in his claim that the "typical" media portrayal was "that a victory for Flood would mean the collapse of our national pastime. God profaned! Flag desecrated! Motherhood defiled! Apple pie blasphemed!"[19] Like Clemente, Flood forced change in baseball and beyond by pushing against these connected grains and entrenched attitudes.

CONTINUED RELEVANCE

The system of teams acquiring the rights of international players received recent scrutiny in the labor negotiations of the major-league owners' lockout that lasted from December 2, 2021, to

March 10, 2022. The possibility of an international draft entered negotiations as a potential bargaining chip between the owners and the players. The owners framed it as a means of giving stability to an international signing system known for exploitation and corruption. The players did not disagree with this claim but refused owner insistence on a strictly regulated qualifying-offer system that would take away player leverage. Ultimately, the two sides dismissed the topic, keeping the current system of only players from the United States, Canada, or a US territory such as Puerto Rico being eligible for the first-year player draft. The international signing system remains unchanged. Outside observers noted the absence of Latin American player representation in these talks and suggested that it is not surprising that a largely North American players union would not fight hard for something largely affecting Latin American players.[20] Significant differences of opinion among Latin American players on the matter further skewed the representation of their overall perspectives. Perhaps this lack of representation reflects the continued confluence of the causes of Clemente and Flood. In the 2022 case, the players union did not want an international draft because it saw this as inhibiting the free market, akin to Flood's cause.[21] It appears such a draft could have improved the overall experience of Latin American players, more analogous to Clemente's agenda.

SWINGING AWAY AT ADVERSITY

The persistence of injustice did not dissuade Clemente and Flood from fighting for structural change. One exchange from a 1963 interview with Clemente conveys this spirit beautifully, in the moment spoken of baseball but reflective of much more. Interviewer Clifford Evans asked, "Roberto Clemente, sometimes you swing at bad balls as if you are impatient. Now, when you are in the batter's box, are you sometimes impatient?" Clemente quickly responded, "I don't think so. I think I'm very relaxed at the plate. I just swing at the bad balls because I'm a good bad ball hitter."[22] This unflinching belief in the ability to turn less-than-ideal circumstances into positive opportunities lies at the root of Clemente's and Flood's stories. They believed that overcoming discrimination and inequality was possible. By seeing the potential for change and taking a swing at challenging circumstances, they improved the plight of future generations. While these efforts would not come to full fruition in their lifetimes, significant progress under the Antitrust Reform Act of 1997 and the prominence of high-earning Latin American major leaguers in the twenty-first century reflect their triumphs in these ongoing struggles.[23]

NOTES

1   Adrian Burgos Jr., *Playing America's Game: Baseball, Latinos, and the Color Line* (Berkeley: University of California Press, 2007), 227; Stuart L. Weiss, *The Curt Flood Story: The Man Behind the Myth* (Columbia, Missouri: University of Missouri Press, 2007), 229-230, Kindle edition.

2   Burgos, 225.

3   Bill Francis, "Baseball Digest Still Enthralling Fans in Eighth Decade," *Baseball History Series* (The National Baseball Hall of Fame and Museum, 2022), https://baseballhall.org/discover/baseball-history/baseball-digest-still-enthralling-fans-in-eighth-decade?fbclid=IwAR125K39N4IZeUaDzY_Mwu6XwNwC9qdOvXW91xS8eIK6ciOsT0CpJPEe1Vs.

4   *Baseball Digest*, September 1972: 1.

5   Burgos, 193.

6   *Baseball Digest*, February 1971: 1; William Gildea, "Curt Flood – Baseball's Angry Rebel," *Baseball Digest*, February 1971: 55-60.

7   Jerome Holtzman, "Richie Relieves Monotony," *The Sporting News*, May 8, 1971: 11, https://paperofrecord.hypernet.ca/paper_view.asp?PaperId=834&RecordId=14&PageId=7612168.

8   Curt Flood and Richard Carter, *The Way It Is* (New York: Trident Press, 1971), 16, https://archive.org/details/wayitisfloo00floo.

9   Ursula McTaggart, "Writing Baseball into History: The Pittsburgh Courier, Integration, and Baseball in a War of Position," *American Studies* vol. 47, no. 1 (Spring 2006): 118, https://www.jstor.org/stable/40604900.

10 Brad Snyder, *A Well-Paid Slave: Curt Flood's Fight for Free Agency in Professional Sports* (New York: Plume, 2007), 69, Kindle edition.

11 Snyder, *A Well-Paid Slave*, 76, 79.

12 Weiss, *The Curt Flood Story*, 155-157.

13 Flood and Carter, *The Way It Is*, 193.

14 Stuart Banner, *The Baseball Trust: A History of Baseball's Antitrust Exemption* (New York: Oxford University Press, 2013), 187-188, https://archive.org/details/baseballtrusthis0000bann.

15 Flood and Carter, *The Way It Is*, 18.

16 Curtis C. Flood, "Letter to Bowie K. Kuhn, Commissioner of Baseball from Curtis C. Flood stating that he had the right to consider offers from other baseball clubs before signing a contract," December 24, 1969, Record Group 21: Records of District Courts of the United States, 1695-2009, Series: Civil Case Files, 1938-1995, National Archives at New York (New York, NY), https://catalog.archives.gov/id/278312.

17 Flood and Carter, *The Way It Is*, 16.

18 Banner, *The Baseball Trust*, 191.

19 Flood and Carter, *The Way It Is*, 18.

20 Alden Gonzalez and Marly Rivera, "'Something Needs to Be Done': Why an MLB International Draft is Such a Big Deal," ESPN, March 10, 2022, https://www.espn.com/mlb/story/_/id/33463929/needs-done-why-mlb-international-draft-such-big-deal.

21 James Wagner, "M.L.B. Cancels Another Week of Games as Lockout Continues," *New York Times*, March 9, 2022, https://www.nytimes.com/2022/03/09/sports/baseball/mlb-lockout.html?smid=url-share; Chelsea Janes, "MLB, Players Union Reach A Deal, Clearing the Way for Baseball's Return," *Washington Post*, March 10, 2022, https://www.washingtonpost.com/sports/2022/03/10/mlb-lockout-deal/; Gonzalez and Rivera, "Something Needs to Be Done," ESPN, March 10, 2022.

22 "Roberto Clemente (1963)," SABR Oral History Collection (Society for American Baseball Research), accessed May 12, 2022, 1:11-1:29, https://sabr.org/interview/roberto-clemente-1963/.

23 U.S. Congress, "H.R.704 - 105th Congress (1997-1998): Major League Baseball Antitrust Reform Act of 1997," February 12, 1997, https://www.congress.gov/bill/105th-congress/house-bill/704?s=1&r=36.

CLEMENTE AND KING: IN THE SERVICE OF OTHERS

BY BENJAMIN SABIN

"Any time you have an opportunity to make a difference in this world and you don't, then you are wasting your time on earth."

– Roberto Clemente[1]

Death comes to us all. It may happen when we are young and carefree, when we are middle-aged with the weight of the world on our shoulders, or when we are old and living life day to day. Martin Luther King Jr. was 39 years old when he died. Roberto Clemente was 38.

King was gunned down on the balcony of his second-floor room at the Lorraine Motel in Memphis, Tennessee. He was in Memphis to march in support of striking sanitation workers. It was 6:05 P.M. on April 4, 1968. King was on his way to dinner at the house of Memphis minister Samuel "Billy" Kyles, but first he was scheduled to speak with members of the Southern Christian Leadership Conference, who were waiting in the parking lot below his room. When he stepped out on the balcony, a single shot from an assassin's gun struck King in the face. He was pronounced dead an hour later.[2]

Clemente was killed in a plane crash off the Puerto Rican coast on December 31, 1972. He was on his way to Nicaragua. That country had suffered a devastating earthquake, and Clemente had collected supplies on his own accord and decided to deliver them personally. The plane took off at 9 P.M. and made it to an altitude of only 200 feet before apparently suffering engine failure and plummeting into the ocean. Rescue crews were never able to find the bodies.[3]

Since their untimely passing, both Dr. King and Clemente have been revered as great humanitarians. And even in the moments of their deaths, they were fighting for the betterment of humanity.

A CROSSING OF PATHS

Clemente signed a big-league contract when he was a teenager and came to the US mainland

Even at the field, Clemente took time for the fans. Les Banos photograph courtesy of The Clemente Museum.

from Puerto Rico in 1954. This was at the beginning of the Civil Rights Era and Clemente experienced Jim Crow segregation for the first time during spring training in Florida.[4] In Puerto Rico, integration was the status quo and Clemente wasn't used to being unable to eat in the same restaurants or go to the same movie theaters as his White teammates. Clemente said he learned that being a person of color was "bad over here [United States]."[5]

The following year, 1955, King and other civil-rights activists were arrested in Montgomery, Alabama, for leading a boycott of a transportation company that required nonwhites to give their seats to White passengers. The boycott attracted national attention. King went on to lead many nonviolent protests and demonstrations, and fought for the civil rights of people of color until his assassination over 10 years later.

Since Clemente's first experience of racial inequality, he had become more enterprising in the face of this gross disproportion. As his social awakening continued, he listed Martin Luther King Jr. as one of the top people he admired.[6] The beginning of Clemente's great esteem for King began after he witnessed a speech by King on February 16, 1962, in San German Puerto Rico. Afterward King came to Clemente's farm on the outskirts of his hometown, Carolina.[7] It is not known what the two discussed, but it is clear that Clemente came away from the meeting with a newfound respect for King.

A VOICE

Clemente's admiration for King "was not his philosophy of nonviolence, but his ability to give a voice to the voiceless."[8] He said that King "changed the whole system of American style. He put the people, the ghetto people, the people who didn't have nothing to say in those days, they started saying what they would have liked to say for many years that nobody listened to. Now with this man, these people come down to the place where they were supposed to be but people didn't want them, and sit down as if they were white and call attention to the whole world. Now that wasn't only the black people, but the minority people. The people who didn't have anything, and they had nothing to say in those days because they didn't have any power, they started saying things and they started picketing, and that's the reason I say [King] changed the whole world. ..."[9]

After the Pirates' victory in the 1971 World Series, Clemente took his chance to give a voice to the voiceless as Dr. King had. He had carried the Pirates on his back through much of the Series, and after their victory he chose to address the media and the world in Spanish. This was the first time anybody had spoken Spanish on a nationally televised English-speaking broadcast in the. United States. He spoke to his family, saying, "En el dia mas grande de mi vida, para los nenes la bendicion. [In the most important day of my life, I give blessings to my boys and ask that my parents give their blessing]."[10] Not only did his family hear him, but he managed to give a voice to the Spanish-speaking world.

RESPECT

Dr. King's passing affected many people in many ways. It caused great sadness, suffering, and anger. Riots broke out in dozens of US cities. The country was in turmoil. Jackie Robinson, interviewed the night of King's death, said, "It is the most disturbing and distressing thing we've had to face in a long time."[11] What does one do in the face of such tragedy? They mourn. They pay respect.

The day after King's assassination, the Pirates, who had 11 people of color on their team, the most in the major leagues, held meetings spurred by Clemente. They decided that they wouldn't play the first two games of the season against the Houston Astros. "We are doing this because we white and black players respect what Dr. King

has done for mankind. ... We owe this gesture to his memory and his ideals," said Clemente and pitcher Dave Wickersham in a joint statement.[12] After the players' decision to postpone the start of their 1968 season, Major League Baseball also postponed the remaining games on April 8 and April 9 (the day of King's funeral), choosing instead to start the season on April 10.

LEGACY

Roberto Clemente and Martin Luther King Jr. shared a common bond. They believed that all people are equal regardless of their skin color or their standing in life. Clemente was inspired by King in 1962 and continued to be until his death in 1972. Even now, a half-century after Clemente's and King's deaths, the United States and the world still celebrate the social justice that these two worked hard for.

NOTES

1   Sean Collier, "This MLK Day, Learn About the Humanitarian Side of Roberto Clemente," *Pittsburgh Magazine*, January 14, 2021. https://www.pittsburghmagazine.com/this-mlk-day-learn-about-the-humanitarian-side-of-roberto-clemente/.

2   "Assassination of Martin Luther King, Jr.," *Martin Luther King Jr. Encyclopedia*, Stanford University. https://kinginstitute.stanford.edu/encyclopedia/assassination-martin-luther-king-jr.

3   "Baseball Star Roberto Clemente Dies in Plane Crash," https://www.history.com/this-day-in-history/baseball-star-dies-in-plane-crash.

4   Christopher Klein, "How Puerto Rican Baseball Icon Roberto Clemente Left a Legacy Off the Field," History.com, October 13, 2021. https://www.history.com/news/roberto-clemente-humanitarian-accomplishments-pittsburgh-pirates.

5   Dave Zirin, "Common Bond for Uncommon Men: Roberto Clemente and Martin Luther King," CommonDreams.org, April 7, 2008. https://www.commondreams.org/views/2008/04/07/common-bond-uncommon-men-roberto-clemente-and-martin-luther-king.

6   David Maraniss, *Clemente: The Passion and Grace of Baseball's Last Hero* (New York: Simon & Schuster, 2007), 148.

7   Kevin B. Blackistone, "'More Than a Ballplayer': After MLK Shooting, Roberto Clemente Halted MLB Opening Day 1968," *Washington Post*, March 28, 2018. (online)

8   Maraniss, 221.

9   Maraniss, 221.

10   Maraniss, 264.

11   Bill Francis, "National Tragedy Brought Baseball to a Halt for Two Days in 1968," National Baseball Hall of Fame, https://baseballhall.org/discover/martin-luther-king-jrs-assassination-brought-baseball-to-a-halt-in-1968.

12   https://baseballhall.org/discover/martin-luther-king-jrs-assassination-brought-baseball-to-a-halt-in-1968.

WHY NICARAGUA?
CLEMENTE AS AN ADOPTED SON

BY TONY S. OLIVER

New Year's Day, 1973: As the world awoke to the awful news and details emerged about the accident that claimed Roberto Clemente's life, fans could only ask why. Why Clemente? Why was such a kind human taken at such a young age? Why had the plane malfunctioned? But one "why" stood above the others – why had Clemente chosen to *personally* deliver the supplies?

Math tells us the shortest distance between two points is a straight line. But given the brazen corruption of the Nicaraguan government, Clemente felt the 1,413-mile line between the collected supplies in San Juan and the needy Managua victims went *through him*.

Clemente first visited the country in 1964 as a member of the San Juan Senators, champions of the Puerto Rican Winter League that now bears his name, to play in the Inter-American Series. The competition pitted squads from several nations and had replaced the Caribbean Series, last played in 1960.[1]

The Senators boasted a formidable lineup, anchored by big leaguers Clemente, Orlando Cepeda, Luis Arroyo, José Pagán, and Juan Pizarro, but fell to the local Cinco Estrellas (Five Stars) team.[2] By then, Clemente was an established All-Star, known not just for his prowess on the field but also for his humanitarian nature. He established a close bond with the Nicaraguan people, under the yoke of the Somoza family dictatorship that had ruled since 1936.

The Somozas were unabashed in their corruption. The United States, mindful of the threat of communism (both real and imagined) in Latin America, threw its support behind two generations of strongmen, giving the financial and military backing that was interpreted as a blank check to oppress Nicaraguans.

Against this backdrop, Clemente returned in November 1972 to manage the Puerto Rican team in the amateur World Series (later renamed the Baseball World Cup).[3] Cuba ransacked the field en route to a 14-1 record, while the United States and Nicaragua both finished 13-2.[4]

Only a few weeks later, a devastating earthquake destroyed most of the capital. Cruelly, it occurred on December 23, as the country prepared for Christmas. It shook the capital around 12:30 A.M., thereby catching most of its inhabitants asleep. Its 6.3 magnitude was followed by large two aftershocks within an hour, adding panic and confusion to the sea of people crowding its damaged, darkened streets. The calamity was the first humanitarian mission handled by the fledging organization Medicins Sans Frontieres (Doctors Without Borders), now a leader in medical relief.[5]

Amid the destruction, foreign aid rushed in, only to be met with inadequate distribution schemes and a government all too eager to withhold goods for its own benefit. Major Raúl Pellegrina, who delivered one of the first loads of aid collected by Clemente, was ordered by the armed forces to hand over the cargo. He refused, stating he "had told the soldiers that if they didn't let him through, he would reload his aircraft and fly back to San Juan and tell the great Roberto Clemente what was happening."[6]

Clemente's role has been well chronicled. He personally organized relief efforts, and after hearing about the dictatorship's craven behavior firsthand, chose to board the ill-fated flight. Despite the plea of his wife, Vera, not to get onto the plane, Clemente remained steadfast in what he saw as a moral mission: "When your time comes, it comes; if you are going to die, you will die. And babies are dying. They need these supplies."[7] His death added to the disaster's toll, estimated to be between 4,000 and 11,000 people with almost two-thirds of a million displaced.[8]

In the 1970s, domestic and international criticism of the regime mounted, and Anastasio Somoza Debayle turned even more restrictive.[9] The Frente de Liberación Nacional Sandinista (National Sandinista Liberation Front) toppled the government in 1979 but, seduced by power, ruled in a similar autocratic fashion.[10] Tensions remained as US-based contra-revolutionaries fought a guerrilla war that engulfed the entire nation. Peace came in 1990 with free elections, won by a coalition of anti-Sandinista parties. Democracy and peaceful transitions were sustained into the twenty-first century, though Daniel Ortega's return to power in 2006 has brought repression and contested elections. Political opponents have been frequently jailed since 2015.

While baseball was already the country's favorite sport, no Nicaraguan had reached the major leagues before Dennis Martínez ("El Presidente") in 1976. Since then, 14 others have joined the big show, influenced by Clemente's passion.[11] Martínez, who played in the Puerto Rican Winter League, was direct in his praise: "I had two idols — one as a pitcher, Juan Marichal, and the other, Clemente, as a human being. I took him as an example. He got me to think more about helping your neighbor, helping children, which was his goal and now mine too."[12] In 2019, a Clemente statue was erected in the main lobby of the Dennis Martínez National Stadium in Managua, forever linking both luminaries.[13]

Beyond Puerto Rico and Pittsburgh, no other place honors Clemente's memory as much as Nicaragua. His eldest son, Roberto Jr., joined the Board of Directors of the International Baseball Academy of Central America (IBACA).[14] The Masaya stadium is named after Clemente, as are schools all over the nation. In a touching moment of humanitarian partnership, the Rotary Club of Pittsburgh provided financial assistance for the creation of the Roberto Clemente Health Clinic in Nicaragua, which serves tens of thousands of needy patients.[15]

Clemente is seen as a unifying figure by both pro- and antigovernment groups. On December 31, 2013, then-Vice President Rosario Murillo Zambrana and the Nicaraguan parliament honored Clemente with the "Hero in Solidarity" award, the nation's highest civilian honor.[16] A large mural of "The Great One" was unveiled six years later at the Luis Alfonso Velásquez Flores Park in Managua, with 400 Little Leaguers in attendance.[17] Sports journalist Carlos Reyes addressed the crowd, noting,

"[D]espite not being born in Nicaragua, Roberto Clemente was the most important baseball player of Nicaragua, because giving one's life for others … has enormous meaning."[18]

A year later, at the height of the global coronavirus pandemic, four juvenile teams played a one-day tournament in the Roberto Clemente Youth Stadium, with organizers proclaiming, "Roberto Clemente is a symbol of respect, a symbol of greatness and above all of solidarity. We, the youth, the Nicaraguan youth, the sports promoters, the athletes, remember his example and continue the example of solidarity."[19]

Sadly, politics has tainted the memory. As the Ortega regime repressed its opponents – more than 300 were killed in 2018 alone – the government seized Clemente's memory for a series of exhibition games pitting the Puerto Rican and Nicaraguan national teams. Middle son Luis Clemente spoke with great sadness: "I just feel a little concerned that we were not approached by those who know us from Nicaragua that could have let us know ahead of time what was the ulterior motive behind all of this. We were left in the dark totally."[20] Even Martínez, the greatest living baseball icon of the country, agreed, stating his opposition to a "stadium made for baseball" being used as barracks for the military.[21]

Marlon Torres, chair of the Nicaraguan Sports Institute, had previously stated: "As a sportsman and as a person, Clemente is worthy of imitation; we should remember and maintain his memory all year long, not just on this date."[22] Almost three decades earlier, the government had taken such a step, issuing a set of postage stamps celebrating baseball players, including Clemente.[23]

Nicaragua's affection for Clemente is unique. It was not ordained like Puerto Rico's, where he was born and belonged, nor was it based on the luck of the Rule 5 draft, which allowed Pittsburgh to pluck him from the Brooklyn Dodgers' system. Instead, it was earned through acts shaped by his ethical conviction.

A large mural of Clemente adorns Parque Luis Alfonso Velasquez Flores in Managua, Nicaragua. Courtesy of Steven A. Melnick, Ph.D.

Vera Clemente stated that her husband's bond with Nicaragua was rooted in the similarities between the two nations: "We came to Nicaragua and found the people as we had been in Puerto Rico 30 years ago. Roberto saw himself in the boys in the streets – without shoes, living in a one-room house – much like it had been when his father worked for the sugar mill in Carolina. He changed a twenty-dollar bill into coins each morning and called boys over as we walked to ask them about their families. What work did their father do? What had they eaten for dinner last night? And then he dug into his pockets for them."[24] It's fitting both winter leagues have retired number 21 from being worn on the field, but to forever remain in people's hearts.[25]

NOTES

1   The first version of the Caribbean Series (1949-1960) featured a four-nation round-robin tournament pitting Cuba, Panama, Mexico, and Puerto Rico against one another. After Fidel Castro's ban on professional baseball, the competition was not held until 1970, with Venezuela and the Dominican Republic replacing the departed Cuba and Panama. In the past decade, Cuba and Panama have returned, and Colombia has been added.

2   Néstor Duprey Salgado, "Clemente en la víspera de la gloria." Self-published book, 2017, 381.

3   "XX Campeonato Mundial de Béisbol Amateur: Managua, Nicaragua (1972)," Deportes, Cine, y Otros, https://deportescineyotros.com/2017/01/01/xx-campeonato-mundial-de-beisbol-amateur-managua-nicaragua-1972/.

4   "XX Campeonato Mundial de Béisbol Amateur: Managua, Nicaragua (1972)."

5   "Doctors Without Borders: History," Doctors Without Borders, https://www.doctorswithoutborders.org/who-we-are/history/founding.

6   David Maraniss, Clemente: The Passion and Grace of Baseball's Last Hero (New York: Simon & Schuster, 2006), 302.

7   "Beyond Baseball: The Life of Roberto Clemente," Smithsonian Institution Traveling Exhibition Service, http://www.robertoclemente.si.edu/english/virtual_story_nicaragua_09.htm.

8   "On This Day: 23 December," BBC News, http://news.bbc.co.uk/onthisday/low/dates/stories/december/23/newsid_2540000/2540045.stm.

9   Anastasio Somoza García, the patriarch, ruled until 1956. His eldest son, Luis, took over until 1963, and Anastasio (Junior) governed until 1979. Puppet presidents briefly ruled during the time, but the Somozas were the unquestionable leaders.

10 The movement was named after Augusto Sandino, who organized an ultimately unsuccessful revolution against American economic dominance in the 1920s. For more information, see http://www.sandinorebellion.com/.

11 As of the conclusion of the 2021 season.

12 Antolín Maldonado Ríos, "Dennis Martínez Fue Influenciado por Clemente," El Nuevo Día, January 4, 2013.

13 "Rinden Homenaje a Roberto Clemente en Nicaragua," El Nuevo Día, March 16, 2019, https://www.elnuevodia.com/deportes/beisbol/notas/rinden-homenaje-a-roberto-clemente-en-nicaragua/.

14 "Rinden Homenaje a Roberto Clemente en Nicaragua."

15 "Clinic Timeline," The Roberto Clemente Health Clinic, https://nicaclinic.org/clinictimeline/.

16 "Nicaragua Recuerda al Héroe de la Solidaridad, Roberto Clemente," Viva Nicaragua/Canal 13, December 31, 2019, https://www.vivanicaragua.com.ni/2019/12/31/sociales/nicaragua-heroe-solidaridad-roberto-clemente/.

17 Iris Varela, "Nicaragua Recuerda a Roberto Clemente como 'Héroe del Amor y la Solidaridad,'" Diario Barricada, December 31, 2019, https://diariobarricada.com/nicaragua-recuerda-a-roberto-clemente-como-heroe-del-amor-y-la-solidaridad/.

18 "Nicaragua Recuerda a Roberto Clemente como Héroe de la Solidaridad," Archivo Informativo TN8, December 31, 2019, https://www.youtube.com/watch?v=KPBJ6Px2laU.

19 "Recuerdan a Roberto Clemente a 48 Años de su Mayor Hazaña de Solidaridad," Viva Nicaragua/Canal 13, December 31, 2020, https://www.vivanicaragua.com.ni/2020/12/31/sociales/roberto-clemente-hazana-solidaridad/.

20 Stephen J. Nesbitt, "Peace or Propaganda? In Nicaragua, a Tug of War over Roberto Clemente's Legacy," Pittsburgh Post-Gazette, March 6, 2019, https://www.post-gazette.com/sports/pirates/2019/03/06/roberto-clemente-puerto-rico-nicaragua-baseball-series-dennis-martinez-stadium/stories/201903060029.

21 Nesbitt.

22 "Nicaragua en Deuda con Roberto Clemente," Impacto Latino, December 30, 2012, https://impactolatino.com/nicaragua-en-deuda-con-roberto-clemente/.

23 "Stamp Catalog: Roberto Clemente (Puerto Rico)," Colnect, https://colnect.com/en/stamps/stamp/356277-Roberto_Clemente_Puerto_Rico-Baseball_Players-Nicaragua.

24 Rob Ruck, "Mission of Love: Displays of Respect for Her husband Ease Pain of Vera Clemente's Nicaragua Visit," Los Angeles Times, June 15, 1989, https://www.latimes.com/archives/la-xpm-1989-06-15-sp-2522-story.html.

25 Renso Gómez, "Nicaragua Pone el Ejemplo y Retira Número de Roberto Clemente," El Fildeo, November 2, 2020, https://elfildeo.com/mlb/nicaragua-mlb-roberto-clemente-numero-noticias/142965/2020/v

THE RESPONSE TO CLEMENTE'S DEATH

BY JUSTIN KRUEGER

The death of Roberto Clemente on December 31, 1972, caused shock waves across the globe. He was just a few months removed from being the 11th player, and the first Latin American, to record 3,000 hits in the major leagues. The 38-year-old right fielder for the Pittsburgh Pirates was on a humanitarian mission taking aid to the people of Nicaragua, who had recently been devastated by an earthquake.

Clemente's sudden death felt incomprehensible. It was a jolt.

As a public figure, Clemente was larger than life. He was both man and myth and respected as each. The immediate aftermath of Clemente's death saw an outpouring of responses. Words of condolence, political statements, and civilian acts of remembrance were ubiquitous and continued long after the memorial services that were held in Clemente's hometown of Carolina, Puerto Rico, and in Pittsburgh.[1]

RESPONSE FROM POLITICAL LEADERS

The death of Clemente was both widely and quickly reported. Responses from politicians followed in kind.

Outgoing Puerto Rican Governor Luis A. Ferré issued a proclamation for three days of official national mourning for "the death of the great Puerto Rican, Roberto Clemente."[2] It was one of Ferré's last official acts as governor.

The newly elected governor, Rafael Hernández Colón, who was sworn in on January 2, 1973, canceled all inauguration-related social activities but the state banquet.[3] His inauguration, which would have typically enjoyed widespread celebration, was muted.

At the beginning of Hernández Colón's inauguration ceremony, Puerto Rico's secretary of state, Fernando Chardón, said: "We have with us today the spirit of a man, Roberto Clemente, who helped teach independentistas, statehooders and commonwealthers how to play good baseball and become better citizens."[4]

Clemente Tributes and Pictures on Six Inside Pages

Pittsburgh Post-Gazette

Sun-Telegraph

First Newspaper West of the Alleghenies

Cold
Partly cloudy; high near 30; low tonight in mid-teens.
[Weather Detail on Page 18]

Final City Edition
(1-2-73)
187th Year

VOL. 46—NO. 133 •••••••• TUESDAY, JANUARY 2, 1973 In Three Sections TEN CENTS

Clemente Dies In Plane Crash

SAN JUAN, P. R. (AP)—Baseball star Roberto Clemente and his four companions on a mercy mission were feared dead yesterday in the crash of a cargo plane that plummeted into the ocean within sight of San Juan's luxury hotels.

The four-engined DC7 was loaded with relief supplies for survivors of the Managua, Nicaragua, earthquake. It went down at 9:22 p.m. Sunday about 1½ miles north of San Juan International

Read an editorial, "Roberto Clemente, The Great One," and see a Hungerford cartoon, "Mourning," Page 6.

Airport, from which it had just taken off. The plane, carrying a crew of three and one other passenger, came down in heavy seas a mile and a half from shore. Coast Guard planes circled the area, trying to locate the plane by the light of flares. The wreckage was not found until 5 p.m. yesterday in about 100 feet of water. There were no signs of survivors. The search for bodies will resume this morning.

FRIENDS OF THE FAMILY said the plane had originally taken off at 4 p.m. Sunday and then apparently returned to get mechanical trouble repaired before leaving again.

A Coast Guard spokesman said rescue

units "have found a suitcase, a hatch cover, metal pieces, a wheel and life jackets" but no survivors.

Gov. Luis A. Ferre officially declared the Pittsburgh Pirates' All-Star outfielder dead and ordered three days of mourning because of "the death of the great Puerto Rican, Roberto Clemente."

Ferre said he issued the special proclamation because "Clemente's premature death took place while on a noble mission of charity and neighborly love."

Clemente, 38, had agreed to head Puerto Rico's earthquake relief operation when he got word of the disaster Dec. 23. His relief organization had collected $150,000 in cash and tons of food, clothing and medicine for the survivors.

Cristobal Colon, a friend of Clemente who was working on the committee to raise funds and collect clothing for the earthquake victims, said he had driven Clemente and his wife, Vera, to the airport.

"After we put him on the plane, Vera and I went to the arrivals area of the airport," Colon said.

MRS. CLEMENTE SAID she was concerned that the plane seemed old and overloaded, but her husband assured her that everything would be all right. When the pilot did not show up until late, she

said he told her, "if there is one more delay, we'll leave this for tomorrow."

Colon said Clemente had insisted on going with the flight to make certain that the supplies got into the hands of the people who needed them.

"He had received reports that some of the food and clothing he had sent earlier had fallen into the hands of profiteers," said Colon.

Clemente had been asked to take part in the collection of funds by Luis Vigoraux, a television producer.

"He did not just lend his name to the fund-raising activities the way some famous personalities do," said Vigoraux. "He took over the entire thing, arranging for collection points, publicity and the transportation to Nicaragua."

Airport officials said the plane crashed after making a normal left bank while climbing after the takeoff. They were unable to pinpoint the cause of the crash.

A Puerto Rico Ports Authority official said that beside Clemente, the occupants of the plane were the pilot, Jerry Geisel; the copilot and owner, Arthur Rivera; the flight engineer, Rafael Matias, and a radio newsman identified only by his last name, Lozano.

A Federal Aviation Administration of-
(Cont'd on Page 2, Column 1)

Pittsburgh Pirate superstar Roberto Clemente, 38, killed flying mercy mission to victims of earthquake.

'The Great One' Is Dead
Tragedy Evokes Tears,

Peace Talks To Be Marked

S. Vietnam Cease-Fires End
U.S. Switches Raids

He concluded by calling for a moment of silence from the crowd.

Hernández Colón, at the end of his address, acknowledged:

> "In my greeting there is also my sympathy with Puerto Rico's bereavement today on the death of our Roberto Clemente. ... Our youth have lost an idol and an example. Our people have lost one of their glories. All our hearts are saddened by his tragic parting in a mission of aid to the victims of Nicaragua."[5]

New York City Mayor John Lindsay gifted the newly inaugurated Governor Hernández Colón a plaque that read:

> "There are many things that bind the eight million people of New York and the people of Puerto Rico

together. None of them are more outstanding today than the grief felt over the loss of Roberto Clemente, an outstanding baseball player and humanitarian."[6]

Pittsburgh Mayor Peter F. Flaherty on January 2 proclaimed Roberto Clemente Week. During this time of remembrance, a portrait of Clemente hung in the lobby of the City-County Building in downtown Pittsburgh.[7]

The White House issued the following statement by President Richard M. Nixon on January 2:

> "Every sports fan admired and respected Roberto Clemente as one of the greatest baseball players of our time. In the tragedy of his untimely death, we are reminded that he deserved even greater respect and admiration for his splendid qualities as a generous and kind human being.

He sacrificed his life on a mission of mercy. The best memorial we can build to his memory is to contribute generously for the relief of those he was trying to help – the earthquake victims in Nicaragua."[8]

In a White House ceremony in May, Clemente's widow, Vera, accepted the Presidential Citizens Medal from President Nixon on behalf of her late husband. The medal recognizes "citizens of the United States of America who have performed exemplary deeds of service for their country or their fellow citizens" (per Executive Order 11494; November 13, 1969).

Anastasio Somoza, the Nicaraguan dictator, whose acts of corruption against his own citizens had prompted Clemente's own desire to travel to Nicaragua himself to ensure the delivery of resources to those who needed them the most, sent a cable expressing his condolences to the Clemente family. Somoza stated, "He died a hero, leaving his family in order to aid humanity."[9]

RESPONSE FROM MAJOR LEAGUE BASEBALL

After his death, Pirates players Manny Sanguillén, Bob Johnson, and Rennie Stennett, along with Governor Ferré traveled to Clemente's hometown and offered their support to his family: Vera and the couple's three young sons, Roberto Jr., Luis Roberto, and Roberto Enrique.[10]

One of Clemente's closest teammates on the Pirates was Manny Sanguillén. Clemente had taken the young Sanguillén under his wing during his rookie season in 1967. Sanguillén was from Panama. He and Clemente had shared similar experiences, a kinship, both being from Latin America. The death of Clemente was especially hard for him.

Instead of attending Clemente's funeral, he joined a search party that went looking for victims of the crash. Despite rough waters and no diving experience, Sanguillén felt compelled to look for Clemente. He went back to the beach several times in the weeks after the crash. As he noted later, "God sent [Clemente] so people would realize that Latinos were talented."[11]

Of his efforts, Sanguillén lamented: "I [kept going back] to see if the ocean had brought him back."[12]

Teammate Steve Blass noted Sanguillén's efforts:

"It was so genuine, his reaction. We're at the memorial, and he's down at the beach, still not being able to tear himself away from the proximity, as close as he could get to where the tragedy happened."[13]

At Clemente's funeral in Puerto Rico, Blass concluded his eulogy by noting:

Let this be a silent token
Of lasting friendship's gleam,
And all that we've left unspoken
– Your friends on the Pirate team.[14]

Blass added, "Roberto Clemente touched us all and we're all better players and people for having known him. I think we all learned from him."[15]

From his home in Greenwich, Connecticut, pitcher Tom Seaver commented that Clemente was "emotional, sincere, a compassionate type of person," adding, "I could not believe what I heard on the radio, that he was gone. It was just chills, period. It's a horrible loss, not only to his family and teammates but to all of us, especially the young players. I mean, you look up to Henry Aaron and Sandy Koufax and Roberto Clemente."[16]

Baseball Commissioner Bowie Kuhn commented: "Words seem futile in the face of this tragedy, nor can they possibly do justice to this unique man. Somehow, Roberto transcended superstardom. His marvelous playing skills rank him among the truly elite. And what a wonderfully good man he was. Always concerned about others. He had about him a touch of royalty."[17]

Kuhn, like many others, saw Clemente as a gentleman, dignified in his actions and one who cared about others.

Pirates chairman of the board John Galbreath echoed a similar sentiment, commenting: "He was one of the greatest persons I knew. If you have to die, how better could your death be exemplified than by being on a mission of mercy? It was so typical of the man. Every time I was down there, someone was always saying how he contributed to the youth and needy of his island; how he was going to make that his life's work. He did these things without fanfare or anything – just what he thought was right to help somebody else."[18]

Clemente's longtime manager with the Pirates, Danny Murtaugh, commented, "It was so typical that he'd meet his death in such a fashion – helping people less fortunate. ... I thought Roberto was the greatest player I've ever seen."[19]

With tears in his eyes, Willie Stargell said, "Pittsburgh lost a heck of a man. ... Clemente's work with the relief effort was typical. Roberto was always trying to help someone."[20]

Around baseball, people similarly commented on Clemente's athletic greatness. Oakland A's manager Dick Williams said, "Clemente was the greatest player I have ever watched." Los Angeles Dodgers pitcher Jim Brewer said, "Clemente was a fantastic outfielder, the best hitter in the National League and someone who constantly gave everybody fits."[21]

On January 2 Jack Lang, the secretary of the Baseball Writers' Association of America, noted that there was precedent for Clemente's immediate enshrinement in the National Baseball Hall of Fame. A waiver on the waiting period of enshrinement had been issued in 1939 for the ailing Lou Gehrig.[22]

Joe Heiling, the president of the BBWAA, commented: "We consider Clemente like Stan Musial and Sandy Koufax. He would have been elected and inducted in his first year as an eligible. So why wait." Immediate plans were to set a meeting with Commissioner Kuhn and Paul Kerr, the president of the Baseball Hall of Fame, to decide how to move forward.[23]

Within a few months of his death, on March 20, 1973, Clemente was elected to the Hall of Fame, following a special election in which the five-year waiting period was waived. Other inductees that year were Monte Irvin, George Kelly, Mickey Welch, Billy Evans, and Warren Spahn.

Later in 1973, the Commissioner's Award, presented annually by Major League Baseball to honor a major-league player for his sportsmanship, community involvement, and contributions in the community and on the field, was renamed the Roberto Clemente Award. Since 2002 the major leagues also celebrate Roberto Clemente Day in September.

RESPONSE FROM CITIZENS

In Puerto Rico immediately after the crash, many people went to a beach area close to the airport from which Clemente's plane had taken off. His friend and former major-league pitcher José Santiago noted: "[I]t was packed with people. It was devastating news for everybody. People were going, 'Are you sure he boarded the plane? Maybe he didn't.' Or claiming, 'Oh, he's got to be alive.' Some would say, 'He's clinging to a rock in one of those little islands out there.'"[24]

The thought of their national hero dead was devastating for Puerto Ricans. Radio stations all over the island canceled regular programming, instead opting for somber music in remembrance of Clemente.[25]

Hector Lopez, a childhood friend of Clemente's, later remembered: "The country was completely paralyzed by the news. ... The holiday season ended. People took down their Christmas trees and went into a national mourning."[26]

Soon after news of Clemente's death came, some Pittsburgh area residents began circulating a petition to rename Three Rivers Stadium, the Pirates' home ballpark, Roberto Clemente Memorial Stadium.[27] The local Mellon Foundation donated $100,000 to earthquake victims in Nicaragua in Clemente's name.

Ironically, Clemente in death was extolled to a far greater extent than when he was alive. Clemente biographer David Maraniss wrote: "After Clemente died, he was martyred in Pittsburgh and everyone said they loved him, but that was not the case when he was alive. He had to overcome a lot in terms of race and language in Pittsburgh, and did not really win the city over completely until he died."[28]

Wells Twombly, a sports columnist for the San Francisco Examiner, wrote, "No athlete of Clemente's quality has been taken for granted quite so shamelessly. ... Roberto just couldn't make the game of baseball look hard enough."[29]

Twombly added, "Trouble was that Roberto Clemente could never communicate his true self. It was his opinion that newspapermen had a stringent pecking order. They regarded baseball players in the following way: On top were the American whites, followed rapidly by the American blacks. Next were the Latin whites. Way down at the bottom were the Latin blacks. They were nobody's children."[30]

Similarly, the Black Panthers, noting how Clemente was seemingly misunderstood by many, ran an obituary in their newspaper thanking him supporting their breakfast programs and health clinics operated in Philadelphia. The obituary concluded: "It is ironic that the profession in which he achieved 'legendry' knew him the least. Roberto Clemente did not, as the Commissioner of Baseball maintained, 'Have about him a touch of royalty.' Roberto Clemente was simply a man, a man who strove to achieve his dream of peace and justice for oppressed people throughout the world."[31]

Clemente's death also brought about quick memorialization in song. Paul New Stewart wrote "The Ballad of Roberto Clemente" and Ramito, a Puerto Rican country singer, released the album Ramito Canta a Clemente – la Tragedia de Nicaragua [Ramito Sings to Clemente – The Tragedy of Nicaragua].[32]

While responses to Clemente's death were both varied and ubiquitous, a through line of all the responses was the respect people felt for Clemente, whether they knew him well or not. His athletic prowess, his willingness to fight for justice, and his ability to help others showed that he meant different things to different people. It was, however, Clemente's premature death that cemented his legacy as an icon.

SOURCES

In addition to the sources cited in the Notes, information was gathered from Baseball-Reference.com and Baseball-Alamanac.com.

NOTES

1   Rob Biertempfel, "What If ... Roberto Clemente Had Played 3 More Seasons With the Pirates?," *The Athletic*, August 18, 2021. https://theathletic.com/2765112/2021/08/18/what-if-roberto-clemente-had-played-three-more-seasons-with-the-pirates/.

2   Sam Goldaper, "Puerto Rico Goes into Mourning," *New York Times*, January 2, 1973. https://www.nytimes.com/1973/01/02/archives/puerto-rico-goes-into-mourning-the-reactions-greatest-player.html.

3   "Death of Clemente Casts a Pall Over Inauguration of Puerto Rico's 4th Elected Governor," *New York Times*, January 3, 1973. https://www.nytimes.com/1973/01/03/archives/death-of-clemente-casts-a-pall-over-inauguration-of-puerto-ricos.html.

4   "Death of Clemente Casts a Pall Over Inauguration of Puerto Rico's 4th Elected Governor."

5   "Death of Clemente Casts a Pall Over Inauguration of Puerto Rico's 4th Elected Governor."

6   "Death of Clemente Casts a Pall Over Inauguration of Puerto Rico's 4th Elected Governor."

7   "Fame Niche Sought for Clemente," *New York Times*, January 3, 1973. https://www.nytimes.com/1973/01/03/archives/fame-niche-sought-for-clemente-clementes-niche-in-hall-of-fame-in.html.

8   Richard Nixon, "Statement About the Death of Roberto Clemente," online by Gerhard Peters and John T. Woolley, the American Presidency Project. https://www.presidency.ucsb.edu/documents/statement-about-the-death-roberto-clemente.

9   Goldaper, "Puerto Rico Goes into Mourning."

10 Goldaper.

11 Nathalie Alonso, "He Braved Ocean, Sharks to Search for Clemente," MLB.com, April 16, 2020. https://www.mlb.com/news/roberto-clemente-manny-sanguillen-friendship.

12 Alonso.

13 Alonso.

14 Bob Hurte, "Steve Blass," Society for American Baseball Research BioProject. https://sabr.org/bioproj/person/steve-blass/.

15 Goldaper, "Puerto Rico Goes into Mourning."

16 Joseph Durso, "A Man of Two Worlds," *New York Times*, January 2, 1973. https://www.nytimes.com/1973/01/02/archives/a-man-of-two-worlds-clemente-as-deeply-pledged-to-civic-concerns-in.html.

17 Goldaper, "Puerto Rico Goes into Mourning."

18 Goldaper.

19 Goldaper.

20 Goldaper.

21 Goldaper.

22 "Fame Niche Sought for Clemente."

23 "Fame Niche Sought for Clemente,"

24 Jorge L. Ortiz, "Clemente's Impact Wanes in Puerto Rico 40 Years After His Death," USA Today, December 27, 2012. https://www.usatoday.com/story/sports/mlb/2012/12/27/roberto-clemente-40th-anniversary-death-plane-crash-puerto-rico-pirates-humanitarian/1794453/.

25 Goldaper, "Puerto Rico Goes into Mourning."

26 Ortiz.

27 "Fame Niche Sought for Clemente."

28 Harold Friend, "MLB History: Jon Matlack Didn't Know He'd Given Up Roberto Clemente's 3,000th Hit," Bleacher Report, July 8, 2011. https://bleacherreport.com/articles/761414-amazing-jon-matlack-didnt-know-he-had-given-up-roberto-clementes-3000-hit.

29 Wells Twombly, "Super Hero," *San Francisco Examiner*, January 2, 1973.

30 Twombly.

31 Zinn Education Project, "This Day in History: Dec. 31, 1972: Roberto Clemente Dies." https://www.zinnedproject.org/news/tdih/roberto-clemente-dies/.

32 Judy Cantor-Navas, "Remember Baseball Great Roberto Clemente With These Musical Tributes," *Billboard*, December 28, 2017. https://www.billboard.com/music/latin/roberto-clemente-death-anniversary-musical-tributes-8085490/.

BASEBALL REBEL: ROBERTO CLEMENTE

BY ROBERT ELIAS AND PETER DREIER

Robert Clemente was not the first Latino to play major-league baseball, but he was the first Latino superstar. He saw that as both a responsibility and an opportunity. Like Jackie Robinson, he used his athletic celebrity to speak out on behalf of social and racial justice. And like Robinson, he faced racism and pushback from owners, fans, sportswriters, and even some fellow players.

Clemente made his major-league debut in April 1955. Besides his solid hitting, he performed exceptionally on the basepaths and defensively in the outfield, routinely throwing out runners. Clemente introduced an exciting, rambunctious style of play, which endeared him to the fans but also made him more susceptible to injuries. In 1960 he was selected for his first of 15 All-Star Game appearances and helped lead the Pirates to the World Series and to their upset victory over the Yankees. Clemente won the first of his four batting titles in 1961 (with a .351 average) and an MVP Award in 1966. In 1968 he injured his shoulder and had such a hard time swinging the

bat that he thought he'd have to retire. He rallied, however, making a comeback in 1969, hitting a NL second-best .345. In 1971 Clemente again led the Pirates to the World Series. He starred in the seven-game upset of the Baltimore Orioles, hitting .414, and winning the Series MVP. In 1972 Clemente reached 3,000 hits in his next-to-last game of the season, a feat surpassed by only 10 other major leaguers at the time.[1] For his career, Clemente hit over .300 13 times and ended his career with a .317 average, 240 home runs, 1,305 RBIs, and 12 Gold Gloves.

Born in 1934 in Carolina, Puerto Rico, Clemente starred as an all-around athlete in high school. His arm was so strong that he became an Olympic prospect throwing the javelin. But he loved baseball and attracted the attention of Brooklyn Dodgers scout Al Campanis at a San Juan tryout in 1952. After an outstanding 1953 season with the Santurce Crabbers in the Puerto Rican League, the New York Giants and Milwaukee Braves offered Clemente a contract, but he signed with the Dodgers instead in 1954. Under rules at the time, Clemente received a signing bonus that required the Dodgers to keep him on their major-league roster or risk losing him in the offseason draft. Bonus players often just sat on the big-league bench when otherwise they could be gaining experience playing in the minors.

The Dodgers took a chance on losing Clemente by sending him to their Montreal Royals farm team in the International League for the 1954 season. The Royals put Clemente in the lineup for only 87 of their 155 games. Some argue that they did so to hide his skills from other clubs, especially the Dodgers' archrival, the Giants, that might claim him at the end of the season. Others speculate that Clemente wasn't elevated immediately to Brooklyn because they had a quota for Black players.

Clemente struggled initially in Montreal, but his performance improved by the season's end. The Dodgers knew that the Pittsburgh Pirates – by then run by former Brooklyn general manager Branch Rickey – had their eye on Clemente. Dodgers GM Buzzie Bavasi struck a deal with Rickey (his former boss) to have the Pirates draft another player off the Royals roster. Since each minor-league team could lose only one player, Clemente would be protected. But the deal fell through and Clemente became a Pirate after all. In the offseason, Clemente returned to the Santurce Crabbers, joined by Willie Mays in the outfield. Clemente enjoyed a sensational season and the two players led the team to the Caribbean Series championship. Near the end of the winter season, an automobile accident damaged Clemente's back. It would hinder him for the rest of his baseball career.

Clemente bristled over the racist way that sportswriters covered him. Clemente was frequently hurt and sometimes required surgery. He suffered damaged discs, bone chips, pulled muscles, a strained instep, a thigh hematoma, tonsillitis, malaria, stomach problems, and insomnia. Even so, between 1955 and 1972 he played more games than anyone in Pirates history.

Yet some sportswriters, teammates, and managers repeatedly accused him of being lazy or faking injuries if he missed a game. To the contrary, Clemente repeatedly played through pain, and excelled nevertheless. According to Pirates trainer Tony Bartirome, Clemente "... wasn't a hypochondriac, he was a fighter." When a White player pushed through injuries, he was regarded as a hero. "Mickey Mantle is God," Clemente observed, "but if a Latin or black is sick, they say it is in his head."[2] Clemente fought constantly against negative stereotypes of emotional and lackadaisical Latinos.

The racism extended to the names the sportswriters used to identify him. They called him Bobby or Bob, instead of his preferred name, Roberto. Baseball card companies and other merchandisers followed suit even through the end of his career. White players were always asked what they wanted to be called. Sportswriters also made fun of his accent, quoted him in broken English, and paid little attention to his powerful intellect and social conscience. He knew little English when he joined the majors, and naturally spoke with a Spanish accent. After winning the 1961 All-Star Game for the National League, for example, Clemente was quoted as: "I get heet. ... When I come to plate in lass eening ... I say I 'ope that Weelhelm [Hoyt Wilhelm] peetch me outside. ..."[3]

Reporters corrected grammatical mistakes in English for White players all the time, but routinely made Latinos look ignorant, even a highly intelligent thinker like Clemente. The sportswriters thought nothing about not speaking Spanish themselves despite the growing presence of Latinos in major-league baseball.

Despite his stellar play for the Pirates' 1960 World Series champions (.314 average, 16 homers, and 94 RBIs), he placed only eighth in the MVP balloting for an award bestowed on his White teammate Dick Groat. Given the racism he'd experienced throughout his time in the majors, he couldn't help feeling that it influenced the voting. Clemente wasn't a hometown favorite like Groat. Some baseball writers viewed him as brash and moody for speaking his mind, and speaking in Spanish. Clemente believed that Latino players like him didn't receive the recognition they deserved, and he publicly complained about it.

Clemente played in the Puerto Rican League most offseasons, mostly for the Senadores de San Juan, which he also managed in 1964. He felt obliged to play for his Puerto Ricans fans. As Stew Thornley has noted, Clemente was "perhaps the most inspirational figure the island has ever known, and he took that responsibility seriously."[4]

In the 1970-1971 offseason, he managed the Senadores again, competing against Santurce, managed by future Hall of Famer Frank Robinson. Both were top candidates to be the first Black manager in the major leagues, which Robinson achieved in 1975 with the Cleveland Indians.

Clemente was a proud Black man, Puerto Rican, and American. From 1958 to 1964 he served in the Marine Corps Reserve. Coming from Puerto Rico, a more racially integrated island, he was shocked by the segregation he encountered in mainland America, especially during spring training in the Jim Crow South. Black players on the Pirates during Florida spring training in the late 1950s and early 1960s couldn't stay in the same hotels or eat in the same restaurants as their White teammates. While on the road, White teammates had to bring their food out to the team bus. Clemente refused to sit and wait on the bus. He demanded that the Pirates provide Black players with another vehicle so they could drive to Black restaurants where they would be served. He and other Black players were also excluded from the Pirates' annual spring golf tournament at a local country club, while their White teammates participated.

During Clemente's playing days, Pittsburgh had a large Black population but few Latinos.[5] The prejudice against Latinos came not only from the fans and the media, but also his teammates, who used racial slurs when referring to Clemente and other Latino players. He occasionally confronted his bigoted White teammates. Clemente said, "I don't believe in color; I believe in people. I always respect everyone, and thanks to God my mother and my father taught me to never hate, never to dislike someone because of their color. I didn't know about racism when I got to Pittsburgh."[6] Nevertheless, the racism he faced turned "a mild, kind man into a blunt and angry one," wrote biographer Mike Freeman.[7]

Clemente refused to be treated as a second-class citizen, repeatedly protesting Jim Crow segregation. When he encountered racism and stereotypes, he fought back vocally and visibly, even when that made him a bigger target. Clemente pushed back when a reporter called him a "chocolate-covered islander" or when sportswriters otherwise mocked him personally or questioned his abilities. He was confident of his abilities, insisting that "nobody does anything better than me in baseball."[8] Some Whites resented his directness but he demanded their respect.

As MLB.com columnist Joe Posnanski wrote, Clemente "... did rage. In this way, he was like one of his heroes, Jackie Robinson. He was unwilling to simply accept what he saw as injustice."[9] Clemente refused to remain silent. "You writers are all the same," he shouted at one critical reporter. "You don't know a damn thing about me."[10] Clemente didn't want to merely represent Latin Americans; he wanted to improve their lives. He always said: "Remember who paved the way for you," and he paid tribute to Puerto Rican pioneers in major-league baseball like Hiram Bithorn and Luis Olmo.[11]

According to his wife, Vera, Clemente talked "a lot about how being a black Latin coming into baseball meant you had two strikes against you. He wanted the Latino players to get their fair share of the money. He wanted them to be managers ... to get respect."[12] According to Pirates trainer Tony Bartirome, Clemente saw his quest to improve things for the Latin and Black player as "his small way of changing the country for the better."[13]

Clemente was angered by double standards. "When the sportswriters write about a black or Hispanic player, it's always something controversial. When they write about white players, it's usually nice – human interest stuff." He liked to think he made some progress against that practice. "I believe that every human being is equal, but one has to fight hard all the time to maintain that equality. Always, they would say you'd really have to be something to be like Babe Ruth. But Babe Ruth was an American player. What we needed was a Puerto Rican player they could say that about, someone to look up to and try to equal."[14]

In 1970, at Roberto Clemente Night at Three Rivers Stadium, Clemente declared: "I have achieved this triumph for us, the Latinos. I believe it is a matter of pride for all of us, the Puerto Ricans as well as others in the Caribbean because we are all brothers."[15]

Clemente pushed the Pirates to hire more players of color and they listened. By the early 1970s, half the Pittsburgh roster was Black, Latino, or Spanish-speaking, and in 1971, for the first time in National or American League history, the Pirates fielded an all-Black and Latino lineup, thanks largely to Clemente.

Clemente played his entire career with the Pirates, from 1955 to 1972, during the peak of civil-rights activism. He closely followed the movement and identified with its struggles. He witnessed a speech Martin Luther King Jr. gave at a university in San Germán in February 1962.[16] They later became friends. They met often, including a long visit on Clemente's farm on the outskirts of Carolina, Puerto Rico, where they discussed King's philosophy of nonviolence and racial integration. Clemente voiced these ideas both inside and outside the clubhouse. As

teammate Al Oliver recalled: "Our conversations always stemmed around people from all walks of life being able to get along. He had a problem with people who treated you differently because of where you were from, your nationality, your color; also poor people, how they were treated."[17]

King was assassinated in Memphis on Thursday, April 4, 1968, during the last week of baseball's spring training. His funeral was scheduled for Tuesday, April 9, the day after opening day. Immediately, the NBA and NHL suspended their playoff games. Racetracks shut down for the weekend. The North American Soccer League called off games. But major-league baseball waffled. After many players sat out the last few games of spring training to honor King, several owners insisted that Commissioner William Eckert penalize them for refusing to play. But Eckert was more concerned about the start of the regular season.

Clemente was upset that Eckert announced that each team could decide for itself whether it would play games scheduled for Opening Day and the day of King's funeral. Some team owners, torn over what to do, approached their Black players to feel the pulse of their employees.

In response, Clemente observed that "[i]f you have to ask Negro players, then we do not have a great country."[18]

King's murder triggered rebellions in a number of cities with major-league teams. Two teams, the Washington Senators and Cincinnati Reds, postponed their home openers because their stadiums were near the protests. But Houston Astros owner Roy Hofheinz, a businessman and former Houston mayor, insisted that his team would play its opener against the Pirates – the third game scheduled for April 8. "Our fans are counting on it," explained Astros vice president Bill Giles.[19] Under baseball rules, as the visiting team, the Pirates were required to play if the Astros wanted the game to go on.

Courtesy of The Clemente Museum.

On Friday, April 5, the next to last day of spring training in Richmond, Virginia, the Pirates players met in the hotel room of first baseman Donn Clendenon, who at King's urging had attended Morehouse College and who taught school with King's sister, to discuss what to do. The first meeting was attended by all 11 Black players (six of them also Latino), more than any other major-league team. At that meeting, veteran third baseman Maury Wills urged his teammates to refuse to play on Opening Day and the following day, when America would be watching or listening to King's funeral.

The following day, all 25 players came to the meeting at the ballpark. The Black players explained that they had decided to boycott the two games. After Clemente urged his teammates to support Wills' idea, they took a vote. They unanimously supported the idea. Clemente and Dave Wickersham, a White pitcher, contacted Pirates general manager Joe Brown and asked him to postpone the season's first two games. The two players wrote a public statement on behalf of their teammates, which was included in the *Pittsburgh Press* story about the protest the next day: "We are doing this because we (white and black players) respect what Dr, King has done for mankind. Dr. King was not only concerned with Negroes or whites but also poor people. We owe this gesture to his memory and his ideals."[20] Clendenon and Willie Stargell walked into the Astros' locker room and persuaded the Black players to join the protest. The other players agreed and informed the Houston brass: They would not play the first two games, until after King was buried.

St. Louis Cardinals pitcher Bob Gibson and some of his teammates had the same idea. They met in first baseman Orlando Cepeda's apartment and then told Cardinals management that they wouldn't play on April 9, Opening Day for most of the teams. Players on other teams followed their lead. The Los Angeles Dodgers' Walter O'Malley was the last owner to hold out, but when the Phillies players refused to take the field against the Dodgers, his hands were tied. Commissioner Eckert, his back against the wall, reluctantly moved all Opening Day games to April 10. No sportswriter at the time described the players' action as a strike. But that's what it was – a two-day walkout, not over salaries and pensions, but over social justice.

Besides being concerned about racial injustice, Clemente was also a strong proponent of workers' rights and labor unions. He played an important role in the battle to dismantle baseball's reserve clause. He was the Pirates' player representative to the Major League Baseball Players Association and a close ally of Marvin Miller, whom players hired as the union's first executive director in 1966. Three years later, the St. Louis Cardinals traded their star outfielder Curt Flood to the Philadelphia Phillies. Flood didn't want to move to Philadelphia, which he called "the nation's northernmost southern city."[21] The Phillies offered him a $100,000 salary for the 1970 season, a $10,000 boost from his Cardinals salary. But for Flood, it was a matter of principle. He objected to being treated like a piece of property and to the reserve clause's restriction on his (and other players') freedom.

Flood talked with Miller about the possibility of suing in order to overturn the reserve clause. In 1922, in a case called *Federal Baseball Club v. National League*, the U.S. Supreme Court ruled that the Sherman Anti-Trust Act, which was intended to prevent collusion and monopolistic practices by business, did not apply to baseball. The court claimed that baseball was an "amusement" rather than a business engaged in interstate commerce, and thus was exempt from the federal antitrust law. The ruling allowed major-league baseball owners to operate as a monopoly, with teams colluding to deny players their right to bargain with prospective employers. Many scholars believed that this was one of the high court's worst decisions, but it remained in force a half-century later.[22] It was as if, Miller once observed, "the courts were saying, 'Yes, you're an American and have the right to seek employment anywhere you like, but this right does not apply to baseball players.'"[23]

Miller warned Flood that the odds were against him. He pointed out that a lawsuit would be expensive and could take two or more years. Moreover, Miller said, even if he won the lawsuit, he'd probably be unemployable in major-league baseball; the owners would blacklist him as a player and as a future coach or manager. Miller recalled, "I said to Curt, 'Unless some miracle takes place and the Supreme Court reverses itself, you're not going to win,' and Curt, to his everlasting credit, said, 'But would it benefit all the other players and future players?' And I said, 'Yes.' And he said, 'That's good enough for me.'"[24]

At the urging of Clemente, the players union held its annual executive committee meeting in San Juan, Puerto Rico, in early December of 1969. Miller invited Flood to the meeting at the Sheraton Hotel to seek the union's financial and moral support for his lawsuit. Many of the players were skeptical of Flood's idea to sue. After all, two previous legal challenges – by New York Giants outfielder Danny Gardella in 1949 and Yankees minor leaguer George Toolson in 1953 – had failed. Tom Haller, the Dodgers All-Star catcher, bluntly asked Flood if his decision to challenge his trade was based on race. "I didn't want it to be just a black thing," Haller recalled. "I wanted it to be a baseball thing."[25] Flood responded that while being Black no doubt made him more sensitive to injustice, he was doing this for all ballplayers, regardless of color.

The tide turned after Clemente spoke out on Flood's behalf. He declared that Flood was the only player with the courage to take on the owners and the reserve clause. "So far, no one is doing anything," he said.[26]

Clemente explained how as a minor leaguer he'd had turned down a much bigger bonus offer from the Milwaukee Braves because he wanted to played for the Brooklyn Dodgers. He was upset when the Dodgers allowed him to be drafted by the Pirates without any say in the matter because of the reserve clause. He would have preferred to play in New York, with its large Puerto Rican population, rather than Pittsburgh, a more racist city for Latinos. He even offered to refund the Pirates $4,000 in exchange for his freedom, but Joe Brown, the Pirates' general manager, refused. "He had me," Clemente told his fellow players on the union's executive committee. He estimated that over his career with the Pirates, the team had "made $300,000 on me.[27] Clemente no doubt lost lucrative commercial endorsement opportunities in the smaller and whiter Pittsburgh region.

Clemente was one of the few players on the executive committee who was earning at least $100,000.[28] The players understood that Clemente – like Flood – was speaking on behalf of them, younger players, and future players. "Roberto was respected by everyone," recalled Dick Moss, the MLBPA's lawyer. "He was very important to us."[29]

After Clemente spoke, Miller repeated his recommendation that the MLBPA support the lawsuit of their fellow player and union member. The players voted unanimously to back Flood's lawsuit.[30]

Clemente once observed that: "If you have a chance to help others and fail to do so, you are wasting your time on this earth."[31] His activism went beyond fighting against racism and for players' rights. Besides sponsoring philanthropies to distribute food, medical supplies, and baseball equipment, Clemente focused particularly on children. He routinely visited sick kids in hospitals and held frequent baseball clinics for low-income children. He campaigned to use sports to counter drug problems in Puerto Rico and elsewhere. Most ambitiously, he began building a Sports City in Puerto Rico, seeking to replicate it throughout the United States to provide athletics and counseling but also intercity and interracial exchanges to challenge all forms of discrimination.

A lasting bond between Clemente and the Nicaraguan people also began in the 1963-1964 offseason when Clemente played winter ball for the Senadores de San Juan, who represented Puerto Rico in the International Series in Managua, Nicaragua. Clemente became a fan favorite during the series, making many friends and pledging to return.

In 1971 West Point graduate Anastasio Somoza Jr., the third in a succession of US-backed Somoza dictators, canceled Nicaraguan Winter League baseball. However, the Nicaraguan national amateur team thrived. The following year, in front of euphoric home crowds in Estadio Nacional, the amateur team led by future major leaguers Dennis Martinez and Tony Chevez captured a bronze medal in the World Amateur Baseball Championships (WABC), including upsets over perennial champions Cuba and the United States. Those victories sparked national celebration. One of Nicaragua's proudest and most memorable moments was upended three weeks later when a massive earthquake struck Nicaragua, killing nearly 10,000 people and destroying half of Managua.

Clemente had just been in Nicaragua, managing the Puerto Rican team at the WABC games and making more friends in the country, many of whom were poor and needed help. Back home in San Juan, he decided to help the recovery, using the media to organize a massive campaign of food, clothing, and medical assistance. Funded by Clemente, two cargo planes and a freighter began delivering the Puerto Rican aid. But soon word got out that Somoza was siphoning off the international aid flowing into Managua (including $30 million from the United States) and stockpiling it for his corrupt government. President Nixon dispatched a battalion of US paratroopers to Managua, which only further helped Somoza

loot the country. Nixon claimed he didn't want the earthquake to provide opportunities for communists.

Clemente learned that when a private American medical team arrived in Managua, it had to fight local Somoza officials from confiscating the supplies it brought. When Clemente discovered that Somoza was diverting other aid, he was enraged and vowed to personally deliver the relief he had gathered. Well-known and respected in Nicaragua, Clemente believed his presence would ensure that the aid would get to the people who needed it.

On December 31, 1972, the 38-year-old ballplayer boarded a broken-down and overloaded plane. Some warned him against making the trip, but he said, "[B]abies are dying. They need these supplies." Claiming that "the people in charge know what they're doing," Clemente may nevertheless have suspected something was wrong with the plane, but said: "I have to go. I have to make sure everything's okay in Nicaragua."[32] Several minutes after takeoff, the plane crashed into the Atlantic Ocean, killing Clemente and four others.

After Clemente's death, Nixon proposed a Roberto Clemente Memorial Fund, even though the president's support for the dictator Somoza and US foreign policy's long-standing oppression of Nicaragua led directly to Clemente's demise. In 1973 Nixon hosted the Clemente family survivors in the White House, posthumously bestowing the first-ever Presidential Citizen's Medal on the fallen star. Clemente would have likely bristled at Nixon's words: "The best memorial we can build to his memory is to contribute generously ... to those he was trying to help ... in Managua in Nicaragua, one of our friends to the south. [T]hat is the way Roberto Clemente would have wanted it."[33]

As David Maraniss observed, Clemente became "universally loved and admired ... but it wasn't like that in his playing days."[34] It was "glorification after the fact." Clemente's memory was co-opted not only by Nixon, but by other pol-iticians he would have likely despised, including George W. Bush (who posthumously awarded him the Medal of Freedom).

More genuinely, the Pirates retired Clemente's number in 1973 and the Baseball Writers Asso-ciation of America waived the normal five-year waiting period to elect Clemente to the National Baseball Hall of Fame in 1973, the first Latino player ever inducted, if one excepts Ted Wil-liams, whose mother was Mexican-American.[35] The Office of the Commissioner established an annual Roberto Clemente Award (for community service) and a Roberto Clemente Day. In 1974 the Roberto Clemente Sports City opened in Puerto Rico and has since served hundreds of thousands of kids, including future major-league stars Juan González, Bernie Williams, and Iván Rodrí-guez. In 1998 the Sports City complex unveiled a bronze cenotaph, usually reserved for fallen military heroes, describing Clemente as "Son of

Carolina, Exemplary Citizen, Athlete, Philan-thropist, Teacher, Hero of the Americas and the World." Clemente has been honored by dozens of schools, hospitals, coins, stamps, post offices, bridges, parks, housing developments, ballparks, streets, and museums in his name in the United States, Puerto Rico, and Nicaragua.

For all his posthumous veneration, Clemente was, as Maraniss has observed, "no gentle giant or saint" but instead a "fierce critic of both baseball and American society."[36] Clemente's crusade should not be sanitized: "He ranks only behind Jackie Robinson among players whose sociologi-cal significance transcended the sport itself." He raised issues that remain relevant and unresolved to this day. "With the nativist strain in American politics resurgent," wrote Maraniss in 2016, "I wish Clemente were around to respond to ... Don-ald Trump and those who promote fear based on geography and language and race."[37]

NOTES

1   Clemente did appear in one more game on October 3, 1972, in the ninth inning as a defensive replacement, but he did not bat.

2   Clemente Family, with Mike Freeman, *Clemente: The True Legacy of an Undying Hero* (New York: Celebra, 2013), 34.

3   David Maraniss, "The Last Hero, Roberto Clemente, Baseball's Latin Legend," *Washington Post*, April 2, 2006, https://www.washingtonpost.com/archive/opinions/2006/04/02/the-last-hero-span-classbankheadroberto-clemente-baseballs-latino-legendspan/7c38584c-a70d-4ff1-9eea-1febd1c05402/.

4   Stew Thornley, *Roberto Clemente* (Minneapolis: Twenty-First Century Books, 2006), 56.

5   In 1960, Pittsburgh's population of 604,332 was 83.2 percent White, 6.7 percent Black, and less than one percent Hispanic. Campbell Gibson and Kay Jung, "Historical Census Statistics On Population Totals By Race, 1790 to 1990, and By Hispanic Origin, 1970 to 1990, For Large Cities And Other Urban Places In The United States," Washington, D.C. U.S. Census Bureau, Population Division, Working Paper No. 76, February 2005.

6   Matt Snyder, "Remembering Roberto Clemente, 40 Years After His Death," CBSSports.com, December 31, 2012, https://www.cbssports.com/mlb/news/remembering-roberto-clemente-40-years-after-his-death/.

7   Clemente Family, with Freeman, Clemente, 58.

8   C.B. Ways, "'Nobody Does Anything Better Than Me in Baseball,' Says Roberto Clemente," *New York Times*, April 9, 1972: SM38.

9   Joe Posnanski, "A Legacy Cherished: Remembering Roberto: Hall of Famer Synonymous with Heroism Thanks to Charitable Spirit, Baseball Feats," MLB.com, December 28, 2017, https://www.mlb.com/news/roberto-clemente-s-legacy-still-resonates-c264059654.

10 Posnanski, "A Legacy Cherished."

11 Mashkur Hussain, "The Great One," *The Ball Point*, August 26, 2017, https://theballpoint.org/the-great-one-11985eb949c4.

12 Peter Dreier, "Athletes' Racial Justice Protest Last Week Made History. But It Wasn't the First Wildcat Strike in Pro Sports," TalkingPointsMemo, September 3, 2020, https://talkingpointsmemo.com/cafe/athletes-racial-justice-protest-history-wasnt-first-wildcat-strike-pro-sports.

13 Clemente Family, with Freeman, Clemente, 35.

14 "Beyond Baseball: The Life of Roberto Clemente," Smithsonian Institution (http://www.robertoclemente.si.edu/english/virtual_legacy.htm).

15 Roger Bruns, *Finding Baseball's Next Clemente: Combatting Scandal in Latino Recruiting* (Santa Barbara, California: ABC-CLIO, 2015), 79.

16 Kevin Blackistone, "'More Than a Ballplayer': After MLK Shooting, Roberto Clemente Halted MLB Opening Day 1968," *Washington Post*, March 28, 2018, https://www.washingtonpost.com/sports/more-than-a-ballplayer-after-mlk-shooting-roberto-clemente-halted-mlb-opening-day-1968/2018/03/28/658f94b2-3289-11e8-8abc-22a366b72f2d_story.html.

17 David Maraniss, *Clemente: The Passion and Grace of Baseball's Last Hero* (New York: Simon & Schuster, 2006), 220.

18 Blackistone, "'More Than a Ballplayer.'"

19 John Florio and Ouisie Shapiro, "When King Died, Major League Baseball Struck Out," The Undefeated, April 4, 2018, https://theundefeated.com/features/when-martin-luther-king-died-major-league-baseball-struck-out/.

20 Les Biederman, "Pirate-Astro Opener Delayed," *Pittsburgh Press*, April 7, 1968.

21 Flood with Carter, 158.

22 Abrams, "Before the Flood"; Nathanson, "Who Exempted Baseball, Anyway?"; Mitchell Nathanson, interview with Peter Dreier, April 8, 2021.

23 Barra, "How Curt Flood Changed Baseball."

24 Kevin Blackistone, "Baseball's Hall of Fame Cannot Be Complete Without Curt Flood," *Washington Post*, December 25, 2019, https://www.washingtonpost.com/sports/mlb/baseballs-hall-of-fame-cannot-be-complete-without-curt-flood/2019/12/23/68e9a526-25b7-11ea-ad73-2fd294520e97_story.html

25 Snyder, *A Well-Paid Slave*, 76.

26 Maraniss, *Clemente*, 231.

27 Snyder, *A Well-Paid Slave*, 79.

28 David Maraniss's authoritative biography says that Clemente earned over $100,000 in 1969. But Baseball-Reference.com lists his salary that year as $45,000, although acknowledging that other sources indicate different salaries. Baseball Reference says he made $100,000 in 1970, so it is possible that he had signed a contract for that amount by the time of the December 1969 union meeting. https://www.baseball-reference.com/players/c/clemero01.shtml.

29 Maraniss, Clemente, 232.

30   On June 19, 1972, the Supreme Court ruled against Flood by a 5-3 vote. Writing the majority decision, Justice Harry Blackmun admitted that baseball's exemption from federal antitrust laws was an "aberration" but declared that it was up to Congress, not the court, to fix the situation. Miller found another way to dismantle the reserve clause. At the close of the 1975 season, he persuaded Los Angeles Dodgers pitcher Andy Messersmith and Montreal Expos pitcher Dave McNally to refuse to sign contracts with their teams, claiming that they were free agents because the reserve clause should only apply for one year. The union had already won the right to a three-person board to hear all grievances. On December 23, 1975, the neutral arbitrator Pete Seitz ruled in favor of Messersmith and McNally, agreeing with Miller that owners didn't have the right to perpetually renew contracts, that renewals could only be a one-time thing, and that players should be free to negotiate with another team.

31   "Roberto Clemente Quotes," Baseball-Almanac.com, https://www.baseball-almanac.com/quotes/roberto_clemente_quotes.shtml.

32   Clemente Family, with Freeman, Clemente, 78.

33   Richard Nixon, "Remarks at a Ceremony Honoring Roberto Clemente," The American Presidency Project (May 14, 1973), https://www.presidency.ucsb.edu/documents/remarks-ceremony-honoring-roberto-clemente.

34   David Maraniss, "No Gentle Saint: Roberto Clemente Was a Fierce Critic of Both Baseball and American Society," The Undefeated, May 31, 2016, https://theundefeated.com/features/roberto-clemente-was-a-fierce-critic-of-both-baseball-and-american-society/.

35   Williams never publicly acknowledged his Latino heritage, but it may have made him sensitive to racial bigotry. In his Hall of Fame induction speech in 1966, Williams made a plea for adding Negro League players to Cooperstown. See Bill Nowlin, Ted Williams – The First Latino in the Baseball Hall of Fame (Cambridge, Massachusetts: Rounder Books, 2018).

36   Maraniss, "No Gentle Saint."

37   Maraniss, "No Gentle Saint."

ROBERTO CLEMENTE —
THE FIRST PLAYER FROM LATIN AMERICA TO BE INDUCTED IN THE NATIONAL BASEBALL HALL OF FAME

BY BILL NOWLIN

In the immediate aftermath of Roberto Clemente's New Year's Eve plane crash while on a mercy mission to Nicaragua, there were calls for him to be inducted by acclamation into the National Baseball Hall of Fame. His qualifications were never questioned; he was only the 11th player to reach 3,000 base hits and was a 15-time All-Star. The only thing standing in the way was a Hall of Fame rule that a player cannot become eligible for induction until five years after his playing career ended.

On January 2, 1973, Joe Heiling, the president of the Baseball Writers' Association of America (BBWAA), said, "We feel that Clemente, like Sandy Koufax and Stan Musial, would be a first-ballot inductee, so why wait?" Secretary-treasurer Jack Lang said that BBWAA leadership had reached out to Commissioner Bowie Kuhn and that Kuhn had offered his "complete support."[1]

Joseph Durso of the New York Times wrote that Clemente "doubtlessly will become the first Latin player elected to baseball's Hall of Fame."[2]

And the Boston Globe's Harold Kaese wrote, with perhaps a bit more precision, "Prediction: Roberto Clemente will be the first Latin-American player in baseball's Hall of Fame."[3]

The sports editor of the Chicago Defender wrote that Clemente was "one of the many great black superstars, who never got the right break in the mainstream of publicity. But now that he is gone, his accomplishments on the field have assured him a sport in baseball's Hall of Fame."[4]

In the aftermath of Clemente's death, the board of directors of the Hall voted on January 3 to amend the eligibility rules.[5] An editorial in The Sporting News endorsed the idea, its final sentence reading, "If induction into the baseball shrine enhances Roberto's reputation, his name will add luster to the Hall of Fame, too."[6]

There were those who recommended not being so hasty. Among the first to speak out was Richard Dozer of the Chicago Tribune, who said he would vote against admission before the five-year period, giving a number of reasons, one of which was that Clemente's children would then be ages 13, 12, and 9 and would then better "realize the scope of the honor. All they know now is that Daddy's gone."[7]

Bob Broeg, writing in the *St. Louis Post-Dispatch*, noted how proud a man Clemente had been and suggested, "[T]he way I see it, to steamroller Roberto into the Hall of Fame now is really a disservice to the proud person who liked to feel that he was best in life, not in death."[8] Broeg argued that Clemente himself wouldn't be able to appreciate an induction ceremony and that "[f]ive years from now, all of us could benefit anew by renewing the faith, so to speak, by a reminder and restatement of the compassion and consideration of the outstanding athlete and humanitarian who died on a mission of mercy to the helpless and homeless of Managua."[9]

Those arguments notwithstanding, at a January 27 meeting, the Hall of Fame Committee of the BBWAA and the Hall of Fame Veterans Committee agreed to hold a special election.[10]

The results were reported in late March, 393 to 29 with two abstentions. It was the largest number of ballots cast in any Hall of Fame vote.[11]

The Associated Press story declared Clemente "the first Latin-American player voted into the Hall."[12]

The actual induction took place at Cooperstown on August 6, as part of the annual ceremony. Others inducted that day were pitcher Warren Spahn, the sole player elected in 1973,[13] Monte Irvin, voted in by a Special Committee on the Negro Leagues,[14] and three selected by the Veterans Committee: umpire and executive Billy Evans, George "Highpockets" Kelly, and Mickey Welch.

Vera Clemente attended the induction ceremonies, along with her mother-in-law and her three sons. Described as speaking with "her composure shaken and her voice cracking under the strain," she said, "This is Roberto's last triumph."[15] The *Los Angeles Sentinel* offered her comments in some detail.[16] Among those present was Mrs. Lou Gehrig.

THE FIRST LATIN AMERICAN PLAYER IN THE HALL OF FAME

Who was the first player from Latin America to be inducted into the National Baseball Hall of Fame?

Was it Ty Cobb, Walter Johnson, Christy Mathewson, Babe Ruth, or Honus Wagner? No, it was not. They were the first five inducted into the Hall of Fame, in the first class back in 1936. All were born in the continental United States.

The first person born outside the United States was inducted just two years later, in 1938 – Harry Chadwick, a pioneer/executive who came from Exeter, England.

In 1953, two more British natives were added to the Hall in the same class – executive Harry Wright (Sheffield) and umpire Tommy Connolly (Manchester). Wright had played baseball in Boston from 1871 to 1877.

In 1962 Jackie Robinson became the first Black ballplayer voted into the Hall.

Roberto Clemente had lived to see Satchel Paige added to the Hall of Fame in 1971, and both Josh Gibson and Buck Leonard added in 1972.

A native of Carolina, Puerto Rico, with his 1973 induction, Clemente was the first player from Latin America to be inducted into the Hall, via special election after his tragic death on December 31, 1972. As noted, also inducted in 1973 was Negro Leaguer and eight-year National League ballplayer Monte Irvin.

LATER PLAYERS FROM LATIN AMERICA IN THE HALL OF FAME

Four years after Clemente's induction, Martin Dihigo of Cidra, Cuba, was inducted in 1977. Had the five-year waiting period been maintained, Clemente would have first become eligible in 1978, and thus might have been the second Latin American inductee.

The mission Clemente had been on when he lost his life inspired many, in Puerto Rico, throughout Latin America, and around the world. With no disrespect to Martin Dihigo, honoring Clemente in the Hall of Fame in 1973 was part of an outpouring of activity that resulted in many tributes that produced good works of one kind or another, such as the construction of Ciudad Deportiva Roberto Clemente in Carolina, Puerto Rico (Roberto Clemente Sports City).

It was Clemente's dream to build such a sports complex, a dream that had been noted by the *New York Times* more than a year before his death.[17] As early as February 20, 1973, Vera Clemente announced the securing of a 602-acre site in Carolina, Clemente's hometown.[18] An article on the History.com website says, "The Roberto Clemente Sports City has served more than one million children, including future major leaguers Bernie Williams, Ivan Rodriguez, Juan Gonzalez, and Benito Santiago."[19]

After Clemente, it was 10 more years before the next player from Latin America was named to the Hall of Fame. Such players named since Clemente's induction are:

1983 – Juan Marichal, of Laguna Verde, Dominican Republic

1984 – Luis Aparicio, of Maracaibo, Venezuela

1991 – Rod Carew, of Gatun, Panama Canal Zone.

1999 - Orlando Cepeda, of Ponce, Puerto Rico

2000 – Tony Perez, of Camaguey, Cuba

2006 – Jose Mendez, of Cardenas, Cuba

2006 – Cristobal Torriente, of Cienfuegos, Cuba

2011 – Roberto Alomar, of Ponce, Puerto Rico

2015 – Pedro Martinez, of Manoguayabo, Dominican Republic

2017 – Ivan Rodriguez, of Manati, Puerto Rico

2018 – Vladimir Guerrero, of Nizao, Dominican Republic

2019 – Mariano Rivera, of Panama City, Panama

2022 – Orestes "Minnie" Miñoso, of La Habana, Cuba

2022 – Tony Oliva, of Pinar del Rio, Cuba

2022 – David Ortiz, of Santo Domingo, Dominican Republic

Edgar Martinez was born in New York City but raised in Puerto Rico. He was voted into the Hall of Fame in 2019.

One can be sure that many more will eventually be so honored, given the obvious demographics in major-league baseball over the past 25-plus years.

Recent reports state that Hispanic or Latino ballplayers make up around 30 percent of current major-league players.[20]

As perhaps a point of interest, four natives of other countries are enshrined in the Hall of Fame:

Fergie Jenkins (1991), born in Chatham, Ontario, Canada

Barney Dreyfuss (2008), born in Freiburg, Germany

Bert Blyleven (2011), born in Zeist, The Netherlands

Larry Walker (2021), born in Maple Ridge, British Columbia, Canada

SIDEBAR: FIRST LATIN PLAYER IN THE HALL OF FAME?

Ted Williams was inducted into the National Baseball Hall of Fame in 1966, seven years before Roberto Clemente. Joseph Durso – in an article written the very day it was learned that Clemente had been killed in the airplane crash – said that Clemente would without doubt become "the first Latin player" elected to the Hall of Fame. From the next day onward, newspaper accounts always referred to him as the "first Latin American player." Why the distinction? We don't know. Almost certainly, none of the writers had Ted

Williams in mind at the time. It was nearly 30 years later before that question was raised.

In 2002, I wrote an article for the *Boston Globe Magazine* entitled "El Splinter Esplendido, Ted Williams's Latino Heritage."[21] In it, I explored his family background, which included both maternal grandparents having been born in Mexico. He knew his grandmother Natalia Venzor, for whom Spanish remained her primary language. My research continued, and a much longer essay appeared in a book co-authored with eight other SABR members, *The Kid: Ted Williams in San Diego.*[22]

I ultimately devoted an entire book to the subject, building on that 2005 essay. Published in 2018, it was entitled *Ted Williams; First Latino in the Baseball Hall of Fame.*[23] Most of the rest of this sidebar is drawn from this 2018 book.

Awareness that Ted Williams had been Latino began to spread. The National Baseball Hall of Fame gift shop offered a T-shirt for a while that listed Latino Hall of Famers, with Ted Williams top of the list. A minor controversy arose in August 2005, when Major League Baseball didn't seem to have gotten the message. Richard Sandomir led a story in the *New York Times* writing, "When Major League Baseball unveiled its ballot for the Latino Legends team Tuesday, the 60 nominees excluded two of the greatest Hispanic players ever: Ted Williams and Reggie Jackson."[24] MLB argued that neither Williams nor Jackson were publicly linked to their Latino heritage, that they didn't "represent the Latin community." Sandomir wrapped up his article: "Jackson, whose grandmother was Puerto Rican, said he is 'proud of my Latin blood,' but not upset at being left off the ballot. But he is offended by any suggestion by baseball about his connection to those roots. 'They have no right to pass judgment on what I claim about my Latin heritage,' said Jackson, whose middle name is Martinez. 'I just don't run my mouth off about it.'"[25]

Photograph by Duane Rieder.

What was MLB's rationale? J.A. Marzán explained: "Sandomir cited Carmine Tiso, a baseball 'spokesperson,' who explained that lineage is not baseball's standard for identifying a player as Hispanic: '[Baseball] ... applied a litmus test that went beyond statistics: the nominees had to have a direct connection to their Latino heritage.' A second cited spokesman, Richard Levin, said the players should 'represent the Latin community.' Tiso added a defense of Williams: 'It's not that he was ashamed of his heritage, but we felt that we didn't find enough connection from Ted to that Latino heritage.' Levin appended an additional consideration: that Williams's name 'would distort the ballot' and 'cause havoc' because his ethnicity is not widely known."[26]

One could mock the notion of resultant "havoc," but the explanation offered by the Major League Baseball spokesmen shares similarity to that later rationally argued by scholar Adrian Burgos Jr. that Ted Williams should not be considered Latino because he "did not identify as

Latino nor was he racialized as such during his legendary career."[27] Ted hadn't had to anglicize his surname, suffer ridicule for his accent, or bear discrimination at contract time.

Ted Williams was able to live as Anglo – fairly easily, since he'd been largely raised as such. If he didn't publicly identify as Latino, does that disqualify him from being considered Latino? We have the evidence that Ted knew he could have been considered Latino. As he wrote in his autobiography, "If I had had my mother's name, there is no doubt I would have run into problems in those days, the prejudices people had in Southern California."[28] *Ted Williams: First Latino in the Hall of Fame* demonstrates that he *did* identify as partially Latino – but, for a cluster of reasons, informed by time and place, wanted to avoid that perception.

Burgos is by no means incorrect. He further argues that "it is also important that we do not rewrite the history of Latinos and baseball by retroactively inserting Williams because he chose not to do so on the grandest platform he was provided."[29] That platform was the occasion of his 1966 induction into the National Baseball Hall of Fame. Ted talked about the playground director who'd worked with him as a kid, his coach in high school, and other influences. He could have made something of his Latino heritage, but he did not. The absence of this acknowledgment could be considered underscored by his use of the bully pulpit to call for the recognition of Satchel Paige and Josh Gibson as "symbols of the great Negro players who are not here only because they weren't given the chance." Here was an opportunity for Williams to state what he, three years later, expressed in *My Turn at Bat*, that he himself *could have* suffered from prejudice, too. One could perhaps understand that he wasn't ready to throw open windows in public that he had long been accustomed to keeping closed. One could also argue that – had he been tempted – he might have preferred not to muddy the waters, the better

to keep the focus on his point about the Negro Leaguers. They *had* suffered discrimination; he had not had to.

Needless to say, it's a complex question. There is identity, and there is public acknowledgment of identity. If one wants to avoid being "branded" as of such-and-such a heritage, the human psyche is such that one can even deny something to the point where one's own consciousness is deceived by the masking and denial. Williams never denied he was Latino; he just didn't want to go there. Had he been born a couple of decades later, or lived a decade or two longer, this might have been otherwise.

Major League Baseball itself had perhaps changed its tune by 2012. On September 25, 2012, during Hispanic Heritage Month, Jesse Sanchez, a writer for MLB.com, released his "All-Time Latino Team." The outfield featured Ted Williams in left field, Reggie Jackson in center, and Roberto Clemente in right field.[30]

Full-length Williams biographies by Leigh Montville (in 2004) and Ben Bradlee Jr. (2013) helped better establish the popular awareness of this side of Ted Williams's ancestry.

All that said, Roberto Clemente was, in fact, both the first Latin-American player inducted into the National Baseball Hall of Fame and the first player publicly identified as Latino to have been inducted. That public identification mattered a great deal. It was Clemente who inspired thousands upon thousands of Latinos, in so many ways.

ROBERTO CLEMENTE – AN INSPIRATION TO LATINO PLAYERS OF ANY BACKGROUND

That detour aside, there is no question whatsoever that for the past near-half-century, it is indeed Roberto Clemente who has inspired other Latinos – players, fans of the game, and those writing about baseball, sport, and matters of history and society. He was in the forefront.

Courtesy of Thomas Van Hyning.

Adrian Burgos Jr., editor-in-chief of LaVidaBaseball.com, spoke of the ongoing impact that Clemente has had in Puerto Rico alone, on top of the players who have come through Ciudad Deportiva Roberto Clemente. "One thing that's really fascinating is that we saw a generation of players – Hall of Famers like Clemente, Cepeda – who weren't able to enjoy big-money free agency. So Alomar and Pudge [Rodriguez] ... they got to enjoy the money that came with being a star in the league. They're also parlaying that into the development of baseball in Puerto Rico," said Burgos. "That's how you honor Clemente, by making sure that the next generation has the opportunity, you give to the impoverished community, you seek out ways to help them have that opportunity. ... It's not trite, not passé, not rote, it's deeply meaningful in the culture of Puerto Rico, particularly in baseball but also in education: How do you honor the spirit of Clemente? How do you carry on that tradition?"[31]

Both Edwin Correa and Carlos Beltran have followed in Clemente's footsteps and established baseball academies of their own in Puerto Rico.[32]

NOTES

1. United Press International, "Writers Move to Induct Clement into Hall," *Boston Globe*, January 3, 1973: 52.

2. Joseph Durso, "A Man of Two Worlds," *New York Times*, January 2, 1973: 48.

3. Harold Kaese, "Press Ignored Clemente, Cooperstown Won't," *Boston Globe*, January 3, 1973: 51.

4. Norman O. Unger, "Great Hall for 'Beeg Boy'?," *Chicago Defender*, January 3, 1973: 24. This day's edition of the newspaper misspelled the author's first name as Noman.

5. "Way Paved to Put Clemente in Hall Now," *Washington Post*, January 4, 1973: F6. The rule had been suspended once before, though at the time it was only a one-year rule – for the induction of Lou Gehrig after he had been diagnosed with ALS. That suspension allowed Gehrig to experience the induction while he was still alive. For more details on Gehrig's induction, and other rule changes over the year, see Harold Kaese, "Hall Rules Suspended Twice, Changed Often," *Boston Globe*, January 7, 1973: 107. Kaese's own view, he said, was that making an exception "does not diminish the splendor of the Hall – which is kind of a paper peacock in any case – and shows that, after all, the hearts of most baseball writers are in the right place."

6. "A Man of Quality," *The Sporting News*, January 20, 1973: 12.

7. Richard Dozer, "Fame Vote Now Could Be Disservice to Clemente," *Chicago Tribune*, January 5, 1973: C3.

8. As rendered in The Sporting News, see Bob Broeg, "Quick Enshrinement Disservice to Roberto," *The Sporting News*, January 20, 1973: 38. The original article appeared as "Instant Enshrinement Is a Disservice to Clemente," *St. Louis Post-Dispatch*, January 7, 1973: 32. For comments from a couple of other sportswriters of the day, see Vince Guerrieri, "The Writers Are Bad": Clemente and the Press," in this volume.

9. Broeg, "Quick Enshrinement Disservice to Roberto."

10. Jack Lang, "Writers to Cast Ballots on Clemente," *The Sporting News*, February 10, 1973: 48.

11. Jack Lang, "Writers Okay Clemente Induction," *The Sporting News*, March 31, 1973: 32. See also United Press International, "Clemente Makes Hall of Fame," *Chicago Tribune*, March 21, 1973: F1, which reports on the reaction of Vera Clemente to the honor. She had flown to St. Petersburg for the announcement.

12. Associated Press, "Writers Vote Clemente Into Cooperstown Shrine," *Hartford Courant*, March 21, 1973: 59A. It was reported that the majority of the votes against Clemente's induction were accompanied by an explanation that the voter was opposed to waiving the five-year rule.

13. Associated Press, "Spahn Goes Solo to the Hall of Fame," *New York Times*, January 25, 1973: F1.

14. Joseph Durso, "Irvin Named to Hall of Fame in Special Vote for Blacks," *New York Times*, February 8, 1973: 55.

15 United Press International, "Clemente's Widow Shaken at Ceremony," *Los Angeles Times*, August 7, 1973: B3.

16 Milton Richman, "Mrs. Clemente Remembers Roberto," *Los Angles Sentinel*, August 9, 1973: B2.

17 Murray Chass, "Clemente's Dream: A Utopian Sports City," *New York Times*, October 21, 1971: 62.

18 United Press International, "Site Picked for Clemente Sports City," *New York Times*, February 21, 1973: 28. The land was provided by the government of Puerto Rico. Initial funding was provided by $500,000 donated by the Pittsburgh Pirates and "a local newspaper and bank."

19 Christopher Klein, "How Puerto Rico Baseball Icon Roberto Clemente Left a Legacy Off the Field," History.com, October 13, 2021. https://www.history.com/news/roberto-clemente-humanitarian-accomplishments-pittsburgh-pirates. Accessed January 20, 2022.

20 For instance, the Institute for Ethics and Diversity in Sports stated, "The percentage of Hispanic or Latinx players saw a decrease from 29.9 percent in 2020 to 28.1 percent on 2021 Opening Day rosters." See Dr. Richard Lapchick, "The 2021 Gender and Racial Report Card," Institute for Ethics and Diversity in Sports. 138a69_0fc7d964273c45938ad7a26f7e638636.pdf (tidesport.org), accessed January 21, 2022. According to an Infogram post in October 2020, the percentage was 31.9 percent. See https://www.routine.com/blog/post/mlb-player-demographics/, also accessed January 21, 2022.

21 Bill Nowlin, "El Splinter Esplendido, Ted Williams's Latino Heritage," *Boston Globe Magazine*, June 2, 2002.

22 Bill Nowlin, ed., *The Kid: Ted Williams in San Diego* (Burlington, Massachusetts: Rounder Books, 2005), published in collaboration with the Ted Williams (San Diego) Chapter of the Society for American Baseball Research.

23 Bill Nowlin, *Ted Williams; First Latino in the Baseball Hall of Fame* (Cambridge, Massachusetts: Rounder Books, 2018).

24 Richard Sandomir, "Williams and Jackson Omitted from Latino Ballots," *New York Times*, August 26, 2005: D1.

25 Sandomir.

26 J.A. Marzán, "Ted Williams: Throw the Heat; Hold the Tortillas," *New English Review*, November 2014. https://www.newenglishreview.org/custpage.cfm/frm/170995/sec_id/170995. Accessed January 20, 2022.

27 Adrian Burgos Jr., "No, Ted Williams Was Not Baseball's First Latino Superstar," *The Sporting News*, June 24, 2015.

28 Ted Williams with John Underwood, *My Turn At Bat* (New York: Fireside Books, 1969), 28.

29 Burgos.

30 Jesse Sanchez, "Clemente Heads All-Time Latino Team," MLB.com, September 25, 2012. http://mlb.mlb.com/mlb/events/alltimelatino/index.jsp. Accessed January 20, 2022.

31 Chris Davies, "The Past, Present and Future of Baseball in Puerto Rico," *Hardball Times*, April 17, 2018. https://tht.fangraphs.com/the-future-of-baseball-in-puerto-rico/. Accessed January 24, 2022.

32 For a story on the Beltran Academy, see Jason Margolis, "Baseball Academies Are Helping Puerto Rican Students on the Field and in the Classroom," theworld, July 1, 2016. https://theworld.org/stories/2016-07-01/baseball-academies-are-helping-puerto-rican-students-field-and-classroom. Accessed January 24, 2022.

¡QUE VIVA CLEMENTE!:
ROBERTO CLEMENTE LIVES ON IN THE HEARTS OF LATINO MAJOR LEAGUERS

BY JAMES FORR

Long after most of the city has descended into slumber, Roberto Clemente rises again.

For Latin American baseball players, a road trip into Pittsburgh often means a midnight pilgrimage to the Roberto Clemente Museum, located, incongruously enough, in a restored nineteenth-century firehouse, a little off the beaten path but not far from downtown.

The tours usually begin after a game and last until 2:00 or 3:00 A.M. Young players making their first visits grow wide-eyed as they grip Clemente's bat or trace the outline of the number 21 on his jersey; the old heads stand in the background, smiling knowingly and nodding. All of them coming closer – photograph by photograph, anecdote by anecdote, moment by moment – to a man Washington Nationals manager Dave Martinez calls "the baseball god of Latin players."[1]

Some Latino players whose careers overlapped with Clemente's played well into the 1980s and carried his memory forward. Later generations had watched him on TV or heard stories from their parents. Players coming up today may know nothing about Clemente beyond, at most, what they have read on his Wikipedia page. Nonetheless, all of these men have held Clemente in reverence and his legacy has assumed many forms.

CLEMENTE THE BALLPLAYER

Ironically, Clemente's baseball exploits are only a small part of the inheritance he has passed down. Those who saw him play, though, will never forget.

His teammate Manny Sanguillen raved, "I've never seen a better ballplayer than Roberto Clemente, not only in right field. He was the most complete ballplayer ever."[2]

"When I first played against Clemente I was a fan. I wanted to watch him. That arm!" gushed Cincinnati's Tony Pérez, who learned about that arm firsthand very early in his career.[3] He was on first base when a teammate blooped a single to shallow right field. Clemente was playing deep. Pérez was sure he could take the extra base.

"I didn't even look at the third-base coach," he said. "I just ran because I was going to make it easy." But when Pérez arrived, the ball was waiting for him. "Our third-base coach, a Cuban guy named Reggie Otero, said to me in Spanish, 'Chiquito, go to the dugout. Do you know who that was? That's Roberto Clemente.'"[4]

Seattle Mariners great Edgar Martinez, who was born in New York and grew up in Puerto Rico, says Clemente was part of a formative childhood memory. "I was about 9 years old, and my aunt was watching what probably were highlights of Roberto Clemente (in the 1971) World Series, and he homered and she was just screaming," Martinez recalled. "I remember after that I got really interested in the game. Right away I went outside and started hitting rocks with a broomstick, and I kind of fell in love with the game."[5]

Modern players speak relatively little of Clemente's on-field prowess. It is understandable – there isn't much for them to go on beyond tables of statistics and some grainy video clips. But some of them may have picked up a gauzy glimpse of Clemente from their elders, like a legend passed down from one generation to another.

Toronto pitcher José Berrios heard the tales from his father. "He said, 'We're not going to see another arm like his in right field.'"[6]

Julio Ricardo Varela, founder of the digital media site Latino Rebels, sees a little of Clemente in Fernando Tatis Jr. of the San Diego Padres. "He's also bringing the Dominican, Caribbean, Latino, Latin-American energy of the baseball that I grew up with, of the baseball I remember. It was OK to wear it on your sleeve."[7] The son of a major leaguer, Tatis has demonstrated an appreciation for baseball history. On Roberto Clemente Day in 2021, he sported a pair of baseball shoes with an image of a sliding Clemente on one side and a Puerto Rican flag on the other. Across the toes were Clemente's career statistics and a quote attributed to him: "I was born to play baseball."[8]

"The way [Clemente] played the game was kind of how my dad wanted to play the game," said Francisco Lindor. "By ... playing the game like that, even though he didn't play the game professionally, my dad taught me the game that way. Being aggressive, having fun."[9]

CLEMENTE THE HUMANITARIAN

Even Lindor admits Clemente the player is secondary to Clemente the man. "[H]e was not great just on the field, but he was outstanding off the field. That's why we're wearing number 21 [on Roberto Clemente Day]. It's not because he got 3,000 hits and won a World Series and got 12 Gold Gloves. It's not because of that. It's because how good he was off the field."[10]

Clemente's work on behalf of those in need has come to define him, largely because of the tragic nobility of his death in a plane crash delivering relief supplies to earthquake-ravaged Nicaragua.

The Roberto Clemente Award is presented annually to a player who "best represents the game of baseball through extraordinary character, community involvement, philanthropy, and positive contributions, both on and off the field." Yadier Molina of the St. Louis Cardinals was named the winner in 2018 for his work with Fundación 4, which helps Puerto Rican children struggling to overcome abuse, poverty, or medical issues. He called the award "a dream come true."[11]

"[Clemente] did a lot of things off the field to help people, and he had a lot less than we do these days," Molina said. "If he did it, why shouldn't we help others?"[12]

"Once [I started] playing baseball, everybody was like, 'Oh, you have a good arm like Roberto,' 'You hit like Roberto,' stuff like that," recalled 2021 Clemente Award winner Nelson Cruz. "Then, I started to find out what kind of person he was and what he did for his community and what he did for all Latin Americans, and definitely, it's a guy that you want to follow, an example that you want to go after."[13]

Cruz's impact is felt everywhere in his hometown of Las Matas de Santa Cruz in the Dominican Republic. Among other initiatives, he has funded the purchase of emergency vehicles, financed the construction of a police station, and donated money to help families in need of food, medicine, and financial support during the COVID-19 pandemic. Through his Boomstick23 Foundation, Cruz also is helping to build a new technical center that will provide better job opportunities for young people.

Boston manager Alex Cora said of Clemente, "If there's a Hall of Fame above the Hall of Fame, off the field, he's in that Hall of Fame."[14] Cora has done his best to emulate that example. Before signing his contract with the Red Sox in October 2017, he made the organization pledge to send relief to Puerto Rico, which had been devastated by Hurricane Sandy a month earlier. Subsequently, Cora, along with members of the front office and a handful of Red Sox players, accompanied a plane that delivered 10 tons of supplies to his hometown of Caguas – much as Clemente was trying to do on his fateful flight on New Year's Eve 1972.

Clemente's close friend Luis Mayoral believes Clemente would have dedicated his post-baseball life to philanthropic work. "I see him as more of a sociologist, not necessarily a politician. He was trying to help people better themselves."[15]

CLEMENTE THE ACTIVIST

Clemente wasn't just a caring man who helped people. He was also a proud, fierce man who wasn't afraid to make good, necessary trouble.

"Latin American Negro ballplayers are treated today much like all Negroes were treated in baseball in the early days of the broken color barrier," Clemente told *Sport* magazine in 1962. "They are subjected to prejudices and stamped with generalizations. Because they speak Spanish among themselves, they are set off as a minority within a minority, and they bear the brunt of the sport's remaining racial prejudices. 'They're all lazy, look for the easy way, the short cut' is one charge. 'They have no guts' is another. There are more."[16]

Clemente was a fearless counterpuncher. Speaking for his Latino major-league brethren, Pérez called him, "our leader."[17] Manny Mota, Clemente's teammate from 1963 to 1968, agreed. "He didn't permit injustices in regard to race. He was very vocal, and that was difficult. He was very misunderstood. But he would not accept injustices with Latins nor with players of color. He was always there to defend them."[18]

In a 1983 article, Rod Carew, who grew up in Panama, complained that a decade after Clemente's death, baseball still wasn't doing enough to help Latino players adjust to life in the States. Aurelio Rodriguez of the Chicago White Sox believed the void left by Clemente was yet to be filled. "We need somebody to speak for us but not just to talk. The thing about Clemente is that he had something to say."[19]

Bias in American culture is endemic and complex. Today's bigotry may not always be as overt or malicious as that which confronted Clemente; in many cases, the bias may not even be conscious. But it is still there.

Even well into the twenty-first century, broadcasters and scouts frequently use coded, stereotyped language to describe the abilities of Latino players.[20] When a Black or Latino player celebrates a home run or a strikeout with too much exuberance, he still may hear a lecture about "playing the game the right way," which is to say, the White way.

In 2016, a *Houston Chronicle* columnist quoted the Astros' Carlos Gómez, a nonnative English speaker, without cleaning up his grammar, a courtesy typically extended to all players.[21] It was the same kind of thing that infuriated Clemente 50 years earlier, when writers would directly quote his "broken English," thus reducing this highly intelligent and thoughtful man to sounding, in print, like a buffoon.

"I know how he felt," said Blue Jays manager Charlie Montoyo in 2021. "I came to the States with no English at all. So, I know what the English barrier does, not knowing what people are telling you and stuff. I've gone through all that."[22]

Clemente didn't restrict himself to issues solely germane to Latin American players. As an admirer of Martin Luther King Jr., Clemente was sensitive to all the bitter flavors of injustice. "Our conversations always stemmed around people from all walks of life being able to get along well, or no excuse why that shouldn't be," said Pirates teammate Al Oliver. "He had a problem with people who treated you differently because of where you were from, your nationality, your color, also poor people, how they were treated."[23]

After King's assassination in April 1968, Clemente led a group of Pirates who refused to take the field on Opening Day, which fell the day before King was to be buried. "[W]hen Martin Luther King died, they come and ask the Negro players if we should play," he said. "I say, 'If you have to ask Negro players, then we do not have a great country.'"[24] The Pirates' protest led Commissioner William Eckert to postpone all games until April 10.

A year later, at a meeting of the executive committee of the Major League Baseball Players Association, Curt Flood announced his plans to sue Major-League Baseball to end the reserve clause. Other players greeted the news with skepticism, even ridicule – until Clemente piped up. He spoke with passion of how the reserve clause limited his earning potential and chained him to a city where, although he was beloved, he frequently encountered ignorance and prejudice. As author Brad Snyder put it, "The tenor of the meeting soon shifted from whether the players would back Flood, to how."[25]

Today's generation of Latinos in baseball doesn't talk much about Clemente's role as an activist. His humanitarian activities overshadow his harder-edged and more challenging political side. Nonetheless, that part of Clemente likely will never be extinguished completely.

A video clip of Clemente thanking his parents in Spanish following the Pirates' World Series victory in 1971 resonates with Alex Cora. Cora hadn't even been born yet, but Clemente's message was timeless. "On national television, he asked for a moment to speak Spanish. No one does that," Cora said in 2021. "He taught us resolve and conviction. In many ways, he showed the world that we have to fight for what we believe in and we have to stand up for our rights, and he did it the right way."[26]

"I think Roberto would be disappointed with what's going on in today's society," mused Starling Marte, who got to know some of Clemente's former teammates and his sons while with the Pirates from 2012 to 2019. "He was the kind of guy that was fighting against all the hatred and injustice that's happening today. Today, current players are still fighting, though. We're using his spirit. Even though he's not here today, it's important to continue to fight for equality and justice, the way he would have."[27]

Pittsburgh sportscaster Sam Nover had a different perspective than Luis Mayoral about where Clemente's road would have taken him after baseball. "He would have run for political office. He would have been the Puerto Rican equivalent to someone like Kennedy."[28]

CLEMENTE THE DEITY

The metaphors that players use to describe Clemente suggest he has almost transformed from a flesh-and-blood person who actually walked this earth to a sacred, almost otherworldly symbol.

Pedro Martinez: "Clemente is beyond everything we can think of. … Kind of like an angel that God had here for the perfect time."[29]

Courtesy of The Clemente Museum.

Benjie Molina (Yadier's brother): "In many houses when I was growing up, including ours, the portraits of two famous men hung in honored spots among the family photos: Jesus and Roberto Clemente."[30]

Carlos Beltrán: "Even though he passed away a long time ago, he is still alive."[31]

Orlando Merced: "I feel as if I knew him. He has that look that speaks to you. He's like Elvis. He's still alive."[32]

For Puerto Rican players in particular, Clemente's uniform number 21 has taken on sacramental qualities. For most, that number has been strictly off-limits. A 2019 *New York Times* article noted that since Clemente's death, 235 Puerto Rican-born players had appeared in the major leagues, but only 16 had worn the number 21 — and none of them in the previous five seasons.

"No Puerto Ricans will use that number because of Roberto Clemente," insisted Carlos Correa.[33]

When Beltrán joined the Cardinals in 2012, his preferred number, 15, was taken. He told the equipment manager, "'Man, I don't want 21.' I feel like – I cannot touch that number. It's like, no, no, not 21. That's something I want to leave."[34]

Eddie Rosario remembers being a kid in Guayama, Puerto Rico, and backpedaling even then when a youth coach offered him that number. "I'm not Roberto Clemente. I can't wear that," he thought.[35]

"You can use it to honor him or you can see it as something you don't want to touch, because the way he carried the No. 21 is hard for another player to do in the same way," according to Beltrán. "It's not impossible, but it'll be really hard. You'll always have that shadow of Clemente, and many players avoid using that."[36]

One player willing to shoulder that burden was Carlos Delgado, who wore 21 in 1996 with Toronto and again from 2006 to 2009 with the New York Mets. "I thought he was so important that this was a way to recognize him. I understand

the other side of the coin, not using the number to honor him, but as long as you honor his memory and his career, I think it's O.K."[37]

Delgado has done just that, as a humanitarian and activist. In 2004 he protested the United States' military involvement in Iraq and Afghanistan by refusing to stand for the playing of "God Bless America" during the seventh-inning stretch. "As an athlete, you have a platform with a lot of followers. You can push positive things, you can push movements and support movements."[38]

Beginning in 2020, Major League Baseball has invited all players, coaches, and managers of Puerto Rican descent to wear 21 to commemorate Roberto Clemente Day, which is celebrated around the league each September 15.

"It's a blessing to be able to wear his number on a day like that," according to Lindor. "It's super special. It shows our roots."[39]

"Obviously, this jersey is going to be in a special place in my house," said Javier Baez after he wore 21 in 2020.[40]

The Mets' Edwin Diaz is one of many who has called for 21 to be retired across the league. "It would be a tremendous honor if they did retire the number 21," he told reporters. "Obviously, in the history of the game, there have been a lot of number 21s, but I think he trumps them all. You look at his numbers on the field and they are there, but also what he was able to do off the field and all the people he was able to help, not only in Puerto Rico but in every other country he used to help out in."[41]

For the true believers, seeing and interacting with the personal effects housed in the Clemente Museum is almost like receiving the Eucharist. Through those artifacts, they absorb a small part of Clemente's legendary spirit.

Albert Pujols was the first active major leaguer to visit the museum, in April 2007, less than a year after it opened. Word spread within baseball's Latin American community, and now museum founder and curator Duane Rieder finds himself giving private tours all summer. "It all depends on the major-league schedule, but if they are in for four days, I'm getting them. For some of these guys, it's a ritual."[42]

Dave Martinez, who was raised in New York by Puerto Rican parents, led a busload of his Washington Nationals players to the museum in 2021. "I got great feedback from our young guys, especially our Latin guys, that went. They loved it," Martinez said. "It was awesome to just kind of communicate with them [about] what they enjoyed, what it meant for them to see something like that, and they all started talking about it."[43]

Few players who visit the museum arrive completely ignorant about Clemente. "To give you an example of what kind of an impact he had on Puerto Rico and the game of baseball, even in the schools they teach about Roberto Clemente," according to Victor Caratini of the San Diego Padres. "We had sections [of the curriculum] entirely dedicated to him and what he did not only [in] baseball, but [on] the humanitarian side of things."[44]

But there is so much more to learn, as Martín Maldonado discovered when he visited as a member of the Milwaukee Brewers. "That's when I got shocked," Maldonado remembered. "I never knew he served in the military. They told him about a movie and he was going to be the guy that had to [hit into a triple play]. He told the guy he wasn't going to do the movie because he doesn't [hit into triple plays.] That was one of the most impressive things I've ever heard."[45]

"When you grow up, you think a lot about Clemente," said the Nationals' Luis García. "Everybody says that name in the Dominican. You go to Google and you put in Roberto Clemente and you see the photo, you see the biography — you only see that. But when you go to the museum, it's very different. You feel that."[46]

Rieder recalled when Yadier Molina brought Puerto Rican hip-hop legend Daddy Yankee to get schooled. It was Molina's third or fourth trip, so he knew what to expect. Daddy Yankee is known for his humanitarian work and, as it happens, was once a promising baseball player, but his knowledge of Clemente didn't run deep until that visit.

"I remember looking at Yadi's face and he was giggling, and then I looked at Daddy's face and his mouth is open," Rieder remembered. "He goes, 'Wow. I didn't know any of this stuff. Keep going.' Yadi was in the background saying, 'Let him have it. Tell him all the stories.' Two hours later, we're still there and I am still telling him the story.

"He goes, 'I gotta apologize. I didn't know any of this.' And Yadi is there snickering in the background. It was one of those beautiful moments."[47]

After players visit a couple of times, they acquire their own favorite stories. "The third time he was there, Pujols was translating [what I was saying] into Spanish to some of the guys," Rieder said. "[That] was really cool, just to see him getting so excited about being there and seeing new things and learning more. Because the story is still evolving. We're still finding out new stuff constantly."[48]

Rieder does something unusual when he shows the players around – he lets them touch things.

"I got to touch the Rawlings spikes [Clemente] wore when he used to run down fly balls in right field," wrote Carlos Beltrán. "I got to hold the bats he used to get some of his 3,000 hits. I got to run my fingers across the stitching of the number 21 on the back of a jersey he actually wore in a game. I never felt closer to my hero than I did that night."[49]

"I want to give them the mojo," laughed Rieder. It is almost as big a thrill for him as it is for the players. "I let them swing a bat that he actually touched and they get goose bumps. Carlos Beltrán wanted to put Clemente's cleats on his wife because she was Puerto Rican. He put the cleats on her and the oversized jersey and she was getting teary-eyed. Those moments go a long way."[50]

On a 2018 visit, a group of Chicago Cubs was admiring a suit that Clemente wore to the 1971 All-Star Game. With its wide lapels and head-turning black, white, and silver pattern, the suit was a relic from the era of mod fashion, yet somehow still contemporary and cool. Rieder noticed that Javier Baez was roughly the same size as Clemente and offered to let him wear the suit jacket.

"I put the jacket on him and he was just freaking out," Rieder recalled. "He was sending video to his family in Puerto Rico and he did an Instagram post that went all over."[51] ESPN's Eduardo Pérez arranged to have Baez wear the jacket at the Home Run Derby. He rocked it so well that Topps used an image of Baez in the jacket on his 2019 baseball card.

"We're getting this whole generation of young players hooked on Clemente," said Rieder. "It's so awesome. They don't know much when they come, but they do when they leave."[52]

"I think it's important for them to learn the history," explained Dave Martinez. "[T]he battles that he had to fight, I think it's important for them to understand that, and what it meant for him to play the game, and what it means to each individual now to represent and play the game."[53]

Ozzie Guillen, then the manager of the White Sox, once ignited a small brush fire when he suggested that Clemente was only the third-best baseball player from Puerto Rico, behind Roberto Alomar and Ivan Rodriguez.[54] Talk like that is almost heretical; however, Guillen, who named a son after Clemente and boasts a vast collection of Clemente memorabilia, understands that the emotional connection Latin American players have with Clemente has relatively little to do with his statistics.

Yes, Clemente's baseball skills merit respect and his humanitarian efforts command admiration. And, of course, he died in service of his personal mission. But he also is venerated, in no small part, because of his refusal to kneel to a culture that even today can be cold, condescending, and cruel.

"He lived racism. He was a man who was happy to be not only Puerto Rican, but Latin American," said Guillen. "He let people know that. And that is something that is very important for all of us."[55]

NOTES

1   Patrick Reddington, "Washington Nationals News & Notes: Davey Martinez on Roberto Clemente Day; Resting Young Players, and Watching Young Players," SB Nation: Federal Baseball, September 16, 2021, https://www.federalbaseball.com/2021/9/16/22675978/washington-nationals-news-davey-martinez-roberto-clemente-day-resting-young-players-luis-garcia.

2   Charlie Vascellaro, "My Clemente: Manny Sanguillen," *La Vida Baseball*, June 19, 2017, https://www.lavidabaseball.com/manny-sanguillen-roberto-clemente/.

3   Danny Torres, interview with Tony Pérez, Talkin' 21 Podcast, podcast audio, October 2020, https://open.spotify.com/episode/1uPgRBs5rrcj6o7x24UJQQ?si=TOejy34cTyqIagYwOYXCjw.

4   Torres interview.

5   "Edgar Martinez Tours Hall of Fame, Reflects on His Baseball Journey and Childhood Idol," Seattle Times, July 11, 2019, https://www.seattletimes.com/sports/mariners/edgar-martinez-tours-hall-of-fame-reflects-on-his-baseball-journey-and-childhood-idol/.

6   Julia Kreuz, "What Roberto Clemente Day Means for Blue Jays with Puerto Rican Roots," Yahoo! Sports, September 16, 2021, https://news.yahoo.com/mlb-what-roberto-clemente-day-means-for-blue-jays-from-puerto-rico-180047013.html?fr=sycsrp_catchall.

7   Julia O'Connell, "The Huddle: Baseball's Unwritten Rules & Roberto Clemente," *Global Sport Matters*, August 22, 2020, https://globalsportmatters.com/listen/2020/08/22/the-huddle-baseballs-unwritten-rules-roberto-clemente/.

8   R.J. Anderson, "MLB Celebrates Roberto Clemente Day as Players Wear No. 21, Call for Number to Be Retired," CBSSports.com, September 9, 2020. https://www.cbssports.com/mlb/news/mlb-celebrates-roberto-clemente-day-as-players-wear-no-21-call-for-number-to-be-retired/.

9   Mandy Bell, "Lindor on Clemente's No. 21: 'Super Special," MLB.com, September 7, 2020, https://www.mlb.com/news/francisco-lindor-21-roberto-clemente-day.

10 Bell.

11 "Cardinals Catcher Wins Roberto Clemente Award," ESPN.com, October 24, 2018, https://www.espn.com/mlb/story/_/id/25072934/cardinals-yadier-molina-wins-roberto-clemente-award.

12 Jorge Ortiz, "Clemente's Impact Wanes in Puerto Rico 40 Years After His Death," *USA Today*, December 27, 2012, https://www.usatoday.com/story/sports/mlb/2012/12/27/roberto-clemente-40th-anniversary-death-plane-crash-puerto-rico-pirates-humanitarian/1794453/.

13 Do-Hyoung Park and Anthony Castrovince, "Nelson Cruz Wins Roberto Clemente Award," MLB.com, October 27, 2021, https://www.mlb.com/news/nelson-cruz-wins-2021-roberto-clemente-award.

14 Chris Cotillo, "Why Are Boston Red Sox Players, Coaches Wearing No. 21? Kiké Hernández, Alex Cora, and Others Honoring Clemente," Masslive.com, September 15, 2021, https://www.masslive.com/redsox/2021/09/why-are-boston-red-sox-players-coaches-wearing-no-21-kike-hernandez-alex-cora-and-others-honoring-roberto-clemente.html.

15 Gene Collier, "Pride and Petulance," *The Sporting News*, December 28, 1992: 34-36.

16 Howard Cohn, "Roberto Clemente's Problem," *Sport*, May 1962: 54-56.

17 Danny Torres, interview with Tony Pérez.

18 George Diaz, "Clemente 30 Years After His Tragic Death, the Influence of baseball's First Hispanic Superstar Is Stronger Than Ever," *Orlando Sentinel*, March 31, 2002, https://www.orlandosentinel.com/news/os-xpm-2002-03-31-0203300030-story.html.

19 Robert Heuer, "Clemente's Legacy for Latin Ballplayers," *New York Times*, January 2, 1983: Sec 5, 2.

20 Adam Felder and Seth Amitin, "How MLB Announcers Favor American Players Over Foreign Ones," *The Atlantic*, August 27, 2012, https://www.theatlantic.com/entertainment/archive/2012/08/how-mlb-announcers-favor-american-players-over-foreign-ones/261265/; Alex Speier, "How Racial Bias Can Seep Into Scouting Reports," *Boston Globe*, June 10, 2020, https://www.bostonglobe.com/2020/06/10/sports/how-racial-bias-can-seep-into-baseball-scouting-reports/.

21 Craig Calcaterra, "Houston Chronicle Editor Apologizes for Column about Carlos Gomez," NBCSports.com, May 16, 2016, https://mlb.nbcsports.com/2016/05/16/houston-chronicle-editor-apologies-for-column-about-carlos-gomez/.

22 Kreuz, "What Roberto Clemente Day Means for Blue Jays with Puerto Rican Roots."

23 David Maraniss, "No Gentle Saint," TheUndefeated.com, May 31, 2016, https://theundefeated.com/features/roberto-clemente-was-a-fierce-critic-of-both-baseball-and-american-society/.

24 Phil Musick, "Intense Pride Still Rages in Roberto Clemente," *Pittsburgh Press*, July 28, 1969: 24.

25 Brad Snyder, *A Well-Paid Slave: Curt Flood's Fight for Free Agency in Professional Sports* (New York: Penguin Publishing Group, 2006), 79.

26 Nathalie Alonso, "Clemente Continued What Robinson Started," MLB.com, December 15, 2021, https://www.mlb.com/news/roberto-clemente-day-celebrated-for-2021.

27 Jerry Crasnick, "Roberto Remembered," MLBPlayers.com, accessed January 13, 2022, https://www.mlbplayers.com/roberto-remembered.

28 Danny Torres, "Rare Interview Sets Tone for Roberto Clemente's Legacy," Metsmerized Online, September 9, 2020, https://metsmerizedonline.com/2020/09/rare-interview-sets-tone-for-roberto-clementes-legacy-2.html/.

29 "What Roberto Clemente Means to Pedro Martinez," La Vida Baseball, September 17, 2019, https://www.lavidabaseball.com/pedro-martinez-my-clemente/.

30 Bengie Molina with Joan Ryan, Molina: The Story of the Father Who Raised an Unlikely Baseball Dynasty (New York: Simon and Schuster, 2015), 26.

31 Derrick Gould, "Beltran Strives to Follow in Clemente's Footsteps," Stltoday.com, September 2, 2013, https://www.stltoday.com/sports/baseball/professional/beltran-strives-to-follow-in-clementes-footsteps/article_ab563518-2176-58b2-bde0-289384b39ccc.html.

32 Steve Wulf, "December 31: ¡Arriba Roberto!" Sports Illustrated, accessed November 28, 2021, https://vault.si.com/vault/1992/12/28/december-31-arriba-roberto-on-new-years-eve-in-1972-roberto-clemente-undertook-a-mission-of-mercy-his-death-that-night-immortalized-him-as-a-man-greater-than-his-game.

33 James Wagner, "For Many Latino players, Roberto Clemente's Number Is Off Limits, Too," New York Times, April 17, 2019: Sec B, 9.

34 Gould.

35 Wagner.

36 Wagner.

37 Wagner.

38 Jorge Castillo, "Remembering Roberto Clemente as a Black Man Who Fought Against Racial Injustice," Los Angeles Times, September 8, 2020, https://www.latimes.com/sports/dodgers/story/2020-09-08/roberto-clemente-fought-racial-injustice.

39 Castillo.

40 Anderson.

41 Anthony DiComo (@AnthonyDiComo), "It Would Be a Tremendous Honor if [MLB] Did Retire the Number 21," September 9, 2020, https://twitter.com/AnthonyDiComo/status/1303799232869130247.

42 Duane Rieder, telephone interview with author, January 13, 2022.

43 Reddington, "Davey Martinez on Roberto Clemente Day."

44 Barry Bloom, "Puerto Rican Players Pushing MLB to Retire Clemente's Number," Global Sport Matters, July 8, 2019, https://globalsportmatters.com/culture/2019/07/08/puerto-rican-players-pushing-mlb-to-retire-clementes-number/.

45 Chandler Rome, "What Roberto Clemente Means to Astros Catcher Martin Maldonado," Houston Chronicle, September 9, 2020, https://www.houstonchronicle.com/texas-sports-nation/astros/article/Roberto-Clemente-means-Astros-Martin-Maldonado-15555451.php.

46 Jessica Camerato, "Nats Take 'Amazing' Trip to Clemente Museum," MLB.com, September 15, 2021, https://www.mlb.com/news/nationals-visit-roberto-clemente-museum-in-pittsburgh.

47 Rieder interview.

48 Rieder interview.

49 Carlos Beltrán, "How We Play Baseball in Puerto Rico," The Players' Tribune, June 1, 2016, https://www.theplayerstribune.com/articles/2016-5-31-carlos-beltran-yankees-puerto-rico-roberto-clemente.

50 Rieder interview.

51 Rieder interview.

52 Rieder interview.

53 Reddington, "Davey Martinez on Roberto Clemente Day."

54 "ChiSox's Guillen Creates Controversy with Clemente Talk," ESPN.com, April 8, 2008, https://www.espn.com/mlb/news/story?id=3336775.

55 Diaz, "Clemente 30 Years After His Tragic Death."

CLEMENTE REMEMBERED

BY NORMAN MACHT

In the 1950s and '60s, most of what baseball fans knew about their home team players came from the sportswriters they read. In the case of Puerto Rican and other Latino players, much of what was written was mean-spirited and demeaning, caricaturing those players' cultural differences and language hurdles more than their struggles and successes as color-segregated major league ballplayers. Roberto Clemente was no exception; in fact, as a proud and private eventual Hall of Fame outfielder, he became a lightning rod for writers' barbs. If he was hurting — and he was often hurting — he was called lazy, a chronic complainer, looking for a day off. And that was all the fans knew about him.

This is the Roberto Clemente that opposing players, his Pirates' teammates and other team employees knew, and the public didn't know:

Pirates manager Bill Virdon: "You got him going on a plane or bus telling jokes and stories and he had everybody in stitches."

Trainer Tony Bartirome: "Clemente was the funniest man I ever saw in a clubhouse, but only among the players. He had the knack of getting a team up, if they were in a slump, by making everybody relax and feel good. He was at the center of the noise and life and laughter in the clubhouse, but as soon as the writers came in, he clammed up. They never saw it."

A life-size wax statue of Clemente stood in the team's offices. One day Bartirome carried it down to the clubhouse. "I took it into an empty room adjacent to the clubhouse. It was dark and cold in there. The only light came from a nearby bathroom. I laid it on a platform and covered it to the chin with a blanket while some of the players watched. Then I called the team doctor and told him, 'Bobby's real sick, doc, you better do something. We put him in the side room in case the writers came in.'

"The doctor touched the statue's hand. It was as cold as ice. He put his ear to the statue's chest. No heartbeat. 'My God,' he cried. 'He's dead!' By this time everybody in the clubhouse was roaring with laughter, Clemente the loudest of all."

Phillies outfielder Richie Ashburn: "Bobby and I were at one of those winter banquets in Pittsburgh. The snow was deep on the roads. After it was over he offered to drive me to the airport. I figured it was on his way, or he was going there too, so I said, 'Okay.' I found out later that he was really going to the other side of the city and it was far out of his way."

While the writers played up other Pittsburgh players for the team's success, National League fans and players who had the chance to see Clemente in action didn't need the writers to tell them he was the most exciting player they would ever see. Veteran manager Sparky Anderson said, "In my 22 years as a manager, I never saw a better player." Hall of Fame pitcher Don Sutton called him "the best player I competed against and the most exciting I ever saw." Richie Ashburn named him "the best right fielder I ever saw in 40 years."

It was not just a strong and accurate arm that impressed them. It was speed, daring, unpredictability, and baseball smarts that dazzled teammates and opponents alike.

Pitcher Johnny Podres: "He would hit pitches thrown over his head, down by his ankles, inside, outside. I'd get two quick strikes on him and never get the third one. No matter where I threw it, he'd hit it."

Podres called him a team player. "If a double was needed, he would go for that. If there were two out and the Pirates needed a run, he would go for the home run. But he would not swing for the fences if his team was down by three or four runs. He would just try to get on base. That's a team player."

Joe Torre learned about Clemente's strong, accurate arm as a rookie in 1961. "I got a hit to right field and rounded first base as most runners do. Clemente picked up the ball, faked a throw to second and threw it so fast behind me to first base I was caught and tagged out. It was my most embarrassing moment on the field."

Veteran pitcher Nelson Briles was traded from St. Louis to Pittsburgh in 1971. "I never gave him credit for his ability until I was on the same team. One day I was pitching and Willie McCovey, a left-handed pull hitter, was at bat. Clemente was not playing him to pull, so I waved Robby a few steps closer to the right-field line. I was ready to pitch and I glanced out there at him and he had moved back. So I waved him over again and he took a few steps toward the line. I pitched and McCovey hit a screaming line drive into the right-center field gap. I knew it was good for a double and I ran over to back up third base. When I got there, I discovered that Clemente had caught the ball. Back in the dugout Clemente said, 'I bet you, Nellie, you no figure out how I made that catch. It is because the great Roberto knows how to play the hitter and the pitcher each day. You were pitching good and I knew that hitter could not pull the ball on you, so I move back after you moved me.'"

Teammate Al Jackson described Clemente's intimidating baserunning tactics. "He was the only player I ever saw who would hit a single to left field and run so hard he would get halfway to second, and have to hit the dirt and slide to stop himself, then pop up and get back to first base. If the left fielder bobbled the ball, he'd be into second easily, but he always got back to first if he had to. He played that hard and intensely all the time."

Pitcher Harvey Haddix: "In Pittsburgh I was as close to Roberto Clemente as anybody. A fine guy. I liked him. He would not start a conversation, but if you wanted to talk with him, he would. We talked a lot on airplane rides and in spring training. He would not let you get close to him. He wanted his privacy, never went with our groups to dinner. He went by himself. One day he came out and I laughed at him. He was rubbing a white suntan lotion all over him. He said, 'You know why? You see so and so over there? He too black. You see me? Nice and tan.' Was he a hot dog? I haven't seen a guy yet who didn't like to show off his skills. I was called a hot dog a lot of times; I could catch a ball behind my back and other ways. He did not want any attention.

Teammate Richie Hebner: "Robby led by example. When he was 36, if he hit a tap back to the pitcher, he still roared down to first base like the cops were chasing him. When we young players saw that, we told ourselves if he's bearing down like that after 16 years in the majors, we'd better do that, too, or we'll look bad."

SOURCES

All quotations are selected by Norman Macht from interviews he did with the players in question.

THE ROBERTO CLEMENTE AWARD

BY JOHN BLANKSTEIN

It was fitting that Nelson Cruz received the Roberto Clemente Award in 2022 as the 50th anniversary of Clemente's untimely passing approached. Both Clemente and Cruz hailed from Caribbean islands, and each used his wealth and status derived from playing major-league baseball to help improve the lives of the less fortunate there as well as around the United States. From an early time in his career, Cruz arranged medical and dental treatment for people in his native Dominican Republic who could not afford proper treatment on their own. Among other things, Cruz's efforts assisted more than 1,000 families through various challenges caused by the COVID-19 pandemic. Clemente, of course, lost his life in a plane accident while he was deeply engaged in a fight to help Nicaraguans after a more typical natural disaster, a tremendous earthquake that struck in the final days of 1972.

When we think of memorials, our minds usually jump to something physical: a building, a statue, a painting, a mural. These things connote permanence because they are tangible and often enormous. But they aren't forever; statues can be torn down. Ballparks, too, can be torn down or renamed again and again after a succession of corporations. Awards achieve a different type of permanence; there is every reason to believe that the Roberto Clemente Award will remain intact and awarded each year.

Clemente biographer David Maraniss suggests strongly that Clemente intended to stay involved in the game after his retirement, which surely would have come a few years after 1972.[1] Maybe he would have coached, maybe he would have managed. Certainly he would have remained involved in issues of the day outside baseball. Could we have imagined him extending his career another seven years to still be Willie Stargell's teammate on the 1979 World Series champions? It seems unlikely, but he may have been in uniform as a coach on his way to being a manager, or maybe he would have been the manager already. As of 2022 Stargell was one of two Pittsburgh Pirates to win the Roberto Clemente Award, the other being Andrew McCutchen.

The prize that honors Clemente was not created in his name. Started in 1971 as the Commissioner's Trophy, or the Baseball Achievement Award, it is now "bestowed annually to the player who best represents the game of Baseball through extraordinary character, community involvement, philanthropy, and positive contributions both on and off the field."[2] Willie Mays and Brooks Robinson were the first two recipients of the award.

After his death on the final day of 1972, the trophy was renamed in Clemente's honor. Little fanfare was involved in the first new award in 1973: "A memorial was dedicated to Clemente today: the trophy given by the Commissioner each year to a ballplayer of high reputation was named the Roberto Clemente Award. It was given tonight at the annual Governor's Dinner to Al Kaline, 38-year-old outfielder for the Detroit Tigers."[3] The Governor's Dinner was held in St. Petersburg, Florida, on March 20, 1973 Vera Clemente was introduced and presented the renamed award. Commissioner Bowie Kuhn said of its prior name, "I have never liked that name. It is awkward. But we have renamed it as well and as fittingly as we ever could. We have renamed it the Roberto Clemente Award and we present it to a man noted for his unassuming ways and his flawless and perfect execution on and off the field."[4] Kuhn said the award would be "given annually hereafter ... to the major leaguer whose onfield and off-field conduct best exemplifies the best traditions of the game."[5] It's not clear whether Kaline knew in advance that he'd be receiving the award.

It had been quite a day for Vera Clemente. That morning, the announcement had been made that in a special election, her husband had been named to the National Baseball Hall of Fame.

A round of broadcast and newspaper interviews followed. That evening, at the dinner, Commissioner Kuhn made the announcement regarding the naming of the award, and Vera made the presentation to Kaline, although she was unable to complete her remarks after being overcome with tearful emotion.

The process for selection is outlined on mlb.com: "Every year, each MLB Club nominates a player to be considered for the Award in tribute to Clemente's achievements and character. This year's list of nominees features players whose various community and philanthropic activities have focused on important issues ranging from awareness & fundraising to support those with cancer and other illnesses or special needs, education for young people, natural disaster relief, outreach to underserved children & communities in the United States and abroad, and more."[6]

The description submitted by the Minnesota Twins on behalf of their 2021 nominee Cruz runs 10 paragraphs. It detailed his personal efforts to provide food and funds to 1,200 families in Las Matas de Santa Cruz, his Dominican hometown, so they could comply with stay-at-home orders during the early months of the COVID-19 pandemic. Cruz's work resulted in a $400,000 donation from MLB, the MLBPA, and the Players Trust. The veteran power hitter had previously donated an ambulance, a fire truck, and related supplies, and has annually arranged for dentists and optometrists to visit the town to offer checkups, medicine, and eyewear.[7]

The following is a listing of the recipients of the Roberto Clemente Award (including the 1971 and 1972 Baseball Achievement Awards):

YR	Player	Team	LG	POS	Year	Player	Team	LG	POS
1971	**Willie Mays**	San Francisco Giants	NL	OF	1997	Eric Davis	Baltimore Orioles	AL	OF
1972	**Brooks Robinson**	Baltimore Orioles	AL	3B	1998	Sammy Sosa	Chicago Cubs	NL	OF
1973	**Al Kaline**	Detroit Tigers	AL	OF	1999	**Tony Gwynn**	San Diego Padres	NL	OF
1974	**Willie Stargell**	Pittsburgh Pirates	NL	OF	2000	Al Leiter	New York Mets	NL	P
1975	**Lou Brock**	St. Louis Cardinals	NL	OF	2001	Curt Schilling	Arizona Diamondbacks	NL	P
1976	Pete Rose	Cincinnati Reds	NL	3B	2002	**Jim Thome**	Cleveland Indians	AL	1B
1977	**Rod Carew**	Minnesota Twins	AL	1B	2003	Jamie Moyer	Seattle Mariners	AL	P
1978	Greg Luzinski	Philadelphia Phillies	NL	OF	2004	**Edgar Martinez**	Seattle Mariners	AL	DH
1979	Andy Thornton	Cleveland Indians	AL	1B	2005	**John Smoltz**	Atlanta Braves	NL	P
1980	**Phil Niekro**	Atlanta Braves	NL	P	2006	Carlos Delgado	New York Mets	NL	OF
1981	Steve Garvey	Los Angeles Dodgers	NL	1B	2007	**Craig Biggio**	Houston Astros	NL	2B
1982	Ken Singleton	Baltimore Orioles	AL	DH	2008	Albert Pujols	St. Louis Cardinals	NL	1B
1983	Cecil Cooper	Milwaukee Brewers	AL	1B	2009	**Derek Jeter**	New York Yankees	AL	SS
1984	Ron Guidry	New York Yankees	AL	P	2010	Tim Wakefield	Boston Red Sox	AL	P
1985	Don Baylor	New York Yankees	AL	DH	2011	**David Ortiz**	Boston Red Sox	AL	DH
1986	Garry Maddox	Philadelphia Phillies	NL	OF	2012	Clayton Kershaw	Los Angeles Dodgers	NL	P
1987	Rick Sutcliffe	Chicago Cubs	NL	P	2013	Carlos Beltran	St. Louis Cardinals	NL	OF
1988	Dale Murphy	Atlanta Braves	NL	OF	2014	Paul Konerko	Chicago White Sox	AL	1B
1989	**Gary Carter**	New York Mets	NL	C	2014	Jimmy Rollins	Philadelphia Phillies	NL	SS
1990	Dave Stewart	Oakland Athletics	AL	P	2015	Andrew McCutchen	Pittsburgh Pirates	NL	OF
1991	Harold Reynolds	Seattle Mariners	AL	2B	2016	Curtis Granderson	New York Mets	NL	OF
1992	**Cal Ripken Jr.**	Baltimore Orioles	AL	SS	2017	Anthony Rizzo	Chicago Cubs	NL	1B
1993	**Barry Larkin**	Cincinnati Reds	NL	SS	2018	Yadier Molina	St. Louis Cardinals	NL	C
1994	**Dave Winfield**	Minnesota Twins	AL	DH	2019	Carlos Carrasco	Cleveland Indians	AL	P
1995	**Ozzie Smith**	St. Louis Cardinals	NL	SS	2020	Adam Wainwright	St. Louis Cardinals	NL	P
1996	**Kirby Puckett**	Minnesota Twins	AL	OF	2021	Nelson Cruz	Twins / 2021 Rays	AL	DH

Names in bold have been inducted into the National Baseball Hall of Fame.

The on-field profile of the players connected to Clemente through this award has changed over the years. Six of the first seven players honored were later inducted into the Hall of Fame, and the seventh was Pete Rose. The honorees were all Clemente's contemporaries and arguably his near-equal in playing greatness. From 1978 to 1991, in contrast, only two honorees – Phil Niekro and Gary Carter – have made it into the Hall of Fame. Niekro is also one of only 12 pitchers who have been included among the 52.

Aside from Clayton Kershaw, who won the award as a 24-year-old, most honorees have been well into the latter portion of their career, and most were still producing at a high level at that age, as Clemente himself was. Four honorees won in years in which they were integral pieces in a World Series championship – Pete Rose of the 1976 Cincinnati Reds, Steve Garvey of the 1981 Los Angeles Dodgers, Curt Schilling of the 2001 Arizona Diamondbacks, and Derek Jeter of the 2009 New York Yankees.

The Roberto Clemente Foundation offers interesting perspectives on the award:

So what exactly is the award? It's been given out for nearly 50 years, but it doesn't get as much publicity as, say, the Cy Young Award. So what makes it stand out among the many (some would say too many) awards the MLB gives out each year? The Clemente Award is the only MLB award not based on field performance. Make no mistake, the recipient is always an outstanding player, but this is not a statistics award. It's intended for athletes who embody Roberto's values on the diamond and in the community. Because of that, it stands out as unique (because it is) and is simultaneously easy to ignore during the blitz of press that always comes with the end of the World Series. But while its media footprint may be relatively small, it has established itself as one of the sport's most prestigious awards.[8]

The Foundation also thoughtfully notes, "Some of these players, since receiving their awards, have gone on in the intervening years to exhibit deficiencies in character that Roberto certainly would not have approved of. It's worth noting that such cases are exceptions, and most of these men have shown themselves to have exemplary character, at least in public. If anything, those exceptions serve as case studies to show that it's always a mistake to hold up entertainers and athletes as paragons of virtue. Roberto himself wasn't perfect, nobody is. What matters is the effort put in to use your platform to make the world a better place."

On receiving the award in 2021, Cruz said, "I never was doing what I was doing to be recognized or win awards, but it's always nice when people recognize the work that you put on to help others. I know all 29 other players that were nominated really deserved to win it. I just thank God that I was the one."[9]

The selection process, as described for the 2021 award: Cruz was selected from a list of 30 players, one from each major-league team. Voting members for the award included Commissioner Rob Manfred; Roberto Clemente's children, Enrique, Luis, and Roberto Jr.; former players (including former Roberto Clemente Award winners), and journalists from MLB Network, Fox Sports, ESPN, TBS, and MLB.com. Additionally, fans were given the chance to vote via MLB.com/Clemente21.[10]

The emphasis on philanthropy has evolved over the years. It is a welcome evolution and, as the Clemente Foundation has noted, differentiates the award from other awards in professional sports.

ACKNOWLEDGMENTS

Thanks to Bill Nowlin and John Thorn for assistance in preparing this article.

NOTES

1   David Maraniss, *Clemente: The Passion and Grace of Base-ball's Last Hero* (New York, Simon and Schuster, 2006), 284-5.

2   https://www.mlb.com/community/Roberto-Clemente-Award

3   Joseph Durso, "A Rare Honor for Clemente," *New York Times*, March 20, 1973   http://archive.nytimes.com/www.nytimes.com/packages/html/sports/year_in_sports/03.20.html?scp=8&sq=11th%2520Day&st=cse Accessed June 29, 2022.

4   Jack Lang, "Proud Mrs. Clemente Presents Award," *The Sporting News*, April 7, 1973: 37.

5   Bill Clark, "Griffith Honored by Askew," *Orlando Sentinel*, March 21, 1973: 26.

6   https://www.mlb.com/community/roberto-clemente-award. Accessed February 6, 2022.

7   https://www.mlb.com/community/roberto-clemente-award. Accessed May 9, 2022. The materials submitted in support of each nominee by all 30 major-league clubs is presented.

8   https://robertoclementefoundation.com/clemente-award/ Accessed May 9, 2022.

9   Do-Hyoung Park and Anthony Castrovince, "Nelson Cruz Wins Roberto Clemente Award," MLB.com, October 27, 2021. https://www.mlb.com/news/nelson-cruz-wins-2021-roberto-clemente-award#:~:text=%22I%20never%20was%20doing%20what,that%20I%20was%20the%20one.%22

10 The balloting completed, the ballot item at the site has been removed.

Photograph by Duane Rieder.

ROBERTO CLEMENTE, HUMANITARIAN

BY THOMAS KERN

"Any time you have an opportunity to make a difference in this world and you don't, then you are wasting your time on Earth."

– Roberto Clemente Walker

For a sports figure to be idolized for his or her greatness is not uncommon. Roberto Clemente received the accolades and adulation of many in his native Puerto Rico and his adopted home of Pittsburgh. Yet Clemente may have been revered even more for his compassion and altruism than his baseball career. It was in his DNA to care deeply for others, particularly those less well off. He brought an unremitting drive to excel on the baseball diamond. This same relentlessness fueled his passion to do good. Clemente's fundamental character underpinned this passion. Wrote biographer Kal Wagenheim, "[H]e believed passionately in the virtue and dignity of hard work … that a man should revere his parents, wife and children, his country, and God. He believed just as fiercely in his personal worth and integrity."[1] These values would foreshadow, indeed form his motivations on and off the playing field.

Any elaboration on Clemente's humanitarianism can best consider him and his legacy in three ways. First was his generosity, his dedication to the well-being of those whose needs were under-addressed by the communities in which they lived. This compassion would eventually bring about his early death, and he shared privately with family and friends that he knew this would happen.

Second was his attentiveness to civil rights, seen through the prism of a Puerto Rican Latino and as a Black man in American society in the 1950s and 1960s.

Third was that his exemplar of humanitarianism was shared, embraced, and practiced by his wife, Vera, and his sons, Roberto Jr., Luis, and Enrique. The Clemente Foundation is one manifestation of this, but Vera's work with the Roberto Clemente Sports Complex in Puerto

Rico prior to the foundation's creation is equally profound. Added to the family's embodiment of Clemente's selflessness is recognition by Major League Baseball of Clemente as the face of its own humanitarian initiative.

As Clemente's baseball talents emerged and flourished in the late 1950s and into the 1960s, so too did the attention that was paid him by fans and the media. Publicly Clemente was a reserved man. His seeming aloofness and his detachment were accentuated and often misinterpreted by an audience that did not share his native language of Spanish. On the diamond, Clemente was the consummate two-way player, as both his offensive and defensive numbers portrayed. This was fueled by his passion for excellence. That same passion motivated him to fight inequity and hardship, and it rallied in him an equal intensity to improve of the lives of others.

In Puerto Rico Clemente, as one of the first Latino superstars in the majors, was revered. Yet he used this sentiment not to feed his own ego but to seek change in the barrios of San Juan and beyond.

When it came to his charitable commitments, these were reflected both in individual ways and in wider settings. Throughout his career in Pittsburgh, he would tirelessly sign autographs for the fans, focusing often on the young. A little more than a week after the opening of Three Rivers Stadium on July 16, 1970, a park some christened "The House That Clemente Built" by virtue of his being the face of the franchise for a decade, the Pirates honored him with Roberto Clemente Night on July 24. True to Clemente's character, while he accepted the honor graciously, he also requested that the Pirates incorporate a benevolent element and raise funds for Pittsburgh's Children's Hospital.

According to biographer Bruce Markusen, "[W]ith the help of a local sports organization, Roberto had asked all fans to make donations to a fund in his name. 'I want the money to help poor kids,' said Clemente, who made sure that all $5,500 in donations were designated for crippled children whose parents could not afford medical costs."[2] In fact, the selection of Children's Hospital was not coincidental. "'One of the things he really liked to do was go to Children's Hospital in Pittsburgh and visit kids,' recalled Joe Christopher, a former teammate of Clemente's and later a Pirates official. 'That's something that many people don't write about. That's where his real passion was — making other people feel important.'"[3] He was also known to visit the sick in hospitals on the road as well. Pirates general manager Joe Brown summed it up: "I don't think Clemente turned down many people who wanted his help — if anybody."[4]

After the July 24, 1970, game played in his honor, he spoke to the press. "We are on the field doing what we love to do," he said." [The fans] have to work in the mill or other places eight hours a day and work much harder than us and they pay their way in."[5]

Clemente's passion for racial equality always existed, but according to Markusen, "[I]n the mid-sixties, a little-known encounter with one of the country's most famous civil rights leaders provided Clemente with a further insight on the subject of racism." Sportswriter and family friend Luis Rodriguez Mayoral remarked, "Somewhere along the road in his major-league career, he befriended Martin Luther King. I think that was also a key relationship in the development of Roberto Clemente the fighter for social equality." The men met in 1964 in Puerto Rico, "when King went down there to a little farm that Roberto had in the outskirts of Carolina." Markusen further reflected, "Although one was African American and the other Latino, the two men found common grounds of interest" and became friends. Clemente was later quoted in a 1972 interview: "I believe that this man [King] not only changed the lifestyle of the American black, he changed the life of everybody."[6] Clemente was once asked about his heroes and he placed King at the top of the list.[7]

Clemente's dedication to racial equality was both personal and societal. It was personal because of the segregationist practices he and other minorities on the Pirates faced when playing in the South, most notably in spring training. Clemente protested these conditions to Pirates officials, including Brown, who eventually introduced measures to work around local laws, including the team renting its own hotel during spring training.

But Clemente also advocated for the status of all minority players, Black and Latino alike. He believed they suffered from a two-tier status when it came to recognition, and remarked to reporters that "the Latin American player doesn't get the recognition he deserves. Neither does the Negro player unless he does something really spectacular like Willie Mays."[8] He added, "I am an American citizen ... [but] to the people here, we are outsiders, foreigners."[9] This bigotry troubled Clemente deeply and energized him to serve as a spokesman for all people of color in the game. For that, he was revered not only by his fellow Puerto Ricans, but by those from elsewhere in Latin America and African Americans as well.

The assassination of Martin Luther King in April 1968 precipitated a movement by several teams, spearheaded by the Pirates, to not play on Monday, Opening Day, April 8, out of respect for King. After lengthy deliberations, both major leagues canceled the first two games (April 8 and 9, the latter the day of King's funeral). Clemente and other minority players, while supportive of the outcome, were disappointed with the indecisive way in which their teams and the leagues responded to the tragedy. Clemente remarked later, "If you have to ask Negro players (whether or not to play), then we do not have a great country."[10] Clemente lamented that the shared, common values a nation should aspire to were still lacking.

Later in his career, Clemente acknowledged and celebrated the progress to open sports to minorities, citing the 1971 Pirates squad that included a dozen Black (including Latino) players. At the same time, he advocated for Curt Flood's challenge to baseball's reserve clause and its restrictive contractual arrangements that owners held over the players, White and Black alike. He called on owners to hire Black managers and on sponsors to offer more endorsements to minority players, and he disputed the media's characterization of minorities insofar as "they made it look like we were entirely different from the white players."[11]

In October 1972, on the heels of his 3,000th hit, and then a disappointing playoff loss to the Cincinnati Reds that kept the Pirates from returning to the World Series, Clemente held a wide-ranging interview with a Pittsburgh reporter. He ended by saying, "My biggest worry – to live for my kids to be people that people look at them and respect them and they respect other people."[12]

Clemente's connection to Nicaragua was a long-standing one, what with his relationships with many Latin American ballplayers from the Caribbean and Central America. But it was heightened by his 1972 postseason travel to the country in his capacity as the manager of the Puerto Rican national team that played in the Amateur World Series in Managua from November 15 to December 5. Cuba won the series and the United States finished second. Puerto Rico finished with a 9-6 record, tied for sixth.[13] Clemente's short stay left him finding the Nicaraguan people warm and embracing of him. While there, "Roberto had become attached to a teenage orphan [Julio Parrales] who had lost both his legs and for whom he [and others on the Puerto Rican team] arranged to be provided artificial limbs."[14] Clemente promised to make him batboy for the Puerto Rican team the next year. His sensitivity to the plight of the young knew no boundaries.

When the December 23 earthquake wrecked Managua, Clemente felt a personal mission to lead relief efforts from Puerto Rico. Reflected Osvaldo Gil, a close friend of Clemente's, "When the earthquake occurred, Roberto called his Nicaraguan friends, who told him they were in great despair for there was no food, clothes, medicine. These words struck Clemente very hard and from that moment on [he] promised himself to do whatever, even the impossible, to help his friends."[15] About Clemente's stay in Nicaragua, his wife, Vera, reflected, "He liked to talk to the poor people. He used to tell me it was the same way Puerto Rico was years ago."[16] She later wrote, "We lost some very good friends in the earthquake."[17] Clemente "committed himself so fully to the effort that he regularly refused meals, barely slept, and never opened the Christmas presents that he had received. He even visited the houses of the wealthier sections of San Juan — literally going door to door — asking people to make donations."[18] Thanks significantly to him, the relief effort generated more than $150,000 and 26 tons of supplies.

Even during his relief efforts, Clemente kept his commitments to run a series of baseball clinics in Puerto Rico. "On the 27th," according to Yuyo Ruiz, "Roberto went to the Colon Baseball Park in Aguadilla to offer what would be his last technical clinic."[19] It was, according to Ramiro Martinez, a local sports announcer, one more opportunity for Clemente "to please children as they deserved. ... For him, it was much more important to give than to take, to please than be pleased."[20]

The rest of the story is tragic: Clemente arranged for a broken-down supply plane that should never have been okayed to fly, sending him and the four others on the plane to their death in the waters north of San Juan just minutes after takeoff at 9:23 P.M. on New Year's Eve. Roberto thought it was crucial that he fly with the supplies because of the rampant corruption of the Somoza regime in Nicaragua and Clemente's

belief that he could personally ensure that the supplies would not be commandeered by the dictator's cronies.[21]

Pirates great Willie Stargell spoke for many – players and fans alike – when he tearfully reflected immediately after the news, "Clemente's work with the relief effort was typical. Roberto was always trying to help someone. ... Just the way he lost his life, leaving home on the 31st of December. ... It's [January 1st] one of the most sacred days in Puerto Rico; it is a very religious day. It's when families traditionally are together. He somewhat broke that tradition because he felt the need to go to Nicaragua to help those families who were victims of the earthquake. As a result, he gave his life. ..."[22]

Clemente's death shook Puerto Rico deeply. And it left its imprint across the United States. President Nixon somberly reflected, "He sacrificed his life on a mission of mercy." Nixon himself donated $1,000 to the Roberto Clemente Memorial Fund.[23]

Vera Clemente reflected on her husband's final days and how his heroic efforts were memorialized:

> "When he passed away, all the funds that were raised were used to build a pediatrics wing at the Masaya Hospital [in Nicaragua]. That expansion for a pediatrics department was built with those funds, with the collaboration of engineers over there, and we'd transfer funds to them. ... A lot of people from [Puerto Rico] went to that inauguration. ... The hospital was decorated, it had air-conditioning, color TV, very pretty, pediatric, it was for children"[24]

In the months after Clemente's death, Nixon presented Vera with the Congressional Gold Medal in his memory. Thirty years later, she similarly accepted the Medal of Freedom from President George W. Bush at the White House.

In the last years of his prematurely shortened life, Clemente had focused his energies on the notion of a sports city in Carolina, his home, southeast of San Juan. Said Efren R. Bernier, a family friend, "He felt that sports were one of the best ways to imbue in youth the values of good citizenship. ... With sports the child learned in a natural way, at an important stage of his life, that one must sacrifice a bit for the common good."[25] Clemente remarked at the time that the government spent "millions for dope control in Puerto Rico, but they attack the problem after it is there. Why don't they attack it before it starts? It would help to get kids interested in sports and give them somewhere to learn."[26] Clemente's vision was clear and is worth repeating from Wagenheim in detail:

> He dreamed of building a large complex where children from all social classes could stay for weeks at a time. "I want to have three baseball fields, a swimming pool, basketball, tennis, a lake where fathers and sons can get together, all kinds of recreational sports. It's not enough to go to a summer camp and have one or two instructors for a little time and then you go home and forget everything. You go to a sports city and have people like Mays and Mantle and Williams, and kids would never forget it. If I was president of the United States, I would build a sports city and take in kids of all ways of life. What we want to do is exchange kids with every city in the United States and show all the kids how to live and play with other kids."[27]

In early 1972 Clemente worked with local authorities to solicit support and learned that a US naval base in San Juan would soon be turned over to the commonwealth, providing facilities already in place that could house Sports City. The land was deeded to Clemente just weeks before he died. Clemente did not see his vision fulfilled, but his death provided impetus for the Puerto Rican government to provide land to start the complex. Vera Clemente embraced the project, and it became her own – Ciudad Deportiva.[28]

Vera Clemente's *New York Times* obituary in 2019 shared what had been her resolve to fulfilling Roberto's, indeed their joint, dream of a sports community for Puerto Rico's youth.

"When he died, I felt the responsibility to at least make a reality of a sports city, to give children the opportunity not just to become stars but good citizens," she told the *Times* in 1994. "My main purpose was to do what he was planning to do."[29]

She said she was compelled to carry out her husband's wishes not only because of the way he died but also because of the way he had lived. "If he had died in a common way, people would still remember him," she said. "But December 31, it was a special day, and his was a special mission. I admire him for that, as a person, as a human being. So his image I keep alive. I feel happy doing what I am doing."[30]

The family's hard work eventually led to a sports and recreational complex spanning 300 acres with the range of sports fields and supporting infrastructure that Clemente hoped for. According to the Roberto Clemente Foundation website, the complex included a baseball park, football and soccer fields, a swimming pool, tennis courts, an athletic track, and a batting-practice field. It also had an entertainment area, a gym, and meeting rooms.[31]

Ciudad Deportiva/Sports City served thousands of youths in its earlier years, but recently the complex, poorly situated to begin with on marshland, has suffered from extreme weather (most recently 2017's Hurricane Maria), and due to the economic problems it has faced to keep it going, has been all but shut down. Occasional use is procured by local residents.[32]

Nonetheless, the Clemente family has continued to embrace Roberto's legacy, taking the long view in serving Clemente's two extended families, in Puerto Rico and Pittsburgh. Roberto Clemente Jr. offered this tribute to his father in O'Brien's 1994 remembrance of Clemente:

> My father was much more than a baseball player. He was a man with humanitarian vision – a dream of a better life for all children through sports and education. His dream was first manifested in 1974

Clemente conducting a sports clinic in 1972 with the youth of his native Carolina, only months before his tragic death. Courtesy of The Clemente Museum.

with the creation of the Roberto Clemente Sports City in Puerto Rico. Hundreds of thousands of children have benefited from its sports and educational programs. We established the Roberto Clemente Foundation to provide children in the Pittsburgh area with the opportunity to learn, enjoy, and participate in sports of all kinds in order to instill in them the qualities of responsibility, character and leadership. The foundation will emphasize the importance of education through supplemental tutoring and will rehabilitate local parks, playgrounds, and ballfields.[33]

Roberto Jr. helped establish Major League Baseball's Reviving Baseball in the Inner Cities (RBI) program in Puerto Rico in 1992 and then returned to the mainland in 1993 to help set up the foundation in his father's name. Roberto Jr. learned

that Pittsburgh did not have its own RBI program and was involved in its establishment in 1994.

"I don't do community service just because my father did it," Roberto Jr. said. "I do it because I can make a difference. I know what it's like to grow up without a father, and I can relate to kids when I tell them my story."

The founding of the Roberto Clemente Foundation in the early 1990s provided a focal point for the Clemente family and charitable donors to serve those in need. The foundation's website frames its purpose as follows:

The Roberto Clemente Foundation is a 501.C.3 non-profit organization founded to honor and perpetuate the legacy, legend and courage and character of

Roberto and Vera Clemente. The Foundation maintains the values which Roberto embodied on and off the field of hard work, faith, love, service and helping those less fortunate. The Foundation promotes sport and play, particularly through baseball and softball and has conducted numerous clinics with several partners. In addition to hospital and school visits, the Foundation has led disaster relief efforts, military and veteran support initiatives, conducts equipment drives and supports the Clemente Cup for NAIA and Division III college baseball teams.[34]

In 2009 the Public Broadcasting Service released as part of its *American Experience* series a documentary of Roberto Clemente's family and legacy. In it, son Luis Clemente said:

I would like for people to see my father as an inspiration. To see him as a person who came from, you know, not a rich neighborhood or anything, but from a noble house in Puerto Rico. Probably with no hopes of knowing what he was going to become but carrying himself in such a way that always had – you know, the values. That was always first. The caring and respect for the parents and siblings, and towards people. Zero tolerance against injustice. Not putting up with being put down. Becoming an activist and letting his message get across very strongly. That should be an inspiration to everyone … understanding how a single individual really truly makes a difference.[35]

Another lasting tribute to Clemente is the Roberto Clemente Award. The award "is given annually to the major-league player who 'best exemplifies the game of baseball, sportsmanship, community involvement and the individual's contribution to his team,' as voted on by baseball fans and members of the media. … Originally known as the Commissioner's Award, it has been presented by Major League Baseball since 1971. In 1973, the award was renamed for Clemente after his death."[36]

The story of Clemente's humanitarian ideals remains alive and a 2020 collaboration between the Clemente Museum in Pittsburgh and the Roberto Clemente Foundation created a temporary exhibit in San Juan to share in depth Clemente's life and legacy. Delayed in its opening by the worldwide pandemic, when it opened in October 2021, it was said the exhibit "highlights the humanitarian and charitable initiatives of the Roberto Clemente Foundation … and captures the story of Vera Clemente, a leader and humanitarian in her own right."[37]

Wrote Luis Clemente in the announcement of the exhibit's opening, "It was time to honor both of their legacies; we haven't dropped the ball; we continue to work on his legacy and all that he stood for."[38]

Today, the focus by brothers Roberto Jr. and Luis on their father's two homes keeps them attentive to the needs of both communities. The Roberto Clemente Foundation continues to inform their work on the mainland; likewise, their father's vision for Sports City, despite its current problems, remains the beacon of service, community, and opportunity for the streets and fields of Carolina and beyond. Revitalizing Ciudad Deportiva is uppermost in their minds.

Both acknowledged that development in the first years of Sports City was slow; the marshland deeded for the project was a lackluster property requiring significant expenditure to make it usable. The local community saw little progress – emerging structures were not visible from the road and vital early momentum was lost. In recent times, efforts by the nonprofit board overseeing Sports City to bring improvements to the complex have failed to gain government acceptance. One idea was a partnership with Legacy Sports USA, whose complex in Mesa, Arizona, offered a model for Sports City. Instead, the Puerto Rican government has sought to reclaim the land on which Sports City is located, and with it, establish direct government control replacing the nonprofit organization's oversight.

Recent legislative actions have further muddied the waters with the passing of a law to collect revenue through the sale of commemorative Clemente license plates and the mandatory purchase of registration stickers highlighting Roberto's accomplishments and values. Revenue would go in part to a Fondo del Distrito Roberto Clemente (not to be confused with the family's foundation). According to Julio Pablon:

> Clemente's middle son, Luis Clemente learned of this sticker, [of the] license plate with his father's image, like everyone else, he saw it in the news. He was taken aback and went on social media with the following statement: "Not even the Roberto Clemente Foundation, much less my family, has any influence on that charge, and even more so, we are not the beneficiaries of this fund." He added, "In fact, our approval was not sought for the use of our father's image on the commemorative registration stickers and license plates. Image to which we legitimately have the rights to use. In addition, the government of Puerto Rico did not seek or obtain the approval of other entities that claim the rights involved in the image."[39]

Guest columnist Mayra Montero for *El Nuevo Día* at the time the legislation was announced wrote:

> "The situation is very simple: as politicians find it increasingly difficult to raise money for their luxuries, their legislative offices full of party friends, their trips, petty cash, whims, and those campaign promises that, because this is a bankrupt country, they cannot and will not comply, they have found a way to rob citizens and extract $5 a head. That to start. It is an experiment that could be extended."[40]

It is worth asking what is next. In 2022, time is understandably set aside to celebrate Clemente's 3,000th hit and then honor the 50th Anniversary of Roberto's ultimate sacrifice, dying while delivering relief supplies to earthquake torn Nicaragua. Major League Baseball, the Pittsburgh Pirates, the city of Pittsburgh, and yes, the people of Puerto Rico will all stop and reflect on the life and loss of a great icon. However, real measures can and should accompany these remembrances. The Clemente brothers continue to tell their story and seek partnerships and collaboration that will reestablish Sports City and take it to the next level. They know that the people of Puerto Rico and the fans of Roberto are ready, willing, and able to honor Roberto properly by taking the "opportunity to make a difference in this world." May a genuine partnership among all who hold Roberto's legacy dear take place.

NOTES

1 Kal Wagenheim, *Clemente!* (New York: Olmstead Press, 2001), 3.

2 Bruce Markusen, *Roberto Clemente: The Great One* (Chicago: Sports Publishing, Inc., 1998), 195.

3 Markusen, 196.

4 Markusen, 196.

5 Markusen, 196.

6 Markusen, 125-127.

7 David Mariniss, *Clemente: The Passion and Grace of Baseball's Last Hero* (New York: Simon & Schuster, 2006), 148.

8 Markusen, 150.

9 Markusen, 151.

10 Markusen, 173.

11 Wagenheim, 179.

12 Mariniss, 285.

13 Baseball-Reference.com, https://www.baseball-reference.com/bullpen/1972_Amateur_World_Series, accessed October 28, 2021.

14 Markusen, 311.

15 Yuyo Ruiz, *The Last Hours of Roberto Clemente* (San Juan, Puerto Rico: Yuyo Ruiz, 1998), 85.

16 Jim O'Brien, *Remembering Roberto: Clemente Recalled by Teammates, Family, Friends, and Fans* (Pittsburgh: James P. O'Brien Publishing, 1994), 38.

17 Markusen, 311.

18 Markusen, 311.

19 Ruiz, 42.

20 Ruiz, 47.

21 Mariniss, 304.

22 Mariniss, 317.

23 O'Brien, 34.

24 "Clemente's Family and Legacy," American Experience, PBS.org. https://www.pbs.org/wgbh/americanexperience/features/roberto-clemente-his-family-and-his-legacy/accessed November 4, 2021.

25 Wagenheim, 182.

26 Wagenheim, 182.

27 Wagenheim, 182.

28 https://robertoclementefoundation.com/veras-vision/, accessed December 30, 2021.

29 Katharine Q. Seelye, "Vera Clemente, Flame-Keeping Widow of Baseball's Roberto, Dies at 78," *New York Times*, November 18, 2019.

30 Seelye.

31 www.robertoclementefoundation.com, accessed November 4, 2021.

32 El Vocero, March 19, 2022, https://www.elvocero.com/gobierno/legislatura/el-representante-ngel-matos-pide-agilizar-el-traspaso-de-la-ciudad-deportiva-roberto-clemente/article_84f81086-a72e-11ec-9fe9-4b0391309be5.html.

33 O'Brien, 12.

34 https://latinobaseball.com/pittsburgh-designates-sept-15-as-robert-clemente-day-weeklong-events-celebrate-pirates-legend/, accessed December 30 2021.

35 American Experience, PBS.org.

36 Markusen, 340.

37 "The Roberto Clemente Museum in Puerto Rico to Re-Open for a Limited Engagement," *Latinx Newswire*, October 14, 2021.

38 Latinx Newswire.

39 Julio Pablon, January 18, 2022, Latinosports, "Big Controversy in Puerto Rico over Imposed Clemente Registration Sticker & License Plates."

40 Pablon.

SAINT ROBERTO CLEMENTE?

BY RICHARD J. PUERZER

Roberto Clemente is one of the greatest players in the history of baseball, exhibiting remarkable skills both in the field and at the plate. Likewise, Clemente is widely regarded as an admirable human being. He was not only a good teammate, husband, and father, but he was also a responsible world citizen and faithful Catholic. His virtuous reputation as both a ballplayer and person was eternally cemented by the circumstances of his death: He died while still an active player trying to bring aid to Nicaraguan earthquake victims.

We generally consider professional ballplayers for no greater honor than induction into the National Baseball Hall of Fame, a status that Clemente achieved soon after his death. However, unlike every other ballplayer and very few other human beings, some have desired to further scrutinize Clemente's life. They have asked if Clemente led a life of heroic virtue and was holy. They have asked if, in death, Clemente was responsible for a miracle. They have asked that serious consideration be given to the solemn question: Was Roberto Clemente a saint?

In the summer of 2014, a story appeared on the *National Catholic Reporter* website titled "Could Baseball Player Roberto Clemente Become a Saint?"[1] The article documented the work of Pittsburgh native Richard Rossi, a former evangelical minister, in promoting the idea of Clemente as a saint. Rossi produced and directed a 2013 movie-length dramatization of Clemente, titled *Baseball's Last Hero: 21 Clemente Stories.*[2] As he contemplated Clemente's life, Rossi came to believe that Clemente had led a saintly life. In 2014 this belief led Rossi to reach out to Pope Francis and Archbishop Roberto Gonzalez Nieves of San Juan, Puerto Rico, and seek their support. At the time, it appeared that Rossi had little more than his personal conviction motivating him to promote the notion of Clemente as a saint. However, the idea resonated with others, and over the next year stories appeared in the media, from the *Los Angeles Times* to *The Sporting News*, all presenting this idea with something much closer to curiosity, and even possibility, rather than skepticism.[3]

Any discussion of making Clemente a saint would be incomplete without detailing the checkered past of its primary proponent, Rossi. Raised a Catholic, he became a born-again Christian in his college years and later started his own churches and held healing clinics, events akin to faith healing. In 1994 Rossi's life took a much darker turn when he was charged with attempted murder after his wife was found near death on a roadside near Pittsburgh. She initially accused Rossi of attacking her but later recanted the story. The subsequent trial became a sensationalized event and ended in a hung jury. Rossi served 96 days in prison after a plea bargain. He and his family moved to California, where he once again found himself in legal trouble, charged with diverting money from a church for his personal use.[4]

In the summer of 2017, stories regarding the campaign for Clemente's sainthood were revived as it was reported that Clemente had perhaps been responsible for a miracle. Jamie Nieto, the actor who played Clemente in *Baseball's Last Hero*, was purported to have been a part of the miracle.

Besides being an actor, Nieto was a former Olympic high jumper who broke his neck in an accident in 2016. Nieto was married on July 22, 2017. Despite being told that he might never walk again, Nieto walked down the aisle at his wedding. Rossi claimed that Nieto's recovery and ability to walk again as he took part in the marriage sacrament was miraculous and attributed the miracle to Clemente.

Additionally, Rossi claimed that this miracle further qualified Clemente for sainthood.[5] After Rossi's claim was made, it was reported that "church sources" stated that Pope Francis had officially declared Clemente as "blessed." This moved Clemente just one step from becoming a saint in the Catholic Church. Again, this story received wide, and generally earnest, media attention.[6] However, a few days later, the Vatican officially denied the claim of beatification of Clemente.[7]

No new information concerning the possibility of sainthood for Roberto Clemente has appeared since 2017.

While it seems unlikely that Clemente will be ever truly be considered for sainthood, he remains an inspirational figure for his humanitarian work. A quote attributed to Clemente reflects his beliefs in serving others: "Any time you have the opportunity to accomplish something for somebody who comes behind you and you do not do it, you are wasting your time on Earth."[8] As the stories regarding the possibility of sainthood for Clemente were met almost exclusively with curiosity and wonder rather than disbelief, clearly they struck a chord with the public. In life and in death, Clemente evokes thoughts beyond the baseball diamond. Baseball fans will continue to admire, revere, and venerate Roberto Clemente as a good, if not saintly, human being who lived a grace-filled life.

NOTES

1   Heather Morrison, "Could Baseball Player Roberto Clemente Become a saint," *National Catholic Reporter*, June 28, 2014, https://www.ncronline.org/news/people/could-baseball-player-roberto-clemente-become-saint.

2   *Baseball's Last Hero: 21 Clemente Stories*, written and directed by Richard Rossi, 2013.

3   Michael McGough, "Roberto Clemente Be a saint? He's in the Ballpark," *Los Angeles Times*, June 13, 2014, https://www.latimes.com/opinion/opinion-la/la-ol-clemente-miracles-sainthood-20140613-story.html; Justin McGuire, "Should Roberto Clemente Be a Saint? Some Fans Think So," *The Sporting News*, June 23, 2014, https://www.sportingnews.com/us/mlb/news/roberto-clemente-saint-sainthood-canonization-pirates/1lbioj3z5yrjm1nctddwzes6dd.

4   Steve Levin, "Rev. Rossi Back in News as Hollywood Success Story," *Pittsburgh Post-Gazette*, May 4, 2008, https://old.post-gazette.com/pg/08125/878975-85.stm; Diana Nelson Jones, "Saint Roberto Clemente?: Former Pittsburgh Pastor Seeks Sainthood for the Pirates Great," *Pittsburgh Post-Gazette*, January 11, 2015, https://www.post-gazette.com/local/city/2015/01/11/Saint-Roberto-Clemente-Richard-Rossi-Pirates/stories/201501110144.

5   "Will Pope Greenlight Clemente Canonization? – Some Claim Miracle Requirement Met," *Catholic News Wire*, July 22, 2017, http://catholicnewswire.blogspot.com/.

6   Marissa Payne, "After July 'Miracle,' Pope Francis Reportedly Moves Roberto Clemente Closer to Sainthood," *Chicago Tribune*, August 17, 2017, https://www.chicagotribune.com/sports/ct-roberto-clemente-closer-to-sainthood-20170817-story.html.

7   "No, Pope Francis Did Not Beatify Roberto Clemente," *Catholic News Agency*, August 18, 2017, https://www.catholicnewsagency.com/news/36643/no-pope-francis-did-not-beatify-roberto-clemente.

8   This quote was in Clemente's acceptance speech for the Tris Speaker Award in Houston, Texas. It is mentioned in the article "Standing Cheer for Roberto," *The Sporting News*, February 20, 1971: 44.

REMEMBRANCE AND ICONOGRAPHY OF CLEMENTE IN PUBLIC SPACES

BY JUSTIN KRUEGER

Stories about Roberto Clemente are numerous. He is much more than a man who died at age 38 in a plane crash carrying humanitarian aid to Nicaragua. In the half-century since his untimely death, Clemente has transcended to cultural icon and been honored with numerous public remembrances. Public remembrances are value statements. In one part, the act is about not forgetting. It is about saying that a person, place, idea, or event is worthy of public recognition, of public space. That there is value to a wider public rather than to a small group or individual. But remembrance is also about those who enact the remembrance. What is it that the remembrance is supposed to evoke? Or mean? For whom is the remembrance meant?

According to Dr. Chris Stride, a senior lecturer and applied statistician at the University of Sheffield in England who also helps run The Sporting Statues Project, Clemente has more statues worldwide than any athlete other than Pelé.[1]

Clemente's remembrance, however, is far more than public statues and memorials. His name, face, and figure has often been utilized in public spaces of high volume: parks, schools, thoroughfares, bridges, stadiums, even postage stamps. In all these avenues, despite diverging depictions or different focal points, Clemente is remembered as an inspiration.

PUERTO RICO

One of the first public spaces in remembrance of Roberto Clemente was dedicated shortly after his death. A newly minted indoor events arena in San Juan, Puerto Rico, was named Roberto Clemente Coliseum (Coliseo Roberto Clemente). It opened in early 1973, barely a month after the ballplayer's death, and for a time, it was the largest indoor arena in Puerto Rico.[2]

Clemente's hometown of Carolina, has several spaces of public remembrance. Vera Clemente, Roberto's widow, established his dream 'sports city, the Roberto Clemente Municipal Sports Complex (Ciudad Deportiva Roberto Clemente), between Carolina and San Juan. It currently covers 304 acres and includes numerous athletic fields, and a statue of Roberto Clemente. However, a direct hit by Hurricane Maria, a category five hurricane, in 2017 left extensive damage to the facilities. In 2020, FEMA pledged millions of dollars to help rebuild the complex.

Also located in Carolina is Roberto Clemente Stadium (Estadio Roberto Clemente). It opened in 2000 and serves as the home of Gigantes de Carolina of the Puerto Rican Professional Baseball League. Outside the home plate entrance to the stadium is a statue of Clemente in stride, getting his 3,000th hit. Another statue, located outside the stadium at the center-field gate, shows him tipping his cap after reaching that milestone.

A nearby road is named in his honor, and multiple Clemente statues greet visitors to a roundabout fountain near downtown Carolina.

PITTSBURGH

Clemente in public remembrance is nowhere more evident than in Pittsburgh.

In 1976, Pittsburgh renamed a road that ran along the old Forbes Field in the Oakland neighborhood, Clemente Road. It was renamed Roberto & Vera Clemente Drive in 2021 by City Council approval. The change in name occurred after the Clementes' sons petitioned the city of Pittsburgh to add their mother's name.[3]

On July 8, 1994, during All-Star Week in Pittsburgh, a 12-foot-tall bronze statue of Clemente was placed at Gate A of Three Rivers Stadium.

At the dedication, Dan Galbreath, read a letter that Clemente had written to him and his father, John W. Galbreath, after the 1971 World Series. The Galbreaths had owned the Pirates from 1946 to 1985. In the letter, Clemente insisted that he would never tarnish his legacy by playing just to cash a paycheck. He wrote: "Whenever you don't think I can contribute to our team's success, I will retire. I will never play for any other team, ever."[4]

A portion of the Legends of Pittsburgh wall mural by Michael Malle, featuring images of Bill Mazeroski, Clemente, and Honus Wagner. Courtesy of The Clemente Museum.

Before Clemente's death, John W. Galbreath had named one of his racehorses Roberto in honor of the star outfielder. The horse went on to win the prestigious Epsom Derby of Surrey, England, in 1972.

After the Pirates moved to PNC Park in 2001, the statue was moved to its new location outside the center-field gate where it now stands between the ballpark and the Roberto Clemente (6th Street) Bridge.

Other Pirate greats with statues at PNC Park include Hall of Famers Honus Wagner, Willie Stargell, and Bill Mazeroski.

The 6th Street Bridge was renamed in honor of Clemente in August 1998. To many, the renaming was public appeasement for PNC Financial Services gaining naming rights to the new ballpark. Before naming rights to the new ballpark had been announced, there was hope among fans that the stadium would be named in honor of "The Great One."

SABR helps commemorate the location of second base, Three Rivers Stadium. Courtesy of The Clemente Museum.

Roberto Clemente Bridge stretches across the Allegheny River and is part of the "Three Sisters" built in the 1920s, which also includes the 7th Street (now the Andy Warhol Bridge) and 9th Street (now the Rachel Carson Bridge) bridges.

Beyond daily vehicular use, Clemente Bridge also serves as a pedestrian thoroughfare when the Pirates play at home.

Pittsburgh is also home to the non-profit Clemente Museum. The museum is in Engine House 25 in the Lawrenceville neighborhood and includes a large collection of photos and other memorabilia from his baseball career and humanitarian work. As noted on their website:

"Clemente dedicated his 3000th hit to the Pittsburgh fans and people of Puerto Rico. We are honored to be part of Pittsburgh's dedication to him. Some will come to remember. Some will come to learn. All will leave inspired."[5]

AND THE REST OF THE UNITED STATES

In 2018, four members of Puerto Rican descent in the U.S. House of Representatives sponsored a bill to get Roberto Clemente's crash site in Loíza, Puerto Rico, added to the National Register of Historic Places. The bill stated:

"Roberto Clemente's passion and advocacy demonstrated the positive influence that professional athletes could have in improving the lives of others... Roberto Clemente challenged the stereotypes that had marginalized native Spanish speakers in this Nation and remains an icon to many Puerto Ricans and Latinos in the United States and Latin America."[6]

A similar resolution was sent by 11 U.S. senators in December 2021 to the Secretary of the Interior.[7]

In the fall of 2020, the Orange County School Board in Florida voted unanimously to change the name of Stonewall Jackson Middle School to Roberto Clemente Middle School. The student population of the school is predominantly Hispanic. Prior to the renaming, it was the last school in central Florida named for a Confederate general.[8] Artist Neysa Millán added a mural of Clemente at the school after being asked by the local Little League.[9]

Additionally, the Orlando City Council renamed Stonewall Jackson Road in Clemente's honor in June 2021. Commissioner Tony Ortiz noted that "it was the people who aimed for change." The newly renamed Roberto Clemente Middle School is located on the road.[10]

On the occasion, Orlando mayor Buddy Dyer, tweeted:

"Thanks to community efforts, we're now able to honor Roberto Clemente, a hero to many, and make our city more welcoming with this newly renamed road. Each day... students will get to school via this street that recognizes a humanitarian who uplifted those in need."[11]

There are also numerous other public remembrances of Clemente throughout the United States. A section of Route 21 in Newark, New Jersey was designated by the New Jersey Legislature at Roberto Clemente Memorial Highway in summer 2016. The Osceola County Board of County Commissioners in Florida dedicated the Roberto Clemente Memorial Roadway in 2015.

Schools named in Clemente's honor are located in Pennsylvania, Connecticut, New York, New Jersey, Illinois, and Maryland.

Several other parks also are named for Clemente. Roberto Clemente State Park, located in the Bronx, is a 25-acre multipurpose park located alongside the Harlem River. It has playgrounds, basketball courts, numerous ball fields, swimming pool, recreation building, and waterfront promenade. Each year, the park holds a Roberto Clemente Week with special events that celebrate the former ballplayer's life.[12]

In 2013, park officials unveiled a life-size bronze statue of its namesake. The statue, commissioned and donated by Goya Foods, shows Clemente raising his helmet in acknowledgement of the crowd after his 3,000th hit.[13] The four-foot base upon which the statue stands has the inscription of Clemente's famous quote:

> "Any time you have an opportunity to make a difference in this world and you don't, then you are wasting your time on Earth."

It was also the first statue in New York to honor a person of Puerto Rican heritage.

At the dedication of the statue, Clemente's son, Roberto Jr. noted:

> "For the children who use this park, who play here, this is a great way for them to see who the man was... They will see the statue and be able to learn about Roberto Clemente, not only the baseball player but the human being."[14]

Park director Frances Rodriguez commented:

> "We are absolutely honored to receive this statue... The significance is great because we are here to serve the community and Clemente was a true humanitarian. He truly cared about other people."[15]

In November 2018 the Roberto Clemente Plaza for bus and subway commuters opened in the South Bronx. Like Herald Square in Midtown Manhattan, Clemente Plaza was envisioned as an urban green space and serves about 75,000 visitors daily.[16]

The monument *Para Roberto* was unveiled at the plaza in October 2019. Below is a description:

> "The entire sculpture is cast in bronze with twelve sugar cane stalks (representing Clemente's 12 Golden Glove wins) surround a chair made of baseball bats, baseballs, and stickballs with the Puerto Rican flag as the back of the chair."[17]

The artist, Melissa Calderón noted:

> "The sculpture features an empty 'Abuelo' chair- the type a grandfather might use in Puerto Rico, reminiscing and telling stories filled with history and wisdom which represents Clemente in his retirement, had he lived. I'm grateful for the City's support of this commission and thrilled to see it installed in the heart of the South Bronx where it can become a part of the neighborhood fabric and inspire future generations with Clemente's example."[18]

Another well-known public space named after Clemente is located at Back Bay Fens in Boston. Roberto Clemente Field is part of Boston's Emerald Necklace, a 1,100-acre chain of parks that was originally designed by Frederick Law Olmsted in the late 1800s. While the field is city property, it is managed by the athletic department of Division III Emmanuel College and used for Saints softball, women and men's soccer, lacrosse, and track and field.[19]

A Little League in Branch Brook Park in Newark, New Jersey, is named in Clemente's honor. A cast of the Clemente statue that is located outside PNC Park was unveiled at Branch Brook in 2012. Young ballplayers play games at Roberto Clemente Field.

A neighborhood park near downtown Miami, Florida, and a city park in Cleveland, Ohio, also are named in Clemente's honor.

The Louisville Slugger Museum & Factory unveiled its statue of Clemente, crouched in a batting stance, during the summer of 2021. The statue is the sixth at the museum and follows

Clemente's number is displayed on the RF porch of Parque Luis Alfonso Velasquez Flores in Managua, Nicaragua. Courtesy of Steven A. Melnick, Ph.D.

Babe Ruth, Ted Williams, Ken Griffey Jr., Derek Jeter, and Jackie Robinson.

Bailey Mazik, the museum's curator and exhibits director, noted at the ceremony unveiling the statue:

> "Clemente had so much talent on and off the field, and what a tremendous understatement that is...He connected people through service and sport. He did what needed to be done for his team and his community."[20]

The National Baseball Hall of Fame unveiled bronze statues of Roberto Clemente, Jackie Robinson, and Lou Gehrig at an exhibit in 2008 called Character and Courage. Also, in 2015, a bronze bust of Clemente was unveiled in Boston's South End at the corner of West Dedham and Washington Street.[21]

Clemente has also been honored with U.S. Postal Service stamps issued in 1984 and 2000.

CONCLUSION

Roberto Clemente was a great ballplayer. In his death, he has transcended the limitations he once lamented during the 1971 World Series:

> "I feel that I would be considered to be a much better athlete if I were not a black Latin...I play as good as anybody. Maybe I play as good as anybody who plays the game. But I am not loved. I don't need to be loved. I just wish that it would happen. There are many people like me who would like that to happen. I wish it for them. Do you know what I mean?'[22]

Clemente is an iconic figure. In life, he demonstrated that through his athleticism, through his humanitarian efforts, and in his efforts and desire for the world to be a more just place. He is remembered. In the 50 years since his death, he has become a symbol of admiration.

SOURCES

In addition to the sources cited in the Notes, information was gathered from Baseball-Reference.com and Baseball-Alamanac.com.

NOTES

1   Hayes Gardner, "A bronze age for college football: Behind the culture that honors sports figures with statues," *Louisville Courier Journal*, January 7, 2020.

2   Judy Cantor-Navas, "Remember Baseball Great Roberto Clemente With These Musical Tributes," *Billboard*, December 28, 2017. https://www.billboard.com/music/latin/roberto-clemente-death-anniversary-musical-tributes-8085490/

3   "New street sign unveiled for 'Roberto & Vera Clemente Drive' in Pittsburgh's Oakland neighborhood," WTAE, December 2, 2021. https://www.wtae.com/article/roberto-vera-clemente-street-signs-pittsburgh/38415251

4   Rob Biertempfel, "What if...Roberto Clemente had played 3 more seasons with the Pirates?," *Athletic*, August 18, 2021. https://theathletic.com/2765112/2021/08/18/what-if-roberto-clemente-had-played-three-more-seasons-with-the-pirates/

5   "The Museum," The Clemente Museum, https://clementemuseum.com/museum/

6   Jose E. Serrano, H. Res. 792, December 10, 2018. https://www.congress.gov/bill/115th-congress/house-resolution/792/text

7   S. Res. 481, December 16, 2021. https://www.govinfo.gov/content/pkg/BILLS-117sres481is/html/BILLS-117sres481is.htm

8   Andrew Limberg, "School in Florida renamed in honor of Roberto Clemente," 93.7 The Fan, September 23, 2020. https://www.audacy.com/937thefan/news/pittsburgh-pirates/school-in-florida-renamed-in-honor-of-roberto-clemente

9   Ezzy Castro, "Central Florida artist creates mural for Roberto Clemente Middle School," ClickOrlando.com, March 26, 2021. https://www.clickorlando.com/news/local/2021/03/26/central-florida-artist-creates-mural-for-roberto-clemente-middle-school/#//

10 Ezzy Castro, "City of Orlando unveils new Roberto Clemente street sign," ClickOrlando.com, June 23, 2021. https://www.clickorlando.com/news/local/2021/06/23/city-of-orlando-unveils-new-roberto-clemente-street-sign/

11 Alex Galbraith, "Later, loser: Orlando renames road named for Confederate general to honor Roberto Clemente," Orlando Weekly, June 23, 2021. https://www.orlandoweekly.com/news/later-loser-orlando-renames-road-named-for-confederate-general-to-honor-roberto-clemente-29545752

12 "Roberto Clemente State Park," New York State Parks, Recreation and Historic Preservation, https://parks.ny.gov/parks/robertoclemente/details.aspx

13 Denis Slattery, "Baseball legend Roberto Clemente immortalized with statue at his namesake state park," *New York Daily News*, June 27, 2013. https://www.nydailynews.com/new-york/bronx/inside-the-park-homer-roberto-clemente-article-1.1384602

14 Slattery.

15 Slattery.

16 "Roberto Clemente Plaza," Third Avenue Business Improvement District. https://www.thirdavenuebid.org/roberto-clemente-plaza

17 Ed García Conde, "NYC's Newest Monument is a Tribute to Puerto Rican Humanitarian and Baseball Legend Roberto Clemente in The Bronx," Welcome2TheBronx.com, October 4, 2019. https://welcome2thebronx.com/2019/10/04/nycs-newest-monument-is-a-tribute-to-puerto-rican-humanitarian-and-baseball-legend-roberto-clemente-in-the-bronx/

18 García Conde.

19 "Roberto Clemente Field," Emmanuel College: Centers, Partnerships & Institutes. https://www.emmanuel.edu/discover-emmanuel/centers-partnerships-and-institutes/community-partnerships/roberto-clemente-field.html

20 Hayes Gardner, "With sons present, Roberto Clemente statue unveiled at Louisville Slugger Museum," *Louisville Courier Journal*, August 18, 2021. https://www.courier-journal.com/story/sports/mlb/2021/08/18/louisville-slugger-museum-unveils-statue-famous-latino-athlete/5557290001/

21 Amanda Hoover, "Roberto Clemente honored with statue in South End," Boston.com, November 19, 2015. https://www.boston.com/news/local-news/2015/11/19/roberto-clemente-honored-with-statue-in-south-end/

22 Wells Twombly, "Super Hero," *San Francisco Examiner*, January 2, 1973.

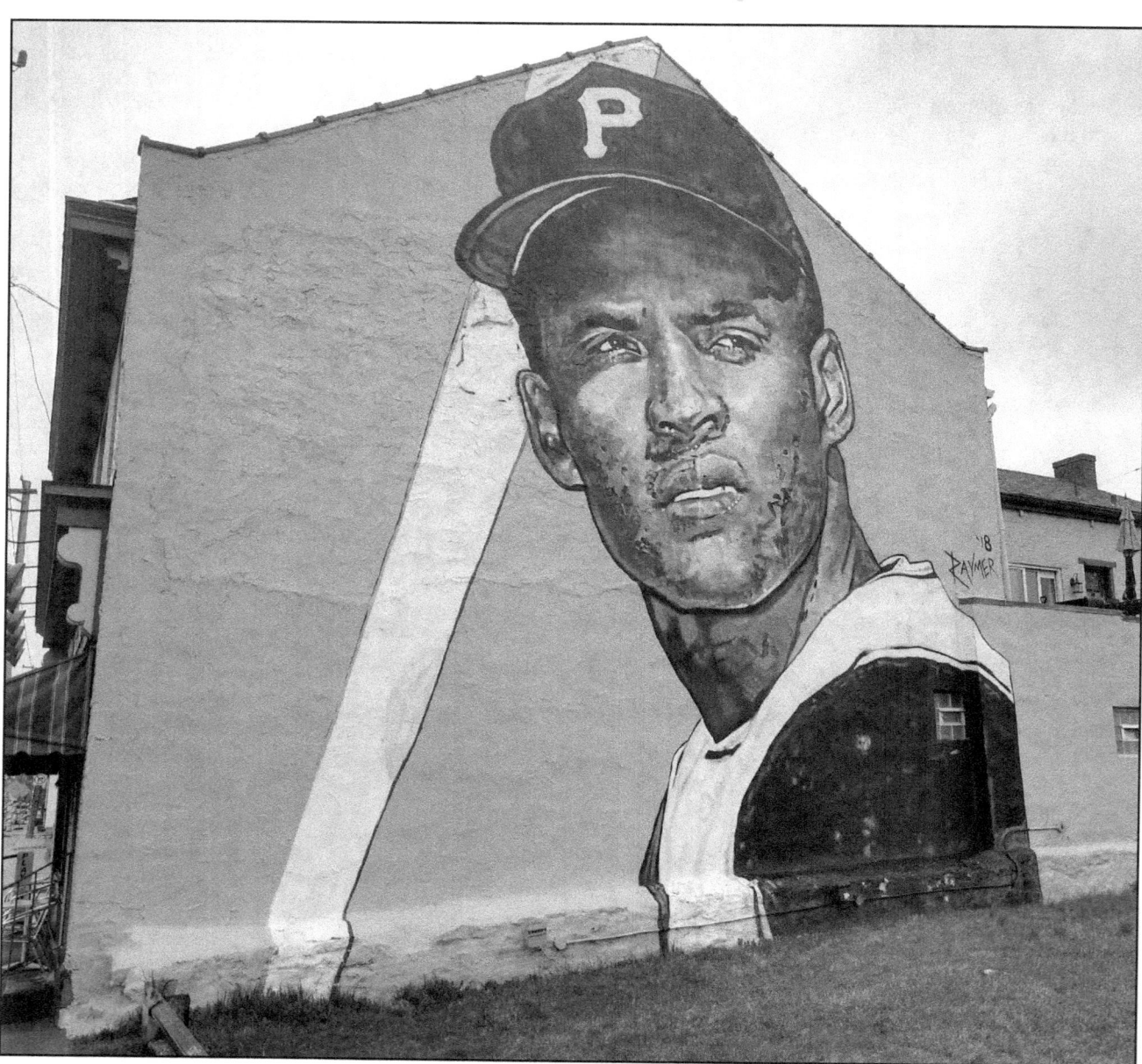

Courtesy of The Clemente Museum.

ROBERTO CLEMENTE POSTAGE STAMPS ACROSS THE WORLD

BY TONY S. OLIVER

What if postage stamps could talk? Would they be beholden to secrecy, sworn to maintain the integrity of the content of their envelopes? Would they be blind to their mission, knowing only they serve to accompany letters from origin to destination? Or would they be eager to tell stories of their voyage and the messages they carry?

One can only imagine the 1984 and 2000 Roberto Clemente US Postal Service stamps would beam with pride to carry monetary assistance, moral support, words of encouragement, and other acts of human kindness. There would be no better way to honor their subject.

Clemente is one of four baseball players (along with Jackie Robinson, Babe Ruth, and Lou Gehrig) to be depicted on more than one USPS stamp.[1] Even the most diehard baseball fans are unaware of the process and the numerous steps to earn this honor. Like the sport itself, the methodology is independent of time and prone to managerial strategy.

The USPS Citizens' Stamp Advisory Committee (CSAC), established in 1957, evaluates stamp design topics. While anyone can submit suggestions, the meetings are confidential and the minutes are not released to the public. Current rules prevent living persons from consideration, and three years must pass after someone's death before they can be considered. Over 40,000 proposals are received each year, so projects are carefully researched for several years.[2] Once a theme is officially selected, external artists and design experts are tasked with bringing the concept to life.[3]

The 20-cent stamp was issued on August 17, 1984, on the eve of what would have been Clemente's 50th birthday.[4] The ceremony was held in his namesake sports city in Carolina, Puerto Rico. The limited color palette takes away all but the essential components: Clemente's head is shown against a waving Puerto Rican flag, his brown skin popping against the white border. Clemente's face is determined, much as it was between the foul lines, and reflective, as it was during interviews. The light blue background makes the stamp almost angelic; the absence of the traditional Pirates color and the "P" on the cap paints an almost ethereal reverence. More than 119 million units were printed by the American Bank Note Company, but its origin story dates back several years.[5]

The stamp was designed by Yale School of Art graduate Juan López-Bonilla, originally from Puerto Rico. In 1981 his professor and mentor Bradbury Thompson notified him about the dream opportunity, given that López-Bonilla idolized Clemente.

"I had a good relationship with my professors, especially Bradbury Thompson. He asked me about my baseball idols: Cepeda, Clemente, among others. I shared that on New Year's Eve 1972 we were going to a party in Carolina. ... As we passed the airport, I told my wife that the motor on a plane seemed to be backfiring. When we reached the party, it was like a funeral. I asked 'did someone die?' I hadn't heard ... and when my friend told me my hair stood on its end. Thompson told he served on the CSAC and asked whether I would be interested in submitting a design for the Clemente stamp."[6]

There was a family connection as well, as López Bonilla's uncle Héctor, an architect, had designed the Sports City. López-Bonilla submitted two designs: one with the Pirates star at bat, and the chosen one, which looks remarkably complete in a preliminary sketch he shared with the author. While few guidelines were given him, one stood out: "try to capture not just his sportsmanship, but also his sense of humanity."[7] Almost four decades later, López-Bonilla still receives mail about his work on the stamp, a source of immense pride: "The greatest honor, the greatest privilege, and the greatest gift, was not only that I was able to do the stamp ... but that Bradbury Thompson went to Puerto Rico for the first day of issue. That was one of the most significant moments of my life."[8]

The Postal Service sent 500,000 of the 20-cent Clemente stamps to Pittsburgh. Fans formed a line at the McKnight station, "decorated in black and gold against a backdrop of Pirate memorabilia," and bought 22,506 Clemente stamps, or four times the typical figure for a first-day offering. "Customers got a taste of Clemente birthday cake" and popcorn, while former Pirate Frank Thomas signed autographs. The downtown office also did a booming business, with sales up by 25 percent.[9]

Sixteen years later, Clemente was selected as one of 20 Hall of Famers for the "Legends of Baseball" stamp series. The 33-cent piece highlights Clemente, regal in the classic 1950s/1960s sleeveless Pirate uniform, in a batting stance against an azure background.

Phil Jordan served as the art director: "USPS manager Carl Burcham and I spent a couple of days at the Baseball Hall of Fame in Cooperstown. The director Bill Guilfoile consulted with us on how to manage a sheet of 20 subjects. The players were selected by the Baseball Hall of Fame."[10] Jordan, who retired in 2014, would also later work on the "Major League Baseball All-Stars" series released in 2012.[11]

The 20 players were among the hundred considered for the All-Century Team, announced during the 1999 season.[12] Three designers were commissioned to produce concepts for consideration, with Don Truesdell's submission being chosen. Truesdell, a noted baseball fan, partnered with illustrator Joe Saffold. This relationship is akin to the battery, as both must be in lockstep: "The designer manages, arranges, and organizes all aspects of the product – illustration, photography, typography and mechanics. The illustrator produces art for the subject."[13]

Saffold's submission for consideration had local connections. "They asked me to do a preliminary piece of artwork ... from the state of Georgia, you have to do Ty Cobb."[14] His drawings used colored pencils, and oil and acrylic paints to bring his subjects to life, a task made harder by the black-and-white sources given the eras of many players: "When we got into the job, the Postal Service had a baseball committee of experts to help them choose the Hall of Fame players. They gave me reference photos, which was helpful, and they were very supportive about providing the best available photos I could use to work with. One of the most invaluable books was the bible of baseball uniforms through history … that became one of the stickiest points of everything since a lot were done from black-and-white photographs."[15]

The finished product was released on July 6, 2000, in Atlanta, five days before Turner Field hosted the All-Star Game. A total of 225 million stamps were printed by Ashton-Potter, with each design appearing once in the 11.25 million sets.[16]

Other nations have also issued stamps honoring Clemente. Turks and Caicos, a British Overseas Territory in the Caribbean, was the first; a 1980 landscape design shows Clemente's face and a batting scene. The words "human rights" adorn the left column while Clemente's year of birth and death (1934-1972) are shown on the bottom. Nicaragua, forever linked to Clemente, paid its respects in 1984 as part of a "Famous Baseball Players" panel.

Grenada, capitalizing on the baseball-card fever that characterized the 1980s, partnered with Major League Baseball Properties, Inc. and the Major League Baseball Players' Association on a nine-stamp panel showcasing Ruth, Bob Feller, Clemente, and six active players.[17] While the USPS forbids honoring living persons with stamps, other countries have no such restrictions.[18] The government was forthcoming in its rationale, noting an expected fiscal windfall, while competing camps of collectors – baseball card and philatelic – argued the merits of the 1988 product.[19] Estimates ranged from $30 million to $50 million to be derived from the issue, a combination of the sales price being above the face value and the likelihood that collectors would not use them for mailing letters.[20] In essence, the government was printing money.

Another Caribbean country, Saint Vincent and the Grenadines, produced a stamp in 1992, as part of a series of sports figures. The year of Clemente's Hall of Fame election, 1973, is shown on the left side. Nicaragua produced a stunning "starting nine" titled "Siglo XX Grandes Jugadores de Beisbol" (co-titled in English as "Baseball's Hall of Fame Dream Team") with one Cooperstown-enshrined player per position.[21]

St. Vincent seized on the 50th anniversary of Robinson breaking the sport's color barrier by commemorating his feat. Sixteen other Black players, captured in photographs rather than drawings, accompany Robinson in the panel. Laos, a country with no baseball history, chose Clemente among other American sports figures in a 1999 collection titled "Great People of the 20th Century." A 3x3 grid panel captures him in mid-swing in a black-and-white photograph; the bottom right corner is the stamp itself, while the remaining eight portions reproduce the image with a sepia tint.

Angola's "Millennium 2001" series is perhaps the most puzzling. A collection of contemporary and retired baseball players adorns the offering with instantly recognizable drawings or photographs. However, Clemente's shows a young boy with a bat and ball in hand, while a black-and-white insert captures an outfielder about to catch a fly ball. While both images can be interpreted as depicting Clemente, his name on the left side confirms the identity, as do the three different photographs on the borders of the panel. The same year, the Democratic Republic of the Congo became the third African nation to honor the Pittsburgh baseball star. This stamp is unique in juxtaposing Clemente's baseball and family lives; a well-known picture with his wife, Vera, and their three children adorns the bottom the right corner.

In 2002 Somaliland and the Falkland Islands paid tribute to the Queen Mother, King George VI's widow and mother to Queen Elizabeth

II, with a "woman of the century" series. Male historical figures, among them Clemente, were shown on the sheet, but they were not part of the actual stamps.

A typical eBay search reveals dozens of specimens for sale, ranging from individual items to commemorative first-day-of-issue cachets. The pieces, at the intersection of baseball and stamp memorabilia, are cherished by rabid Clemente collectors. While there is no way to measure how many were used in circulation, it is likely those who affixed Clemente's visage to the letters and packages did so with an extra sense of pride and satisfaction.

Collage of Clemente Stamp Materials by Juan López-Bonilla. Background: Uncut panel of 20-cent 1984 United States Clemente stamp. Foreground, from left to right: Poster commemorating the 1984 stamp release, the Puerto Rican newspaper "El Mundo" article from 1982 denoting the design selection, the design sketch for landscape version of stamp, the signature of designer, and the original sketch submission for Clemente stamp.

ACKNOWLEDGMENTS

Phil Jordan for graciously answering my questions via email.

Alicia Leathers, library assistant for the American Philatelic Society and its Research Library, for graciously answering my philatelic questions via email.

Juan López-Bonilla for his time and knowledge discussing his role in the 1984 Roberto Clemente USPS stamp via a telephone interview.

Joe Saffold for his time and knowledge discussing his role in the 2000 Roberto Clemente USPS stamp via a telephone interview.

The curators of the "Baseball Is My Life" blog for their thorough checklist on baseball postage stamps.

NOTES

1   "The Black Experience: African-Americans on Postage Stamps," Smithsonian National Postal Museum, https://postalmuseum.si.edu/exhibition/the-black-experience-sports-baseball/roberto-clemente.

2   Paulette Bee, "Put a Stamp on It: How Art Director Greg Breeding Helps the USPS Create New Stamps," National Endowment for the Arts, July 15, 2020, https://www.arts.gov/stories/blog/2020/put-stamp-it-how-art-director-greg-breeding-helps-usps-create-new-stamps.

3   Paulette Bee.

4   "1984 Roberto Clemente," *Baseball Is My Life*, https://baseballismy.life/baseball-stamps/1984-roberto-clemente/.

5   1984 Roberto Clemente.

6   Phone interview and subsequent email exchange between Juan López-Bonilla and the author, July 20, 2021.

7   López-Bonilla interview.

8   López-Bonilla interview.

9   Alvin Rosensweet, "Clemente Stamp Draws Crowds," *Pittsburgh Post-Gazette*, August 21, 1984.

10 Email interview of Phil Jordan by the author, July 29, 2021.

11 "Saluting Art Director Phil Jordan," http://www.photoassist.com/saluting-art-director-phil-jordan/.

12 Baseball All-Century Team, Baseball Almanac, https://www.baseball-almanac.com/legendary/limc100.shtml.

13 Jordan interview.

14 Phone interview with Joe Saffold, July 22, 2021.

15 Saffold interview. Jordan references the book by Marc Okkonen, *Baseball Uniforms of the 20th Century* (Sterling Publications, 1991).

16 "2000 Legends of Baseball," Baseball Is My Life, https://baseballismy.life/baseball-stamps/2000-legends-of-baseball/.

17 These are the first stamps to have the team names and logos. The uncut panels have the Major League Baseball® logo (white batter silhouette with red and blue background) and the Major League Baseball Players® logo (shield-format, with hitter making contact with the ball and red and blue background).

18 Ed Stephan, "Baseball on Stamps," http://www.edstephan.org/webstuff/bbstamps/as.html.

19 Tom Palmer, "The Bambino from Grenada: Ruth and Other U.S. Stars Appear on Foreign Stamps," *Sports Illustrated*, November 26, 1990, https://vault.si.com/vault/1990/11/26/the-bambino-from-grenada-ruth-and-other-us-stars-appear-on-foreign-stamps.

20 Bill McAllister, "Play Ball, Grenada Style," *Washington Post*, February 24, 1989, https://www.washingtonpost.com/archive/lifestyle/1989/02/24/play-ball-grenada-style/c902722c-4113-4d0f-86ee-290ef3109479/.

21 Like the 1988 Grenada issue, this set shows the team logos, although not the team names. The panel shows the Major League Baseball® logo and states that "Major League Baseball trademarks and copyrights are used with the permission of Major League Baseball Properties, Inc."

THE CLEMENTES
AND THE KANTROWITZES

BY HOWARD ELSON

Most baseball fans know about Roberto Clemente's heroics at bat and in the field for the Pittsburgh Pirates. Many know of his humanitarian efforts. The award bestowed annually to the player who "best represents the game of Baseball through extraordinary character, community involvement, philanthropy, and positive contributions, both on and off the field" is named for Clemente. And of course, many know that he lost his life on December 31, 1972, in the humanitarian effort to fly emergency relief supplies to Nicaragua from his native Puerto Rico, after a devastating earthquake. He is especially revered in his birthplace, the Commonwealth of Puerto Rico, and by Hispanic players and baseball fans everywhere, many of whom never saw him play, almost 50 years after his untimely death at age 38. He had so much more to accomplish, on the baseball field, and in the world. Much of that humanitarian work is still being carried out by the Roberto Clemente Foundation.

What isn't well-known is the small, personal story of a lasting friendship between the Clemente family and a Jewish family living in the Squirrel Hill neighborhood of Pittsburgh, the Kantrowitzes.

This story was told to me by Richard Kantrowitz and, after Richard's death in April 2022, by his son, Sam. Richard's father, Henry Kantrowitz, a second-generation American, lived with his wife, Pearl, in Squirrel Hill, a neighborhood in Pittsburgh known for its Jewish personality. Henry, a CPA by profession, was a sports fan holding season tickets for both the Steelers and the Pirates. Henry was a big fan of the young Roberto Clemente, plucked from the Dodgers' Montreal farm club in 1954, who, by the late 1950s and early '60s was a star at nearby Forbes Field. Henry could literally hear the cheers from the old ballpark in his home on Fair Oaks Street.

Henry had a friend in the Pirates organization and invited him to dinner at their Squirrel Hill home. Henry asked his friend if he could bring Clemente ... which he did ... and they hit it off. Henry became a close friend and a tax and financial adviser to Clemente. When Clemente

198

Roberto, in the middle, flanked by the Kantrowitz brothers, Richard on the left. Courtesy Sam Kantrowitz personal collection.

complained about "not being used to the cold in Pittsburgh," Henry gave him a warm winter coat. Even before Roberto married Vera Zabala in 1964, Pearl Kantrowitz, Henry's wife, befriended Vera, took her shopping, and helped her learn English. When their sons, Luis and Roberto Jr., were born, the Kantrowitzes baby-sat for them.

Henry and Pearl Kantrowitz visited the Clementes in Puerto Rico on many occasions and were with them during that fateful month of December 1972. The Kantrowitzes flew home a week before Roberto's death, in part because Roberto was so busy with the relief flights to Nicaragua.

Henry and Pearl's son, Richard, lived at home and like his father, became a CPA. He was always around when the Clementes would visit and became their accountant and confidant, working with Vera and the Clemente sons in starting the Roberto Clemente Foundation, serving over the years as both treasurer and president.

The next generation of Clementes and Kantrowitzes continues the friendship. Roberto Jr. was a pallbearer at both Roz (Richard's wife) Kantrowitz's and Richard Kantrowitz's funerals. It was at Richard's funeral that I talked with Sam and Roberto Jr. Sam knew I had been trying to get in touch with his father to interview him for SABR's 2022 book, to ask about the families' friendship. He agreed to talk with me, in his father's stead. I also spoke with Roberto Jr. about the SABR project, and he told me that he'd had conversations with those involved.

Sam Kantrowitz and Luis and Roberto Jr. continue to keep in touch – texting, phoning, and visiting when the Clemente boys travel to

Wilmington, North Carolina, where Sam is a school principal, to play in the Willie Stargell Charity Golf Tournament, held annually in "Pops'" hometown.

Roberto Clemente Jr. visited Richard Kantrowitz, the day before he died ... to say goodbye and thank him for all he'd done for the Clemente family.

The family friendship that had begun nearly 70 years earlier still endures.

Top row L to R: Orlando Zabala (Vera Clemente's brother), Henry Kantrowitz, Pearl Kantrowitz, Vera Clemente, Luisa Walker (Robert Clemente's mother). Second row: Richard Kantrowitz and Roberto Clemente holding a stained glass image of Clemente glued onto canvas. To the right is a snapshot of Vera Clemente holding the item. Courtesy Sam Kantrowitz personal collection.

THE CLEMENTE MUSEUM

BY THOMAS KERN

"My mother and father never taught me to hate anyone, or to dislike anyone because of their race or color. ... I don't believe in color. I believe in people."

– Roberto Clemente Walker

The establishment of the Clemente Museum in the Lawrenceville neighborhood adjoining downtown Pittsburgh was the brainchild of local photographer Duane Rieder. Clemente played his entire major-league career in Pittsburgh and died tragically in an airplane crash on December 31, 1972. One of baseball's greatest humanitarians, he was organizing relief supplies for earthquake-torn Nicaragua when the plane he had hired to fly supplies to Managua on New Year's Eve crashed into the waters off Puerto Rico's north coast. All five people on the plane, including Clemente, perished. Clemente's remains were never found.

During his 18-year playing career with the Pirates, Clemente was always admired, yet sometimes misunderstood because of his reserved, almost aloof demeanor. But his Hall of Fame career – which included exactly 3,000 hits, 12 Gold Gloves, 15 All-Star Games, and a post-season role in helping lead the Pirates to World Series championships in 1960 and 1971 – made for an unrivaled legacy that his selfless commitment to those less fortunate and the sacrifice of his own life even further solidified.

Few great sports figures have a museum to extol their legacy, but in Rieder's view, the Clemente Museum seemed a natural addition to Pittsburgh's cultural scene.

The fortuitous convergence of events that shaped the museum's creation have established it as a fitting legacy to Clemente and a beacon for those wishing to learn more about and honor the Great Roberto. Major-league teams visiting Pittsburgh and the Pirates and other civic organizations have made the museum a focal point for social and cultural events.

The story of the museum begins in the early 1990s, when local entrepreneur Duane Rieder's photography business needed a place to grow. His career began while he was in art school, and he officially opened a business in 1986. The 12,000-square-foot Lawrenceville firehouse, built in 1896, closed its doors in 1972 and was scheduled for demolition. For Rieder, it was an ideal setting for his work. Why Lawrenceville? The area had suffered from years of downturn following the city's industrial decline. Local efforts took shape in the 1990s to attract new businesses to the neighborhood. According to Rieder, "I was one of the first persons to go to Lawrenceville [to relocate a business]. They wanted me to come in and be a sort of role model for what it could be. I opened up officially in 1996, at the beginning of the movement."[1]

The derelict firehouse offered a sizable ground floor for photo shoots (where the bays for the fire engines had been) and an upstairs that could serve as a studio. Rieder could stage the renovations to the building over time to affordably upgrade

the rundown structure. In sum, Engine House 25 at 3339 Penn Avenue was ideal for the new Rieder studio.

Although it was not on Rieder's radar at the time, several quirks made it seem preordained that the firehouse should host the Clemente Museum. According to Rieder, "The walls are 21 inches thick in the building. There's a steel beam upstairs from Carnegie Steel, stamped 1896, that's 21 inches deep. It's holding up a rubber roof, there's no need for it to be that thick!"[2]

Images courtesy of The Clemente Museum.

Alongside Rieder's business interests was his love of sports. Photography would become a natural platform for him to combine the two for the native of St. Marys in northwestern Pennsylvania, about 120 miles from Pittsburgh. Rieder's Pennsylvania ties and love of baseball forged a link to the team he grew up with – the 1960s and early 1970s Pirates led by Clemente, Vernon Law, Bill Mazeroski, and Willie Stargell. "We were poor and there were five of us, so we would play baseball all day long in the summer, rain or shine," Rieder recalled. In 1971, he said, he got Clemente's autograph along with a few others while at a Pirates game. Roberto was kind to him, Rieder remembered. Unfortunately, he no longer has that autograph. He was 11 when Clemente died in the plane crash. Like all baseball fans, and not just those in Pittsburgh, Rieder was devastated by Clemente's untimely death at the age of 38. "I thought, he's a professional athlete in great shape, surely he'll just swim to shore."[3]

In a rare move, the National Baseball Hall of Fame immediately inducted Clemente into the Hall in the summer of 1973, dispensing with the five-year wait embedded in its rules. His career accomplishments alone were compelling; the addition of Clemente's character made his unusually timed induction an easy decision. Rieder later learned of another coincidence surrounding the engine house and Clemente when he learned that Lou Gehrig had stayed in the building one night in 1927.[4] Apparently, Gehrig knew one of the local firefighters. The bond between Gehrig and Clemente was unique: the only two players elected to the Hall of Fame via special election.

Rieder first met the Clemente family – his widow, Vera, and his sons Luis, Roberto Jr., and Roberto Enrique – in the run-up to the 1994 All-Star Game scheduled to take place in Pittsburgh. In 1993 Rieder's sports photography partnered with the Clemente family to produce a calendar as a memento for publication around the time of the 1994 All-Star Game in Pittsburgh. This was before he purchased Engine House 25 as his studio.

Rieder told the story as follows: "I was asked in 1993 to do a calendar full of pictures of Clemente. I went to his house in Puerto Rico and found that a lot of the photos of him had been damaged by water, from hurricanes and humidity. I retouched the photos for the family, preserving them, and was named his official archivist in 1996."[5] The trip to Puerto Rico led to the longstanding friendship with the Clementes and was, for Rieder, transformational. "When I hugged [Vera Clemente] for the first time, it was like I was hugging an angel, and from that moment on, I decided I wanted to help her."[6]

Vera Clemente died in 2019, but the connection with the Clemente sons remains strong.

And the 1994 Clemente Calendar? "I'm a fan of old baseball," said Rieder. "I love the look of the old sepia-toned images."[7] And so, the calendar brought that look to bear and won accolades.

The growing friendship between Rieder and the Clementes sharpened the photographer's interest in and collection and preservation of artifacts and helped the Clementes restore and add to their own memorabilia. Phil Dorsey, a friend of the Clementes, died in 2002, and Rieder inherited much of his Clemente memorabilia. "I really got hooked on the photos of Roberto," Rieder said. "I started buying and collecting negatives, collecting photos, to help Vera with her archive. And it just grew and grew."[8] Over time, Rieder bought signed articles and found documents from Roberto's career in both the military and baseball.

Fast-forward to 2006, when the Pirates hosted another All-Star Game. Thirty days before the game, Vera Clemente contacted Rieder to ask if the family could host an event at the Engine House. He recalled, "We hurried and slapped some paint on the interior and dressed it up in one month. … Vera Clemente was coming into town for the All-Star Game, and we wanted to show her the space and the collection."[9]

Courtesy of The Clemente Museum.

Rieder decided to transform the ground floor from his studio into a showcase for his collection of memorabilia, eventually including a reproduction of the Forbes Field scoreboard. "Vera told me; it looks like a museum here. And the seed was planted there."[10]

This party and his work with the Clemente family was the catalyst for Rieder to put together the Clemente Museum, and it opened on July 10, 2006. Rieder would be the first to admit that he had not started out years previously to open a museum. Instead, things just happened. His passion as a photographer became a catalyst for his sports interests, his relationship with the Clementes, and finally, a place to honor Roberto. "Without photography, none of this would be possible," he said. "It has afforded me the opportunity to do all this, so when a client calls, that takes precedence."[11]

As the years went by and while motivated by the circumstances surrounding Clemente's passing, Rieder believed it important that the former ballplayer's story be told to future generations as a reminder of what all might aspire to: excellence in one's chosen profession for sure, but also a commitment to serve those less fortunate.

Not surprisingly, on the façade of the building next to the museum, where a mural painted by Kyle Holbrook stands, alongside is Roberto Clemente's famous quote, "Any time you have an opportunity to make a difference in this world and you don't, then you are wasting your time on Earth."[12] The story of Clemente's life as told in the museum focuses equally on his humanitarianism alongside his baseball accomplishments.

For Rieder, this summed up his resolve to make the museum a reality. "Everybody knows how he died – helping people. He was doing that his whole life, for a lot of people in Pittsburgh and in Puerto Rico. I'm doing this because of the person he was, not because he was a great baseball player."[13]

As plans took shape to house a museum at the Engine House, Rieder learned that the building was vacated on December 31, 1972. The day Clemente died. Another coincidence.

Vera Clemente served on the museum's board for many years, and although the Clemente family is not formally involved in the museum's operation, the special relationship the family has with Rieder in his capacity as executive director has allowed him to use Clemente's name, image, and likeness. Rieder confers with the family on important matters, works closely with them on events designed to honor Roberto, and assists them in whatever capacity he can. The commitment is simple – to help tell the whole story about one of baseball's all-time greats.

The museum's collection, according to its website, "showcase[s] the world's largest exhibited collection of baseball artifacts, works of art, literature, photographs, memorabilia, and related materials which focus on Roberto Clemente, his teammates, his personal life, and his humanitarian causes. Whether it is the Gold Gloves, Clemente's 'Momen' bat, the Silver Slugger Award, the cleats, and home base from the '71 series or the name of his wife, Vera, scratched into a vase Roberto made for her, visitors to the Museum will leave knowing, more fully, what made Roberto Clemente a great man."[14]

The Clemente family has loaned many pieces. These include several of Clemente's Gold Gloves, his Silver Slugger Award bat from 1961, and the Hall of Fame plaque when Cooperstown corrected the inscription and gave the first one to the family. All else is either "from Rieder's personal collection amassed over the years through purchase in auctions, trade, or from people who chose to donate their own Clemente artifacts."[15]

A sad reminder of Clemente's passing is "a propeller from the Douglas DC-7 plane, later determined to be overloaded, that crashed just after takeoff on Dec. 31, 1972. It was given to Rieder by the captain [of the Coast Guard ship] who retrieved it."[16]

Emblematic of Rieder's research and acquisition for the museum collections is the story about the *Angel in the Outfield* photograph. As one enters the museum, on the right is a floor-to-ceiling artwork depicting a Clemente catch in the outfield in spring training at Fort Myers in 1960. It is worth capturing the story in full as written by fellow photographer Al Tieleman:

The most impressive piece, which hangs just inside the front door, is a huge, quartered photograph of Clemente, jumping in the air, a ball just about to settle into his mitt. Very typical of the posed-action images photographers shot in the past, this image however, has a cloud formation that appears to give Clemente angel wings.

Rieder claims this image was part of a Pittsburgh newspaper collection which he purchased after it was discarded and retrieved from the trash. He explains the image was never published and was simply a series of several images a *Sun Telegraph* photographer took the same day. (There is a similar, smaller Mazeroski print displayed adjacent to this print with no cloud formation.) If this image was truly never published, I would consider it one of the all-time gaffes in photojournalism. If it was published, or even known to exist, well, that would be worse. The image is stunning, and borders on unbelievable because of its perfection: A beloved athlete, killed on a mercy mission, levitating perfectly in front of clouds that make him appear angelic.

(Here's a comment from Alabama photographer Kevin Glackmeyer regarding the origin of the Clemente image noted in the blog post below. "The iconic, seemingly fabricated photograph of Roberto Clemente jumping for a fly ball at Terry Park is one of the most recognizable photos in baseball history but the story behind the photo is the incredible part. Clouds shaped like wings of an angel appear in the background behind Clemente. The negative of the photo was taken some time before 1960 at Terry Park [by Ed Salamony] of the *Pittsburgh Post-Gazette*. It was recovered from a trash container in 1991 in pieces and was reconstructed to display the amazingly well-timed photograph. The photo was stored in a box for seven years and then bought and displayed at the Clemente Museum in Pittsburgh where it remains today.")[17]

The museum and its collections are open by appointment only and, assisted by several docents, hosts multiple tours daily. It can also be rented for special events. It is important to note that the museum is separate from both the nearby Western Pennsylvania Sports Museum at the Senator John Heinz History Center and other Clemente charities. Nor is it connected to the Clemente Foundation, based in the United States, or to Sports City, the recreation complex built by the Clemente family in his hometown of Carolina, Puerto Rico.

One other note. As a sidelight, Rieder has made wine for years. He noted that the wine came in handy as a punctuation mark, "putting his work on the labels as a way to stand out to potential clients."[18]

Rieder launched his winery, Engine House 25, in 2009 in the basement of the museum. It became a wine cellar and a place to host private gatherings. The wine is also sold to support the museum and local charities. It is yet another coincidence that Roberto Clemente preferred red wine, thanks to former Pirates player and trainer Tony Bartirome's home winemaking that he shared with Clemente.

SOURCES

Unless otherwise noted, the basis for this article is several interviews with Duane Rieder, the museum's executive director, and one of its docents, Gary Euler. The museum's website has also provided content: https://clementemuseum.com/.

Two videos on YouTube capture tours by Duane Rieder of the museum:

Tour of Roberto Clemente Museum Part One - https://www.youtube.com/watch?v=xavubPgolnA&t=265s

Roberto Clemente Museum Tour Part Two - https://www.youtube.com/watch?v=JVJEAksztzk&t=8s

NOTES

1   Will Schuster, "From Igloo to Igloo: Perspective: My Interview with Photographer Duane Rieder," willschuster.blogspot.com, April 10, 2013. https://willschuster.blogspot.com/2013/04/perspective-my-interview-with.html, accessed November 18, 2021.

2   Kevin Creagh, "Off The Beaten Path – The Clemente Museum; One in a Series of Sporadically-Timed Articles Highlighting Hidden Pittsburgh gems," *City Life: The Point of Pittsburgh*, March 5, 2015. https://thepointofpittsburgh.com/off-the-beaten-path-the-clemente-museum/, accessed November 18, 2021.

3   Creagh.

4   Christine H. O'Toole, "On the Fast Track: Duane Rieder," *Pittsburgh Magazine*, October 12, 2010.

5   Schuster.

6   Joe Wojcik, "Ariba Roberto: Duane Rieder Pieces Together Memorabilia for the Clemente Museum," *Business Times* (Pittsburgh), December 13, 2017.

7   O'Toole.

8   Wojcik.

9   Creagh.

10 Author interview with Duane Rieder, July 29, 2021.

11 Creagh.

12 There are multiple sources for Clemente's famous quote.

13 Jennifer Baron, "Cleveland's The Plain Dealer Scores a Home Run at Pittsburgh's Clemente Museum," *Pittsburgh in the News*, April 12, 2016.

14 Clemente Museum, https://clementemuseum.com/museum/, accessed October 24, 2021.

15 Creagh.

16 Baron.

17 Al Tieleman, "Angel in the Outfield," http://altielemans.com/blog/angel-in-the-outfield, accessed October 24, 2021.

18 Schuster.

MONTREAL DEFEATS HAVANA ON ROBERTO CLEMENTE'S WALK-OFF HOME RUN

JULY 25, 1954
MONTREAL ROYALS 7, HAVANA SUGAR KINGS 6
(GAME ONE OF DOUBLEHEADER),
AT DE LORIMIER STADIUM, MONTREAL

BY GARY BELLEVILLE

Max Macon, the new manager of the Montreal Royals, knew exactly what was expected of him.[1] The Royals, a Brooklyn Dodgers Triple-A affiliate, were not unlike most minor-league teams in the 1950s: Turning a profit usually took precedence over player development.[2] "The only orders I had were to win and draw big crowds," Macon acknowledged.[3] Given the strength of the Royals roster and the quality of International League pitching in 1954, it wasn't all that surprising that a raw, 19-year-old Roberto Clemente had difficulty finding playing time with Montreal in his first (and only) minor-league season.[4]

The Royals had won the Governors' Cup in five of the previous eight seasons, and they were the defending Junior World Series champions.[5] They were expected to challenge for the pennant once again in 1954.[6]

Macon had given Clemente plenty of opportunities in spring training to show what he could do.[7] The youngster hit only .200 in 40 spring at-bats, the lowest mark among the five outfielders who came north with the Royals to start the season.[8] As a result, Clemente started the regular season buried in the depth chart behind more seasoned outfielders.[9]

A closer look at Clemente's spring-training at-bats shows just how overmatched he was in the early going. The Royals had a relatively easy spring schedule, with 12 of their 22 games against teams at Double A or below.[10] One of those games was a seven-inning affair on April 1 against a team known simply as the Civilians, a group of ex-servicemen who were waiting to be assigned to one of the Dodgers minor-league affiliates.[11] The Civilians had Robert Virkstis and Lester Fessette toss six of the seven innings that day – pitchers who spent the 1954 season in Class-D and Class-B ball, respectively. Clemente went 3-for-4 in the game, including an inside-the-park home run. But set aside his offensive outburst against a weak Civilian squad and Clemente hit only .139 (5-for-36) with no extra-base hits in the other spring-training games.[12]

Despite Clemente's spring-training struggles, Macon, who was a strong proponent of the platoon system,[13] penciled his young Puerto Rican outfielder into the starting lineup the first four times the Royals faced a left-handed starting pitcher in the regular season.[14] Clemente went 4-for-8 in Montreal's first five games, but Macon had him on a short leash with four more experienced outfielders at his disposal. After a 0-for-10 stretch between April 30 and May 8, Clemente was shifted into a bench role and he was mainly used as a pinch-runner and late-inning defensive replacement until June 3.

Clemente's chances for regular playing time decreased significantly when the Royals upgraded their already strong outfield twice in early May. Gino Cimoli replaced Bert Hamric on May 8, and a few days later Brooklyn optioned the 1953 International League batting champion, Sandy Amorós, to Montreal.[15] Amorós picked up where he left off the previous season with the Royals, and he reeled off a 27-game hitting streak from June 16 to July 7.[16] When the Dodgers recalled Amorós on July 12, Clemente didn't move up the Royals depth chart, because Brooklyn had also optioned 30-year-old outfielder Don Thompson to Montreal after he refused to report to their other Triple-A affiliate, in St. Paul.[17]

Even with the logjam of quality outfielders, Clemente got a second chance as a platoon player. Between June 4 and July 9, he started eight games – all against left-handed starting pitchers – but he went only 6-for-34 (.176). He was relegated to a bench role once again. Between July 10 and July 24, Clemente appeared in only one of Montreal's 16 games and that was as a pinch-runner in the first game of a July 21 twin bill.[18]

Clemente's breakthrough came on July 25 in Montreal when the Havana Sugar Kings faced the Royals in a Sunday afternoon doubleheader. Montreal started the day in third place with a 53-43 record, one game ahead of fourth-place Havana.[19] Royals hurler Ken Lehman (12-5) got the start in the opener, while the Sugar Kings countered with 32-year-old right-hander

Saul Rogovin, who had won the 1951 American League ERA title with the White Sox before running into arm troubles. As had been the case since July 8, Clemente was on the bench to start the game. The struggling rookie was hitting .207 with just one extra-base hit in 58 at-bats.

Lehman kept Havana off the scoresheet in the top of the first inning, but the teams scored multiple runs in their next four at-bats, with the lead changing hands four times. When the dust had settled, Havana led, 5-4, after 2½ innings. Both pitchers helped their own cause, as Rogovin drove in two runs with a double and Lehman smacked a two-run home run.[20] The other big blast was a two-run shot by Havana first baseman Paul Smith.

Smith notched his third RBI of the game in the top of the fifth to extend Havana's lead to 6-4. Lehman's day came to an end four batters later when he walked Luis Morales, loading the bases with two out. Reliever Art Fabbro came in and retired the side without allowing any further damage.

Montreal drew back within a run in the bottom of the fifth on an RBI single by center fielder Thompson.

Macon sent left-handed-hitting Dick Whitman in to pinch-hit for left fielder Cimoli in the bottom of the eighth to gain the platoon advantage against Rogovin. The move failed to spark the Royals offense, as Whitman was unable to reach base and the score remained 6-5 through eight innings. Since Whitman normally played right field, Macon sent Clemente out to left for the ninth. With no more outfielders on the bench, Clemente was in the game until its conclusion.

Montreal rallied to put runners on the corners with one out in the bottom of the ninth against a tiring Rogovin, and so lefty Ken Raffensberger was brought in to face slugger Rocky Nelson. Nelson came through with a clutch sacrifice fly and the game was tied, 6-6. Havana's top reliever, righty Charlie "Bubba" Harris, replaced

Raffensberger on the mound. Harris got out of the inning unscathed, sending the see-saw battle into extra innings.

After Havana failed to score in the top of the 10th, Harris retired Thompson to open the bottom of the frame. The next batter, Clemente, capitalized on his opportunity by slamming a 350-foot home run to left field, giving Montreal a thrilling 7-6 walk-off victory.[21]

Macon rewarded Clemente by giving him the start in the second game of the doubleheader against 34-year-old left-hander Hooks Iott.[22] Clemente recorded the eventual game-winning RBI with a double in the second inning, and he finished the doubleheader with two extra-base hits in three at-bats. For the remainder of the regular season and the playoffs, Clemente got the start whenever the opposing pitcher was a southpaw.[23] Between July 25 and the end of the regular season, he hit a much-improved .289 in 90 at-bats and Montreal played .593 baseball.

The Royals finished in second place with an 88-66 record. They dispatched third-place Rochester in six games in the playoff semifinals, with the series-clinching RBI coming off the bat of veteran Dixie Howell in Game Six with two outs in the bottom of the ninth inning. Howell had been inserted as a pinch-hitter for Clemente against Rochester ace Jack Faszholz, whose streak of eight consecutive victories against Montreal was thus snapped.[24]

Toward the tail end of the playoff series with Rochester, Macon was interviewed by *Montreal Gazette* columnist Dink Carroll about the top prospects in the International League. Macon referred to Clemente as a "wonderful prospect" before making an interesting disclosure. "But I don't know if we can hold him," he admitted. "Clyde Sukeforth scouted him and I'm pretty sure the Pirates intend to draft him [in the Rule 5 draft]."[25] Clemente had caught Sukeforth's eye at the beginning of June when he was in Richmond to scout Montreal pitcher Joe Black.[26] Sukeforth,

who had managed Macon in Montreal between 1940 and '42, had a conversation with his former player about Clemente in Richmond.[27]

The Royals were upset by fourth-place Syracuse in seven games in the Governors' Cup final.

Clemente saw limited action in the playoffs, as Montreal's opponents used a left-handed starting pitcher in only three of its 13 postseason games. He was limited to three singles and one RBI in seven at-bats.[28]

After the season, Clemente played in the Puerto Rican Winter League, and he was turning heads with a .380 batting average when the Rule 5 Draft was held in late November in New York.[29] Just as Macon had feared, Pittsburgh selected Clemente (with the first overall pick). But the Dodgers may have lost the future Hall of Famer even if Sukeforth hadn't been so observant during his fateful June scouting trip. According to Pittsburgh vice president Branch Rickey Jr., Clemente was "the number one draft choice on at least four or five clubs."[30]

SOURCES

In addition to the sources cited in the Notes, the author consulted Baseball-Reference.com, *The Encyclopedia of Minor League Baseball*, and Retrosheet.org.

NOTES

1 In 1954 Macon took over the managerial duties from Walter Alston, who had managed the Montreal Royals during the previous four seasons. Alston began his 23-year tenure as manager of the Brooklyn/Los Angeles Dodgers in 1954.

2 The theory that the Dodgers attempted to hide Clemente in Montreal was debunked by SABR researcher Stew Thornley in 2006. Stew Thornley, "Clemente's Entry into Organized Baseball: Hidden in Montreal?," *The National Pastime* (SABR, 2006), http://research.sabr.org/journals/files/SABR-National_Pastime-26.pdf, accessed September 23, 2021.

3 Thornley.

4 Macon was under the impression that Clemente was one year younger than he was. That is, he thought Clemente was only 18 when the season began. "Macon Denies Hiding Clemente from Scouts," *The Capital* (Annapolis, Maryland), November 25, 1971: 19.

5 The Governors' Cup was awarded to the playoff champion of the International League. The champions of the American Association and the International League met annually in the Junior World Series.

6 Dink Carroll, "Playing the Field," *Montreal Gazette*, April 21, 1954: 20; Jean Barrette, "Autour des Buts," *La Patrie*, April 18, 1954: 107.

7 Clemente collected 40 at-bats in 16 spring-training games. The most at-bats by a Montreal outfielder (Bert Hamric) that spring was 44 – only four more than Clemente had.

8 "Royals' Batting Averages," *Montreal Gazette*, April 21, 1954: 20.

9 The other outfielders on Montreal's Opening Day roster were 34-year-old Jack Cassini, 33-year-old Dick Whitman, 29-year-old Ken Wood, and 26-year-old Bert Hamric. Cassini, Whitman, and Wood had previous big-league experience, while Hamric was coming off a season in which he hit .298 in Double A. On May 8 the Brooklyn Dodgers sent 24-year-old outfielder Gino Cimoli to Montreal from their other Triple-A affiliate, in St. Paul; Hamric was transferred in the opposite direction that same day. Cimoli had played for the Royals between 1949 and 1952. The 1953 International League batting champion, Sandy Amorós, was demoted by the Dodgers in May 1954 and occupied one of the three starting outfielder positions with Montreal between May 13 and July 11. Wood was sent to the Richmond Virginians to free up a roster spot for Amorós, who remained with the Royals until he was recalled by Brooklyn on July 12. On June 28 Brooklyn optioned 30-year-old outfielder Don Thompson to St. Paul, but he refused to report to the Saints. He reported to Montreal, where he had enjoyed great success in 1950 and 1952. Thompson had 167 at-bats with the Royals between July 10, 1954, and the end of the regular season.

10 The Royals played one game against a Brooklyn Dodgers "B" squad. Their other spring games were against nine Triple-A teams, three Double-A teams, eight Single-A teams, and one unclassified squad. The author compiled a list of the Royals' 1954 spring-training games using box scores in Montreal newspapers. The spreadsheet, which includes Clemente's game log, can be found at https://docs.google.com/spreadsheets/d/1XDBpPQZMquGbTdHweArQwq-GOEIkRCLNsoID-I6hrofg.

11 Canadian Press, "Clemente Paces Royals to Win," *Montreal Gazette*, April 2, 1954: 22.

12 Clemente also recorded two singles in five at-bats in Montreal's final spring-training game, on April 16 against the Class-A Elmira Pioneers. All five of those at-bats were against lefty Emerson Unzicker, a pitcher who posted a 5.08 ERA and 1.941 WHIP in Class-A ball that season.

13 Thornley.

14 The author compiled a 1954 game log for Clemente's regular-season and playoff games using box scores in Montreal newspapers. The spreadsheet can be found at https://docs.google.com/spreadsheets/d/1hVW48dTMqo01utBWYaKQBw_JjUtAT-latNtUdgP1Y54.

15 Ken Wood was sent from the Royals to the Richmond Virginians to free up a roster spot for Amorós. "Hamric Sent to St. Paul; Nelson Back," *Montreal Gazette*, May 8, 1954: 8.

16 Amorós's 27-game hitting streak broke his own team record of 26, which was set in 1953.

17 "Royals Play Host to Ottawa," *Montreal Gazette*, July 13, 1954: 18.

18 Clemente was also announced as a pinch-hitter in the ninth inning of the first game of a July 11 doubleheader in Syracuse. But when the Chiefs brought in a right-handed pitcher to replace a lefty on the mound, Macon called Clemente back to the bench and used a left-handed pinch-hitter instead – pitcher Tommy Lasorda. The future Dodgers manager was retired on a popup. Associated Press, "Royals Lose Doubleheader to Syracuse Chiefs, 10-8, 2-0," *Montreal Gazette*, July 12, 1954: 16.

19 The top four teams in the standings qualified for the International League playoffs.

20 Dink Carroll, "Clemente, Lasorda Bright Spots as Royals Take Double," *Montreal Gazette*, July 26, 1954: 20.

21 Associated Press, "Sugar Kings Drop Pair to Royals," *Richmond Times-Dispatch*, July 26, 1954: 18.

22 The second game of the twin bill was a seven-inning affair.

23 Clemente did not start a single game in the regular season or playoffs in which the opposing starter was a right-hander.

24 Dink Carroll, "Royals Dispose of Wings 4-3 as Howell Singles in Ninth," *Montreal Gazette*, September 24, 1954: 24.

25 Dink Carroll, "Playing the Field," *Montreal Gazette*, September 21, 1954: 18. At the time, the Rule 5 Draft was commonly referred to as the Major-League Draft.

26 Black had been recently demoted to Montreal by Brooklyn. He had posted an 11.57 ERA in five relief appearances with the Dodgers in April and May.

27 Thornley; Stephen J. Nesbitt, "Hide and Seek: The True Story of How the Dodgers Lost Roberto Clemente," *The Athletic*, December 17, 2019.

28 Clemente game log compiled by the author at https://docs. google.com/spreadsheets/d/1hVW48dTMqo01utBWYaKQBw_ JjUtAT-latNtUdgP1Y54.

29 Associated Press, "Majors Pick 13 Players," *Racine* (Wisconsin) *Journal-Times*, November 23, 1954: 13.

30 The other teams that were believed to be poised to take Clemente with their first pick included the Baltimore Orioles, Chicago White Sox, Kansas City Athletics, New York Giants, and St. Louis Cardinals. Kansas City held the second overall pick. Associated Press, "Majors Pick 13 Players"; Hy Turkin, "'Good Prospects Fewer' – Only 13 in Majors' Draft," *The Sporting News*, December 1, 1954: 4.

GAMES OF SUNDAY, JULY 25
AT MONTREAL

Cubans.	AB.	H.	O.	A.	Montreal.	AB.	H.	O.	A.
Nicholas, cf-rf	5	1	4	0	Cassini, rf..	5	2	4	0
Delis, lf....	5	2	3	0	Fernandez, ss	3	1	4	2
Smith, 1b...	4	1	9	1	C.Thompson,c	4	0	3	1
Noble, c.....	5	0	7	0	Roebuck.....	0	0	0	0
Formental, rf	4	3	0	0	Howell, c....	0	0	1	0
Scull, cf....	0	0	0	0	Nelson, 1b...	3	2	11	0
Morales, 2b.	4	0	1	2	Wilson, 3b...	5	1	0	1
Garcia, 3b...	4	0	0	2	D.Thompson,cf	5	2	2	1
Lipon, ss...	5	2	3	1	Cimoli, lf....	3	0	0	0
Rogovin, p..	4	1	0	2	aWhitman...	1	0	0	0
Raff'sberger,p	0	0	0	0	Clemente, lf..	1	1	1	0
Harris, p....	0	0	1	0	Young, 2b...	4	1	4	6
	—	—	—	—	Lehman, p...	1	1	0	1
Totals ...	40	10	d28	8	Fabbro, p....	1	0	0	0
					bMacon.....	1	0	0	0
					Hood, p.....	0	0	0	0
					Totals	37	11	30	12

Cubans	....	0	3	2	0	1	0	0	0	0—6
Montreal	....	2	2	0	0	1	0	0	0	1¹	1—7

aFlied out for Cimoli in eighth. bStruck out for Fabbro in eighth. cRan for C. Thompson in ninth. dOne out when winning run scored in tenth. R—Nicholas, Delis, Smith, Formental, Garcia, Lipon, Cassini, Fernandez 2, Nelson, Clemente, Young, Lehman. E—Fernandez 2, Rogovin. RBI—Wilson, D. Thompson 2, Lipon, Rogovin 2, Lehman 2, Nelson, Clemente. 2B—D. Thompson, Rogovin, Delis, Lipon, Cassini, Fernandez. HR—Lehman, Smith, Clemente. SB—Nicholas. SH—Fernandez. SF—Nelson. DP—Fernandez and Young; D. Thompson and Nelson. LOB—Cubans 8, Montreal 8. BB—Lehman 1, Fabbro 2, Rogovin 3, Hood 1. SO—Lehman 2, Fabbro 2, Rogovin 6, Hood 1. Hits—Lehman 9 in 4⅔, Fabbro 13 in ⅓, Rogovin 10 in 8½, Raffensberger 0 in ⅓. HP—Rogovin (C. Thompson). WP—Lehman. Winner—Hood (3-2). Loser—Harris (11-6). T—2:33.

CLEMENTE AND MAYS HOMERS BOOKEND SANTURCE'S 11-INNING CARIBBEAN SERIES WIN OVER MAGALLANES

FEBRUARY 12, 1955
SANTURCE CRABBERS 4, MAGALLANES NAVIGATORS 2 (11 INNINGS), AT ESTADIO UNIVERSITARIO, CARACAS, VENEZUELA

BY THOMAS E. VAN HYNING

Herman Franks had managed the 1953-54 Magallanes Navigators to a 39-37 record in the Venezuelan four-team Winter League and led the Santurce Crabbers to the Caribbean Series the next season.[1]

Franks recalled, "When Santurce arrived in Caracas, they asked me what I was doing there. They said, we [Santurce] didn't have a chance to win as Almendares from Cuba would take it all. I told them the only reason I brought this [Santurce] team there was for them to see Willie Mays and Roberto Clemente."[2]

Magallanes represented Venezuela in the 1955 Caribbean Series, Phase I (1949-1960) of a four-team round-robin tournament, which also included teams from Cuba, Panamá, and Puerto Rico. Magallanes finished second (4-2), one game behind Santurce.[3] Teams played each opponent twice. Phase I of the Caribbean Series was discontinued in February 1961, due to issues between Fidel Castro, the Caribbean Confederation, and the discontinuation of the Cuban Winter League.

Santurce won the Caribbean Series in 1951 (5-1), 1953 (6-0), and 1955 (5-1) and was the first team to win three titles. The Crabbers' 1951 and 1953 squads were reinforced by players from other league teams, a common practice throughout the Caribbean. The 1955 edition, though, had only Santurce players on its 22-man roster. Six February 2022 Caribbean Series teams had 32-man rosters, 10 more than 1955.[4]

The 1954-55 Crabbers went 47-25 and beat Caguas in the league finals. They used 20 of 22 roster players in Caracas, 6 pitchers and 14 position players. Roberto Clemente was Santurce's only native position player who started all six contests. Teams were allowed nine imports. Franks' two coaches, Dick Seay and Ramón "Monchile" Concepción, once played in the Negro Leagues. Santurce's main series lineup, including its February 12 game versus Magallanes, was:

Don Zimmer, SS
Roberto Clemente, LF
Willie Mays, CF

Buzz Clarkson, 3B
Bob Thurman, RF
George Crowe, 1B
Harry Chiti, C
Ron Samford, 2B
Sam Jones, P

Santurce played three "home games" in the series. Clemente was 1-for-8 in his first two games, vs. Cuba's Almendares Blues (0-for-4) on February 10; then, 1-for-4 against Panamá's Carta Vieja Yankees the next day.[5] On opening Night, against Almendares, Clemente played in front of the largest crowd (40,000 total, paid attendance 34,000) as of that moment of his career. Rubén Gómez bested Almendares in the series opener.[6]

Sam Jones started and finished against Magallanes on February 12. He allowed three hits, two by Chico Carrasquel and one by Ramón Monzant.[7] (Monzant was Franks' 1953-54 workhorse with a 14-6 won-lost record, and Magallanes' 1954-55 ace, 11-7 W-L.)[8] Magallanes' lineup for skipper Lázaro Salazar comprised the following:[9]

Chico Carrasquel, SS
Jack Lohrke, 2B
George Wilson, RF
Bob Skinner, 1B
Bob Lennon, CF
Luis "Camaleón" García, 3B
Dalmiro Finol, LF
Luis "Güigüi" Lucas, C
Ramón Monzant, P

Magallanes took a 1-0 lead off Jones when it loaded the bases, and Skinner grounded into a double play. Clemente cracked a solo homer in the first — a long drive over the center-field fence — after Zimmer was retired. Güigüi Lucas scored a go-ahead run in the second, after he walked, advanced to second on a Monzant base hit, and dashed home on Carrasquel's run-scoring single. Crowe's triple in the fourth scored Clarkson, to tie the game, 2-2.[10] Santurce threatened in the

seventh, with two-out hits by Samford and Jones, but Zimmer flied to center.[11]

The clock struck midnight when Clemente stepped to the plate and singled in the home half of the 11th. Enriqueta Marcano Zorrilla, niece of Santurce owner Pedrín Zorrilla, remembered the crowd mocking Mays, 0-for-12 until then, with a whispering sh ... sh ... sound, as if to say, he "was being silenced."[12] Mays' walk-off 385-foot homer to left-center, at 12:03 A.M., ended the 2-hour 25-minute contest. Clemente scored the winning run, followed by Mays, in the 4-2 win.[13]

Santurce was the "home team" vs. Almendares on February 13. The Crabbers were losing, 6-0, in the sixth when Zimmer singled and Clemente doubled. Mays tripled and Crowe singled to cut the deficit in half.[14] Thurman's eighth-inning double drove in Mays to make it 6-4. Almendares' Red Munger retired Chiti and Samford in the ninth, but Alfonso Gerard drilled a pinch-hit single, followed by Zimmer's two-run homer, to tie the game (6-6).[15]

Clemente drew a two-out walk. Bobby Bragan, Almendares' skipper, summoned Al Lyons to pitch. Mays singled to right, and Clemente never stopped running. Right fielder Lee Walls bobbled the ball but got it to second baseman Al Federoff, who threw it wide of the plate.[16] "That winning run by Clemente from first was terrific," recalled Zimmer. "What a great effort!"[17]

Clemente's two triples vs. Carta Vieja on February 14, after Magallanes beat Almendares, propelled Santurce and Bill Greason to an 11-3 series-clinching win. His first three-bagger sparked a three-run rally in the top of the first, followed by a third-inning triple. The Crabbers lost a meaningless game to Magallanes the next night.[18]

Table I has Clemente's hitting stats. He scored one-fourth of Santurce's 32 runs, per Table I. The Crabbers' winning share was $650 apiece. Total attendance was 122,000, with $206,000 in gate receipts.[19] Zimmer, the Series MVP, called these Crabbers "the greatest Winter League ballclub ever assembled." He got emotional recalling Clemente as a Santurce teammate and someone he managed with the 1967-68 San Juan Senators. "I appreciated his hustle and dedication as a Santurce teammate, and as someone I managed with San Juan."[20]

Thurman, a Santurce role model for Clemente in 1952-1956 during 3½ Winter League seasons, noted, "We were just like a big family; everyone would do something for somebody else. ... It just jelled 'cause we had the talent to play the game. I often thought that we could beat any major-league club with the set-up we had. Roberto played left field because I had a better throwing arm than he did."[21]

Clemente arrived at Santurce's Isla Grande Airport at 3:26 P.M. on February 16. Over 50,000 fans waited for the plane's arrival. Enriqueta Marcano Zorrilla recalled that "Santurce, Campeón Séptima Serie del Caribe" (Santurce Champion Seventh Caribbean Series) was inscribed on the plane.[22] A day earlier, Pedrín Zorrilla received this congratulatory telegram from Puerto Rican governor Luis Muñoz Marín: "I commend Puerto Rico's representative for their resounding triumph. ... It exemplifies the fighting spirit of our people."[23]

TABLE I: SANTURCE CRABBERS HITTING STATS, 1955 CARIBBEAN SERIES

Player	G	AB	R	H	2B	3B	HR	RBI	AVG	SLG
Don Zimmer	6	26	6	10	2	0	3	4	.385	.808
Roberto Clemente	6	26	8	7	1	2	1	3	.269	.577
Willie Mays	6	25	6	11	1	2	2	9	.440	.880
Buzz Clarkson	5	16	3	6	0	0	0	3	.375	.375
Bob Thurman	6	22	1	7	1	0	0	3	.318	.364
George Crowe	6	20	3	4	1	1	0	3	.200	.350
Harry Chiti	4	15	2	5	2	0	1	4	.333	.667
Ronnie Samford	6	23	1	2	0	1	0	2	.087	.174
Valmy Thomas	2	7	0	2	0	0	0	0	.286	.286
William Figueroa	2	7	0	2	0	0	0	0	.286	.286
Alfonso Gerard	2	2	1	1	0	0	0	0	.500	.500
Luis R. Olmo	2	2	0	1	0	0	0	0	.500	.500
José St. Claire	4	2	0	0	0	0	0	0	.000	.000
Pedro Arroyo	1	1	0	0	0	0	0	0	.000	.000
Bill Greason	2	6	1	2	0	0	1	1	.333	.833
Rubén Gómez	2	5	0	0	0	0	0	0	.000	.000
Sam Jones	1	3	0	1	0	0	0	0	.333	.333
Eleuterio López	2	1	0	0	0	0	0	0	.000	.000
George Sackie	2	1	0	0	0	0	0	0	.000	.000
Luis R. Cabrera	1	0	0	0	0	0	0	0	.000	.000
Totals	6	210	32	61	8	6	8	32	.290	.500

#21 – Clemente – watches a celebrating Willie Mays, #24. Courtesy of Jorge Colón Delgado.

The championship and welcome home concluded a special winter for Clemente, who led all 1955 Caribbean Series players with eight runs scored, including the game-winning dash from first on Mays' single on February 13. Clemente developed a special bond with Mays, via late-morning practices during the 1954-55 season at Sixto Escobar Stadium, with Luis Olmo, Franks, and batboy Orlando Cepeda, who also attended these practices.[24]

ACKNOWLEDGMENTS

Special thanks to Herman Franks, Bob Thurman, and Don Zimmer for their thoughts and insights on Clemente and the 1955 Caribbean Series. Enriqueta Marcano Zorrilla shared firsthand observations. Jorge Colón Delgado furnished Clemente reference materials.

NOTES

1   Caribbean Series teams from Phase I (1949-1960) through Phase II (1970-present) tend to represent League All-Star Teams, instead of the ballclub that won the given country's postseason series. The 1954-55 Santurce Crabbers were an exception since they did not reinforce themselves with players from the four other Puerto Rico Winter League teams, unlike their opponents from Cuba, Panamá, and Venezuela.

2   Herman Franks interview with Thomas Van Hyning, December 14, 1998.

3   Hosts rotated among the four countries, with Venezuela hosting the 1951, 1955, and 1959 events, held in February. https://www.1800beisbol.com/baseball/deportes/serie_del_caribe/venezuela_primera_etapa_de_la_serie_del_caribe/, accessed February 17, 2022. Phase I was the first 12 Caribbean Series events, February 1949 through February 1960. A separate Phase II began in February 1970 and continues through today. The February 1981 Caribbean Series was canceled due to a players strike in Venezuela. The Caribbean Series was discontinued from 1961 to 1969. Another series: Inter-American Series, took place, from 1961-1964, plus a February 1965 Series between two Dominican and two Venezuelan teams. But there have been only two Caribbean Series phases: I and II.

4   The Caribbean Confederation coordinates and runs this annual event. It dictates who the host country is; team roster limits; and many other particulars. Six countries have competed in this event since February 2019. Currently, Colombia (2020-present), Mexico (1971-present), and the Dominican Republic (1970-present), Panamá, Puerto Rico, and Venezuela play a five-game round-robin, followed by the semifinals and finals.

5   Jorge Colón Delgado, *La Maquinaria Perfecta* (San Juan, Puerto Rico, 2007), 169.

6   Franklin E. Whaite, "Latin Championship Tournament Proves Another Giant Romp," *The Sporting News*, February 23, 1955: 28. Marcos Evangelista Pérez Jiménez, Venezuela's president, threw out the first pitch. The author and Pérez Jiménez's son were co-workers in the city of San Juan, Puerto Rico, 1979. And the author was a Santurce, Puerto Rico, grade-school classmate of Rafael Gómez, son of Rubén Gómez.

7   Whaite: 28.

8   Monzant was a workhorse; Franks appreciated his work ethic and dedication to his craft. https://www.pelotabinaria.com.ve/beisbol/mostrar.php?ID=monzram001, accessed February 18, 2022.

9   Colón Delgado, 149.

10 Colón Delgado, 150.

11 Colón Delgado, 150.

12 Enriqueta Marcano Zorrilla interview with Thomas Van Hyning, Santurce, Puerto Rico, November 1997.

13 Thomas E. Van Hyning, *The Santurce Crabbers: Sixty Seasons of Puerto Rican Winter League Baseball* (Jefferson, North Carolina: McFarland & Company Inc., 1999), 70.

14 Colón Delgado, 154.

15 Van Hyning, 70.

16 Van Hyning, 70.

17 Don Zimmer interview with Thomas Van Hyning, Winter Haven, Florida, March 1992.

18 Whaite, 30.

19 Whaite 27.

20 Zimmer interview, March 1992.

21 Bob Thurman appearance with Thomas Van Hyning, sports radio talk show, Ponce, Puerto Rico, October 1991.

22 Marcano Zorrilla, 1997.

23 Van Hyning, 71.

24 Franks hit flies and grounders to Mays, Clemente, and Olmo, who in turn threw the ball back to Cepeda, one of Santurce's 1954-55 batboys. This created a bond between Clemente and Mays, who wanted Roberto to charge the ball more efficiently and release the throw more quickly. Matt Monagan, "Mays, Clemente in the Same Outfield? It Happened: The Two Legends Won a Championship Together in Puerto Rico." https://www.mlb.com/news/willie-mays-and-roberto-clemente-on-same-team, accessed February 16, 2022. See Thomas Van Hyning, "Roberto Clemente's Puerto Rico Winter League Career (Part 1)," in Bill Nowlin and Glen Sparks, eds., *"¡Arriba!": The Heroic Life of Roberto Clemente* (Phoenix: SABR, 2022).

ROBERTO CLEMENTE'S FIRST HIT AND FIRST RUN SCORED

APRIL 17, 1955
BROOKLYN DODGERS 10, PITTSBURGH PIRATES 3
(FIRST GAME OF DOUBLEHEADER)
AT FORBES FIELD, PITTSBURGH

BY JANE SCHUPMANN HEWITT

Roberto Clemente, the first great Latin American baseball star to enter major-league baseball and make it into the Hall of Fame, debuted for the Pittsburgh Pirates in right field as a 20-year-old on April 17, 1955.

This was only one year after the Pirates' acquisition of Curt Roberts, the African American second baseman from the Kansas City Monarchs, broke the team's color barrier. Roberts helped the young Clemente, one of only four *boricua,* or Puerto Ricans, in the major leagues at the time, to learn the ropes. No one could see into the future that day, but according to Puerto Rican broadcaster and journalist Luis Mayoral, "Clemente was our [Puerto Rico's] Jackie Robinson. He was on a crusade to show the American public what a Hispanic man, a black Hispanic man, was capable of."[1]

The 1955 season had just begun. Brooklyn was undefeated at 4-0. The 0-3 Pirates had yet to win a game. Since fielding some great players in the 1930s and '40s, among them shortstop Arky Vaughan and slugger Ralph Kiner, from 1938 to 1955 the Pirates rarely finished closer than eighth and last, and came in second only once, in 1944. In 1952 the club sank to its worst record ever, finishing 54½ games behind the Dodgers. In the five seasons since 1950, they had finished last four times and seventh once.

On this spring day in 1955, working the first game of a Sunday doubleheader at Forbes Field was Pirates pitcher Jake Thies. He had gone 3-9 for the Pirates in his 1954 rookie season. Young lefty Johnny Podres, now in his third season, started for the Dodgers. The 22-year-old was just months away from becoming a Dodger hero forever. On October 4, he threw a 2-0 shutout to win Game Seven of the World Series against Brooklyn's archrival, the New York Yankees.

Dodgers outfielder Sandy Amoros and catcher Roy Campanella also played vital roles in that Series win, and all three were on the field for Clemente's inaugural game. Still, Pittsburgh's rookie right fielder wasted no time in showing glimpses of what was to come in his own stellar career of 18 seasons in a Pirates uniform.

Before stepping to the plate for the first of four chances against Podres that afternoon, Clemente chose his bat, a typical Hillerich & Bradsby Louisville Slugger, from the rack. On the barrel of the bat, the manufacturer had etched his signature, *Momen Clemente* – a name based on his childhood habit of telling family and friends to wait a moment, *un momentito*, when they wanted his attention. This name was on every bat he used through 1960.[2]

After two outs in the bottom of the first – a fly ball by Earl Smith and a line drive to deep center field by Gene Freese – Clemente, batting third, lined Podres' pitch off Dodgers shortstop Pee Wee Reese's glove for a single. Frank Thomas belted a triple to right field, bringing Clemente home, so that in his first major-league inning, Clemente achieved the first of 3,000 career hits and scored his first run. Thomas followed by scoring on a fielding error and the Pirates took a 2-0 lead, their only lead of the day.

The Dodgers scored in the second when Gil Hodges doubled to left, moved to third on Amoros' fly ball, and headed home on Jackie Robinson's sacrifce fly. The Pirates had no action in the second, with only a walk.

In the third inning the Dodgers scored another run. Jim Gilliam walked, Reese moved him to third with a line-drive double to left, and Hodges drove him home with a fly to center. The score was tied, 2-2.

Brooklyn added four more runs in the fourth, the first thanks to an error by Pittsburgh's Gene Freese and the second on a passed ball by catcher Jack Shepard. Duke Snider's two-run homer to right field off reliever Nellie King made it 6-2, but not before Clemente had a chance to impress the crowd with his skills in the field. In what the *Pittsburgh Post-Gazette* called "a heart-stopping catch," he leapt high to grab Gilliam's hard-hit fly to right and returned it with a bullet throw home.[3] This superb skill in the field endeared him to Pittsburgh fans throughout his career and

earned him 12 Gold Gloves, one for every season from 1961 through 1972.

"Momen" developed the skill and strength in his right arm by playing baseball and softball at an early age, as well as by excelling in throwing the javelin for his hometown track and field team at Julio Vizcarrondo Coronado High School in Carolina, Puerto Rico.

Still in his teens, Clemente played in the Puerto Rico winter league, alongside major leaguers like the New York Giants' Willie Mays and Rubén Gómez, the first Puerto Rican pitcher to start and win a World Series game. Only three years older than Clemente, Mays had much more professional experience, having played a year with the Birmingham Black Barons of the Negro Leagues at age 17, as well as three years with the Giants. Mays took time to advise Clemente on fielding and throwing techniques in the outfield, since Clemente's early experience had been in the infield.

After the Pirates added a run in the sixth inning when first baseman Preston Ward doubled to left field and catcher Shepard drove him home with a single to right, the Dodgers followed by scoring three times in the seventh. Dodgers All-Star catcher Campanella, at the start of a phenomenal comeback year from hand and knee injuries the previous season, capped the ninth with a solo home run off Pirates pitcher Vern Law.

Clemente's history-making on the field mattered little to the final outcome; the game ended with a score of 10-3.

Later, in the nightcap, Clemente hit leadoff and continued to show skill and potential. He doubled in the sixth and rapped out a single on a fly to short center in the eighth. He raced past first, tapping his tremendous speed, but had to scramble back. When Don Zimmer's throw went astray and the ball sailed into the dugout, baserunner Dick Smith was allowed to score and Clemente was given third. Dick Cole scored him with a single to center.

The final score of 3-2 was more even-handed in the second game, but still went down as a loss for the Pirates. Clemente was left standing in the on-deck circle, with the tying and winning runs on base when Gene Freese hit a game-ending popup.

The 1955 Pirates, managed by Fred Haney, finished last. Clemente's rookie numbers were not exceptional, either; he batted only .255 with 121 hits and 47 RBIs. But Pittsburgh fans were hungry for a hero. Bobby Bragan took the helm in 1956, but was replaced in midseason 1957 by Danny Murtaugh, who eventually led young Clemente and the Pirates on a steady climb out of the cellar and toward a first-place finish in 1960.[4] Along the way, Clemente adapted and learned, creating his own style and perfecting the skills that took him from *Momen* to *el Magnifico*.

SOURCES

In addition to the sources cited in the Notes, the author consulted Baseball-Reference.com, Retrosheet.org., *Total Baseball* (1989 edition), and the following:

Maraniss, David. *Clemente: The Passion and Grace of Baseball's Last Hero* (New York: Simon & Schuster, 2006).

NOTES

1 Harold Friend, "Roberto Clemente: Prejudice, Pride, Boasting, and Greatness," bleacherreport.com, September 23, 2011. https://bleacherreport.com/articles/862283-roberto-clemente-prejudice-pride-boasting-and-greatness. Accessed April 14, 2022.

2 Stephen Tsi Chuen Wong, "Roberto 'Momen' Clemente 1960 Louisville Slugger Professional Model Game Used Bat," Smithsonian Institution National Postal Museum Blog: *Baseball: America's Home Run*. April 6, 2022. https://postalmuseum.si.edu/roberto-"momen"-clemente-1960-louisville-slugger-professional-model-game-used-bat.

3 Jack Hernon, "Unbeaten Bums Sweep Winless Bucs, 10-3, 3-2," *Pittsburgh Post-Gazette*, April 18, 1955: 18, 20.

4 Frederick Ivor-Campbell, "Team Histories," in John Thorn and David Reuther, eds., *Total Baseball* (New York: Warner Books, 1989), 89.

CLEMENTE'S FIRST HOME RUN AND FIRST OUTFIELD ASSIST — IN THE SAME INNING OF THE SAME GAME

APRIL 18, 1955
NEW YORK GIANTS 12, PITTSBURGH PIRATES 3
AT THE POLO GROUNDS, NEW YORK

BY JOE LEISEK

A day after dropping both ends of a Sunday doubleheader to the Brooklyn Dodgers at Forbes Field, the winless Pittsburgh Pirates traveled to New York City to take on the defending World Series champion Giants on Monday, April 18, 1955.

It was yet another loss for the visitors, in front of fewer than 3,000 paying customers at the Polo Grounds. The Pirates, managed by Fred Haney, were just six games into what became their fourth consecutive last-place National League finish – which would have been five straight if they hadn't narrowly escaped the cellar in 1951.

In a little over a week, any early-season optimism had vanished – especially among those who covered the team for the *Pittsburgh Press*, the *Post-Gazette*, and the *Sun-Telegraph*. Lester J. Biederman, writing in the *Press*, pulled no punches in his game story lede:

"The Buccos had the daylights thrashed out of them by the slumping Giants yesterday in their first Polo Grounds appearance, 12-3, and within a

half hour after the shambles ended, three Pirates pitchers were sent back to the minors.

"However, the way the Pirates have been playing since the season started, losing all six games, cutting a team of this caliber shouldn't be difficult."[1]

Post-Gazette sportswriter Jack Hernon added a heavy dose of sarcasm to his report:

"The Pirates rallied for two runs in the ninth here this afternoon, falling only ten runs short of beating the Giants, and thus lost their sixth in a row, 12-3.

"Unfortunately, before that 'rally,' the World Champs had put an eight on the scoreboard in the fourth inning, and that was about the size of it."[2]

Despite the shambles, the game was noteworthy for two plays in the fifth inning involving Roberto Clemente, the Pirates' 21-year-old rookie from Puerto Rico – plays that provided an early glimpse of the power, speed, and defense that would define Clemente's brilliant 18-year career.

By the fifth inning, the rout was already on. Led by Whitey Lockman and Willie Mays, the

Giants scored two runs in the first inning, another in the third, and eight in the fourth, all before the Pirates tallied their first run.

In all, the defending champions pounded out 15 hits. Among Lockman's four hits were a homer and a double, while Mays had three hits, including an RBI triple. Hank Thompson homered in the first inning. Pirates starter Max Surkont, a journeyman who finished the season with a record of 7-14 and an ERA of 5.57, was lifted in the fourth inning after surrendering eight hits and seven earned runs.

In the top of the fifth, with the Pirates already trailing 11-0, center fielder Earl Smith led off by lining out to pitcher Don Liddle, an Illinois native who had started and won Game Four of the World Series the previous year. Second baseman Gene Freese grounded out to third.

Clemente stepped to the plate with two out. He had made his major-league debut just the day before, starting both games of the doubleheader against the Dodgers, the team that originally signed him out of the Puerto Rican League. In the opener, he singled off starter Johnny Podres in the first inning for his first major-league hit, and scored his first run when the next batter, outfielder Frank Thomas, tripled to right. In the nightcap, Clemente doubled to right with one out in the sixth off Dodgers starter and future Pirates teammate Clem Labine. He added an infield single in the eighth.

Now, in the fifth inning of his third big-league game, Clemente hit a drive to deep left-center field. The ball sailed over the head of Lockman, playing left field instead of his customary first-base position because right fielder Don Mueller had just left the game with an ankle injury. Left fielder Monte Irvin was now in right field.

Pittsburgh Press writer Biederman, in his column "From the Scoreboard," wrote that Lockman "tried to make a stab for (the ball) in front of the Pirate bullpen."[3] It's important to note that in the cavernous Polo Grounds, the visitors bullpen

was located in the field of play in front of the left-center-field wall — more than 440 feet from home plate.[4]

Lockman retrieved the ball and threw wildly to Mays, whose relay was too late to give the infield any chance of throwing out the flying Clemente. In the third-base coaching box, manager Haney gave Clemente the "go" sign, and the speedy outfielder slid past Giants catcher Wes Westrum and was called safe by home-plate umpire Dusty Boggess.

Pittsburgh Sun-Telegraph staff writer Charles J. Doyle wrote: "Clemente displayed more speed than this writer has seen any Pittsburgh player show in recent years."[5] In a column appearing in the same issue, he wrote: "The Bucs still are talking about the speed and slide used by Roberto Clemente in his first major league homer."[6]

It was the first of nine inside-the-park home runs Clemente hit in his major-league career, which places him second among players since 1950.[7]

After this display of power and speed, Clemente showed off his legendary right-field throwing arm — for which he is still widely known more than 65 years later.

Leading off the home half of the fifth, pitcher Liddle popped out to shortstop. Second baseman Davey Williams walked. The next batter, shortstop Alvin Dark, hit a line drive to Clemente in right field. Clemente caught the ball and threw to first baseman Preston Ward, doubling off Williams and earning Clemente his first major-league outfield assist.

Clemente led all National League right fielders with 16 assists in 1955. Over his career, he led the league in outfield assists five times and ranks second all-time among right fielders with 266.[8]

In other game highlights, Clemente singled in the seventh and hit a sacrifice fly in the ninth, driving in Dick Groat for Pittsburgh's second run. His line on the day: four at-bats, two hits, one home run, one run scored, two runs batted in, one putout, one assist.

Clemente's home-run dash around the bases may have stunned teammates and the small crowd, but probably not anyone who knew him well – and especially not Clemente himself. Two months after the game against the Giants, Biederman wrote in *The Sporting News*: "He's very proud of his feats as a track star in Puerto Rico and explains he was considered so good in the 400 meters, the javelin and the hop, skip, and jump that he would have been picked for the Olympics at Helsinki but for the fact that he already had signed a professional baseball contract."[9]

Also of note, Clemente and Mays – who made the relay throw when Clemente hit his home run – were teammates with the champion Santurce Cangrejeros of the 1954-55 Puerto Rican winter league.[10]

Clemente quickly became a fan favorite during his rookie season. Biederman wrote in *The Sporting News*: "The Pittsburgh fans have fallen in love with his spectacular fielding and his deadly right arm."[11]

SABR biographer Stew Thornley described Clemente as "the greatest Puerto Rican player."[12]

That Monday afternoon at the Polo Grounds provided a stunning preview of his legacy on the field.

SOURCES

In addition to the sources cited in the Notes, the author accessed a file provided by the National Baseball Hall of Fame Library, Retrosheet.org, and Baseball-Reference.com.

NOTES

1   Lester J. Biederman, "Bucs Farm Hurlers Thies, Bell, Hall, but 12-3 Drubbing by Giants Qualifies More Pirates for Cut," *Pittsburgh Press*, April 19, 1955.

2   Jack Hernon, "Winless Bucs Lose Sixth, Bow to Giants, 12-3," *Pittsburg Post-Gazette*, April 19, 1955.

3   Les Biederman, "From the Scoreboard," *Pittsburgh Press*, April 19, 1955.

4   https://ballparks.com/baseball/national/pologr.htm.

5   Charles J. Doyle, "Giants' Battling Slump Ends; Cold Weather Shortens Bucs' Stay in N.Y.," *Pittsburgh Sun-Telegraph*, April 19, 1955.

6   Chilly Doyle, "Chilly Sauce," *Pittsburgh Sun-Telegraph*, April 19, 1955.

7   Derek Bain, "Fun Facts About Inside-the-Park Home Runs," Seamheads.com, June 8, 2016. https://seamheads.com/blog/2016/06/08/fun-facts-about-inside-the-park-home-runs/, Accessed February 13, 2022. Carl Reichers researched the dates of Clemente's inside-the-park home runs and found nine: April 18, 1955; July 25, 1956; May 11, 1957; July 23, 1958; August 28, 1959; July 14, 1966; April 21, 1968; September 22, 1968; May 19, 1971.

8   https://www.baseball-reference.com/leaders/A_rf_career.shtml.

9   Les Biederman, "Clemente, Early Buc Ace, Says He's Better in Summer," *The Sporting News*, June 29, 1955: 26.

10 https://baseballhall.org/discover/santurce-cangrejeros-willie-mays-roberto-clemente.

11 Les Biederman, "Clemente, Early Buc Ace, Says He's Better in Summer."

12 https://sabr.org/bioproj/person/roberto-clemente/.

CLEMENTE NOTCHES FIRST CAREER GAME-WINNING RBI AS BUCS TOP PHILS FOR FIRST WIN OF SEASON

APRIL 24, 1955
PITTSBURGH PIRATES 6, PHILADELPHIA PHILLIES 1
AT CONNIE MACK STADIUM, PHILADELPHIA
(FIRST GAME OF DOUBLEHEADER)

BY KELLEN NIELSON

The weather at Connie Mack Stadium in Philadelphia was cold and miserable with 40-mph winds for the Pirates-Phillies game on April 24, 1955. Unfortunately for the Pirates, the 1955 season had so far matched the weather. It was marred by rainouts and eight consecutive losses to start the season and the 14th consecutive loss going back to the end of the '54 campaign. The eighth loss set a franchise record for consecutive losses to start a season and was one shy of tying the all-time record of nine, set by the 1918 Brooklyn Robins.[1]

The 1954 Pittsburgh Pirates finished the year with an abysmal 53-101 record and dead last in the National League. But, with the advent of spring each team has hope, and the 1955 Pirates were no different. General manager Branch Rickey proclaimed, "This 1955 club will be the best Pittsburgh has had in many years. The Pirates will be a happy surprise to our people sooner or later." He tempered that enthusiasm by adding, "That surprise can come this year. It could, but most certainly not later than 1956."[2] The local media was even less

enthused. *Pittsburgh Post-Gazette* sportswriter Al Abrams opined, "[W]e're going out on a shaky limb and predict the Pirates will finally make seventh place this year."[3] But there was hope, most notably in Dick Groat and Roberto Clemente.

Groat had enjoyed success in the 1952 campaign but had spent the previous two years in military service. He was off to a mediocre start, batting .231 with no home runs or RBIs and only one run scored in five games.

Clemente was a highly touted prospect signed by the Dodgers on February 19, 1954, out of Puerto Rico at the age of 19. Clemente's signing bonus was reported to be $10,000, which made him a "bonus baby." This required him to be on the major-league roster for two years or be subject to loss via the Rule 5 draft. Dodgers GM Buzzie Bavasi had persuaded Rickey not to draft the young outfielder and to draft another Dodgers player, John Rutherford, which would have left Clemente a Dodger. Believing he had a deal in place, Bavasi left Clemente unprotected. Bavasi soon learned the deal was off. "It seemed that [Dodgers' owner] Walter O'Malley and Mr. Rickey got in another argument and it seems Walter called Mr. Rickey every name in the book,"[4] Bavasi told Clemente's SABR biographer, Stew Thornley. Despite Bavasi's efforts, when the Dodgers left the young outfielder form Puerto Rico unprotected, Rickey scooped him up with the first pick in the November 22, 1964, draft.

Clemente had been tearing up winter ball in Puerto Rico. He was playing for the Santurce Cangrejeros alongside Willie Mays. Manager Herman Franks called Clemente "the best player in the league, except for Willie Mays."[5] On Opening Day 1955, Clemente was notably absent from the lineup. Instead, another youngster, Roman Mejias, played right field. New York Giants scout Tom Sheehan questioned Clemente's absence from the lineup and was told, "(Manager) Fred Haney thinks he's going to be a good ball player but feels certain pitchers will give him trouble."[6]

Mejias's start to the 1955 season was rough. He went 2-for-11 in the Pirates' first three games with a home run and two RBIs. Clemente's time on the bench was not long and he made his major-league debut on April 17, 1955, against the Dodgers and went 1-for-4 with a run scored.

In the first game of the Sunday afternoon doubleheader, the starter for manager Haney's Pirates was Max Surkont, who was in his second year with Pittsburgh. Surkont was the Opening Day pitcher and making his third start of the season. His previous two starts were disasters. He gave up 13 runs in 10⅓ innings and lost both games. Going for the Phillies was another right-hander, Jim Owens, who was making his second career start.

Owens immediately found himself in trouble. He walked Clemente to start the game and added another walk before getting out of the jam without allowing a run. Surkont followed suit in the bottom half, giving up a two-out double and a walk before retiring Earl Torgesen to end the half-inning.

Owens's fortunes did not improve in the second. Dale Long greeted him with a single to center. Toby Atwell grounded to first and Long advanced to second. Gene Freese knocked a triple to left, scoring Long and giving the Pirates the lead. Freese held third as Surkont grounded out to first. It looked as if Jones might limit the damage. Clemente, up next, instead hit a line-drive single to right to give Pittsburgh a 2-0 lead. The RBI gave Clemente three in the young season. Owens walked Groat and was off to the showers after only 1⅔ innings. Steve Ridzik retired Felipe Montemayor on a groundout to first to stop the bleeding.

Surkont tossed a shutdown inning in the bottom of the second despite allowing a leadoff walk. Both teams were retired without scoring a run in the third. The Pirates broke the game open in the fourth. Atwell walked and Freese reached on an error by Ridzik on a bunt attempt. Surkont attempted to sacrifice but Atwell was forced out at third. Phillies third baseman Willie Jones threw the ball away trying for a double play at second and the runners advanced to second and third. Freese held third as Clemente flied to right, but he and Surkont scored on Groat's double to right. Montemayor singled to right to give the Pirates a five-run lead. Phillies manager Mayo Smith called on Thornton Kipper to relieve Ridzik and Kipper struck out Frank Thomas.

In the Phillies' fourth, Surkont continued to live dangerously, giving up a single and walk before getting a double play off the bat of Willie Jones. Stan Palys flied out to left field to end the inning. The Phillies scored in the bottom of the sixth when Del Ennis launched a home run to deep left field. That proved to be the lone run for the Phillies.

Both teams managed a hit in the seventh with no runs scored. In the eighth, Freese led off with a single off the fourth Phillies pitcher, Dave Cole, and was sacrificed to second by Surkont. Clemente doubled to center field, scoring Freese.

Clemente's second RBI of the day gave the Pirates a commanding 6-1 lead. The inning ended when Groat and Montemayor grounded out.

The Phillies stranded baserunners in the eighth and ninth. Surkont finished off the opposition to gain the complete-game victory and give the Pirates their first win of the young season. Surkont kept the Phillies at bay over his nine innings, allowing eight hits and four walks. Surkont improved his record to 1-2 and lowered his ERA to 6.52. Owens took the loss for the Phillies and fell to 0-2.

The Pirates had several offensive stars in their victory. Freese had three hits and three runs scored. Long had four hits, including a double and a run scored. Groat added two hits and two RBIs, but it was Clemente who sparked the Pittsburgh offense. He was 2-for-4 with a double and two RBIs. Since Clemente's insertion into the lineup, he was batting .381 with two doubles and four RBIs.

The win came on the eve of Haney's birthday and the team "whooped it up" as "flashbulbs popped" in the clubhouse after the game.[7]

Despite the Pirates' struggles over the previous years and a rough start to the '55 season, Clemente seemed to offer some hope for the team's future.[8] His second-inning single had provided the Pirates with their second run in the 6-1 victory, giving him the first game-winning RBI of his career.

SOURCES

In addition to the sources mentioned in the Notes, the author consulted Baseball-Reference.com, SABR.org, and Retrosheet.org

https://www.baseball-reference.com/boxes/PHI/PHI195504241.shtml

https://www.retrosheet.org/boxesetc/1955/B04241PHI1955.htm

NOTES

1   The 1988 Baltimore Orioles set a new record with 21 straight losses.

2   Branch Rickey, "Third Base Weak Spot, GM Admits," *Pittsburgh Post-Gazette*, April 14, 1955.

3   Al Abrams, "Sidelights on Sports," *Pittsburgh Post-Gazette*, April 14, 1955: 14.

4   Stew Thornley, "Roberto Clemente," SABR biography project Roberto Clemente – Society for American Baseball Research (sabr.org).

5   Stew Thornley, "Roberto Clemente."

6   Jack Hernon, "Who's in Left, Center and Right," *Pittsburgh Post-Gazette*, April 15, 1955: 25.

7   Russ Green (United Press), "Pirates Beat Phillies, Snap Losing Streak," *Shamokin* (Pennsylvania) *News-Dispatch*, April 25, 1955: 6.

8   The Phillies won the second game of the doubleheader, 3-0, though the final score was not known until June 28. Heavy rain delayed the start of the game, which was suspended in the eighth inning by a Philadelphia curfew and completed on the June date.

CLEMENTE'S FIVE HITS LEAD PIRATES TO CURFEW-INTERRUPTED WIN OVER PHILLIES

MAY 29, 1955
PITTSBURGH PIRATES 11, PHILADELPHIA PHILLIES 5
(SECOND GAME OF DOUBLEHEADER)
AT FORBES FIELD, PITTSBURGH

BY JOHN FREDLAND

A freak ankle injury sidelined Roberto Clemente for four games in May 1955, momentarily sidetracking his spectacular rookie-year emergence in Pittsburgh. The 20-year-old native of Puerto Rico returned on May 29 with five hits in the Pirates' curfew-interrupted 11-5 win over the Philadelphia Phillies in the second game of a doubleheader – but lost his chance for a sixth hit when he was removed for a pinch-runner.

In November 1954, Pittsburgh plucked Clemente from the Brooklyn Dodgers in baseball's Rule 5 Draft. The Dodgers had signed Clemente for a reported $5,000 salary and $10,000 bonus during the previous winter; baseball's bonus rules required them to keep him on their major-league roster for two years or risk losing him in the draft. When Brooklyn left Clemente unprotected after he spent 1954 in the Triple-A International League, the Pirates selected him with the draft's first pick.[1]

Clemente watched Pittsburgh's first three games of 1955 from the dugout. But manager Fred Haney plugged him into the lineup for game four

on April 17, and it was the genesis of greatness. Through May 22, Clemente had a .281/.307/.450 batting line in 31 games and rave reviews from Pittsburgh's media.

"Here's a young Puerto Rican of 20, with a baseball future as bright as any fellow in the game today," Les Biederman asserted in the *Pittsburgh Press*. "He can do everything well and above all, has the intense desire to play the game."[2] "No one has called him Willie Mays Jr., yet but Roberto Clemente, the young outfielder, isn't far away from that tag," Al Abrams observed in the *Pittsburgh Post-Gazette*.[3] "Roberto Clemente has been the most sensational figure to appear at Forbes Field since Kiki Cuyler rammed that explosive double to right with the bases loaded and won the 1925 [World Series]," Chilly Doyle gushed in the *Pittsburgh Sun-Telegraph*.[4]

But Pittsburgh, eighth-place finishers in the eight-team National League four times in the previous five years, lost 11 consecutive games between May 11 and May 22 and dropped into the league's cellar. A 15-1 win over first-place

Brooklyn at Forbes Field on May 24 snapped the slide; Clemente haunted his former employers with two hits, two runs, and three RBIs.[5] The *Pittsburgh Press* noted that his uniform number had changed from 13 to 21.[6]

A night later, Clemente had two more hits against the Dodgers before rain washed away the game in the fourth inning.[7] During batting practice for the series finale on May 26, Clemente – just five months removed from an auto accident that caused neck and back soreness for the rest of his life[8] – caught his spikes in wet dirt while swinging and sprained his right ankle.[9] He missed that game and games against the Phillies on May 27 and 28; the Pirates lost all three.

Clemente was again on the sidelines for the first game of a Sunday afternoon doubleheader with the Phillies on May 29. The Pirates also lost that one, 5-2, for their 15th defeat in 16 games. Philadelphia ace Robin Roberts earned the win, shrugging off over an hour in rain delays and Pittsburgh slugger Frank Thomas's first home run of the season.

After his four-game absence, Clemente returned to action in the second game of the doubleheader, batting leadoff. Philadelphia, now on a seven-game winning streak after losing 13 straight earlier in the spring,[10] was the Pirates' closest competitor in the standings, but Pittsburgh still trailed their cross-commonwealth rivals by six games.

Veteran right-hander Max Surkont took the mound for the Pirates, hoping to stop their newest losing streak. Surkont, a product of St. Louis's legendary farm system of the 1930s and '40s, lugged a 5.78 ERA into his eighth start of 1955. He retired the Phillies in order in the first inning.

Clemente led off against Philadelphia starter Dave Cole. Only 24 years old, Cole nonetheless was on his fourth major-league team in six seasons. Deploying the opposite-field swing that became one of his trademarks,[11] Clemente hit Cole's first pitch to right field for a double.[12]

Rookie second baseman Gene Freese followed Clemente. The 21-year-old Freese had drawn unwelcome national attention a day earlier when his baserunning error – failing to touch second base from first after fellow rookie Román Mejías's apparent game-ending single – cost the Pirates a win over the Phillies.[13] Freese dropped down a bunt. Cole bobbled the ball for an error, and the Pirates had runners on first and third.

Jerry Lynch drove in Clemente with a single to center. Freese advanced to third on Lynch's hit and scored on Frank Thomas's long fly ball to left. Singles by Preston Ward and George Freese, brother of Gene Freese, brought home Lynch for a 3-0 Pittsburgh lead.

Clemente ignited the Pirates again in the third. With one out, his hit went off second baseman Bobby Morgan's glove. Morgan picked up the ball and threw to first, but his throw landed in Pittsburgh's dugout. Clemente took second; the play was ruled a single and an error. Gene Freese singled in Clemente to push Pittsburgh's advantage to 4-0.

Aided by a double play, Surkont faced the minimum nine batters through three innings, but the Phillies broke through in the fourth. With one out, Glen Gorbous's bunt down the third-base line stayed fair for a single. Del Ennis singled one out later. Willie Jones – along with Ennis and Richie Ashburn the only starters remaining from Philadelphia's "Whiz Kids" 1950 National League championship team – drove Surkont's pitch over the scoreboard in left field for a three-run home run, cutting the deficit to 4-3.

After Clemente led off the bottom of the fourth with a single, giving him the second three-hit game of his young career, first-year Philadelphia manager Mayo Smith replaced Cole with Thornton Kipper. Gene Freese greeted Kipper with another single, but Lynch short-circuited the inning by grounding into a double play.

The relentless Pirates expanded their lead an inning later. Jack Shepard, catching regularly

L to R: Manny Sanguillen, Willie Stargell, Al Oliver, Dave Cash, and Roberto Clemente lined up behind home plate at Three Rivers Stadium. Courtesy of The Clemente Museum.

while Toby Atwell recovered from a broken finger,[14] walked with one out against Kipper and moved to second on Dick Groat's single. Clemente's two-out double down the right-field line, his fourth hit of the game, scored Shepard for a 5-3 Pittsburgh edge.

Surkont dodged Earl Torgeson's two-out triple in the top of the sixth, and Pittsburgh resumed its siege in the bottom of the inning. Thomas, who snapped a string of 33 games without a home run in the opener, batted with one out. He made it a two-homer day by lining Kipper's pitch over the scoreboard in left, increasing the lead to 6-3.

Ward followed with a walk. George Freese doubled him home. Smith summoned Ron Mrozinski

to replace Kipper. One out later, Groat singled to score Freese. The Pirates had an 8-3 lead.

Surkont's scoreless seventh set the stage for Clemente, leading off the bottom of the inning. Clemente doubled to make it five hits — and three doubles — in five plate appearances. Not wanting to risk further injury to Clemente's ankle, Haney sent in Mejías to pinch-run.[15]

But time was running out at Forbes Field. Pennsylvania law forbade Sunday baseball after 7 P.M.[16] The opener's rain delays had set the nightcap on a tighter timeline than originally anticipated. Mrozinski set down the next two Pirates and then the clock struck seven. Play was suspended until Philadelphia's next visit, in July.

On July 8 the Phillies returned to Pittsburgh. The Pirates remained in last place; Philadelphia still occupied seventh. When the game reconvened, Mrozinski was back on the mound. Marv Blaylock was the new Phil at first, replacing Torgeson, who had been sold to Detroit on June 15. Mrozinski retired Thomas to end the inning.

Pittsburgh's eighth-inning defensive alignment also reflected the passage of time. Johnny O'Brien completed a two-year Army tour in June and became the Pirates' everyday second baseman; here, he replaced Gene Freese.[17] George Freese was demoted to the minors; Dick Cole took over at third.[18] Atwell, now recovered from his broken finger, substituted for Shepard at catcher. Surkont continued his start; Ennis's RBI single cut the deficit to 8-4, but the Phillies moved no closer.

The Pirates then sewed it up against left-hander Bob Kuzava. After one out, singles by Cole, Atwell, and Groat – the fourth hit of the game for Pittsburgh's shortstop – produced a run. Kuzava got two strikes on Surkont, but the Pirates pitcher bunted for a hit, loading the bases.

The leadoff spot was due, but this time it was Mejías, who stayed in the game in right field after running for Clemente. There would be no decline in productivity. The 24-year-old native of Cuba singled, driving in Atwell and Groat for an 11-4 lead. Surkont allowed an unearned run in the ninth but closed out the complete-game win.[19]

Clemente missed the chance for six hits when Mejías ran for him, but still had the first five-hit game of his Hall of Fame career. He had seven more five-hit games before his tragic death in a plane crash on New Year's Eve 1972.

AUTHOR'S NOTE

In addition to Clemente's five-hit game, the doubleheader included Frank Thomas's first two home runs of 1955, after he went homerless in the Pirates' first 33 games of the season. Thomas led the 1954 Pirates with 23 home runs, batted .298/.359/.497, and received MVP votes for the second season in a row, but held out during the following spring in a salary dispute with general manager Branch Rickey. The 25-year-old outfielder started slowly after signing, batting only .149/.208/.191 through the first game of Pittsburgh's doubleheader with the New York Giants on May 22. Thomas eventually got on track and posted a .308 batting average after August 20. His 25 home runs again led the Pirates.

At SABR's 48th annual national convention, held in Pittsburgh in 2018, Thomas, then 89 years old, appeared on a panel discussion of Rickey. He spoke bluntly about the contract negotiations. "Mr. Rickey and I had our problems," Thomas remembered. "He treated me like I was dirt on his feet. … If we would have had agents back then … we went in to talk contract by ourselves. They had the upper hand; we were slaves back then. We couldn't go anywhere. We either signed or we couldn't play baseball. And if you loved baseball as much as I did, you signed."[20]

SOURCES

In addition to the Sources cited in the Notes, the author consulted the Baseball-Reference.com and Retrosheet.org websites for pertinent material and the box scores noted below; newspaper game coverage in the *Philadelphia Inquirer* and *Pittsburgh Post-Gazette*; and SABR Baseball Biography Project biographies of several players who participated in the game, especially Stew Thornley's biography of Roberto Clemente, David E. Skelton's biography of Max Surkont, and Austin Gisriel's biography of David Cole. SABR member Steven Weiner provided helpful feedback on an earlier draft of this article.

https://www.baseball-reference.com/boxes/PIT/PIT195505292.shtml

https://www.retrosheet.org/boxesetc/1955/B05292PIT1955.htm

NOTES

1   David Maraniss, *Clemente: The Passion and Grace of Baseball's Last Hero* (New York: Simon & Schuster Paperbacks: 2006), 36-37, 56-57. The Pirates selected Clemente from the Dodgers in accordance with bonus rules in effect from 1953 to 1957. Edgar Munzel, "Bankrolls Now Only Limit on Bonus Bids," *The Sporting News*, December 18, 1957: 11.

2   Les Biederman, "The Scoreboard," *Pittsburgh Press*, May 10, 1955: 31.

3   Al Abrams, "Sidelights on Sports," *Pittsburgh Post-Gazette*, May 23, 1955: 18.

4   Chilly Doyle, "Fans Like Clemente," *Pittsburgh Sun-Telegraph*, May 4, 1955: 26.

5   Clemente batted .345 in 291 career games against the Brooklyn and Los Angeles Dodgers, his best average against any opponent.

6   Les Biederman, "The Scoreboard," *Pittsburgh Press*, May 25, 1955: 37.

7   Lester J. Biederman, "Cleanup Spot Baffles Pirates," *Pittsburgh Press*, May 26, 1955: 24.

8   Maraniss, 65.

9   Jack Hernon, "Bums Profit on Buc Charity at Home, 6-2: Poor Outfielding Yields Five Runs," *Pittsburgh Post-Gazette*, May 27, 1955: 20.

10 Stan Baumgartner, "Mayo, Now Having Seen Worst, Hopes for Better Days for Phils: Team Blew Leads Seven Times in 13-Game Losing Streak," *The Sporting News*, May 25, 1955: 8.

11 Maraniss, 152.

12 Jack Hernon, "Pirates Lose, 5-2, Then Lead at Curfew, 8-3: Thomas Homers in Both Games," *Pittsburgh Post-Gazette*, May 30, 1955: 39.

13 Lester J. Biederman, "'Boner' by Gene Freese Gives Phils 8-4 Victory: Bucs' Winning Run in 10th Is Nullified," *Pittsburgh Post-Gazette*, May 29, 1955: 4, 1; "Freese Pulls a 'Merkle': Bucs Bow in 11, 8-4," *Daily News*, May 29, 1955: C25; "Stupidity Costs Pirates Victory: Rookie Leaves Field on Forced Play," *Selma* (Alabama) *Times-Journal*, May 29, 1955: 6.

14 Charles J. Doyle, "Same Old Story: Bucs Lose Lead," *Pittsburgh Sun-Telegraph*, May 28, 1955: 10.

15 Lester J. Biederman, "Bucs See Wehmeier Slighted by All-Stars," *Pittsburgh Press*, July 9, 1955: 6.

16 In 1959 Pennsylvania abolished the curfew for Sunday games started before 6 P.M. "Sunday Baseball Bill to Get OK," *Pittsburgh Post-Gazette*, July 30, 1959: 1.

17 "O'Brien Twins to Rejoin Pirates Late Next Week: Both Slated for Army Discharge; Out to Win Back Infield Positions," *Pittsburgh Post-Gazette*, June 1, 1955: 22.

18 Charles J. Doyle, "George Freese, Wade Unhappy," *Pittsburgh Sun-Telegraph*, June 16, 1955: 32.

19 Surkont also started the regularly scheduled Pirates-Phillies game on July 8 but was the losing pitcher in Philadelphia's 5-1 win. Jack Hernon, "Pirates Win Suspended Game, 11-5; Lose, 5-1: Surkont Finishes 1st Tilt, Starts 2nd," *Pittsburgh Post-Gazette*, July 9, 1955: 10.

20 Branch Rickey, *The Pittsburgh Pirates Years*, SABR 48, June 23, 2018. sabr.org/latest/sabr-48-listen-highlights-branch-rickey-pittsburgh-pirates-years-panel/.

ROBERTO CLEMENTE HITS AN INSIDE-THE-PARK, WALK-OFF GRAND SLAM TO LIFT PIRATES

JULY 25, 1956
PITTSBURGH PIRATES 9, CHICAGO CUBS 8
AT FORBES FIELD, PITTSBURGH

BY STEVEN C. WEINER

The headline writer for the front page of a daily newspaper is challenged to provide the reader with glimpses of tragedy and joy, victory and defeat, worry and elation, all appropriately befitting the day's news. When Pittsburgh awoke on the morning of July 26, 1956, the headline spread across the front page of the *Pittsburgh Post-Gazette* was "Luxury Liners Collide, 1,100 Abandoning Andrea Doria."[1]

Just before midnight, the Swedish ship *MS Stockholm* struck the Italian ocean liner *SS Andrea Doria* in dense fog off Nantucket Island. The *Andrea Doria* was severely damaged and badly listing before finally capsizing in the morning. The heroic efforts of rescuers saved 1,660 people but tragically, 51 others lost their lives.[2] No doubt the headline, the photo of the *Andrea Doria* and that first two-column story captured the tragedy and the actions taken in response during the early-morning hours.

For the sports fan, the smaller-print box in the middle of the front page, "Clemente Again, Pirates Win in Merriwell Finish, 9-8,"[3] provided that first glimpse of a unique baseball feat never seen before and so far never repeated (as of 2018.) The 20-year-old Roberto Clemente brought his exciting style to Pittsburgh in his 1955 rookie season and earned a spot in the Pirates outfield. On this night, he clouted an inside-the-park grand slam off Cubs relief pitcher Jim Brosnan to end the game in a victory for the Pirates, right then and there.

Clemente was a free swinger, an impatient hitter who swung at almost any pitch including those outside the strike zone.[4] He became known as a primary example of a good "bad-ball hitter."[5] Playing for the Triple-A Montreal Royals in 1954, Jack Cassini was Clemente's teammate. In Stew Thornley's interview for Clemente's biography for the SABR BioProject, Cassini said, "He could hit. He didn't need a strike. The best way to pitch him was right down the middle of the plate."[6] In fact, Clemente walked only 13 times in 572 plate appearances in 1956. In one stretch that season, covering 192 plate appearances, he went 50 games without walking.[7]

For a game pitting two teams that would finish the season last and next-to-last in the National League, respectively, the Pirates started their All-Star pitcher, Bob Friend (12-8, 3.24 ERA), and the Cubs countered with Warren Hacker (2-8, 5.37).

The Pirates started the scoring in the fourth inning when Clemente reached on an infield single and Dale Long hit his 20th home run of the season for a 2-0 lead. That home run set a record for Pittsburgh left-handed hitters, previously held by Hall of Fame shortstop Arky Vaughan, who hit 19 in 1935.[8] The Pirates scored their third run in the fifth inning. After Friend singled and Bill Virdon doubled, Bob Skinner was intentionally walked to load the bases for Clemente. No grand slam this time, just a sacrifice fly to center for a 3-0 lead. In the sixth inning, consecutive doubles by Frank Thomas and Jack Shepard added another run and Warren Hacker's pitching outing was over for the night when he was replaced by Vito Valentinetti.

Meanwhile, Bob Friend was sailing along into the eighth inning on a 4-0 four-hitter, but four singles that produced one run ended his evening. Roy Face, by now being used almost exclusively in relief, came in to pitch and was summarily hammered with doubles by Walt Moryn, Eddie Miksis, and Hobie Landrith each of whom knocked in two runs for a 7-4 Cubs lead. Each team scored once in its next at-bat for an 8-5 Cubs lead. In the case of the Cubs, they scored on three singles against Face after two were out. Nellie King replaced him and ended the top of the ninth inning by striking out Miksis on three pitches.[9] The stage was now set for the dramatic bottom of the ninth inning and the improbable feat about to unfold.

With Turk Lown pitching for the Cubs, a walk to Hank Foiles, a single by Bill Virdon, and another walk to Dick Cole loaded the bases for Clemente. Jim Brosnan relieved Lown and threw one pitch, described by Jack Hernon as "high

and inside."[10] There was no doubt that Clemente would swing. He hit the ball over Jim King's head in left field and after the ball struck the fencing, it rolled along the cinder warning track toward center field. The three runners easily scored and Clemente ignored the outstretched arms and stop sign of Pirates manager and third-base coach Bobby Bragan as the relay throw came in from center fielder Solly Drake to Ernie Banks to catcher Hobie Landrith. The last moments of the improbable were captured in the *Pittsburgh Post-Gazette*: "He slid, missed the plate, then reached back to rest his hand on the rubber with the ninth Pirate run in a 9-8 victory as the crowd of 12,431 went goofy with excitement."[11]

Would Clemente be fined for roaring right past Bragan? The circumstances were ripe. After the game, Bragan's comments reflected conventional baseball strategy, "Clemente tied up the game, for sure and I threw up the stop sign. ... After all, we had some long-ball hitters coming up, no one out and getting Bobby home with the winning run looked easy."[12] Clemente readily admitted his deliberate action to ignore the stop sign.

Bragan was in his first year as Pirates manager, desperately trying to improve their lot after four consecutive years in the eight-team National League's cellar.[13] Bragan's penchant for fining players started early in the season. After a loss to the New York Giants in the second game of the season, he fined Clemente $25 for missing a squeeze-play sign and Dale Long the same amount for using bad judgment in cutting off a relay from the outfield.[14] As Bragan put it, "A manager can get into serious trouble by letting the little things go unnoticed. They soon grow into big things, so let's put a stop to the little things now."[15]

A *Sports Illustrated* feature story by Robert Creamer also explained the rationale for those minor infractions — $5 for reporting late to the park, $10 for failing to throw a pitchout when it was called for, $20 for failing to slide into second base in a crucial moment. "The fines aren't much, but they sting a man's pride. And they help spread Bragan's basic idea that this club is too good to condone carelessness; carelessness is for eighth-place clubs."[16]

Clemente's heroics and the Pirates' victory maintained their position in fifth place. We can only speculate as to the mood of Bobby Bragan after the game. Clemente was not fined.

It would be 32 years before the term "walk-off" entered the baseball lexicon. As noted by Paul Dickson, "The term was coined by Oakland Athletics pitcher Dennis Eckersley for that lonely stroll from the mound after a pitcher gives up the winning run (Gannett News Service, July 30, 1988)."[17] Eckersley's use of the term had a rather negative connotation marking the losing pitcher as he leaves the field.[18] Common usage has evolved now to highlight the achievement of the batter and the celebratory mood of the winning team and its fans.

The drama created by the possibility of any walk-off home run and the elation felt when it occurs happens quite often. In fact, it occurred at another game on that very night. The author, attending the game with his father as a young teenager and avid Dodgers fan, saw Duke Snider hit a walk-off home run in Roosevelt Stadium, in Jersey City, New Jersey, as the Brooklyn Dodgers edged the Cincinnati Reds, 2-1.[19] But what happened in Jersey City pales in comparison to what happened in Pittsburgh!

"What Roberto Clemente accomplished in Pittsburgh on July 25, 1956, stupefied the tobacco-spitting baseball lifers all around him precisely because it transcended baseball, entering the realm of pure theater and then myth. Even his defiance of authority that day — running through hapless Bobby Bragan's sign — enhances the quality of the legend."[20]

Improbable as it may be, the uniqueness of Clemente's game-ending home run could be duplicated someday if the right set of circumstances align. Regardless, the inside-the-park walk-off grand slam is safe at home plate thanks to Roberto Clemente. We should celebrate what Clemente accomplished on this night and take the greatest of pleasures in what he brought to baseball in an exciting style we got to enjoy over his entire career.

This article previously appeared in *Moments of Joy and Heartbreak: 66 Significant Episodes in the History of the Pittsburgh Pirates* (SABR, 2018), edited by Jorge Iber and Bill Nowlin.

SOURCES

In addition to the references cited in the Notes, the author also accessed Baseball-Reference.com and Retrosheet.org.

https://www.baseball-reference.com/boxes/PIT/PIT195607250.shtml

https://www.retrosheet.org/boxesetc/1956/B07250PIT1956.htm

NOTES

1   "Hits Stockholm in Heavy Fog, Italian Ship Listing So Badly She Can't Lower Life Boats; Vessels Racing to Rescue," *Pittsburgh Post-Gazette*, July 26, 1956: 1.

2   Evan Andrews, "The Sinking of Andrea Doria," History.com, July 25, 2016, accessed September 12, 2017, history.com/news/the-sinking-of-andrea-doria.

3   "A Frank Merriwell finish: A dramatic and successful ending to a baseball game in the manner of Burt L. Standish's (pseudonym for Gilbert Patten) fictitious character Frank Merriwell, who triumphed each week in spectacular fashion by performing unmatchable feats of last-minute derring-do. Merriwell's exploits as a scholar sportsman captured the imagination of millions from 1896 to 1914 in Tip Top Weekly, a pulp-fiction magazine for boys." Paul Dickson, *The Dickson Baseball Dictionary*, 3rd Edition (New York: W.W. Norton & Company, 2009), 345.

4   Dickson, 347.

5   Dickson, 43.

6   Stew Thornley, "Roberto Clemente," SABR Baseball Biography Project (telephone interview with Jack Cassini, June 20, 2005).

7   Les Biederman, "Clemente in 50 Games Without Walk," *The Sporting News*, August 8, 1956: 18.

8   Jack Hernon, "Bucs Bounce Back After Losing Lead, Rally in 9th After Chicago's 7-Run 8th; Long Sets HR Mark," *Pittsburgh Post-Gazette*, July 26, 1956: 14.

9   After mention of such a performance, this author feels compelled to acknowledge Roy Face's outstanding 16-year career as captured in his SABR biography written by Gary Gillette. In this season alone, Face led the National League with 68 appearances and tied a major-league record by appearing in nine consecutive games September 3-13, 1956.

10 Hernon.

11 Hernon.

12 "Clemente Ignored Stop Sign on Slam, but Escaped Fine," *The Sporting News*, August 8, 1956: 18.

13 The Pittsburgh Pirates finished the 1956 season in seventh place in the National League with a record of 66-88 and only the Chicago Cubs trailed them; they remained a seventh-place team well into the 1957 season when Bragan was replaced by Danny Murtaugh in August.

14 "Bragan Cracks Down Early, Fines Clemente, Long $25," *The Sporting News*, April 25, 1956: 21.

15 "Les Biederman, "Bear-Down Bragan Means Business, Buc Fans Learn," *The Sporting News*, May 2, 1956: 7.

16 Robert Creamer, "The Sad Song of Bobby," *Sports Illustrated*, May 6, 1957: 54-58.

17 Dickson, 919.

18 Although unconfirmed by the author, it is quite possible that Dennis Eckersley was referring to the Oakland-Seattle game at the Kingdome on July 29, 1988. Eckersley came into the game in the 10th inning seeking his 31st save of the season with the A's leading 3-2. Instead, Steve Balboni hit a three-run game-winning home run for the Mariners and the walk-off began.

19 Steven C. Weiner, "July 25, 1956: Dodgers Win on Snider Walk-Off Home Run in Jersey City," SABR Games Project.

20 Martin Espada, "The Greatest Forgotten Home Run of All Time," *The Massachusetts Review*, Volume 56, Number 2, Summer 2015: 249-255.

ROBERTO CLEMENTE TRIPLES THREE TIMES IN PITTSBURGH'S VICTORY OVER CINCINNATI

SEPTEMBER 8, 1958
PITTSBURGH PIRATES 4, CINCINNATI REDLEGS 1
AT FORBES FIELD, PITTSBURGH

BY THOMAS J. BROWN JR.

The Pittsburgh Pirates went 21-12 in August and upped their record to 70-61 as September arrived. They still trailed the first-place Milwaukee Braves by 7½ games. Their record for the first week of September was 5-3. Despite beating the Braves three times in their four-game series the previous weekend, the second-place Pirates closed the gap by only one game.

Fourth-place Cincinnati was in Pittsburgh on September 8 to make up a game that had been washed out by a storm on September 4. The Redlegs had been playing hot, winning 13 of their previous 16 games before arriving in Pittsburgh. When they took the field on September 8, they were on a five-game winning streak that started with a 7-4 win over the Pirates the previous week and was followed by a four-game sweep of the last-place Philadelphia Phillies.

Rookie Curt Raydon took the mound for the Pirates. The right-hander had spent the previous four seasons in Pittsburgh's minor-league system after arriving as part of a seven-player trade in December 1953.[1] Raydon entered the game with a 7-4 record and a 3.70 ERA. He had faced Cincinnati twice back in April and pitched 2⅔ innings of relief in a pair of losses. Raydon faced the Redlegs again on August 9, this time as the starting pitcher. He threw 8⅓ innings in the Pirates' 5-2 victory to earn his sixth win of the season. He started against Cincinnati again on September 3, going 4⅔ innings in the Pirates' 7-4 loss.

Raydon allowed a two-out single in the first and another one in the second but got the third out each time without any runs scoring. He walked Cincinnati pitcher Tom Acker to start the third, but a double play and a fly ball ended the frame. The next Redleg baserunner came in the fifth when Roy McMillan walked with two outs. Raydon got Acker to fly out for the third out.

Right-hander Acker, given the start by Cincinnati manager Jimmy Dykes, was 10-5 in 1957 but had struggled to match that total in 1958. After struggling as a starter for the first two months of the 1959 season, he pitched out of the bullpen until the Pirates used him as a starter again in late

August. He entered the game with a 3-2 record with all three wins coming in August. His last start was against the Pirates on September 3. He also faced Raydon in that game. Acker went six innings, giving up all four Pittsburgh runs and leaving with the scored tied in Cincinnati's 7-4 victory.

Acker retired the side in order in the first. Bob Skinner led off with a double in the second but went no farther as Acker retired the next three batters on a fly ball and a pair of groundouts. Acker retired the side in order in the third before Roberto Clemente led off the fourth with a triple, "a tremendous poke against the left field tower."[2] Clemente was stranded on third when Acker struck out the next two batters and got Frank Thomas to fly out.

The Pirates got the best of Acker in the fifth when "Acker's defense went sour on him."[3] Bill Hall started the action with a two-out double. Raydon, who had gone 0-for-35 at the plate before this game, hit a bouncer down the first-base line. First baseman George Crowe charged and tried to grab the ball but ended up kicking it instead.

When Crowe finally chased down the hit near the first-base box seats, his throw sailed over the head of catcher Smoky Burgess as Hall raced home to score the Pirates' first run. When the dust settled, Raydon was standing on second and given credit for a single, his first major-league hit. The rookie pitcher crossed the plate when Bill Virdon doubled to center. Clemente made it 3-0 when he tripled to right-center. Clemente "was cut down on a close play at the plate attempting to stretch it into a homer" to end the frame.[4]

Cincinnati got two runners on base in the sixth when Jerry Lynch doubled and, after a groundout, Frank Robinson walked. Raydon maintained his shutout when Burgess grounded out to second.

The Redlegs scored in the seventh. This time, Raydon was a victim of poor defense. Crowe reached when rookie first baseman Dick Stuart booted his groundball. Alex Grammas then singled to left. Don Newcombe,[5] who was hitting .373 so far with 22 hits in 59 at-bats, pinch-hit for McMillan. He hit a groundball to Stuart, who threw wide to second in an attempt to start a double play. Stuart's second error in the inning loaded the bases.

Dykes now pinch-hit left-handed batter Bob Thurman for Acker. Pirates manager Danny Murtaugh countered by bringing in southpaw Don Gross to replace Raydon. Gross had been traded to the Pirates from Cincinnati for Bob Purkey the previous winter. He entered the game with a 3.95 ERA in 37 appearances, mostly out of the bullpen.

Dykes in turn pulled Thurman and sent the right-handed Walt Dropo to the plate. Gross got Dropo to ground into a double play but Crowe crossed the plate with the Redlegs' first run. Gross ended the rally by getting Johnny Temple to pop out.

Pittsburgh picked up its fourth run in the eighth. With two outs, Clemente hit his third triple, to right-center. Stuart's single scored Clemente, giving the Pirates a 4-1 lead. Gross got Cincinnati out in order for the next two innings, including three straight groundouts in the ninth, to earn his seventh save of the season.

Of his triples, Clemente said after the game, "[The] first two I hit, they [were] fast balls. Then I hit (a) curve."[6] He was the 32nd player to hit three triples in a game. Danny O'Connell of the Milwaukee Braves had been the last to accomplish this feat, on June 13, 1956, against the Phillies. The last time a Pirate had done it was when Carlos Bernier's three triples helped Pittsburgh beat Cincinnati at Forbes Field on May 2, 1953. Clemente now had 10 triples for the season.[7]

Clemente was asked if he was trying to hit three home runs in the game, matching his teammate Roman Mejias, who had hit three homers against the Giants on May 4. He responded, "I hit two homers this year against Philadelphia. Third time I come to bat, he (Mejias) say[s] don't hit three homers, please. He [said] I hit three homers and the next day they bench me."[8]

The win gave the Pirates the edge in their season series with Cincinnati, 12 victories to 10. It was the first time they had accomplished that feat since 1949. The victory moved the Pirates to within six games of the idle Braves. It also stopped the Redlegs' winning streak at five, leaving them at .500 and 12 games out of first.

Pittsburgh's win gave the Pirates 10 wins in 17 games. Fans began to believe that their team might catch the Braves but that didn't happen. Despite winning eight of their next nine games, the Pirates lost their final five games to last-place Philadelphia and finished in second place, eight games out.

Clemente, in his fourth major-league season, cemented his place as the Pirates' everyday right fielder. He did not reach .300 that year; his .289 batting average was fourth highest on the team. It was the second time Clemente had hit multiple triples in a game, the first coming in his rookie season when he hit two in a 7-5 win over Brooklyn on July 3, 1955. Clemente finished his career with 166 triples but had only five games in which he hit more than one.[9]

SOURCES

In addition to the sources cited in the Notes, the author used the Baseball-Reference.com and Retrosheet.org websites for box-score, player, team, and season pages, pitching and batting logs, and other pertinent material.

https://www.baseball-reference.com/boxes/PIT/PIT195809080.shtml

https://www.retrosheet.org/boxesetc/1958/B09080PIT1958.htm

NOTES

1   Milwaukee traded Raydon along with Larry Lassalle (minors), Sid Gordon, Sam Jethroe, Max Surkont, Fred Waters, and $100,000 to the Pirates for Danny O'Connell on December 26, 1953.

2   "Rookie Hurler Ignites Bucs' Winning Rally," *Cincinnati Enquirer*, September 9, 1958: 31.

3   "Rookie Hurler."

4   "Rookie Hurler."

5   Newcombe joined the Reds after a June 15, 1958, trade from the Los Angeles Dodgers. Newcombe, Steve Bilko, and Johnny Klippstein went to Cincinnati for Art Fowler and Charlie Rabe. He batted .265 with 28 doubles and 11 home runs in his eight years with the Dodgers so it may not have surprised anyone when Dykes pulled him off the bench as a pinch-hitter.

6   George Esper (Associated Press), "Pirates Clip Redlegs, 4-1," *Indiana* (Pennsylvania) *Gazette*, September 9, 1958: 11.

7   Clemente's three triples were his last three of the season.

8   Esper.

9   Clemente had two triples when the Pirates beat the Phillies 9-1 on May 9, 1959. He hit two triples in an 11-8 victory over Braves on June 12, 1966. The last time he had a multiple-triple game came when he hit two triples against the Houston Astros on July 21, 1967, in the Pirates' 9-1 win.

FORESHADOWING A CHAMPIONSHIP

APRIL 14, 1960
PITTSBURGH PIRATES 13, CINCINNATI REDS 0
AT FORBES FIELD, PITTSBURGH

BY JEFF BARTO

An MVP, a Cy Young, two future Hall of Famers and a world championship, the Pittsburgh Pirates presaged all these honors by battering the Cincinnati Reds, 13-0, in their 1960 home opener. Pirates shortstop Dick Groat scored three runs on three hits including a double while initiating three double plays to spark his eventual MVP campaign. Right-hander Vernon Law launched his push for the Cy Young Award by spinning a seven-hit shutout without a walk. Future Hall of Famers Roberto Clemente and Bill Mazeroski opened at home with their best games of the season. Clemente, perfect at the plate, smacked three hits including two doubles, a sacrifice fly, and five RBIs. Mazeroski knocked in four runs with a double and tape-measure home run while adding three double plays to his career record. The Pirates' 1960 home opener served as a harbinger for the team's first World Series championship since 1925.

The Pirates had lost their season opener on the road to the Milwaukee Braves, 4-3. Two days later, on April 14, they opened at Forbes Field before 34,064 fans, the largest Opening Day crowd in 12 years.[1] Pittsburgh Mayor Joseph Barr threw out the first pitch to signal the 1:30 P.M. start.[2] An odd mix of weather greeted the teams. Days earlier snow covered the outfield, making it spongy and rutted with just patches of grass.[3] Juxtaposing this marsh, an unseasonal 83 degrees created muggy conditions to start the game.[4]

Law, who won 18 games the year before, faced the Reds' 19-game winner Cal McLish. Both right-handers pitched perfect first innings. In the second, first baseman Frank Robinson flied out to Clemente. Law then hit right fielder Tony Gonzalez, setting the stage for the first of three double plays by Groat and Mazeroski. Catcher Ed Bailey provided the grounder to Groat that ended the inning. McLish struggled in the bottom of the second, giving up three runs on three extra-base hits. Clemente hit a one-out double off the left-field wall. Catcher Smoky Burgess followed with a double to the right-field wall to score Clemente. After a groundout, Mazeroski came to bat and stroked a two-run shot that cleared the combined

41 feet of the Longines clock above the left-field scoreboard.[5] A sportswriter later asked him if the blast was the best ball he hit all spring. "The best ball?" Mazeroski said. "It was the ONLY ball."[6] It would not be his last by game's end.

Law protected his three-run lead in the third by stranding Billy Martin, who opened the inning with a double. In the bottom half, the Pirates continued to rain extra-base hits on McLish. Groat found the left-field wall with a one-out double. McLish hit left fielder Bob Skinner with a pitch. That bruise set the table for Clemente's second double, scoring Groat and Skinner and extending the lead to 5-0. In 1⅔ innings, Calvin Coolidge Julius Caesar Tuskahoma McLish yielded nearly as many runs as he had names. Right-hander Brooks Lawrence took over for his overdubbed teammate to end the inning on Burgess's fly to center. Lawrence would retire the Pirates in order the next inning, but disaster awaited him in the fifth.

In the Reds' fourth inning, Gus Bell hit a one-out single. The mild threat ended when Groat and Mazeroski erased him with their second double play. Lawrence easily ended the Pirates half of the fourth inning with a strikeout by center fielder Gino Cimoli and groundouts by Mazeroski and Law.

The Pirates closed out the top of the fifth inning with yet another double play. Gonzalez opened with a single to right field before Bailey fouled out to third. Martin then grounded to Groat, who fed Mazeroski to complete their third twin killing of the afternoon.

The Pirates unloaded on Cincinnati in the fifth inning. Lawrence faced seven batters; six of them scored. Third baseman Don Hoak opened with a walk and took second on another single by Groat. Skinner's hit drove Hoak home and he took second on center fielder Vada Pinson's failed throw to nab Groat at third. An intentional walk to first baseman Dick Stuart loaded the bases. Pinson then saved several runs with the

best defensive play of the game. Clemente ripped a shot toward the 457-foot marker in left-center field. The area was so distant that the Pirates stored their batting cage there. Where the ball landed might have been a home run in most ballparks. Pinson raced to the cage. With his back to the plate, he made an incredible running catch over his shoulder. Pinson's grab limited Clemente to a sacrifice fly that scored Groat.[7] Lawrence loaded the bases again with a walk to Burgess. Cimoli's double scored Skinner and Stuart, chasing Lawrence from the game. Ex-Pirate Bob Purkey took over in relief. Mazeroski greeted him with the team's seventh extra-base hit, a double that plated Burgess and Cimoli and widened the score to 11-0. Law nearly continued the onslaught, but lined out to Martin at second base, after which Hoak ended the inning with a strikeout.

Law breezed through the Reds' sixth inning, sandwiching a strikeout of pinch-hitter Whitey Lockman between fly outs by third baseman Eddie Kasko and shortstop Roy McMillan. In the bottom of the frame, the Pirates concluded the day's scoring with two more runs. Right-hander Raul Sanchez replaced Purkey on the mound to start the inning. Groat singled to right field for his third hit and moved to second when Sanchez walked Skinner. Stuart's weak tap to Sanchez moved both runners up a base. Clemente drove them home with his third hit of the day, a single to right field. As his fourth and fifth RBIs crossed the plate, Clemente tried to stretch the hit into a double. Gonzalez threw a strike to second, where McMillan tagged out Clemente with his only blemish of the day. Burgess ended the inning with a fly to Pinson in center.

With a 13-0 score, Law had room to allow multiple hits at the start of the next two innings. To open the seventh, Pinson and Bell singled, but Robinson forced Pinson at third. Law then stranded both runners, retiring Gonzalez on a pop foul and Bailey on a soft fly

Clemente on Opening Day of the 1960 season. Courtesy of Dennis Morgan/Pittsburgh Courier Archives.

to Stuart. Sanchez pitched a perfect seventh for the Reds.

The Reds opened the eighth, again with two more hits. Martin sliced his second double and Kasko beat out an infield single. Once more, Law left both runners on base by retiring the next three Reds in order. The Reds sent out right-hander Ted Wieand, in only his second major-league game, to pitch the Pirates eighth. The fifth pitcher of the game for the Reds, Wieand sandwiched a walk between two strikeouts before retiring the final Pirates batter, Stuart, on a fly ball to left field.

Joe Christopher replaced Skinner in left field for the Pirates to start the ninth inning. Law easily retired the Reds in order. Christopher, in his brief appearance, caught the final out that mercifully ended the historical

thrashing. Despite the lengthy fireworks, it took only 2:13 for the teams to sweat through the tropical afternoon conditions.

At the time, it was only the Pirates' fourth Opening Day shutout in the twentieth century. The 13 Pirates runs scored were the second-most for any Opening Day, trailing only the 14 tallied in 1892 and 1953. The 13-0 score remains, as of 2020, the largest margin of victory in a Pirates opener.[8]

The 1960 Pirates produced a memorable season for their fans. From the first to the final game, the team transformed the city. The Opening Day play of Groat, Law, Clemente, and Mazeroski previewed their success during the regular season. Groat went on to win the NL MVP Award and Law captured the Cy Young Award. Clemente enjoyed his breakout season, making his first of 15 All-Star Games, hitting .314, driving in 94 runs and posting a 121 OPS+. As for Mazeroski, his Opening Day home run over the scoreboard clock provided the best omen of all. History records a similar home run over Forbes Field's 406-foot marker to end the 1960 World Series. That walk-off home run claimed the Pirates' first World Series championship in 35 years and made Mazeroski a Pittsburgh legend every October 13 at 3:36 P.M.[9]

SOURCES

In addition to the sources cited in the Notes, the author consulted Baseball-Reference.com and Retrosheet.org for play-by-play information and statistics.

https://www.baseball-reference.com/boxes/PIT/PIT196004140.shtml

https://www.retrosheet.org/boxesetc/1960/B04140PIT1960.htm

NOTES

1   United Press International, "Happy Crowd Watches Buccos Bomb Reds in Opener," *Evening Standard* (Uniontown, Pennsylvania), April 15, 1960: 14.

2   "Opening Day Ceremonies," *Pittsburgh Post-Gazette*, April 14, 1960: 22.

3   Ray Kienzl, "Pirate Notes," *Pittsburgh Sun-Telegraph*, April 15, 1960: 12.

4   David Kelly, "Mayor, Burgess Team Up at Opener," *Pittsburgh Press*, April 14, 1960: 1.

5   David Cicotello and Angelo J. Louisa, *Forbes Field, Essays and Memories of the Pirates' Historic Ballpark, 1909-1971* (Jefferson, North Carolina: McFarland Publishing, 2007), 225.

6   Ray Kienzl, "Who Said Bucs Lack Power?" *Pittsburgh Sun-Telegraph*, April 15, 1960: 12.

7   Joe Reddington Jr., "Clemente, Maz, Groat Whip Up Wild 13-0 Win," *Indiana* (Pennsylvania) *Gazette*, April 15, 1960: 14.

8   Pittsburgh Pirates Opening Day History on Baseball Almanac: baseball-almanac.com/opening_day/odschedule.php?t=PIT.

9   Kevin Kirkland, "Game 7 Gang Gathers Again Sunday," *Pittsburgh Post-Gazette*, October 11, 2013: 33. See also Joe Capozzi, "Back to the Wall," *Palm Beach Post* (West Palm Beach, Florida), October 13, 2000: 206. Each year, on October 13, Pirates fans meet at the remnants of the Forbes Field wall. At 1:00 P.M., organizers begin a loudspeaker recording of the entire game that ends with Mazeroski's home run occurring at 3:36 P.M. It is a tradition that began slowly in 1985 by Saul Finkelstein and swelled to gatherings often over 1,000 each year.

CLEMENTE, HADDIX, GROAT LEAD PIRATES OVER CARDINALS

AUGUST 13, 1960
PITTSBURGH PIRATES 4, ST. LOUIS CARDINALS 1
AT FORBES FIELD, PITTSBURGH

BY STEPHEN M. BRATKOVICH

"There are many things we only see clearly in retrospect"[1]

The quote from Japanese writer Haruki Murakami had nothing to do with the August 13, 1960, baseball game between the eventual World Series champion Pittsburgh Pirates and the St. Louis Cardinals. However, in retrospect, the game proved to be important for both the Pirates and Cardinals, as well as Pittsburgh's exciting right fielder, Roberto Clemente.

One week before, the first-place Pirates were playing at home against the San Francisco Giants. In the seventh inning the Giants' Willie Mays ripped a pitch to deep right field off Wilmer "Vinegar Bend" Mizell. Roberto Clemente, in his sixth major-league season and soon to be a bona fide superstar, raced back to the concrete wall and with a one-handed grab snared Mays's drive while crashing face-first into the outfield barrier. Clemente was "rewarded" for his spectacular catch with

a hospital stay from an injured knee and a gash below his mouth. He received five stitches to his chin and missed the next six Pirates games.[2]

Clemente returned to the Pirates lineup on August 12, vs. Bob Gibson of the Cardinals. He went hitless as the Cardinals thrashed the Pirates, 9-2. The game was St. Louis's second straight victory over Pittsburgh and 14th win in 16 games. The victory pulled them to within three games of the league-leading Pirates.

The next day, two left-handers faced each other in game three of the series. Cardinals skipper Solly Hemus selected Ray Sadecki as the starting pitcher. Pirates manager Danny Murtaugh countered with Harvey Haddix.

Sadecki was only 19 years old and in his rookie year when he took the mound. Just one week earlier, he had pitched a six-hit complete game against the Milwaukee Braves, thrusting the Cardinals into second place behind the Pirates.[3]

Haddix was facing his former team and still looking for a victory against them in 1960. For St. Louis, Haddix had been a three-time All-Star and was runner-up for the National League Rookie of the Year Award in 1953. He slipped to a 12-16 mark and a 4.46 ERA in 1955. The Cardinals shocked their fans when they traded him to Philadelphia during the 1956 campaign. After nearly two full seasons, Haddix was traded again, this time to Cincinnati. Haddix came to the Pirates for the 1959 season with Don Hoak and Smoky Burgess in exchange for slugger Frank Thomas and three other players. Haddix is best known for pitching 12 perfect innings in 1959 against the Milwaukee Braves.

With the matchup of southpaws, both managers loaded their lineups with right-handed batters. Consequently, left-handed batsmen, even fan favorites like Stan Musial and others, were relegated to the dugout. However, Musial was in the lineup the two previous evenings and demonstrated that after 18-plus seasons in St. Louis, he still had magic in his bat. He collected four hits against Pittsburgh in the two games, including a game winning 12th-inning two-run home run.

The Saturday afternoon game started ominously for the Pirates and Haddix. The first batter, Julian Javier, doubled and scored on a single by Bob Nieman. At the end of half an inning, the score stood 1-0, St. Louis. Little did the Cardinals know their lead would be short-lived thanks to Clemente and his teammates.

In the home half of the first, Pirates shortstop Dick Groat hit a line drive that eluded Cardinals right fielder Charlie James. The hit resulted in a triple for Groat, his fourth of the year. Clemente immediately knotted the score, 1-1, with an RBI single to left, his first base hit since his August 5 injury.

The second inning was a scoreless frame for both sides. However, the home half of the third resulted in tallies for the Bucs, thanks again to the duo of Groat and Clemente.

After Groat doubled, Clemente brought the more than 30,000 fans to their feet by driving a Sadecki pitch to deep left field.[4] The two-run

homer, which easily cleared the Forbes Field wall, was Clemente's eighth of the season, surpassing his career high of seven in 1956.[5] At the end of three innings, the Pirates were outpacing the Cardinals, 3-1.

The fourth inning was "curtains" for Sadecki. After walking Bill Virdon, Groat followed with a single that moved Virdon into scoring position. Clemente sent Sadecki to the showers with an infield single that scored Virdon. At this point, Clemente had three hits and four RBIs. After the fourth inning, the score stood 4-1 in the Pirates' favor.

For the remainder of the game, scoring opportunities were scarce for both teams. After the first inning, Haddix settled down and scattered four harmless singles the rest of the way. He allowed only one runner to advance to second base. Cardinals relievers Ron Kline and Bob Grim were nearly as stingy, limiting the Pirates to third base only once.

Haddix induced the Cardinals to go quietly in the ninth. The final tally showing on the scoreboard was Pirates 4, Cardinals 1. With the victory, the Pirates once again had a four-game lead over the Redbirds. The Cardinals loss snapped both their six-game winning streak and nine straight road wins.

Pirates shortstop Dick Groat ended his day with four hits and a walk. At year-end, he led all National League hitters with a .325 average.

Clemente, however, was the game's hero. He collected three hits — two singles and a home run — and drove in all four Pirates runs. He was given due credit for the victory in the next day's *Pittsburgh Post-Gazette* sports section. The headline proclaimed, "Clemente's Bat Beats Cards, 4-1." Also, the newspaper's box score shouted the greeting, "Ariba, Roberto!"[6]

The Puerto Rican native, while leading his Pirates to victory, still didn't have the type of high-profile game that sticks in one's mind. For example, the game didn't have an exciting finish like when Clemente slugged a walk-off inside-the-park home run against the Cubs.[7] Or the Cincinnati Reds game when he blasted three home runs and knocked in seven runs.[8] Clemente's catch in Houston, when Astros manager Harry Walker called it "the greatest catch he ever has seen," far overshadowed the excitement of August 13, 1960.[9] No, the contest wasn't remembered in the manner in which some games are easily recalled. A Pittsburgh sportswriter, after acknowledging the heroics of Clemente and Haddix, called the contest after the fourth inning a "seven-eleven game" (seven Cardinals hits and 11 for the Pirates).[10]

However, in retrospect, the game with St. Louis was quite important to Pittsburgh on that sunny afternoon in 1960. The Redbirds were hot and gaining ground on the Pirates, who faced the prospect of losing three straight to a team that was inching closer to their first-place position. "Stopping the bleeding" can be an overused phrase but it seems apropos for this game. Clemente, along with key teammates, "stepped up" and propelled the Pirates to victory over the Cardinals and eventually the NL pennant and World Series Championship.

AUTHOR'S NOTE

The game on August 13, 1960, in Forbes Field, was the first major-league baseball game I ever attended. I was 8 years old.

SOURCES

In addition to the sources cited in the Notes, the author consulted Baseball-Reference.com and Retrosheet.org.

https://www.baseball-reference.com/boxes/PIT/PIT196008130.shtml

https://www.retrosheet.org/boxesetc/1960/B08130PIT1960.htm

NOTES

1   Haruki Murakami. https://www.goodreads.com/quotes/7281105-there-are-many-things-we-only-see-clearly-in-retrospect (Accessed December 2, 2021). Ironically, in 1978 Murakami was in Jingu Stadium watching a baseball game between the Yakult Swallows and the Hiroshima Carp. During the game, Murakami, for an unknown reason, suddenly realized that he could write a novel. He went home and began writing that night. Murakami's first novel, *Hear the Wind Sing*, launched his writing career which as of 2021 totaled over two dozen titles. https://www.harukimurakami.com/author (Accessed August 22, 2021).

2   Les Biederman, "Corsairs Revive Merriwell Saga on Late Flurries," *The Sporting News*, August 17, 1960: 13; Jorge Iber and Bill Nowlin, eds., *Moments of Joy and Heartbreak: 66 Significant Episodes in the History of the Pittsburgh Pirates* (Phoenix: Society for American Baseball Research, 2018), 272.

3   In 1964, Sadecki helped the Redbirds to a world championship as a 20-game winner.

4   The paid attendance was 24,620 plus 6,191 Knot Hole members. Jack Hernon, "Roberto Drives in Four Runs; Haddix Victor," *Pittsburgh Post-Gazette*, August 14, 1960: 3, 1.

5   Clemente finished the 1960 season with 16 home runs.

6   Jack Hernon, "Clemente's Bat Beats Cards, 4-1," *Pittsburgh Post-Gazette*, August 14, 1960: 3, 1.

7   July 25, 1956.

8   May 15, 1967.

9   Charley Feeney, "Greatest Catch? This One by Roberto Will Do," *The Sporting News*, July 3, 1971: 7.

10 Hernon, "Clemente's Bat Beats Cards, 4-1." Seven of the 11 Pirates hits were from the bats of Clemente and Groat.

CLEMENTE DELIVERS NL WIN IN 10TH INNING OF WINDY MIDSUMMER CLASSIC

JULY 11, 1961
NATIONAL LEAGUE 5, AMERICAN LEAGUE 4
AT CANDLESTICK PARK, SAN FRANCISCO

BY RICHARD CUICCHI

Pittsburgh's Roberto Clemente was no stranger to baseball's big stage when he was selected for the National League's starting lineup in the 1961 All-Star Game. He had previously participated as a substitute outfielder with one at-bat in the 1960 All-Star classic and was a key contributor to the Pirates' dramatic win over the New York Yankees in the 1960 World Series. He attained another level of recognition in 1961 when players, managers, and coaches chose him for the starting lineup for the All-Star Game. And he didn't disappoint his teammates or National League fans, as he belted the game-winning hit in a 10-inning contest at Candlestick Park. Unfortunately for Clemente, the game is most remembered for pitcher Stu Miller being "blown off the mound" by a gust of wind that induced a costly balk during his relief appearance.

In 1961 baseball hosted two All-Star Games per year for the third consecutive season. The first game, the 30th in All-Star Game history, was scheduled for July 11 at San Francisco's

Candlestick Park, while the second contest was slated for Fenway Park in Boston on July 31. In the previous season, the two All-Star Games were held during a four-day break in the regular-season schedule. The leagues changed their approach and decided to conduct the games three weeks apart in 1961, in order to minimize the disruption to the regular-season schedule.[1] The usually windy Candlestick Park hosted its first All-Star Game in only the second year of its existence.

The American League held a 16-13 lead in All-Star play, although the National League had won nine of the last 13 contests. The *San Francisco Examiner* declared the AL a 6-to-5 favorite on the strength of the its slugging trio Mickey Mantle, Roger Maris, and Rocky Colavito, who had 84 home runs between them.[2] Mantle and Maris were currently embroiled in a battle for AL home-run leader that ended with Maris breaking the major-league single-season record.

Clemente enjoyed a breakout season in 1960. The Puerto Rican outfielder attained season highs in practically every offensive category.[3] And in

Courtesy of The Clemente Museum.

1961, his seventh major-league season, he was on pace at the All-Star break to exceed those numbers. He boasted a batting line of .357/.393/.573, with 12 home runs and 51 RBIs. Thus, it should have been no surprise when his peers selected him as a starter in the All-Star outfield with hometown Giants Willie Mays and Orlando Cepeda. The National League's reserve outfielders featured perennial All-Stars Hank Aaron, Frank Robinson, and Stan Musial.

The largest crowd (44,115) to attend a game at Candlestick was treated to a pair of former World Series foes, Warren Spahn and Whitey Ford, who drew the starting assignments.[4] The two left-handers had previously squared off against each other in the 1957 and 1958 World Series.

Forty-year-old Spahn was perfect in his three frames, as only one AL batter hit the ball out of the infield. Spahn struck out three, including the potentially dangerous Mantle and Maris. Ford's only trouble occurred in the second inning when he gave up a triple to Clemente, who scored on Bill White's sacrifice fly.

Reds pitcher Bob Purkey relieved Spahn in the fourth inning, after Johnny Temple hit a line drive that Cepeda misplayed in left field, allowing Temple to reach second. It was the first of five miscues by the National League.

In the bottom of the fourth, Frank Lary threw only one pitch before having to leave the game with an arm injury. On that pitch, Mays reached second base on an error by shortstop Tony Kubek, who bobbled a groundball into left field. Senators pitcher Dick Donovan replaced Lary and faced Clemente, who scored Mays on a 400-foot sacrifice fly near the fence in right-center field.

Hitless through the first five innings, the American League finally got on the scoreboard in the sixth inning on a solo home run by pinch-hitter Harmon Killebrew against Giants pitcher Mike McCormick, making the score 2-1.

The score remained the same until the eighth, when Cubs outfielder George Altman gave the Nationals another run with a pinch-hit solo home run off Mike Fornieles, who had just entered the game.

In the top of the ninth, Pirates relief ace Roy Face started the inning for the National League, which was seeking its third consecutive All-Star victory. He gave up a double to Norm Cash, who was replaced by pinch-runner Nellie Fox. Al Kaline followed with an RBI single to close the National League lead to 3-2. Dodgers lefty Sandy Koufax came in to pitch to left-handed-hitting Maris, who managed to get one of only four hits the AL collected for the day.

With runners now on first and second, Miller replaced Koufax. With strong wind gusts swirling around in the ballpark, the 165-pound Giants reliever committed his wind-induced balk on a delivery to Colavito.[5] The American League evened the score, 3-3, when Kaline scored on Colavito's groundball that was fumbled by third baseman Ken Boyer.

The National League nearly gave away the game after catcher Smoky Burgess dropped a foul ball and second baseman Don Zimmer made a bad throw to first on Yogi Berra's groundball. With the bases loaded, Miller retired Hoyt Wilhelm on a fly ball to Frank Robinson to end the inning.

Miller returned to the mound for the 10th inning with the game tied. He struck out the first two batters but walked Fox. The NL lost its lead when Kaline hit a bouncer to Boyer, who made a wild throw to first that allowed Fox to score from first base.

With the NL down 4-3, pinch-hitter Aaron led off the bottom of the 10th against Wilhelm. Aaron singled and took second on a passed ball. Mays hit a double that scored Aaron. After Frank Robinson was hit by a pitch, Clemente delivered the game-winning walk-off single that scored Mays.

Clemente almost single-handedly won the game for the National League, as he contributed to three of his team's five runs. However, the National League's sloppiness in the field nearly handed a victory to the junior circuit after players committed four errors in the crucial ninth and 10th innings. The teams combined to commit an All-Star Game record seven errors. Commissioner Ford Frick said after the game, "I didn't think either one of those team was going win it. They played like Little Leaguers."[6]

Fans booed umpire Stan Landes for calling the balk on Miller. After the game, Landes said, "Miller came to a set position on the mound, leaning forward. Then he jerked back. It was a balk and I called it. Miller complained to me that the wind had blown him back. Perhaps it did, but it was a balk anyway."[7] Miller, who was the winning pitcher and was clearly familiar with the unusual playing conditions at Candlestick, said, "This was as bad a wind as I've pitched in here."[8]

In his broken English, a joyful Clemente recalled his game-winning hit, "I jus' try to sacrifice myself, so I get runner to third if I do. I feel good. But I get heet [sic] and Willie scored and I feel better than good."[9]

Clemente commented about his other at-bats: "In other park(s), I have two home runs. I feel sure the first one [triple in second inning] is over the fence and I am surprised the ball is almost caught. The second one [sacrifice fly in fourth inning], I hit harder than the first one, but she's caught. The wind (kept) the ball from going over."[10]

Clemente finished the season with his best offensive performance to that point in his career. He led the NL in batting average (.351), with 201 hits and 100 runs scored. He hit 23 home runs and had 89 RBIs. He earned a fourth-place finish in the National League MVP voting.

SOURCES

In addition to the sources in the Notes, the author consulted the following:

Associated Press. "A Moment Blown Out of Proportion for Stu Miller," *New York Times*, July 11, 2007.

Einstein, Charles. "It's All-Star Time in Cave of Winds," *San Francisco Examiner*, July 11, 1961: 48.

Einstein, Charles. "44,115 Watch a Windy Finale," *San Francisco Examiner*, July 12, 1961: 49-50.

Norman, Phil. "S.F. Cyclones Hurt Hurlers: Richards," *San Francisco Examiner*, July 12, 1961: 51.

https://www.baseball-reference.com/allstar/1961-allstar-game-1.shtml.

https://www.retrosheet.org/boxesetc/1961/B07110NLS1961.htm.

NOTES

1   David Vincent, Lyle Spatz, and David Smith, *The Midsummer Classic: The Complete History of Baseball's All-Star Game* (Lincoln: University of Nebraska Press, 2001), 190-191.

2   Charles Einstein. "A.L. 6 to 5 Favorite!" *San Francisco Examiner*, July 11, 1961: 47-48.

3   Clemente's 1960 end-of-season batting statistics included a .314/.357/.458 slash line, 16 home runs. and 94 RBIs.

4   Spahn and Ford faced each other as starting pitchers once in the 1957 World Series and three times in the 1958 Series.

5   It has become part of All-Star folklore that Miller was literally blown off the mound by a gust of wind during his delivery to Rocky Colavito in the ninth inning. In fact, the wind caused him to waver back and forth a couple of inches after he went into his stretch position, which resulted in a balk call. Contrary to the popular characterization of the play, Miller wasn't tumbled off the mound by the wind.

6   "'Played Like LLers' – Frick," *Pittsburgh Post-Gazette*, July 12, 1961: 20.

7   "Winds at Candlestick Equally Cruel to Teams," *Pittsburgh Post-Gazette*, July 12, 1961: 20.

8   "Winds at Candlestick Equally Cruel to Teams."

9   "Clemente Explains Game-Winning Hit: 'I Get Heet, I Feel Good,'" *Pittsburgh Post-Gazette*, July 12, 1961: 20.

10   "Clemente Explains Game-Winning Hit."

PIRATES 24-HIT ATTACK PRODUCES NL RECORD-TYING SHUTOUT

AUGUST 3, 1961
PITTSBURGH PIRATES 19, ST. LOUIS CARDINALS 0
AT BUSCH STADIUM, ST. LOUIS

BY GREGORY H. WOLF

"We just got slaughtered," muttered St. Louis Cardinals skipper Johnny Keane following his team's 19-0 drubbing by the Pittsburgh Pirates.[1] Not only did the Bucs hand the Redbirds their worst whitewashing in franchise history, they tied a 55-year-old NL record (since broken) for the most lopsided shutout in league history.

The Pirates and Cardinals were heading in opposite directions when they met for the second contest of a two-game series in the Gateway City. Keane had replaced skipper Solly Hemus about a month earlier and had the sixth-place squad (48-52) playing its best ball of the season, guiding them to a 15-11 record. Manager Danny Murtaugh's reigning world champion Bucs (45-49), however, were in a free fall. They had lost 13 of their last 15 games and had plummeted from third to fifth place, tied with the Cardinals 14½ games behind the front-running Los Angeles Dodgers. "Every game is a crisis these days with the Pirates," wrote beat writer Lester J. Biederman in the *Pittsburgh Press*."[2]

The Pirates were in dire need of strong pitching – something they hadn't recently experienced. During the nosedive, the staff had yielded at least 10 runs in a game three times, including a whopping 16 to the San Francisco Giants. Toeing the rubber for the Bucs was 35-year-old Harvey Haddix, whose 6-5 slate thus far improved his career record to 112-95 in 10 seasons. Known as the Kitten, the 5-foot-9 hurler knew what it was like to pitch when his team didn't score. Two years earlier, he had authored one of the most famous games in baseball history, tossing 12 perfect innings against the Milwaukee Braves, then losing the game in the 13th, 1-0.

Slumping Pirates batters had scored only 13 combined runs in their previous five games, but batting-practice pitcher Virgil Trucks noticed something different about the team's approach before this contest. "They were hitting me hard … before the game," said the former smoke-thrower with 177 big-league wins, "and often that's a tipoff that a team is going to hit the ball well during the game."[3]

It's doubtful that Trucks was a fortune-teller, but the 11,514 spectators in Busch Stadium (formerly called Sportsman's Park), located at the intersection of Grand and Dodier on the north side of St. Louis, witnessed the worst defeat in post-1900 Cardinals history. The Pirates came out swinging against the 31-year-old journeyman Al Cicotte. Cicotte was the great-nephew of former Chicago White Sox pitcher Eddie Cicotte, who was allegedly one of the ringleaders of the 1919 World Series fixing scandal that led to his and seven teammates' lifetime banishment from the game. Al was banished from this game in the third inning. With two on and two out in the initial inning, Roberto Clemente, laced a single to drive in Bob Skinner for the first run of the game. Smoky Burgess, mired in a 6-for-57 slump, sent a towering home run to deep right field that landed "on the roof," noted sportswriter Jack Hernon in the *Pittsburgh Post-Gazette*, to make it 4-0.[4] "I had a sore finger," explained Burgess about his struggles, "and that was affecting my grip on the bat."[5]

Spotted a four-run lead before he threw his first pitch, Haddix was given a "rocking chair assignment," opined Biederman.[6] That's not how the former the Redbird, who won 20 games (1953) and earned three All-Star berths in Cardinals red, approached the game. The Kitten "pitched as though it were a close one," continued Biederman, even as the runs piled up for the Bucs. He set down the first six batters he faced, and encountered trouble only once. In the third inning he loaded the bases on three singles with two outs, but escaped the threat. Haddix yielded only two more baserunners the entire game: Ken Boyer led off the seventh with a single, but was erased in a 6-4-3 twin killing; and Bill White drew a two-out walk in the ninth. "I was just hoping to go nine innings," said Haddix, who whiffed seven and recorded the 20th and final shutout in his eventual 14-year career. "I'm a seven-inning pitcher, you know. I still went full speed with the lead because that's the only way I know how to pitch."[7]

The kitten purred, but this game was about the Bucs blasters, who collected runs like baseball cards. "The slaughter read like a Social Security number on the Busch Stadium scoreboard for the first six innings: 4-2-2-3-6-2," declared sportswriter Neal Russo in the *St. Louis Post-Dispatch*.[8] In the second, Skinner's second of three doubles drove in a pair. In the following frame, Burgess blasted his second round-tripper, his ninth of the season, to deep right-center field for two more runs and ended Cicotte's evening.

In came 22-year-old right-handed mop-up artist Bob Miller, who was obliged to take one for the team. Doubles by Clemente and reigning NL MVP and 1960 batting champ Dick Groat accounted for three more tallies in the fourth. Miller, a St. Louis native who eventually went on to a 17-year career in the big leagues, labored through an inglorious fifth, loading the bases with no outs. Shortstop Bob Lillis's error on Skinner's grounder enabled Haddix to saunter home, then Dick Stuart, en route to a team-high 35 home runs, applied the coup du grace by smashing a grand slam to deep left to give the Bucs a 16-0 lead. Miller hung in there; or was hung out to dry, depending on one's perspective. Clemente doubled again, the fourth of his five consecutive hits. (The Great One would go on to lead the NL with a .351 average in '61, the first of four times he led the NL in batting average.) He scored on Groat's one-out grounder for the sixth and final run of the frame.

The Redbirds' third and final pitcher, Lindy McDaniel, began the sixth in relief of Miller, whose final line (10 hits, seven of nine runs earned, and two walks) was forgettable. Stuart victimized McDaniel for a one-out RBI single. After Clemente loaded the bases with the Pirates' fourth single of the inning, Burgess drew a walk to force in Skinner for the Bucs 19th and final run. McDaniel finished the game by tossing three scoreless innings, though he gave up a trio of hits.

The Pirates' 19-0 victory tied a 55-year-old twentieth-century NL record for most runs in

Roberto Clemente batted .351 in 1961 and won the first of four batting titles. He collected five hits on August 3, 1961. Courtesy of The Clemente Museum.

a shutout, equaling the Chicago Cubs' output against the New York Giants on June 7, 1906, and matched the franchise record achieved against the Washington Senators twice in the nineteenth century.[9] The Bucs whacked 24 hits, including seven doubles and three home runs, and the game was completed in 2 hours and 36 minutes. The offensive heroes were many: Clemente had five hits (two doubles), scored four times, and drove in two runs; Skinner knocked in three on his three doubles and scored four times; Bill Virdon scored three times and singled three times; Burgess drove home six runs and scored three times, and Stuart plated five. "The 19-0 football-score pounding was sort of retribution for Haddix, whose Pirate teammates had failed him two years ago in one of the greatest pitching performances," wrote Neal Russo, seemingly excited for the Kitten whose name went into the record books.[10]

The Cardinals' 19-run loss was the worst shutout the proud franchise had ever experienced. They had been blanked 14-0 four times, most recently by Johnny Podres and the Brooklyn Dodgers in the first game of a doubleheader on July 17, 1953, at Ebbets Field. Manager Keane took the loss with a grain of salt. He was managing in the big leagues for the first time, but had skippered Cardinals farms teams from 1938 to 1958. "In a way," he said in his Texas drawl, "it's better than losing 2 to 1 because we didn't have to look back and see where a mistake here or there cost us a ballgame."[11] He suggested that the team could quickly forget the results of the game, but also found a silver lining. "We were able to detect some flaws," he said. "Our pitchers were tipping off their pitches. I don't know how many the Pirates caught, but we could call quite a few pitches from our bench."[12]

The 1960 World Series champion Pirates didn't find their moxie after their historic triumph. They continued to sputter, finishing under .500 (75-79) and in sixth place, 18 games behind the pennant-winning Cincinnati Reds. Keane proved to be exactly what the Redbirds needed after their worst stretch of baseball in more than four decades, finishing with a losing record in five of the last seven seasons. He led the Cardinals (80-74) to a fifth-place finish, challenged for the pennant two years later, finishing runner-up to the Dodgers, and then won the pennant and World Series in 1964.

SOURCES

In addition to the sources cited in the Notes, the author also accessed Retrosheet.org, Baseball-Reference.com, Newspapers.com, and SABR.org.

https://www.baseball-reference.com/boxes/SLN/SLN196108030.shtml

https://www.retrosheet.org/boxesetc/1961/B08030SLN1961.htm

NOTES

1 Neal Russo, "19-0 Shutout of Cards Worst in Club History," *St. Louis Post-Dispatch*, August 4, 1961: 4B.

2 Lester J. Biederman, "Pirates Must Beat Cards to Hold 5th," *Pittsburgh Press*, August 2, 1961: 40.

3 United Press International, "Two Years Too Late for Haddix," *Pittsburgh Press*, August 4, 1961: 23.

4 Jack Hernon, "Bucs Rewrite Script, Hammer Cards, 19-0," *Pittsburgh Post-Gazette*, August 4, 1961: 12.

5 "Two Years Too Late for Haddix,"

6 Lester J. Biederman, "Record-Tying Barrage a Tonic for Pirates," *Pittsburgh Press*, August 4, 1961: 23.

7 Russo.

8 Russo.

9 The Pirates beat the Senators 19-0 on July 15, 1893, and then again on July 8, 1896, both times at Exposition Park in Pittsburgh.

10 Russo.

11 Russo.

12 Russo.

CLEMENTE, BURGESS LEAD PIRATES TO BLOWOUT WIN AGAINST CARDINALS

JUNE 30, 1962
PITTSBURGH PIRATES 17, ST. LOUIS CARDINALS 7
AT BUSCH STADIUM, ST. LOUIS

BY GLEN SPARKS

The lean, lithe Roberto Clemente and the squat Smoky Burgess ("barely fit enough to play for the Moose Lodge softball team,"[1] according to one critic) made for an odd, but certainly hard-hitting, duo. They batted fifth and sixth, respectively, in the Pittsburgh Pirates lineup for much of the 1962 season.

On June 30, the two led a 22-hit attack as the Pirates knocked off the St. Louis Cardinals, 17-7, at Busch Stadium. A crowd of 22,527 watched the often-sloppy action.

Both teams entered the game with a record of 43-32, in a third-place tie and 5½ games behind the league-leading San Francisco Giants. The Pirates were less than two years removed from their dramatic World Series championship in 1960 against the New York Yankees. The Cardinals hadn't won a pennant since 1946.

St. Louis took the opener of the three-game series, 5-0. Curt Simmons threw a seven-hit shutout and beat Harvey Haddix. Vernon Law, a 6-foot-2-inch right-hander and an 11-year veteran, started on the mound for Pittsburgh in the second game. The Deacon — so-called because he earned that title in the Mormon church at the age of 12 — had a record of 5-3. Ray Washburn, a 6-foot-1 right-hander in his first full season, took the ball for St. Louis. He also had a record of 5-3. Both pitchers hailed from the Northwest, Law from Idaho and Washburn from Washington.

A fast-moving summer storm had turned the field into a soggy mess just a few hours earlier, and neither team took batting practice. Les Biederman noted in the *Pittsburgh Press* the next day that "despite the work of the ground crew, the infield was slippery in spots."[2] The game began 17 minutes late.

Thanks in part to the wet conditions, Pittsburgh grabbed an early lead with a three-run first inning. Washburn opened the frame by striking out Bill Virdon. Dick Groat grounded out and Bob Skinner walked. Dick Stuart beat out a hit after St. Louis first baseman Bill White "slipped"[3] while trying to field the ball. Clemente's single loaded the bases. Burgess's double emptied them.

Pittsburgh scored five more times in the third inning. Once again, remnants of the afternoon storm did damage to the home club. Law began the rally with a one-out single. Cardinals second baseman Julian Javier "slipped" in an ill-fated attempt at fielding the ball.[4] Virdon and Groat followed with base hits. Skinner's single scored two runs. After Stuart popped out, Clemente slammed a three-run homer into the right-field stands.

Washburn's day ended with that big hit and with an ugly pitching line. He gave up eight earned runs over 1⅔ innings, and his ERA ballooned from 3.82 to 4.76. The hometown *St. Louis Post-Dispatch* noted that Washburn's start was both "short" and "mud-splattered."[5] Reliever Bobby Shantz, a veteran left-hander who stood 5-feet-6, ended the inning by getting Burgess to ground out.

St. Louis scored its first run with one out in the second. Stan Musial, playing in his 21st season and with one more campaign to go in a glorious career, began the frame by flying out to left field. The hard-hitting third baseman Ken Boyer followed that by slamming a Law pitch into the left-field seats.

Third baseman Don Hoak, nicknamed "Tiger," led off the Pittsburgh third with an infield single. Bill Mazeroski then smashed a Shantz pitch for a two-run homer that gave the Pirates a 10-1 advantage. After Law reached on an error, Virdon popped out and Groat hit into a double play.

Boyer added two more RBIs in the St. Louis third. His base hit scored Javier and Fred Whitfield after both singled and Musial walked. Law ended the threat by striking out Carl Sawatski and Charlie James and getting Dal Maxvill to hit into a force play.

The Pirates took an 11-3 lead in the fourth inning. Shantz walked Skinner to start the frame. Stuart's groundout advanced Skinner to second base. Clemente stepped to the plate and lined an RBI single to center field. Burgess then lofted a pitch to Curt Flood. The graceful center fielder caught the ball and fired to first base before Clemente, "feeling frisky" according to the *Post-Dispatch*, could get back safely.[6]

Law gave up just two singles over the next three frames. Shantz set down the Pirates in order in the fifth inning and wiggled out of two-out trouble in the sixth after Skinner doubled and Stuart singled to put runners on first and third. Clemente, though, with an opportunity to inflict more damage, flied out to center field.

Ed Bauta, a right-handed sinkerball pitcher from Cuba, took over pitching duties for St. Louis in the seventh inning. Burgess, the first batter, greeted him by hitting a homer to right field. Law added a two-out single before Virdon flied out to Flood.

St. Louis got to Law for two more runs in the seventh inning. Javier led off by doubling to left field and then left for pinch-runner Julio Gotay. A Whitfield fly ball sent Gotay to third. Doug Clemens slammed a Law pitch over the fence to cut Pittsburgh's lead to 12-5.

Pittsburgh put away the game by scoring five runs in the top of the eighth. Groat, the All-Star shortstop, began the inning with a single. He advanced to third on Skinner's double. Stuart's single scored one run and brought up Clemente, who lined a double for his fifth RBI of the game. (It was one of seven five-RBI games that Clemente had in his career. The others were on July 25, 1956; May 26, 1957; April 14, 1960; July 6, 1961; July 6, 1966; and August 7, 1966. He drove home a career-high seven runs on May 15, 1967, against the Cincinnati Reds at Crosley Field.)

Burgess followed by hitting a three-run homer to give him seven RBIs in the game. (The squat catcher had collected a career-high nine RBIs on July 29, 1955. He ripped three home runs that day. Burgess batted .295 lifetime and set a record at the time with 145 career pinch-hits. Joe Garagiola once said, "You could wake [Burgess] up at 3 A.M. on

Christmas morning, with two inches of snow on the ground, throw him a curveball, and he'd hit a line drive."[7])

The Cardinals pushed across the game's final two runs in the eighth inning. Law gave up a single to James and a double to Maxvill. Gene Oliver, pinch-hitting for Bauta, hit a run-scoring single that put Maxvill on third. The light-hitting shortstop scored on Flood's groundout.

After Gotay flied out, Diomedes Olivo took over pitching duties for Pittsburgh. The 43-year-old left-hander from the Dominican Republic gave up a single to Whitfield but got Doug Clemens to ground out. Don Ferrarese, the Cardinals' fourth pitcher on the day, tossed a scoreless ninth. St. Louis, in need of an epic rally, managed only a base hit off Olivo in the final frame.

The next day the Pirates beat the Cardinals 7-2. Al McBean, a second-year right-hander from the US Virgin Islands, scattered six hits in a complete-game effort. Hoak drove home three runs. Burgess added another two RBIs.

Clemente hit a single and scored a run but also struck out three times. He concluded one of the best months of his career. He drove home 27 runs in 30 games and batted .388 with a .416 on-base percentage. He slugged .578 and had a .994 OPS. Just a few weeks earlier, Clemente had complained to reporters about a "nervous stomach. I can hardly eat. … I don't feel too strong and sometimes when I run, I get short of breath."[8] The reporter noted that Clemente's ailments "could mean misery for opposing pitchers. For when the Pittsburgh Pirates outfielder complains of sickness, he's usually a terror at the plate."[9]

Clemente, so good in June, stayed hot in July. He batted .354 with an .889 OPS. The 27-year-old slumped in August (.239 batting average and just a .658 OPS) but put together a solid September (.311 batting average, .771 OPS). He batted .312 for the season, nearly 40 points below his 1961 mark.

The Pirates finished in fourth place at 93-68. The Cardinals ended up in sixth with a record of 84-78.

The Great One played another 10 seasons, won three more batting titles, and earned the Most Valuable Player Award in 1966. Clemente ended his career with exactly 3,000 hits and 12 Gold Gloves. He died in a plane crash on December 31, 1972, while on a mercy mission to help survivors of a devastating earthquake in Nicaragua. Writers voted him into the Hall of Fame in a 1973 special election. Commissioner Bowie Kuhn said Clemente "made the word 'superstar' seem inadequate. He had about him a touch of royalty."[10]

SOURCES

In addition to the sources cited in the Notes, the author consulted Baseball-Reference.com.

https://www.baseball-reference.com/boxes/SLN/SLN196206300.shtml

NOTES

1 Andy Sturgill, "Smoky Burgess" SABR BioProject: https://sabr.org/bioproj/person/smoky-burgess/.

2 Les Biederman, "Pirate Hit Explosion Stuns Cards," *Pittsburgh Press*, July 1, 1962: 53.

3 Biederman.

4 Biederman.

5 Ed Wilks, "Pirates Rout Washburn in Slugging Attack on Cards," *St. Louis Post-Dispatch*, July 1, 1962: 30.

6 Wilks.

7 Andy Sturgill, "Smoky Burgess." SABR BioProject.

8 Associated Press, "When Clemente's Ailing, the Enemy Pitchers Suffer," *Bloomington* (Illinois) *Pantagraph*, June 6, 1962: 12.

9 "When Clemente's Ailing, the Enemy Pitchers Suffer."

10 "Quotes About Roberto Clemente & Quotes by Roberto Clemente": https://www.baseball-almanac.com/quotes/roberto_clemente_quotes.shtml.

CLEMENTE REACHES 2,000 CAREER HITS

SEPTEMBER 2, 1966
PITTSBURGH PIRATES 7, CHICAGO CUBS 3
AT FORBES FIELD, PITTSBURGH

BY GLEN SPARKS

Roberto Clemente stepped into the batter's box in the fifth inning at Forbes Field. More than 13,000 hometown fans watched on September 2, 1966, as the Pittsburgh Pirates superstar took a few practice swings. Ferguson Jenkins, the Chicago Cubs' 23-year-old right-hander, stood on the mound.

Clemente slammed Jenkins' first pitch into the right-field upper deck for a three-run homer. It was the 2,000th hit of his career and helped Pittsburgh gain a 7-3 victory. Clemente also reached the century mark in RBIs for the first time in a single season. "I couldn't have wished for anything better," he said about his big game.[1]

The Pirates entered the evening with a record of 78-56 and in a first-place tie with the San Francisco Giants in the National League race. The Cubs, on the other hand, were struggling with a mark of 47-86, in last place by 30½ games.

Pirates manager Harry Walker sent 30-year-old Bob Veale out to pitch on this Friday afternoon in the first game of a weekend series. Veale, a 6-foot-6-inch left-hander from Alabama, had a 13-9 won-lost mark. Earlier in the season he made the National League All-Star team for the second straight year. The hard thrower struck out 276 batters in 1965 and led the senior circuit with 250 whiffs in 1964.

Cubs skipper Leo Durocher countered with Jenkins, a product of Ontario, Canada, who stood just one inch shorter than Veale. The Cubs acquired Jenkins on April 21, in a deal with the Philadelphia Phillies. He had appeared in just one game for the Phillies in 1966 and only seven in 1965. *Chicago Tribune* sportswriter Richard Dozer called him "the newest darling of the Cub pitching staff."[2] Jenkins shut out the Los Angeles Dodgers for 5⅓ innings in his Chicago debut on April 23. He also hit a home run off LA starter Don Sutton. Dozer told his readers the next day, "The legend of Ferguson Jenkins started in the damp chill of Wrigley Field yesterday."[3]

Jenkins, though, had a record of just 2-7 and a 3.77 ERA as he took the mound against Clemente and the Pirates. Pittsburgh ook a 1-0 lead in the fourth inning. Jenkins plunked the first batter he faced, the young left fielder Willie Stargell. Donn Clendenon grounded out, advancing Stargell to second. The next batter, Bill Mazeroski, knocked an RBI single to right field.

The Cubs threatened in the fifth. Randy Hundley doubled with one out and made it safely to third after Veale threw into center field on a pickoff attempt. But Veale struck out Byron Browne and Jenkins to end the inning.

Veale began Pittsburgh's half of the fifth by reaching on an infield single. Matty Alou sacrificed the pitcher to second and made it safely aboard when Jenkins overran the ball. Gene Alley, the Pirates' next batter, advanced both baserunners with a sacrifice. That brought Clemente to the plate. The right fielder, famous for his powerful throwing arm and line-drive swing, had 22 homers for the season, one shy of the season high he hit in 1962. He had 98 RBIs and a .326 batting average.

The 32-year-old already had won three batting titles, including the last two, with .339 and .329 marks in 1964 and 1965 respectively. Jenkins, though, had struck him out in the first and induced a groundout in the third. Finally, in the fifth inning, Clemente won the battle between pitcher and batter. "I was trying to pull the ball, waiting for an inside pitch," Clemente said. "But the ball was outside. I knew it was a homer right away."[4]

He added, "With two men on base, I was more concerned with driving in a run than getting number 2,000. I set a goal of 100 RBIs and 25 home runs at the start of the season. Usually, I'm not a home run hitter, but I've been hitting more for home runs this season than ever before."[5]

Clemente's manager, Walker, told reporters, "There's just no way to pitch to him. He can hit everything. I don't know why he's hitting home runs this year, though. He's just going into the ball and meeting it."[6]

First baseman Ernie Banks watched as the ball sailed into the seats and Clemente circled the base. Just a few weeks earlier, Banks had entered the 2,000-career-hit club. "I know Roberto had

a wonderful feeling of satisfaction," Banks said. "When you get 2,000 hits it sort of puts you into select company. It's something you remember for a long time."[7]

The Cubs put across two runs in the sixth. Glenn Beckert lofted a one-out single and sprinted to second after Veale uncorked a wild pitch. Billy Williams struck out before Santo and Banks walked to load the bases. John Boccabella's ground-ball single scored the two lead runners. Hundley popped up for the third out.

Catcher Jim Pagliaroni put the Pirates ahead by three runs once again with his RBI single in the bottom half of the sixth. The hit scored Bob Bailey, who had led off the frame with a triple. Jenkins retired the next three batters.

Chicago narrowed Pittsburgh's lead to 5-3 in the seventh. Durocher sent Adolfo Phillips to pinch-hit for Jenkins with one out. Phillips walked, and that ended the night for Veale. Walker brought in Don Cardwell, who promptly threw a wild pitch, sending Phillips to second. Cardwell's problems continued as he made a wild throw on a pickoff attempt, and Phillips headed for third. Don Kessinger's subsequent groundout gave the Cubs an unearned run.

Cubs reliever Curt Simmons, in his second inning of work, gave up two runs in the eighth. Bailey walked with one out and Pagliaroni singled. Cardwell lined a double to center field that scored both runners.

Pittsburgh nearly added a few more runs. Alou lined a single, advancing Cardwell one base, and then stole second. Alley grounded out and Simmons walked Clemente to load the bases. Stargell, though, lifted a fly ball that Browne grabbed for the third out.

Cardwell pitched around a Clendenon error in the ninth and recorded his first save of the season. Winning pitcher Veale improved his record to 14-9, while Jenkins dropped to 2-7.[8]

The next day's copy of the *Pittsburgh Press* included a photo of Clemente standing next to

15-year-old Gary Chick. The youngster from nearby Penn Hills recovered the home-run ball and gave it back to the batter. Clemente traded him a bat and an autographed baseball.

Clemente credited the fans for helping him reach the 2,000-hit milestone. In 1957 serious back problems nearly forced the ballplayer into retirement. Fans, aware of their hero's pain, wrote sympathetic letters that pleaded for Clemente to keep playing. Clemente talked over his injuries with his father. "He encouraged me to stay," the outfielder said. "But I was still undecided until I remembered what the fans wrote. That clinched it."[9]

The Pirates ended the year with an admirable 92-70 won-loss record but in third place behind the San Francisco Giants and the pennant-winning Los Angeles Dodgers. (The Cubs' struggles continued. They finished last with 103 losses, the second time in franchise history that they reached the century mark in defeats.) Clemente batted .317 with a .536 slugging percentage. He set career highs in home runs (29), RBIs (119), and runs scored (105).

Clemente recorded exactly 3,000 hits in his career. His final one came September 30, 1972, a double in the fourth inning off New York Mets left-hander Jon Matlack. Clemente died just a few months later, on December 31, while on a mercy mission to help victims of a devastating earthquake in Nicaragua. He was 38 years old.

The Baseball Hall of Fame waived the requirement that a player must be retired for five years before being considered for enshrinement and honored Clemente with a plaque in 1973. At the induction ceremony, held on August 6, 1973, in Cooperstown, New York, Vero Clemente spoke about her late husband. "Her voice was choked with emotion and there appeared to be tears in her eyes," Bob Smizik wrote in the next day's *Pittsburgh Press*.[10]

She told the assembled crowd, "This would have been Roberto's last triumph. If Roberto had been here, he would have thanked the fans of Puerto Rico, the fans of Pittsburgh and all the fans in the United States."[11]

SOURCES

In addition to the sources cited in the Notes, the author consulted Baseball-Reference.com.

https://www.baseball-reference.com/boxes/PIT/PIT196609020.shtml

NOTES

1   Lester J. Biederman, "Clemente Makes 2000th Hit Big One for Bucs," *Pittsburgh Press*, September 3, 1966: 8.

2   Ricard Dozer, "Jenkins Was Hockey Star," *Chicago Tribune*, April 24, 1966: 93.

3   Richard Dozer, "Sox Lose; Cubs Win with Jenkins, 2-0," *Chicago Tribune*, April 24, 1966: 93.

4   Ira Miller, "Clemente Has Career Highs," *Belleville (Illinois) News-Democrat*, September 3, 1966: 6.

5   Jeff Meyers, "Bucs Edge Back in Front on 7-3 Triumph; Cards Win in 12th over G-Men; LA Wins," *Tyrone (Pennsylvania) Daily Herald*, September 3, 1966: 8.

6   Meyers.

7   Biederman.

8   Jenkins had a 6-8 won-lost record in 1966. He pitched 19 seasons and won 284 games. He entered the Hall of Fame in 1991.

9   United Press International, "Clemente Gives Credit to Fans; Cards Knock Giants from Top," *Pittsburgh Press*, September 3, 1966: 8.

10 Bob Smizik, "Roberto's 'Last Triumph': Induction into Hall," *Pittsburgh Press*, August 7, 1973: 26.

11 Smizik.

CLEMENTE BLASTS THREE HOMERS AND KNOCKS IN ALL SEVEN RUNS IN BUCS' LOSS

MAY 15, 1967
CINCINNATI REDS 8, PITTSBURGH PIRATES 7
AT CROSLEY FIELD, CINCINNATI

BY GREGORY H. WOLF

"It was almost like Roberto Clemente playing the Reds all by himself," gushed sportswriter Les Biederman in the *Pittsburgh Press*, "and coming so close to wrecking them singlehandedly."[1] Affectionately nicknamed "Arriba" by Pirates radio broadcaster Bob Prince, Clemente belted three home runs and knocked in all seven Pirates runs, but his offensive heroics were not enough to overcome dreadful pitching and a relentless Reds hitting attack punctuated by Tony Perez's game-winning, walk-off double in the 10th. "[It was] one of those weird, sloppy but tingling battles that drive scorekeepers slap-happy and customers back to the park," wrote Lou Smith excitedly in the *Cincinnati Enquirer*.[2]

Skipper Dave Bristol's Reds were one of the early-season surprises in 1967. After a seventh-place finish the previous year, they had gotten off to a hot start and occupied first place (21-10), paced by one of the deepest pitching staffs in the league. Two games behind the Reds were manager Harry Walker's Pirates (16-9), the hottest team in baseball and winners of 13 of their last 17 contests. The

Bucs' strength was hitting; they had led the majors in batting average in 1966 (.279) and duplicated the feat in 1967 (.277).

A cool, damp spring evening with temperatures hovering around 50 degrees suggested an advantage for the hurlers. Both clubs sent former All-Stars to the rubber in the first game of a three-game series: The Pirates' 31-year-old southpaw, Bob Veale, one of the hardest throwers in baseball, owned a 63-40 career record, including 5-0 with a stellar 2.49 ERA thus far in '67. The Reds' right-hander Milt Pappas, acquired from the Baltimore Orioles in the trade for the immensely popular Frank Robinson, was a dependable workhorse with a 125-87 career record. Instead of a pitching duel, the paltry crowd of 5,222 spectators at Crosley Field was treated to a memorable offensive explosion.

After Matty Alou, the reigning NL batting champion (.342), led off the game with a single, Clemente belted what Charley Feeney of the *Pittsburgh Post-Gazette* considered a routine fly to right field, but it "got caught in the wind and sailed

Courtesy of The Clemente Museum.

into the seats" for a two-run homer, his fourth of the season.[3] Clemente had gotten off to a slow start in 1967, but had been wielding what Feeney called a "booming bat" in the Pirates surge.[4] In that 17-game stretch, the seven-time All-Star and three-time NL batting king, had gone 29-for-71 (.408) to raise his batting average to a major-league-leading .368. Coincidentally, Clemente's home run also gave him a cycle in his last four at-bats; he had hit a double, triple, and single in his final three at-bats against the Atlanta Braves the day before.

Veale held the Reds hitless through the first four innings, but got a scare in the fourth when Pete Rose reached on Bill Mazeroski's error and moved to third on a wild pitch with no outs. After Perez fanned and Lee May walked, shortstop Gene Alley scoped up Don Pavletich's grounder and did what the Pirates did best: initiate a 6-4-3 twin killing; they led the big leagues with 186 double plays in 1967.

In the fifth the Pirates took advantage of Perez's error on Alou's routine one-out grounder. After Maury Wills forced Alou, and then stole second, Clemente whacked a two-out liner over the nine-foot fence in right field for a 4-0 Pirates lead. Long regarded as one of baseball's best pure hitters, Clemente tailored his game to fit cavernous Forbes Field in the Steel City, stretching doubles into triples. Never considered a power hitter, the reigning NL MVP had belted a career-most 29 round-trippers the previous campaign, well above his average of 17 over the last seven seasons (1960-66).

Veale survived a shaky fifth (single, balk, and walk), and then came unraveled in the sixth. He "lost rhythm on his fastball suddenly," opined Biederman, and threw more pitches in the inning than he had in the previous five combined.[5] Rose, Perez, and May led off with consecutive singles, the last of which resulted in the Reds' first tally. After Veale's wild pitch enabled the runners to each move up a base, Pavletich drove in Perez on a sacrifice fly, and Chico Ruiz's groundout plated

May to pull the Reds to within one, 4-3. Leo Cardenas's single ended Veale's outing, before reliever Pete Mikkelsen ended the frame.

Dubbed a "one-man-show" by the *Cincinnati Enquirer*, Clemente greeted Darrell Osteen, the Reds' third hurler of the game, by spanking a double over Rose's head in left-center to drive in Mikkelsen and Wills (both of whom Osteen had walked) for a 6-3 Pirates lead in the seventh.[6]

Mikkelsen, a rubber-armed middle reliever who had appeared in 71 games the previous season, imploded just minutes later. Rose drew a two-out walk and scored on Perez's double to deep center field. May followed with a single to score Perez and the Reds were back within one run.

Both teams threatened in the eighth, but came up empty. In relief of Osteen, Gerry Arrigo uncorked a wild pitch to the first batter he faced, enabling Mazeroski (who had walked) to scamper to second with no outs. Making his first appearance since tossing a one-hit shutout against the New York Mets on April 29, Arrigo dusted off the cobwebs to escape the jam. In the Reds' half of the frame, pinch-hitter Art Shamsky, who had clouted three homers against the Pirates at Crosley Field on August 12 the previous season, led off with a double, but was stranded on third, setting the stage for two nailbiting innings.

In the ninth the Pirates tacked on an insurance run when Clemente blasted what Cincinnati sportswriter Lou Smith described as a "prodigious" home run that easily cleared the left-field fence.[7]

A two-run lead in the ninth inning on the road would normally have been an ideal situation for longtime Pirates reliever Elroy Face. However, the 39-year-old forkballer had pitched in each of the last three games, picking up two saves and a win versus the Braves, and remained seated. Walker counted on offseason acquisition Juan Pizarro to close the deal. Lee May, in his first campaign as a regular, greeted the former White Sox All-Star with a towering one-out, two-run round-tripper, driving in Perez (on first via a single) to tie the game, 7-7. Arrigo followed with what appeared to be another home run, over the right-field wall. "[T]he ball was over the fence for a home run," said Clemente, "when I jumped and kept it from falling in."[8] Crashing into the fence, Clemente prevented a game-winning clout, but could not hold onto the ball, which fell for a double. As the Bucs' bullpen remained silent, Pizarro ended the frame with runners on second and third.

After Arrigo set down the Pirates 1-2-3 in the 10th, Pizarro yielded a leadoff single to speedy Tommy Harper and punched out Vada Pinson. Third baseman Maury Wills made a "brilliant" backhanded and potentially game-saving stab of Rose's grounder and then fired to Maz at second to force Harper.[9] To the plate stepped Tony Perez, en route to his first of seven All-Star selections in his 23-year Hall of Fame career. With Steve Blass beginning to warm up in the Pirates 'pen, Perez walloped a double over center fielder Manny Mota's head and off the wall to drive in Rose for the winning run to end the game in 3 hours and 18 minutes. (Mota had replaced Alou to begin the ninth inning after the latter had been ejected by home-plate umpire Bill Jackowski for tossing his bat and helmet when he was called outon strikes.)[10]

"It was an unbelievable finish to an unforgettable game," opined Biederman with an air of disappointment.[11] The trio of Rose, Perez, and May victimized Bucs hurlers for eight of the team's 13 hits, scored all eight Reds runs, and drove in six off what Feeney bluntly called "bad" Pirate pitchers.[12] The "Reds had heroes all over the place," gushed Smith, and included Arrigo, who yielded only one hit – Clemente's homer – in three innings to earn the victory.[13]

"This could have been one of Clemente's great moments," wrote Feeney. "The defeat took away any joy he might have known."[14] Clemente became the fifth Pirate to hit three homers in

a game, joining Ralph Kiner (who did it four times between 1947 and 1951), Frank Thomas, and Roman Mejias (both in 1958), Dick Stuart (1960), and Willie Stargell (1965). "[Y]es, my biggest game, but not my best," replied Clemente when asked to comment on his fifth multi-homer game in his 13-year career. "I don't count this one, we lost."[15]

Clemente hit 240 home runs in his 18-year career, which ended prematurely when he lost his life in a humanitarian mission to Nicaragua on December 31, 1972, just about three months after he notched his 3,000th and final hit. On August 13, 1969, he tied his career best by belting three home runs in a 10-5 victory against the San Francisco Giants in Candlestick Park. On 11 other occasions he hit two round-trippers in a game.

This article appears in "Moments of Joy and Heartbreak: 66 Significant Episodes in the History of the Pittsburgh Pirates" (SABR, 2018), edited by Jorge Iber and Bill Nowlin. To read more stories from this book at the SABR Games Project, click here. It also appears in "Cincinnati's Crosley Field: A Gem in the Queen City" (SABR, 2018), edited by Gregory H. Wolf. To read more stories from this book at the SABR Games Project, click here.

SOURCES

In addition to the sources cited in the Notes, the author accessed Retrosheet.org, Baseball-Reference.com, the SABR Minor Leagues Database, accessed online at Baseball-Reference.com, SABR.org, and *The Sporting News* archive via Paper of Record.

https://www.baseball-reference.com/boxes/CIN/CIN196705150.shtml

https://www.retrosheet.org/boxesetc/1967/B05150CIN1967.htm

NOTES

1 Les Biederman, "Clemente's 'Biggest' Game Wasted," *Pittsburgh Press*, May 16, 1967: 34.

2 Lou Smith, Perez's Double Scuttles Pirates in 10th, 8-7," *Cincinnati Enquirer*, May 16, 1967: 23.

3 Charley Feeney, "Cincinnati Overpowers Clemente by 8-7," *Pittsburgh Post-Gazette*, May 16, 1967: 26.

4 Feeney.

5 Biederman.

6 Smith.

7 Smith.

8 Biederman.

9 Smith.

10 Feeney.

11 Biederman.

12 Feeney.

13 Smith.

14 Feeney.

15 Biederman.

CLEMENTE GETS FIVE STRAIGHT HITS, FOUR RBIS IN WIN AGAINST REDS

SEPTEMBER 13, 1967
PITTSBURGH PIRATES 11, CINCINNATI REDS 3
AT CROSLEY FIELD, CINCINNATI

BY GLEN SPARKS

Roberto Clemente made five hits and drove home four runs on the same day that he criticized "a few" Pittsburgh Pirates for not hustling on the field. "They know who they are," Clemente said.[1]

The Pirates were muddling along with a 72-74 won-lost mark, stuck in seventh place. During an interview with a San Juan, Puerto Rico, radio station, on September 13, 1967, Clemente said, "You don't play for one manager and not for another. You play to win."[2]

Hours later, Pittsburgh's All-Star right fielder helped his club beat the Cincinnati Reds at Crosley Field, 11-3. The Associated Press's Ron Rapoport wrote that "Roberto Clemente conducted a short lesson on show and tell Wednesday."[3] Just 4,996 watched the action on a Wednesday night.

The Pirates had high hopes going into the season. In 1966 the team won 92 games. After a solid start (a 12-6 mark after beating the San Francisco Giants, 6-5, on May 6), the '67 club swooned and dropped to .500 on June 29. Just a few weeks later, general manager Joe L. Brown fired manager Harry Walker and replaced him with Danny Murtaugh, the former infielder who had served as the team's manager from midway into the 1957 season through 1964 and led Pittsburgh to a World Series championship in 1960. Walker told reporters, "Maybe a change of managers will help the team, it often does."[4]

The "grumbling" about Walker had started early in the season, Clemente said. "It began to grow and grow. I said when Danny Murtaugh took over, not to blame him for anything. I didn't know what was going to happen, but I knew that anything that would happen would be the players' fault, not the manager's. It was the same way when Harry Walker was here. He shouldn't be blamed."[5]

Pittsburgh Press sports editor Al Abrams, in his "Sidelights on Sports" column, took no issue with Clemente's assertions. The ballplayer was "telling the truth about a sad situation. … He knows the players who are responsible for not meshing as a team and for the cliques and troublemakers who helped grease the chute for Harry Walker's dismissal."[6]

Courtesy of The Clemente Museum.

Clemente, though, had butted heads with Murtaugh during the skipper's first term in Pittsburgh. Murtaugh often needled Clemente for not playing through aches and pains. Once the manager said, "You're making too much money to sit on the bench." The ballplayer countered, "You act like I don't want to play baseball." Bill Mazeroski, the Pirates' slick-fielding second baseman, said Murtaugh handled Clemente the wrong way. "Roberto just wasn't the type of guy you took off and embarrassed in front of the team. He'd crawl into a shell."[7]

Earlier in 1967, Clemente spoke to a sports magazine and put "the zing" on Murtaugh. According to Clemente, "I told (Murtaugh) I made the statements, but I'm also a professional player and I play my best all the time for any manager. Whatever happened in the past is past. We have only one purpose and that is to win."[8]

Clemente, a three-time batting champ, was enjoying another big year after his 1966 MVP effort when he set career highs with 29 home runs and 119 RBIs. His batting average stood at .349 on the morning of September 13.

It was the finale of a three-game series. Cincinnati won the opener, 4-3, after scoring twice in the bottom of the ninth, and took the second game, 15-7. Pete Rose and Tony Perez each had four RBIs. Cincinnati banged out 23 hits.

Murtaugh asked Tommie Sisk to start on the mound and help avoid a sweep. Reds manager Dave Bristol countered with Mel Queen. Both pitchers were right-handers. Sisk had a record of 11-12, while Queen was 13-6.

Pittsburgh broke out on top with two runs in the third. Sisk led off with a "check-swing"[9] single to right field. Maury Wills, acquired from the Los Angeles Dodgers after the 1966 campaign, also singled to right. Tommy Harper misplayed the ball for an error, allowing Sisk to score and Wills to scoot into third. Matty Alou followed by lofting a sacrifice fly to center field. Clemente,

who flied out in his first at-bat, singled but was left stranded at third.

Cincinnati scored its first run in the bottom of the fourth inning. Vada Pinson doubled to right field and advanced to third base on Lee May's fly ball. Pinson crossed home plate on Perez's groundout.

Clemente hit a home run to deep right field in the fifth inning that put the Pirates ahead 3-1. It was his 21st homer of the season, and it gave him at least 100 RBIs for the second straight season.

Neither team scored again until the Pirates put across five runs in the seventh. Wills began the rally by bunting up the third-base line. Perez fielded the ball and "made a two-base wild heave of his playground hopper."[10] The ball landed in the stands and Wills continued to second base. The National League MVP from 1962 advanced to third on a wild pitch. After Alou flied out, Clemente knocked an RBI double. Queen ended his day by walking Willie Stargell. Bristol sent in Don Nottebart to provide some relief.

The Reds' sloppy fielding continued. Nottebart bobbled a ball hit by the first batter he faced, Donn Clendenon. It was Cincinnati's third error of the night. Clemente scored, Stargell advanced to third, and Clendenon made it safely to second. Gene Alley's base hit brought home both baserunners. Manny Sanguillen doubled home Mazeroski. Pittsburgh now led 8-1, with five of the runs unearned.

Pittsburgh added two more runs in the eighth, this time with Sammy Ellis on the mound. Clemente singled Wills home with nobody out. Later, with two outs, Clendenon raced home after Ellis uncorked a wild pitch. The Pirates added a final run in the ninth inning on Clemente's two-out single, his fifth straight hit. Sanguillen scored from third.

Sisk gave up two runs in the ninth inning. Pinson and May singled with one out. Perez hit a sacrifice fly to bring home Pinson. Tommy Helms, the next batter, singled May to third base.

Art Shamsky followed with an RBI base hit. Leo Cardenas grounded out to end the game.

Bristol, whose team fell to 80-67, said afterward, "(The Pirates) kind of turned it around on us tonight, didn't they? Boy, what a hitting team that is over there." Bristol called the Pirates' struggles "one of the biggest mysteries ever. It seems like every time you pick up a paper, they're in double figures in hitting. And that Clemente. When he makes up his mind, he can do anything he wants with that bat."[11]

More than anything, Clemente hoped for his team to go on a winning streak. He sounded indifferent about winning a fourth batting title. "This is the first year I've felt this way," he said. "The title doesn't bother me anymore. Before, I wanted to win it so bad I would check the papers every day to see how each player was doing. Why the difference? I think because I had something to prove before. I didn't get the recognition. Now, I don't have to prove anything. My attitude is different. Now, I just want to help this team win."[12]

The Pirates ended with a mark of 81-81, in sixth place. Clemente batted a career-high .357, the best figure in the National League. He also led the circuit with 209 hits and hit 23 homers with 110 RBIs. He won the seventh of his 12 Gold Gloves and finished third in the MVP race.

SOURCES

In addition to the sources cited in the Notes, the author consulted baseball-reference.com.

https://www.baseball-reference.com/boxes/CIN/CIN196709130.shtml

NOTES

1   Charles Feeney, Clemente Raps 'Few Slacking Players,'" Pittsburgh Post-Gazette, September 14, 1967: 38.

2   Feeney.

3   Ron Rapoport, "Pirates Rip Reds 11-3, Clemente Leads Assault," Marion (Ohio) Star, September 14, 1967: 27.

4   "Walker Says It's All Part of the Game," Pittsburgh Press, July 19, 1967: 59.

5   Feeney.

6   Al Abrams, "Sidelights on Sports," Pittsburgh Post-Gazette, September 14, 1967: 36.

7   David Maraniss, Clemente: The Passion and Grace of Baseball's Last Hero (New York: Simon & Schuster, 2006), 175.

8   "Walker Says It's All Part of the Game."

9   Lou Smith, "Bucs Get Revenge, Lambaste Reds, 11-3," Cincinnati Enquirer, September 14, 1967: 55.

10   Smith.

11   Jim Ferguson, "Clemente, Pirates Turn Things Around," Dayton Daily News, September 14, 1967: 21.

12   Ferguson.

ROBERTO CLEMENTE'S FOURTH FIVE-HIT GAME

JULY 13, 1968
PHILADELPHIA PHILLIES 3, PITTSBURGH PIRATES 2 (16 INNINGS)
AT FORBES FIELD, PITTSBURGH

BY DARREN GIBSON

Coming off a 1967 National League batting championship, his third in four years, Roberto Clemente struggled mightily at the plate for the first two months of the 1968 season.

He was hampered by a nasty shoulder injury he suffered in the offseason at his home in Puerto Rico. As he climbed on a steel railing on his patio it collapsed and sent him hurtling down a hill. Clemente tried to play through the injury but later admitted that he should have at least skipped spring training.[1] The March 23 edition of *The Sporting News* mentioned that Clemente reported late because his mother-in-law had suffered a heart attack, and that he had a noninjury auto accident, without mentioning the home accident.[2]

Clemente hit but .226 in April and .220 in May, before rebounding by hitting .333 in June.[3] A 2-for-28 slump, however, during the first week of July and heading into the All-Star break, dropped Clemente's average from .265 to .245. The Pirates star had collected only one extra-base hit over his final 11 games before the break. Thus, for the first time in nine years, Clemente was not selected for

the National League All-Star team, missing the midsummer classic, which was being held indoors for the first time, at the Astrodome in Houston. It was Clemente's only All-Star absence over a 13-year period from 1960-1972.

The three-day rest served Clemente well; he collected four hits in the first three games of the initial post-break series, at home against the Philadelphia Phillies, and raised his average back above .250, to .252. The Pirates, however, were in a tailspin. Heading into this finale of the four-game set, Pittsburgh was suffering through a seven-game losing streak, its longest such tailspin in three years.[4] The Pirates had dropped the final four games in Chicago against the Cubs before the break, then these first three games at home. The streak had dropped the Pirates to 40-44 and left them in seventh place in the 10-team National League and 14 games behind the St. Louis Cardinals.

The Pirates were led by new skipper Larry Shepard, who secured his first major-league managerial assignment after years soldiering for teams in the minors, Shepard had managed many of the current Pirates in the minors, mainly during his tenure as skipper of the Columbus Jets of the International League.

The day game on this summer Saturday, July 13, drew only 6,869 fans at Forbes Field. (The Pirates wound up ninth out of 10 NL clubs in attendance for the season.) The *Pittsburgh Press* reported that Clemente took the lineup cards to home plate.[5] Woody Fryman took the hill for the Phillies, with Steve Blass getting the assignment for the Pirates. Clemente's outfield mate, left fielder Willie Stargell, did not start the contest, reducing the power in the Pirates lineup.

The visitors plated single runs in each of the first two innings, thanks to Dick Allen's RBI triple and an unearned run following a rare error by Bill Mazeroski. Clemente grounded out in the first, then led off the bottom of the fourth with a single but was stranded. He singled again in the sixth, but was quickly erased on Manny Mota's double-play grounder, which scored Maury Wills with Pittsburgh's first run. Clemente grounded out to shortstop to end the eighth inning. The Pirates tied the game in the bottom of the ninth inning on a two-out RBI single by pinch-hitter Gary Kolb, sending the game into extra innings.

Clemente's two-out single in the bottom of the 10th wasn't cashed in, as Mota struck out looking. Another two-out single by Clemente, with the bases empty in the bottom of the 12th, was also wasted when Mota lined out. In the top of the 14th, rookie Dock Ellis, in the majors less than a month (he had tossed 2⅔ scoreless relief innings the night before), took the mound for the Pirates. In the bottom of the 14th, Phillies starter Chris Short, who had pitched seven innings two days earlier and earned his eighth victory, took the ball for the visitors. Clemente's two-out triple to right-center field in the bottom of the 14th, his eighth of the season (breaking a tie with Cardinals' Lou Brock for the league lead), put the

winning run just 90 feet away. It was the Pirates' only extra-base hit in the game. However, after an intentional walk to Mota, Gene Alley struck out, so the game rolled into the 15th inning. After a scoreless 15th, the grounds crew dragged the infield for the third time.

In the top of the 16th inning, Philadelphia scored an unearned run on an RBI single by pinch-hitter Rick Joseph to take a 3-2 lead.[6] The rally began with a single by Allen and a miscue by Gene Alley when Johnny Callison's grounder went through his legs. Callison took second on a wild throw from left fielder Kolb, the second error on the play. Allen advanced to third. After Ellis intentionally walked Tony Taylor, Luke Walker replaced Ellis. Joseph, batting for first baseman Johnny Briggs, then laced his go-ahead liner to right field that scored Allen.[7]

In the Pirates' 16th, Wills rapped a two-out single to center and stole second base. A foul tip off Clemente's bat injured the finger of Phillies catcher Mike Ryan, who was replaced by Clay Dalrymple. Clemente walked on a full count. Short then got Mota (completing his 0-for-7 day) to ground out to second base and end the 4-hour 44-minute contest, giving the Phillies the road sweep.

The victory was the Phillies' fifth in five extra-inning games so far in the season. Short earned the win with three innings of relief, and Ellis took the loss. The Pirates thus lost their eighth game in a row, on their way to a 10-game losing streak. Manager Shepard called the 10-game schneid "the worst experience of my life."[8] The Pirates scored only five runs in the four-game series with the Phillies. Matty Alou and Wills together reached base in only three of 16 plate appearances in this game, and Wills was 2-for-19 in the series.

Clemente raised his batting average 11 points to .263 after his five-hit performance, aided by the three extra-inning hits. It was the fourth five-hit game of his career, after two in 1961 and a third in September of 1967. He had two more in 1970 and a seventh and final one in 1971.

Clemente soon missed a week with a bad shoulder, but as the 34-year-old lamented, "How could I ever retire? I have to support 13 people?"[9]

Pirates general manager Joe Brown, trying to take heat off rookie manager Shepard, said in early August, "I can't blame Shepard because of injuries and because Roberto Clemente is batting .265 and because Jim Bunning hasn't been able to come up to expectations."[10]

Still, Clemente's performance on July 13 provided one example of his long climb back and was aided by a torrid .370 in September, which gave him a respectable .291 average by the end of the season. He also won his eighth straight Gold Glove award.

SOURCES

In addition to the sources cited in the Notes, the author consulted Baseball-Reference.com.

https://www.baseball-reference.com/boxes/PIT/PIT196807130.shtml

NOTES

1   BaseballCrank website: http://baseballcrank.com/archives2/2012/07/baseball_1968_y.php. Accessed February 12, 2022.

2   Les Biederman, "Clemente to Go Slow – Until the Bell Rings," *The Sporting News*, March 23, 1968: 11.

3   BaseballCrank.

4   Les Biederman, "Stranded Runners Again Ruin Bucs," *Pittsburgh Press*, July 13, 1968: 6.

5   Les Biederman, Phils Outlast Pirates in 16 Innings, 3-2," *Pittsburgh Press*, July 14, 1968: 69.

6   Allen Lewis, "Pinch Hitter Scores Allen to Beat Bucs," *Philadelphia Inquirer*, July 14, 1968: 51.

7   "Phils Sweep 4-Game Set from Bucs," *Lancaster* (Pennsylvania) *Sunday News*, July 14, 1968: 35.

8   Les Biederman, "Why Do Managers Get Gray? Shepard Knows the Answer," *The Sporting News*, August 3, 1968: 19.

9   Les Biederman, "Shoulder Sore; Clemente Says He May Retire," *The Sporting News*, August 24, 1968: 18.

10   Les Biederman, "Brown Takes Full Blame for Bucs' Poor Showing," *The Sporting News*, August 10, 1968: 16.

CLEMENTE'S DEFENSE STANDS OUT ON HIS NIGHT

JULY 24, 1970
PITTSBURGH PIRATES 11, HOUSTON ASTROS 0
AT THREE RIVERS STADIUM, PITTSBURGH

BY MARK SIMON

That the first-place Pirates routed the fifth-place Astros was a side story for most of the 43,290 fans at the recently opened Three Rivers Stadium on this summer Friday night.

Most in attendance were there to honor the home team's right fielder. It was Roberto Clemente Night.

Fans would have a chance to show Clemente how much they loved him. The game was announced in March and partly sponsored by the Allegheny County Civic Sportsmen's Association, an organization that regularly presented Sportsman of the Year awards to local athletes.[1]

It was not intended as any precursor to retirement. At age 35, Clemente was still going strong, having hit .345 in 1969. Just a few months earlier, during spring training, the Cincinnati Reds' Pete Rose said he aspired to be what Clemente was. "I'd say he's the best hitter I've seen since I've been in the big leagues," Rose said.[2]

Local newspapers printed coupons to help fans make donations to a local children's hospital in Clemente's honor.

"I want to make sure that every penny will be used for poor, crippled kids," Clemente said.[3]

On the day of the game, the *Pittsburgh Post-Gazette* ran a story with quotes from every manager about Clemente's excellence.

Among the highlights:

"Clemente and greatness are one and the same word."
– Gene Mauch, Expos

"Clemente is the most complete ball player to wear a baseball uniform. He can do everything to beat you."
– Red Schoendienst, Cardinals

"Every time I hear that Clemente has an ache, I look for him to go four-for-four."
– Gil Hodges, Mets[4]

The ceremony began more than an hour before the game, was bicultural and bilingual, and was broadcast back to Clemente's native Puerto Rico. Hundreds of Puerto Rican residents were flown to Pittsburgh, including Heriberto Nieves, the mayor of Clemente's hometown, Carolina.

Roberto Clemente Day 1970, with the proud father holding Rickey with Luis on the left and Roberto Jr. on the right. Les Banos photograph courtesy of The Clemente Museum.

Cuban-born Puerto Rican baseball broadcaster Ramiro Martínez served as emcee.[5]

Clemente and his family received a truck's worth of gifts as well as news that the Pirates had established a trust fund to handle the college education expenses of Clemente's children. The gifts were donated to the children's hospital.[6]

Clemente cried as he tried to give a speech to the crowd.

"I have achieved this triumph for us the Latinos," he said. "I believe that it is a matter of pride for all of us, the Puerto Ricans, as well as for all those in the Caribbean because we are all brothers."[7] He also told the fans, "I will never wear any other uniform than a Pittsburgh uniform."[8]

As for the game, the Pirates put this one out of reach quickly, scoring six runs in the first inning.

After Matty Alou singled and Richie Hebner walked against Astros starting pitcher Tom Griffin, Clemente singled to load the bases. Al Oliver followed by singling in the first two runs. Manny Sanguillen then drove in Clemente with a sacrifice fly. The bottom of the Pirates lineup contributed to the big frame as Freddie Patek's two-run double knocked Griffin out of the game. Dock Ellis's double drove in the last run.

The Pirates scored twice in the third inning. Dave Cash hit an RBI double and Patek sprinted home on a wild pitch thrown by Astros reliever Jim Bouton. Pittsburgh added one run in the fifth and two runs in the eighth inning, one coming on Willie Stargell's home run.

Clemente walked in the third and singled in the fifth but neither plate appearance factored in the scoring. He finished the game 2-for-3 with a run scored. Seven of the Pirates starters drove in at least one run, with Clemente and Hebner being the exceptions. Patek, who was filling in at shortstop for Gene Alley, had a game-high three RBIs and three runs scored. The Pirates played this game with a different double-play combination than usual with Patek and Cash starting for Alley and

Mazeroski, the latter of whom was 8-for-46 in his previous 14 games.

Even though Clemente didn't drive in any runs, he was still enjoying one the best offensive stretches of his career. In the 25 games spanning July 3 to August 10, Clemente hit .437 with a .529 on-base percentage and an .862 slugging percentage. His 1.391 OPS was his best for any 25-game span in his career.[9]

Pitching on three days' rest, Ellis went the distance, throwing a four-hit shutout. Clemente helped preserve Ellis's effort with two notable defensive plays, a diving catch in the third inning against Joe Morgan and a sliding, sitting catch in the seventh inning against Dennis Menke. He was removed from the game after that inning.[10]

Asked by reporters why he tried to make daring catches in a lopsided game, Clemente simply said, "It's the only way I know how to play."[11]

Ellis, like Clemente, was working on a good stretch. In his past five games, he had a 1.66 ERA over 43⅓ innings.

The win was the Pirates' 22nd in their last 30 games, a hot streak that moved them from four games out of first place to a 2½-game lead in the NL East.

Clemente suffered a bruised knee, presumably from the sliding catch. That was just the beginning of an injury bug that hampered him the rest of the season. He left the game in the eighth inning with a cut on his left leg.

The next day, Clemente was hit on the right wrist by a pitch and didn't start again for two weeks.[12] He had 31 hits and batted .365 in 21 games after returning but missed another two weeks in September with a sprained muscle in his lower back.[13]

Clemente finished the 1970 season with a .352 batting average but played in a career-low 108 games. Baseball writers still voted him 12th in the National League MVP race.

SOURCES

In addition to the sources cited in the Notes, the author consulted Baseball-Reference.com and Retrosheet.org.

https://www.baseball-reference.com/boxes/PIT/PIT197007240.shtml

https://www.retrosheet.org/boxesetc/1970/B07240PIT1970.htm

NOTES

1 Bill Christine, "Ex-Buc Taylor Takes a Fancy To Cards' Way of Doing Things," *Pittsburgh Press*, March 19, 1970: 43-44.

2 Milton Richman (United Press International), "Pete Rose's Aim: Another Clemente" *Latrobe* (Pennsylvania) *Bulletin*, March 18, 1970: 35.

3 "Clemente Goes All Out for Fund," *Pittsburgh Press*, July 19, 1970: 5.

4 Charley Feeney, "Roamin' Around," *Pittsburgh Post-Gazette*, July 24, 1970: 15.

5 David Maraniss, *Clemente, The Passion and Grace of Baseball's Last Hero* (New York: Simon & Schuster, 2006), 238.

6 "Clemente Shines on His Night," *Pittsburgh Press*, July 24, 1970: 6.

7 Maraniss, 238-239.

8 Charley Feeney, "Clemente Has His Night, Pirates Make It a Big One," *Pittsburgh Post-Gazette*, July 25, 1970: 9.

9 Stathead.com, https://stathead.com/tiny/TL03W.

10 In the game box score on Retrosheet and Baseball-Reference, Clemente is listed as being removed to start the seventh inning. This is contradicted by multiple newspaper reports that state that Clemente came out of the game in the eighth inning.

11 "Clemente Shines on His Night."

12 "Swollen Wrist Sidelines Clemente," *Pittsburgh Press*, July 27, 1970: 23.

13 "Clemente Twists Back Swinging, Leaves Game," *York* (Pennsylvania) *Dispatch*, September 5, 1970: 27.

Clemente and family at 1971 Father & Son Day at Three River Stadium. Les Banos photograph courtesy of The Clemente Museum.

CLEMENTE RACKS UP SECOND FIVE-HIT GAME OF WEEKEND IN PIRATES' ROUT OF DODGERS

AUGUST 23, 1970
PITTSBURGH PIRATES 11, LOS ANGELES DODGERS 0
AT DODGER STADIUM, LOS ANGELES

BY JOHN FREDLAND

Days after celebrating his 36th birthday on August 18, 1970 – and hours after his five hits and go-ahead run helped the Pittsburgh Pirates maintain their National League East lead with a Saturday-night extra-inning win over the Los Angeles Dodgers – Roberto Clemente seized a spot in baseball's record books on August 23 at Dodger Stadium. Clemente's three singles, double, and home run made him just the third player in major-league history with back-to-back games of five hits or more, as he led the Pirates to an 11-0 win over the Dodgers.

Clemente's summer – the 16th of his distinguished career in Pittsburgh – had been an eventful one. After initially declining an All-Star Game invitation, he reconsidered and hit a game-tying sacrifice fly in the National League's 12-inning win on July 14.[1] Two days later, the Pirates opened Three Rivers Stadium,[2] and a night honoring Clemente came soon afterward, on July 24.[3] Some of the headlines were bizarre and disturbing: Clemente revealed in August that he had been abducted after a game in San Diego the previous season.[4]

Hit on his wrist by a pitch on July 25, Clemente was sidelined for all but a single pinch-running appearance during a two-week span as August began,[5] but he was back in right field, batting third and ranking second among eligible National Leaguers with a .349 batting average,[6] as the Pirates made their second California trip of the season to open a series in Los Angeles on August 21. "His birth certificate says he is 36-years-old today," the Pittsburgh Post-Gazette asserted.[7] "He is a young 36. A mere baby who happens to play baseball with a certain flair that excites fans."[8]

With club home-run leader Willie Stargell sidelined with a leg injury[9] and youthful teammates like Al Oliver, Bob Robertson, and Manny Sanguillen in their first pennant race, Clemente knew Pittsburgh depended on his leadership. "If we're going to win," he said before the Pirates left for the West Coast, "I might have to have a good trip."[10] In baseball's second season of divisional play, the Pirates were in first place in August for the first time since 1966 and only the second time since their 1960 World Series championship.

In the series opener against the Dodgers, Clemente singled in the tying run in the fifth inning, but the Pirates were otherwise fruitless against Claude Osteen in a 2-1 loss.[11] The second-place New York Mets beat the Cincinnati Reds and were now only 1½ games back,[12] raising the stakes when Pittsburgh's Bob Moose faced Los Angeles's Don Sutton on Saturday evening.

Clemente rapped out three singles against Sutton, tying the game with an RBI hit in the third, but that was the last scoring for a while. Former Pirate Pete Mikkelsen was pitching in the 14th inning, with the score 1-1, when Clemente singled for his fourth hit, but Pittsburgh left the bases loaded.

Clemente led off the 16th against Mikkelsen by hustling out a single to short, his fifth hit of the game, and stealing second. Two outs later, Jerry May singled to left, and Clemente scored the tiebreaking run. Bruce Dal Canton, Pittsburgh's fourth pitcher of the night, closed out the Dodgers in the bottom of the 16th, with Manny Mota's popup settling into Robertson's glove in foul territory outside first base just minutes before midnight in Los Angeles.[13]

The late finish left Clemente with only a short night of rest; a characteristically light sleeper,[14] he was awake at 6 A.M. on Sunday, "his metabolism attuned to Pittsburgh time," the *Pittsburgh Press* reported.[15] But he was on the field that afternoon, a required presence with Stargell still ailing. "We needed [Clemente's] big bat in the lineup with Willie out," manager Danny Murtaugh explained afterward.[16]

Limited to three runs in the first 25 innings of the series, the Pirates quickly found their groove against Los Angeles's Alan Foster. Freddie Patek led off the first with a single. One out later, he raced to third on Clemente's single to center; when Willie Davis threw to third, Clemente took second.

Oliver grounded to third; Patek broke for the plate. Jim Lefebvre appeared to have a play at home but took the out at first as Patek scored and Clemente advanced to third.[17] Robertson's single drove in Clemente, and the Pirates had an early 2-0 lead.

Steve Blass, a three-day beard growing on his unshaven face,[18] took the mound for Pittsburgh. Six weeks earlier, on July 12, a line drive by St. Louis's Joe Torre appeared to break Blass's right elbow.[19] Further examination, however, revealed that it was only a bruise,[20] and the 28-year-old's first two starts back from the disabled list had continued his return to form after he lost six straight decisions earlier in the season: 13 innings pitched, two earned runs allowed.[21]

Against the Dodgers, Blass allowed Mota's one-out single to center in the first, but Mota aggravated an ankle injury rounding the bag, and Matty Alou's throw to Robertson trapped him for the out.[22] Davis followed by grounding a single off first, but Blass retired Wes Parker to keep the Dodgers scoreless.

Blass started up Pittsburgh's offense in the second with a one-out walk. Alou's bunt single moved him to second, and Clemente singled Blass home for a 3-0 lead.

The Pirates broke the game open in the fourth. Patek doubled to lead off the inning; another Alou infield single pushed him to third. Clemente drove in Patek with a double to center, his third hit of the game. Dodgers manager Walter Alston pulled Foster for left-hander Fred Norman.

Norman retired the first two Pirates he faced before allowing Sanguillen's double to left-center. Alou and Clemente scored, and Pittsburgh's advantage was 6-0.

The bottom of Pittsburgh's batting order sustained the attack in the fifth and sixth. Bill Mazeroski, who had his first four-hit game in nearly five years, opened the fifth with a double and took third on Blass's bunt single. Patek singled in Mazeroski for Pittsburgh's seventh run.

Sanguillen started the Pirates in the sixth with a single. Mazeroski singled him to second one out later. Blass, now borrowing some of Clemente's batting equipment, dropped down a bunt toward third; when Norman booted the ball, Sanguillen came in from second. The play was scored a hit and an error on Norman, and the Pirates led, 8-0.

"I was wearing Roberto's batting helmet and using his bat," Blass said.[23] "Why shouldn't I? There was a law passed here this morning that Clemente isn't allowed to make an out anymore."[24]

After giving up the two hits in the first, Blass had hit his stride. Working around a bruised tendon on the middle finger of his right hand by de-emphasizing his fastball and throwing mostly off-speed pitches,[25] Blass retired Los Angeles in order in the second, third, fourth, and fifth innings. Bill Russell broke the streak of 13 outs in a row by walking to lead off the sixth, but Maury Wills lined into a double play one out later, and the Dodgers remained scoreless.

Knuckleballer Charlie Hough, promoted from the Spokane Indians of the Triple-A Pacific Coast League 12 days earlier and making his fifth major-league appearance, replaced Norman in the seventh. Clemente greeted the 22-year-old right-hander – who threw his final big-league pitch nearly 24 years later, in July 1994 – with his fourth hit of the game, a single to left. Oliver, with one hit in his last 19 at-bats, crushed Hough's pitch into the right-field pavilion; the *Pittsburgh Press* observed that Oliver "stopped and admired the shot, Harmon Killebrew style."[26] Oliver's 12th homer of the year made it 10-0.

Clemente capped his big day – and big weekend – by driving another home run into the left-field seats in the eighth. It was his 14th homer of 1970, his fifth hit of the game, and his 10th hit in less than 24 hours against the franchise that had first signed him in 1954, then lost him to the Pirates in that winter's Rule 5 draft.[27]

Murtaugh sent in Gene Clines to play right in the eighth; Clemente's day was done. Blass closed out the shutout, allowing hits in the eighth and ninth to finish with a four-hitter.

Clemente was only the third major leaguer ever – and, as of 2021, the most recent – to have back-to-back games with five or more hits. In 1876 the first season of NL play, Cal McVey of the Chicago White Stockings had consecutive six-hit games, three days apart.[28] The Brooklyn Robins' Hi Myers had back-to-back five-hit games in August 1917.[29]

Only a fifth-inning lineout kept Clemente from a perfect day at the plate. His weekend barrage boosted his season average to .363, tops in the NL.

The league's schedule-maker finally allowed Clemente the opportunity to rest; the Pirates had an offday on Monday, August 24.

"I know that right now my muscles, they ache and that I welcome a day of rest [on Monday]," Clemente said.[30] "When I hit, you see, I look for situations because you know I cannot get a hit all the time because nobody is perfect."[31]

SOURCES

In addition to the Sources cited in the Notes, the author consulted the Baseball-Reference.com and Retrosheet.org websites for pertinent material and the box scores noted below. He also used game coverage from the *Los Angeles Times*, *Pittsburgh Post-Gazette*, and *Pittsburgh Press* newspapers.

https://www.baseball-reference.com/boxes/LAN/LAN197008230.shtml

https://www.retrosheet.org/boxesetc/1970/B08230LAN1970.htm

NOTES

1   Bill Christine, "Clemente Slams Phils, Snubs Stars: Roberto's HR Keys Pirates' 4-2 Win," *Pittsburgh Press*, July 8, 1970: 61; "Clemente Says He'll Play in All-Star Game," *Pittsburgh Press*, July 11, 1970: 6; Roy McHugh, "Roberto's Reverse," *Pittsburgh Press*, July 15, 1970: 63.

2   "Division-Leading Pirates, Reds Open Sports Palace," *Pittsburgh Press*, July 16, 1970: 1.

3   "Clemente Shines on His Night," *Pittsburgh Press*, July 25, 1970: 6.

4   Bill Christine, "Clemente Reveals Abduction," *Pittsburgh Press*, August 10, 1970: 27.

5   "Swollen Wrist Sidelines Clemente," *Pittsburgh Press*, July 27, 1970: 23.

6   Rico Carty of the Atlanta Braves led the NL with a .357 average. "League Leaders," *Pittsburgh Press*, August 21, 1970: 31.

7   Charley Feeney, "The Old Guy," *Pittsburgh Post-Gazette*, August 18, 1970: 19.

8   Feeney, "The Old Guy."

9   Newspaper coverage of the Pirates' final game before their California trip, a 7-4 loss to the San Francisco Giants on August 19, reported that Stargell played despite a pulled muscle in his left leg. Stargell had 25 home runs to date in 1970; his 31 homers in 136 games led the Pirates, but it was the only season from 1968 through 1975 in which he did not finish in the top 10 in the NL in home runs. Charley Feeney, "Giants Crimp Buc Bid, 7-4, as Mets Lose: Juan Marichal Goes Route Under 13-Hit Barrage," *Pittsburgh Post-Gazette*, August 20, 1970: 30.

10 Roy McHugh, "In No Hurry to Hit," *Pittsburgh Press*, August 24, 1970: 26.

11 Bill Christine, "Bucs Lose – Blame Rookie Umpire: Tremblay's Call Causes Downfall, 2-1," *Pittsburgh Press*, August 22, 1970: 6.

12 Dana Mozley, "Kooz Cools Reds, 4-1; Bud Boots 2," *New York Daily News*, August 22, 1970: 30.

13 Bill Christine, "Pirates Nip Dodgers in 16th, 2-1: Moose Goes 10, Snuffs Early Rally," *Pittsburgh Press*, August 23, 1970: 4, 1.

14 "Roberto Clemente – hypochondriac or not, public agonizer or not – didn't sleep worth a damn," wrote Pittsburgh sportswriter Phil Musick in a 1974 biography. Phil Musick, *Who Was Roberto?: A Biography of Roberto Clemente*, (New York: Doubleday, 1974), 180.

15 Roy McHugh, "In No Hurry to Hit," *Pittsburgh Press*, August 24, 1970: 26.

16 Bill Christine, "Clemente Engineers Destruction of Dodgers," *Pittsburgh Press*, August 24, 1970: 26.

17 Christine, "Clemente Engineers Destruction of Dodgers."

18 "I hate to shave," Blass told the *Pittsburgh Press* afterward. Christine, "Clemente Engineers Destruction of Dodgers."

19 "Broken Arm May Sideline Steve Blass for 3 Weeks," *Pittsburgh Press*, July 13, 1970: 26.

20 Roy McHugh, "An X-Ray of Hope."

21 "Blass Ready for Anything: Pitcher Proves He's Not Gun-Shy," *Pittsburgh Press*, August 19, 1970: 70.

22 John Wiebusch, "Dodgers Grow Weary of 'Sleepy' Clemente: Pirate Slugger Tired but Sets Two-Game Hitting Record With 10; L.A. Inexplicably Loses Punch, Blanked, 11-0," *Los Angeles Times*, August 24, 1970: III, 1.

23 Christine, "Clemente Engineers Destruction of Dodgers."

24 Christine, "Clemente Engineers Destruction of Dodgers."

25 Christine, "Clemente Engineers Destruction of Dodgers."

26 "Ellis Hunts Scapegoat: Blames 'Somebody' for Arm Trouble," *Pittsburgh Press*, August 24, 1970: 26.

27 David Maraniss, *Clemente: The Passion and Grace of Baseball's Last Hero* (New York: Simon & Schuster Paperbacks: 2006), 36-37, 56-57. The Pirates selected Clemente from the Dodgers, then based in Brooklyn, in accordance with bonus rules in effect from 1953 to 1957. Edgar Munzel, "Bankrolls Now Only Limit on Bonus Bids," *The Sporting News*, December 18, 1957: 11. Clemente hit well in all three of the Dodgers' home ballparks as a Pirate. In 98 plate appearances at Ebbets Field between 1955 and 1957, he hit .323/.351/.441. His batting line at the Los Angeles Coliseum, where the Dodgers played from 1958 through 1961, was .331/.362/.426. While Dodger Stadium is regarded as a pitchers' park, Clemente hit .377/.419/.481 in 344 plate appearances between 1962 and 1972.

28 McVey had six hits in seven at-bats in the White Stockings' 30-7 win over the Louisville Grays on July 22, 1876. "Pastimes: Seventh Victory of the Whites Over the Louisvilles an Extraordinary Display of Scientific Batting," *Chicago Tribune*, July 23, 1876: 7. The White Stockings' next game, a 23-2 win over the Cincinnati Reds, was three days later; McVey again had six hits in seven at-bats in that game. "Base-Ball: Another Scalp," *Chicago Tribune*, July 26, 1876: 5.

29 On August 21, 1917, Myers had five hits in six at-bats when Brooklyn tied Pittsburgh 3-3 in 13 innings, in a matchup of the same two franchises involved in the August 1970 Dodgers-Pirates series. Rice, "Each Side Scores Two Runs in an Extra Inning Rally," *Brooklyn Daily Eagle*, August 22, 1917: 2. A day later, the Robins outlasted the Pirates 6-5 in 22 innings – in what was at that time the longest game by innings in NL history – and Myers had five hits in 10 at-bats. Rice, "Superbas Winners in 22 Innings and Break League Record," *Brooklyn Daily Eagle*, August 23, 1917: 14.

30 Wiebusch, "Dodgers Grow Weary of 'Sleepy' Clemente."

31 Wiebusch. Clemente finished 1970 with a .352 batting average but a back injury that kept him out of action for two weeks in September left him without enough at-bats to qualify for the batting title. He returned to the lineup in time for the Pirates' three-game sweep of the Mets on September 25-27 that finally clinched the division title for Pittsburgh.

ROBERTO CLEMENTE SHINES LATE IN PIRATES WIN OVER PHILLIES

JUNE 27, 1971
PITTSBURGH PIRATES 10, PHILADELPHIA PHILLIES 9
AT VETERANS STADIUM, PHILADELPHIA

BY STEVE GINADER

The Philadelphia Phillies opened newly built Veterans Stadium for the 1971 season after occupying Connie Mack Stadium in downtown Philadelphia since 1938. (The A's had first opened the park in 1909.) Through its first two months of game action, the new multipurpose facility in South Philadelphia was gaining a reputation as a hitters' park. Describing the hitting environment, Pirates right fielder Roberto Clemente said, "When I look at the outfield fence it is at eye level. I get the feeling I am looking downhill at the fences. This is the best home run park in the league. Better than Atlanta, which was the best by far."[1] During the final weekend in June, the first-place Pirates were in town to take on the last-place Phillies and the ballpark lived up to its hitter-friendly reputation. In the four-game series, the teams combined for 69 runs as the Pirates won three of four.

The bats were as hot as the weather. With highs in the mid-80s under a sunny sky, the Phillies and Pirates were scheduled to complete the series with a Sunday afternoon doubleheader. The first game produced 12 runs; the starting pitchers scheduled for the second game, Ken Reynolds and Nelson Briles, could expect much of the same. Briles had been obtained by the Pirates in an offseason trade after six successful seasons with the St. Louis Cardinals. Reynolds was a rookie for the Phillies and had a 1-2 record with a 3.81 ERA for the struggling cellar-dwellers.

The first five batters for Pittsburgh set the tone for the game. Leadoff hitter Gene Clines stroked a double to center and moved to third on an infield single by Al Oliver. Clines was in the starting lineup to provide rest for regular right fielder Clemente. Bill Mazeroski plated the first run on a sacrifice fly and cleanup hitter Bob Robertson reached on an infield single, setting the stage for José Pagán. Described as a Punch and Judy hitter, Pagan was not known for his power, but he smashed a Reynolds pitch deep over the left-field wall, putting the Pirates on top 4-0. "Any hitter has got a chance to hit a home run here," Clemente said.[2] The Pirates weren't finished. Gene Alley worked a walk. Alley stole second, moved to third on a groundout, and scored the fifth run on a single by Jackie Hernández. The inning ended for Philadelphia when Briles flied out to left.

The Phillies scored a run in the second when Deron Johnson hit a leadoff home run to deep right. The Phillies cleanup hitter was having a remarkable season, ultimately hitting 34 home runs, fourth best in the majors. The Phillies comeback commenced in earnest the next inning when John Vukovich led off with a single to center. Reynolds stepped in and stroked a triple to left center, which turned out to be his only extra-base hit of the year. Briles' day ended when Denny Doyle's single, Larry Bowa's double, and Tim McCarver's single rallied the Phillies to within a run of a tie. It was the shortest start of the year for Briles when manager Danny Murtaugh replaced him with Jim Nelson. Nelson hit Johnson the first batter he faced, with a pitch to load the bases. Willie Montañez doubled to score two more runs and give Philadelphia the lead. Ron Stone received an intentional walk. Nelson stiffened, retiring the side on a run-scoring grounder by Roger Freed, a popup by Vukovich, and a groundout by Reynolds. The six-run rally put the Phillies ahead, 7-5.

Reynolds settled down after his rocky first inning and shut out the Pirates over the next five innings, allowing only a single and two walks. The Phillies threatened in the fourth and fifth innings, then scored two runs in the sixth. After Vic Davalillo hit for Nelson in the top of the inning, Murtaugh tapped Bob Veale to pitch. The 35-year-old Veale had been a successful starter for the Pirates the previous seven years, winning 103 games. After a down season in 1970, this was his first year pitching in relief. Speaking about his new role he said, "I've got more innings pitched in the bullpen than any of our starters. You know, you're not just throwing idly out there. You're throwing for more effort."[3] With one out, Veale allowed a single to McCarver and a two-run homer to Johnson that stretched the Phillies lead to 9-5. Veale

escaped further damage by retiring the next two batters on a groundout and strikeout.

The Pirates battled back in the seventh to tie the game, 9-9. Reynolds was still pitching despite facing Clines and Oliver for the fourth time. The top two hitters in the lineup had five of the six hits he surrendered. Clines led off the seventh with a single to right and Oliver stroked an opposite-field double to left-center, moving Clines to third. When Mazeroski grounded to short, scoring Clines, Phillies manager Frank Lucchesi made a double switch, substituting Bucky Brandon to pitch and Byron Browne to play left field. The first two batters touched up Brandon for the tying runs. Robertson singled to center and Pagán blasted his second two-run homer deep to left. Both Alley and Milt May grounded out to end the inning but the damage was done. After the game, Brandon called the ballpark "a $50 million bandbox."[4]

More managerial wheels turned in the eighth inning. The Pirates summoned Willie Stargell to pinch-hit for Hernández, leading off, and the Phillies turned to Joe Hoerner to pitch. "We decided Hoerner was coming in to pitch as soon as Stargell was announced," said Lucchesi.[5] Hoerner, who had pitched two innings in the first game and earned a save, fanned the dangerous Stargell, who went on to lead the major leagues with 48 home runs in 1971. Murtaugh then turned to Clemente to pinch-hit for Veale and Lucchesi stuck with Hoerner. "If I had a healthy Dick Selma, Joe comes out," Lucchesi said. "But he was my best bet against Roberto."[6] Clemente delivered with a homer to deep center that rattled off the backdrop. Hoerner explained, "It was supposed to be a fastball in. But I hung it about six inches off the plate and that was it."[7] The blast put the Pirates on top, 10-9. The next two batters struck out to end the inning.

With a late-inning lead, the Pirates' focus shifted to pitching and defense. Closer Dave Giusti was called on for the save opportunity;

Clemente stayed in the game to play right field. Giusti walked Johnson and gave up a single to Montañez but kept the Phillies from scoring in the eighth. Hoerner also shut out the Pirates in the ninth, yielding only a single to Pagán. Freed started the bottom of the ninth with a long drive to center field that Oliver caught on the warning track. "I'm still not stroking the ball like I used to," said Freed. "Lately though, I'm trying to go into the ball more, and I think I'm hitting better this last week."[8] After Vukovich flied out for the second out, Browne hit a drive to right-center that reached the wall. Oliver had trouble playing the carom, so Clemente fielded the ball and fired a long strike to hold Browne to a double. "That play to me was more important, gave me more pleasure, than the home run," said Clemente.[9] With Browne on second, Giusti struck out Joe Lis to end the game.

Before Clemente entered in the eighth inning, the teams accumulated 18 runs on 25 hits, furthering the ballpark's growing reputation. Then Clemente's greatness dominated, as he stroked a homer for the lead run and executed a key defensive play to secure the win. Clemente said, "The homer won the game, but the play in the field might have kept them from winning."[10] The 1971 Pirates left town with a four-game lead in the National League East and continued on to win the pennant and their first World Series since 1960, led by the talented Clemente.

SOURCES

In addition to the sources cited in the Notes, the author relied on Baseball-Reference.com and Retrosheet.org.

https://www.baseball-reference.com/boxes/PHI/PHI197106272.shtml

https://www.retrosheet.org/boxesetc/1971/B06272PHI1971.htm

NOTES

1 Bill Conlin, "'$50M Bandbox' Takes Pounding in Phils' Split," *Philadelphia Daily News*, June 28, 1971: 52.

2 Conlin.

3 "Veale Adjusts to Relief Role," *Pittsburgh Courier*, June 19, 1971: 14.

4 Conlin.

5 "Bucs and Phils Split Doubleheader 10-9 and 8-4," *Uniontown (Pennsylvania) Morning Herald*, June 28, 1971: 20.

6 "Bucs and Phils Split Doubleheader 10-9 and 8-4."

7 "Bucs and Phils Split Doubleheader 10-9 and 8-4."

8 Allen Lewis, "Phils Split with Pirates as Freed Begins to Hit," *Philadelphia Inquirer*, June 28, 1971: 9.

9 Conlin.

10 Conlin.

FIVE FOR THE FINAL TIME
ROBERTO CLEMENTE'S FINAL FIVE-HIT
MAJOR LEAGUE GAME

AUGUST 25, 1971
PITTSBURGH PIRATES 13, ATLANTA BRAVES 6
AT ATLANTA STADIUM

BY KEVIN LARKIN

Roberto Clemente played his entire 18-year career with the Pirates and recorded exactly 3,000 base hits, one of 32 players to reach that coveted mark as of 2021. He had a .317 batting average in 2,433 games.

Clemente had four hits in 39 games and five hits in eight games, the final time on August 25, 1971, against the Atlanta Braves.

Entering the final game of a four-game series in Atlanta, the Pirates had a record of 76-55, which placed them atop the National League East standings with a 4½-game lead over the second-place St. Louis Cardinals.[1] The Braves were in third place in the National League West standings with a record of 68-65 and trailed the first-place San Francisco Giants by 9½ games. Pittsburgh was trying for its second straight division championship, while the Braves hoped to improve on a fifth-place finish in 1970.

In its 10 previous games, Pittsburgh had five wins and five losses, while Atlanta was 4-6. Pittsburgh won the first two games of the series. Atlanta came back with a win in game three.

Clemente began August with a .336 batting average and entered the series finale with a .329 mark. The star right fielder already had 40 multi-hit games in the 1971 season and had enjoyed a four-hit game three times: May 8, May 19, and June 23.

Atlanta was dealing with a controversy before the game. The slugger Rico Carty was involved in a brawl that left him with two black eyes, a split finger, and bruises that Atlanta Mayor Sam Massell called a case of "blatant brutality." White police officers C.T. Turner and L.B. Smith were both off-duty when the fight happened. Officer J.R McEarchern tried to break up the brawl but was struck by Carty. The incident began after Carty and his brother-in-law, Carlos Martinez, pulled behind a patrol car before midnight on August 25. Another car pulled beside the patrol car, and the driver said, "These n------ are harassing me." Carty left his car and a fight ensued. Massell suspended all three officers without pay and said they would have to stand trial before the aldermen's police committee. Carty was charged with "[having] created a turmoil and simple battery on a police officer." (Carty led the NL with a .366 batting average in 1970 but would miss the entire 1971 season due to a knee injury.)[2]

Pirates manager Danny Murtaugh chose as his starter rookie Bruce Kison, who had three wins and four losses with a 3.09 earned-run average in 10 appearances (nine of them starts.) Kison was matched against Pat Jarvis, who was in his sixth season and making his 21st start of the campaign. Jarvis was 5-11 with a 3.74 earned-run average.

The 5-foot-10-inch, right-handed Jarvis found himself in quick trouble. Rennie Stennett, Al Oliver, and Clemente all singled to load the bases in the first inning. Jarvis nearly wiggled out of the jam. He struck out Willie Stargell and Bob Robertson but then gave up consecutive singles to Milt May, Dave Cash, Jackie Hernandez, and Kison that gave the Pirates a 5-0 lead. Atlanta manager Lum Harris replaced Jarvis with right-hander Bob Priddy. Priddy gave up another single, to Stennett, that scored Hernandez. The Pirates took a 6-0 lead before the Braves had even batted.

After Hank Aaron slammed a two-run homer in the bottom of the first inning,[3] the Pirates resumed their scoring onslaught in the second. Clemente reached on his second single of the game and scored on Stargell's two-run homer. Robertson followed Stargell by slamming another home run to give Pittsburgh a 9-2 lead.

In the second inning, Kison, a slender 6-foot-4 righty, gave up inning-opening singles to Mike Lum and Sonny Jackson. After Marty Perez's grounder forced Jackson at second base, with Lum taking third, Kison committed a balk that allowed Lum to score and narrow Pittsburgh's lead to 9-3.

Pittsburgh did not score in the third inning, but Clemente got his third hit of the day, a single. In the Atlanta half of the third, Kison allowed singles to Ralph Garr and Aaron, and was replaced on the mound by Bob Moose. Earl Williams doubled to score Garr, with Aaron taking third base. A sacrifice fly by Darrell Evans scored Aaron, and after Lum popped out to third base, Jackson singled to score Williams.

The Pirates led 10-6 going into the top of the fifth inning and, with one out, Clemente got his fourth single of the day off the new Braves pitcher, Jim Nash, and scored on a single by Stargell and an error by Jackson in center field. After Robertson struck out, a single by May scored Stargell to give the Pirates a 12-6 lead.

In the seventh inning, Clemente flied out to center field off Steve Barber, who had replaced Nash.

Hernandez led off the top of the ninth with a single and went to second on a passed ball. Bob Miller walked and Stennett's sacrifice advanced the runners to second and third. Tom Kelley had come on in relief for Atlanta to start the ninth and, with one out, Oliver hit a sacrifice fly to score Hernandez and give Pittsburgh a 13-6 advantage.

Clemente was the next batter, and he singled, his fifth single of the day. Stargell struck out to end the inning.

Miller remained in the game and after two fly outs he gave up a single to Williams. He got Evans to ground out to end the game. The Pirates came away with the 13-6 victory.

The *Atlanta Constitution*'s Wayne Minshew wrote, "Ringling Brothers would have paid a fortune for some of the things seen in the game and Ed Sullivan would still be on the air if he had them."[4]

Clemente's five hits and three runs scored led the Pirates. May (three hits, three RBIs), Cash (three hits, including a double and a triple), and Hernandez (three hits, two runs scored, two RBIs) also made significant contributions, as did Stargell and Robertson with their home runs The Pirates maintained their five-game lead in the National League East.

Moose got the win in relief of Kison and improved his record to 9-7, while Miller secured his eighth save.

Garr, Lum, and Jackson, who all had three hits, led the Atlanta offense. Jarvis, who left in the first frame, took the loss. The Braves used five relievers to finish the game – Priddy, Ron Herbel, Nash, Barber, and Kelly.

Pittsburgh went on to capture the division title by seven games over the St. Louis Cardinals, defeated the San Francisco Giants in the National League Championship Series three games to one, and bested the Baltimore Orioles in seven games in the World Series.

The Braves finished the season in third place in the West, eight games behind the Giants.

Clemente hit a team-high .341 in 1971 and finished fourth in the NL batting race. (The Cardinals' Joe Torre led the league with a .363 average.) Clemente finished the season with 2,882 hits. The next season he got his 3,000th career hit in the next-to-last game of his career, a double off Jon Matlack in the fourth inning of a 5-0 Pirates win over the New York Mets on September 30.

SOURCES

In addition to the game story and box-score sources cited in the Notes, the author consulted the Baseball-Reference.com and Retrosheet.org websites.

https://www.baseball-reference.com/boxes/ATL/ATL197108250.shtml

https://www.retrosheet.org/boxesetc/1971/B08250ATL1971.htm

NOTES

1   Baseball-Reference.com reflects the 4½-game lead over the Cardinals and Cubs on August 24. The Cardinals won the suspended game of August 1, which was made up on September 7. Were one to count the August 1 game in the August 24 standings, the lead would have been five games.

2   "3 Charged in Beating of Carty," Philadelphia Inquirer, August 26, 1971: 13.

3   It was the 38th home run of the season and the 630th of Aaron's career. See New York Daily News, August 26, 1971: 61.

4   Wayne Minshew, "Pirates Thunder by Braves, 13-6," Atlanta Constitution, August 26, 1972: 67.

THE FIRST ALL-BLACK LINEUP

SEPTEMBER 1, 1971
PITTSBURGH PIRATES 10, PHILADELPHIA PHILLIES 7
AT THREE RIVERS STADIUM, PITTSBURGH

BY RICHARD J. PUERZER

The 1971 Pittsburgh Pirates were a special team in a multitude of ways. They were probably the most diverse team in the major leagues, featuring 13 players of Latin or African-American descent on their roster, including their best two players, Willie Stargell and Roberto Clemente. That season the Pirates went on to win the World Series, but along the way they also achieved a first in the history of major-league baseball. On September 1, 1971, the Pirates fielded an all-Black lineup of African-American and Latino players.

The historic game was played between the Pirates and division rivals the Philadelphia Phillies on a Wednesday night at Three Rivers Stadium in Pittsburgh. The Pirates entered the game with a record of 81-56, and were in first place in the National League East by 4½ games over the St. Louis Cardinals. The Phillies were a lowly 57-77 and in last place in the division. The attendance for the game was 11,278, all of whom got to see history made.

The starting lineup for the Pirates was: batting leadoff and playing second base, Rennie Stennett; batting second and playing center field, Gene Clines; batting third and playing right field, Roberto Clemente; batting cleanup and playing left field, Willie Stargell; batting fifth and catching, Manny Sanguillen; batting sixth and playing third base, Dave Cash; batting seventh and playing first base, Al Oliver; batting eighth and playing shortstop, Jackie Hernandez; and batting ninth and pitching, Dock Ellis.[1]

Aside from the pitcher, the one position and really the only position where a White player was generally more likely to start at this point in the season, was at first base.[2] Bob Robertson generally played first for the Pirates in 1971, especially against left-handed pitching. Despite the fact that the Phillies were starting former-Bucco Woodie Fryman, a lefthander, lefty-swinging Al Oliver got the start at first base for the Bucs.

The occasion of the first all-Black lineup came without any warning. Pirates manager Danny Murtaugh posted the lineup, and may not have realized himself that he had started the game with all Black players. The players themselves did not realize until the game was underway. Al Oliver stated that he had not noticed the lineup until an inning or two into the game when Dave Cash came up to him and said, "Hey Scoop, we've got all brothers out there."[3]

The first inning started out very poorly for Dock Ellis as he walked the first two Phillie batters, Ron Stone and Larry Bowa, to lead off the game. Ellis then righted the ship, getting Tim McCarver to fly out, and striking out Deron Johnson. Ellis was not able to get out of the inning unscathed however, as shortstop Jackie Hernandez was not able to handle a groundball hit by Willie Montanez. The play ended with Stone scoring, Montanez at first, and Bowa at third. Oscar Gamble then singled down the third-base line, allowing Bowa to score. Ellis finally got out of the inning after Terry Harmon, flied out to center. The Pirates roared back in the bottom of the first, with six of the first seven batters reaching base on singles or doubles. By the end of the inning, the Pirates had batted around, knocked out starter Fryman who was replaced by Bucky Brandon, and scored five runs.

Ellis was not very sharp in the second inning either, walking leadoff batter John Vukovich and giving up a home run to Ron Stone for his second long-ball of the season. After walking Larry Bowa, Ellis was relieved by Bob Moose. Moose had started the game the previous night but had gone only 2 1/3 innings. Two batters later, Moose gave up a two-run home run to Deron Johnson, allowing the Phillies to take the lead, 6-5 on the slugger's 29th blast of the year. Once more, the Pirates came back. After a Gene Clines single, stolen base, and advance to third on an errant throw by McCarver, and a Roberto Clemente walk, Willie Stargell hit a sacrifice fly scoring Clines and Manny Sanguillen hit a home run scoring Clemente. The Pirates finished the inning leading 8-6.

In the third, after Moose gave up a two-out single to Phillies pitcher Brandon putting runners on first and second, Pirates manager Danny Murtaugh chose to replace him with hard-throwing

reliever Bob Veale. With Veale's entrance into the game, the Pirates once more fielded an all-Black lineup in the field. Veale struck out Phillies batter Ron Stone to get out of the inning. In the bottom of the third, the Pirates manufactured yet another run on a single by Al Oliver, fielder's choice by Jackie Hernandez, sacrifice bunt by Veale, and single by Stennett. The Phillies brought in veteran reliever Dick Selma, who got them out of the inning. The Pirates now led the game by a score of 9-6.

Luke Walker replaced Veale on the mound to start the fourth inning, and the seasoned southpaw promptly loaded the bases with a walk, single, and walk to the first three Phillie batters. Willie Montanez then hit a sacrifice fly allowing Larry Bowa to score. However, Tim McCarver was thrown out attempting to advance to third base on the sacrifice resulting in a double play. Walker got out of the inning, and the Pirates remained ahead of the Phillies by a score of 9-7. The Pirates were held in check in the bottom of the fourth, the first time in the game that they did not score in an inning. Neither team scored in the fifth inning, but the Pirates put together another rally in the sixth, with Clines reaching base on a double, and scoring on a Clemente single, bringing the score to 10-7. Luke Walker then took control of the game, not allowing a Phillie batter to reach base in the seventh, eighth, or ninth innings.

Luke Walker got the win, his seventh of the season, after pitching the final six innings of the game. Bucky Brandon took the loss for the Phillies. Six Pirates batters had two hits apiece, but it was Manny Sanguillen's two-run home run during the second frame, just his sixth of the season, that put the Pirates ahead for good in this rollicking game.

Immediate recognition of the unprecedented event by the press was mixed. There was no newspaper coverage of the event in Pittsburgh as all of the papers were closed due to a strike. The Philadelphia papers did not really recognize the event either. It was not mentioned in the game account in the *Philadelphia Inquirer*,[4] and the only allusion to the unique Pirates lineup in the *Philadelphia Daily News* was reporter Bill Conlin's reference to Danny Murtaugh's "all-soul lineup," with no further explanation.[5] However, a United Press International story that focused upon the all-Black lineup that was published in several newspapers around the country. In that article, Danny Murtaugh was quoted as saying, "When it comes to making out the lineup, I'm colorblind, and my athletes know it. They don't know it because I told them. They know it because they're familiar with how I operate. The best men in our organization are the ones who are here. And the ones who are here all play, depending on when the circumstances present themselves."[6] Pirates pitcher Steve Blass commented on Murtaugh's approach to the game, stating, "He treated it with the respect it deserved, but didn't act like it was as big of a deal as they were making — he just put out the nine best Pirates and didn't care if they were white, black, Latino, whatever. It was a tremendous response to that whole thing, which was a big deal."[7]

With the win, the Pirates improved to a record of 82 and 56. They completed the season with a record of 97-65. They went on to defeat the San Francisco Giants in the National League Championship Series three games to one, and then defeated the Baltimore Orioles in the World Series in seven games. Historically, the fielding of an all-Black team certainly ranks with that World Series victory.

SOURCES

In addition to the sources cited in the Notes, the author also consulted:

Baseball-Reference.com

Markusen, Bruce. *The Team That Changed Baseball: Roberto Clemente and the 1971 Pittsburgh Pirates* (Yardley, Pennsylvania: Westholme Publishing, 2006).

https://www.baseball-reference.com/boxes/PIT/PIT197109010.shtml

https://www.retrosheet.org/boxesetc/1971/B09010PIT1971.htm

NOTES

1   On Saturday, June 17, 1967 at Connie Mack Stadium, the Pittsburgh Pirates almost fielded an all-Black lineup. Pirates manager Harry Walker's starting lineup was Matty Alou in center field, Maury Wills at third base, Roberto Clemente in right field, Willie Stargell at first base, Manny Mota in left field, Jose Pagan at shortstop, Andre Rodgers at second base, and Jesse Gonder catching. Dennis Ribant was the starting pitcher for that game, but the Pirates also had several Black pitchers including Bob Veale, Al McBean, and Juan Pizarro who all started games that season.

2   Richie Hebner, hospitalized with a viral infection, would have likely been the third baseman since he started 93 games there in 1971, with Jose Pagan (38 games at third base), and Dave Cash (22 games at third base) taking up the slack. Also, Gene Alley (97 games started at shortstop in 1971) was being rested due to a sprained left knee.

3   Al Oliver and Andrew O'Toole, *Baseball's Best Kept Secret: Al Oliver and His Time in Baseball* (Pittsburgh: City of Champions Publishing, 1997), 51.

4   Mark Heisler, "Pirates' Sweep Saddles Phillies With Last Place," *Philadelphia Inquirer*, September 2, 1971: 29-30.

5   Bill Conlin, "Kerplunk! Phils Last," *Philadelphia Daily News*, September 2, 1971: 44.

6   "Pirates Field First All-Black Starting Team," *Tyrone Daily Herald*, September 2, 1971: 5.

7   Colleen Hroncich, *The Whistling Irishman: Danny Murtaugh Remembered* (Philadelphia: Sports Challenge Network, 2010), 178-179.

THE FIRST GAME THE PIRATES WON WHEN ROBERTO CLEMENTE HAD TWO OUTFIELD ASSISTS

SEPTEMBER 14, 1971
PITTSBURGH PIRATES 4, CHICAGO CUBS 3
AT WRIGLEY FIELD, CHICAGO

BY BILL NOWLIN

Over the course of his 18-year major-league career, Pittsburgh Pirates right fielder Roberto Clemente recorded 4,514 putouts at the position.1 He earned 266 outfield assists, throwing out that number of baserunners – an average of a little more than 14 per year.

As one looks through Clemente's career, one comes across the occasional game in which he recorded more than one outfield assist.

There were 14 games in which Clemente earned two outfield assists.2

The first two were both in 1958. The first was on April 17 in Milwaukee against the Braves. He threw out Del Crandall in the third inning and Hank Aaron in the fifth. On July 18, in San Francisco against the Giants, he threw out Valmy Thomas in the third inning and Orlando Cepeda in the fifth.

The next 10 games in which Clemente had two outfield assists were:

May 1, 1959 – a 7-6 home loss to the Cardinals

August 10, 1961 – a 3-2 home loss to the Cardinals

September 4, 1961 – a 9-4 loss to the Cardinals, an away game

May 3, 1962 – an 8-4 loss to the Giants, an away game

May 17, 1964 (1) – a 3-2 loss to the Dodgers, an away game

May 13, 1965 – a 5-4 home loss to the Braves

May 12, 1966 – a 3-0 home loss to the Giants

June 13, 1967 – a 7-4 home loss to the Cardinals

July 7, 1967 – a 6-2 home loss to the Reds

August 12, 1969 – a 6-3 loss to the Giants, an away game3

Finally, after 12 two-assist games – with every one of them a Pirates loss – Clemente recorded two assists in a game his team won. It was at Wrigley Field on September 14, 1971.

It was late in the season. With only 14 games remaining on the schedule, the 89-59 Pirates had a very healthy 6½-game lead in the NL East over second-place St. Louis. They'd been in first place since June 10 and had won 11 of their last 14 games, but they still had to win in order to clinch. The Cubs had lost nine of their last 11 games and were 14 games behind Pittsburgh.

Manager Leo Durocher had Ferguson Jenkins start. The 6-foot-5-inch right-hander already was a 20-game winner with a 21-12 record and a 2.90 ERA. Pirates manager Danny Murtaugh started right-hander Bob Johnson (9-9, 3.52).

Pittsburgh was the first to score, with two runs in the top of the third. With one out, shortstop Jackie Hernandez reached on an error charged to Cubs first baseman Pat Bourque, for coming off the bag too soon on Ron Santo's throw.[4] Johnson sacrificed him to second. Pirates second baseman Rennie Stennett singled to center, driving in Hernandez. Center fielder Vic Davalillo hit a shot to right field that got away from Brock Davis and went for a triple, scoring Stennett.[5] Clemente struck out.

The Cubs claimed one back right away when catcher Frank Fernandez led off the bottom of the third with a home run into the left-field bleachers. Though they loaded the bases with just one out, Johnson escaped any further damage.

The first two batters in the Pirates fourth reached on singles, but Jenkins shut them down before they could score. Jenkins then came to bat in the bottom of the fourth, with two outs and Fernandez on first after a base on balls. The Cubs pitcher homered into the seats in left field, giving Chicago a 3-2 edge. It was his fifth home run of the season.

Center fielder Cleo James followed with a double to right field, but Clemente fielded the ball and threw it in, relayed by Stennett to first baseman Al Oliver – to erase James, who had rounded second base too far.

Bob Moose – more frequently used as a starter – took over pitching for the Pirates in the bottom of the fifth and gave up a pair of singles but was rescued by Bourque hitting into a double play.

Jenkins was tagged for two more runs in the top of the sixth. He struck out Willie Stargell but then gave up a solo home run, a drive that Oliver sent "over the right field seats."[6] Richie Hebner then tripled to right. Catcher Manny Sanguillen was up next, and he struck out – but the ball got away from Fernandez, a passed ball that allowed Sanguillen to reach first base and Hebner to score from third with the go-ahead run.[7] Sanguillen tried to steal second but was thrown out. Hernandez popped up foul to the catcher.

Moose set down the Cubs in order in the sixth. He had just returned after a stint in the military reserve, but clearly had his command.

Jenkins walked Moose leading off the seventh. Stennett bunted for a sacrifice but reached base safely. Davalillo lined into a double play and Clemente grounded out, third to first.

Moose got two outs, but an error by Hebner allowed right fielder Brock Davis to reach first base. Billy Williams doubled to right field. The ball "hit the right field wall and bounced away from Roberto Clemente."[8] Davis – hoping to tie the score – sprinted all the way from first, but Clemente quickly recovered the ball and cut him down at home plate, throwing to Dave Cash (who had just taken over second base from Stennett), who relayed the ball, this time to catcher Sanguillen, who blocked the plate and "then tagging him as he tried to reach around."[9] The play was disputed by the Cubs, who felt that Davis had gotten in before the tag.[10]

Not another Pirate reached base. Jenkins threw a complete game, retiring the side in both the eighth and ninth. Given his two RBIs, the *Chicago Tribune's* Richard Dozer wrote, "It may interest the discerning Cubs fans that Jenkins now has the best ratio for runs batted in per time at bat on the entire ball club."[11] The Cubs pitcher had lost four of his last five decisions. In "referring to sloppy outfield play that has cost him his last two starts," Jenkins said, "I think I'm going to sign up next year as an outfielder."[12]

Moose finished the game for Pittsburgh, working five full innings in relief. He gave up a leadoff single to Santo in the eighth. First baseman Bourque sacrificed him to second, putting the tying run in scoring position with just one out. But Moose got back-to-back groundouts by Paul Popovich and Don Kessinger.

When the game reached the bottom of the ninth still 4-3, Durocher trotted out the pinch-hitters. Fernandez batted first and flied out to left. Johnny Callison pinch-hit for Jenkins. He struck out. Joe Pepitone batted for Cleo James and singled. Bill North was inserted as a pinch-runner for Pepitone. Jim Hickman pinch-hit for Davis and lined out to Stargell in left field for the final out.

Clemente was 0-for-4 at bat, but he had thrown out two Cubs baserunners, either of which could have been the fourth run the Cubs needed to stay in the game.

After the game, Murtaugh said, "Bob Moose did a great job in relief and, of course, those two plays where we hit the cutoff man to get a man at second and another at home helped. They were basic, fundamental plays we worked on all spring. Now they pay off for us in September."[13]

For the Cubs, it was their eighth loss in nine games, and they were mathematically eliminated from the race.

Moose improved his record to 10-7.

After the 13 games in which Clemente had recorded two assists but seen his team lose, at last he finally had a hand in holding down the score through the use of his arm.

After the 1971 season, Clemente was awarded his 11th consecutive Gold Glove. He won his 12th the following year.

The Pirates won the division, then beat the San Francisco Giants, three games to one, in the NLCS. They went on to win the World Series against the Baltimore Orioles, taking Game Seven 2-1. Clemente provided the first of the two runs with a solo homer in the fourth inning. Jose Pagan hit a double to drive in Stargell in the top of the eighth.

SOURCES

In addition to the sources cited in the Notes, the author consulted Baseball-Reference.com and Retrosheet.org.

https://www.baseball-reference.com/boxes/CHN/CHN197109140.shtml

https://www.retrosheet.org/boxesetc/1971/B09140CHN1971.htm

Unfortunately, Pittsburgh newspapers were on strike from May 14 until September 20, 1971, so we are deprived of some of the sources we would normally have available.

NOTES

1   In games where he played other positions, Clemente recorded 122 putouts in center field, 34 in left, and one at second base. All told, he made 4,697 putouts and committed 142 errors for a fielding percentage of .972.

2   There were also two games in which Clemente had two assists, but not both as an outfielder. On May 22, 1956, he had two assists but they were as a third baseman; he had one assist in the eighth and one in the ninth. On July 14, 1956, he had an assist from right field in the fifth inning and then played second base late in the game, and had an infield assist in the seventh. In his entire career, he appeared in only two games at second and one at third. The other game he played at second base was on June 10, 1956. Note: Totals differ between Baseball-Reference.com and Retrosheet. In an email to the author, Retrosheet acknowledges that its fielding statistics for this era have not been fully proofed. Baseball-Reference states on its site, accessed October 6, 2021, "Fielding stats are a combination of official records and Retrosheet records. Both are likely to have substantial errors and will not match perfectly." The figures we have used here are from Retrosheet.

3   The list of "victims" called out may be of interest. Among the 28 are six members of the Hall of Fame, totaling eight of the outs. Willie Mays was thrown out twice, and Orlando Cepeda thrown out three times.

April 17, 1958 – 3rd and 5th innings – Del Crandall and Hank Aaron

July 18, 1958 – 3rd and 5th innings – Valmy Thomas and Orlando Cepeda

May 1, 1959 – 4th and 5th innings – Alex Grammas and Stan Musial

August 10, 1961 – 4th and 5th innings – Ken Boyer and Curt Flood

September 4, 1961 – twice in the 3rd inning – Curt Flood and Charlie James

May 3, 1962 – 1st and 4th innings – Orlando Cepeda and Willie Mays

May 17, 1964 (1) – 2nd and 7th innings – Dick Tracewski and Willie Davis

May 13, 1965 – 8th and 9th innings – Joe Torre and Phil Niekro

May 12, 1966 – 2nd and 8th innings – Jesus Alou and Willie Mays

June 13, 1967 – 1st and 2nd innings – Orlando Cepeda and Curt Flood

July 7, 1967 – 2nd and 7th innings – Lee May and Tommy Helms

August 12, 1969 – 2nd and 8th innings – Ron Hunt and Hal Lanier

September 14, 1971 – 4th and 7th innings - Cleo James and Brock Davis

June 25, 1972 – 6th and 8th innings - Ron Santo and Billy Williams

4   "Cubs Tumble, 4-3," *Chicago Daily Defender*, September 15, 1971: 32. See also Richard Dozer, "Cubs Done for '71!," *Chicago Tribune*, September 15, 1971: C1.

5   George Vass, "Pirates Snuff Out Cubs' Title Hopes," *Chicago Daily News*, September 15, 1971: 42.

6   "Cubs Tumble, 4-3."

7   It was originally scored a wild pitch, but Fernandez took it on himself, explaining that it was indeed a passed ball. See Dozer.

8   United Press International, "Pirates' Magic Number Reduced to 7," *Franklin* (Pennsylvania) *News-Herald*, September 15, 1971: 30.

9   Vass. Two photographs of the play can be seen in the September 15, 1971, *Rockford* (Illinois) *Register-Republic*, on page 33.

10   Dozer.

11   Dozer.

12   Vass.

13   Joe Mooshil (Associated Press), "Chicago's Elimination Sets Stage for Cards-Bucs Battle," *Greenville* (Pennsylvania) *Record-Argus*, September 14, 1971: 20.

KISON'S RELIEF STINT AND MAY'S TIMELY PINCH-HIT BRING BUCS INTO SERIES TIE WITH BIRDS

OCTOBER 13, 1971
PITTSBURGH PIRATES 4, BALTIMORE ORIOLES 3
WORLD SERIES GAME FOUR AT THREE RIVERS STADIUM, PITTSBURGH

BY FREDERICK C. BUSH

After the Pirates lost the first two games of the 1971 World Series to the Orioles in Baltimore, the Series moved to Pittsburgh, and the Pirates rode a complete-game three-hitter by Steve Blass to their first victory. It may have been too much for the Steel City nine to expect Game Four starter Luke Walker to duplicate Blass's feat, but the hope was that he could keep Baltimore's big bats in check well enough for the Pirates to pull out another win and even the Series. As it turned out, Walker failed to make it through the first inning, but reliever Bruce Kison bailed him out. Kison hurled 6⅓ innings of shutout ball, and the Bucs overcame the disappointment of Roberto Clemente's near home run to eke out a 4-3 triumph.

Pittsburgh's Three Rivers Stadium had opened on July 16, 1970, and a record crowd of 51,378 packed the ballpark on this October 13 evening for the major leagues' first World Series night game.[1] Game Four in 1971 took place 11 years to the day from the last World Series game played in Pittsburgh, at old Forbes Field. In that

Game Seven, second baseman Bill Mazeroski hit his famous ninth-inning leadoff homer to defeat the New York Yankees, 10-9, as the underdog Pirates captured the championship. Although Mazeroski would register only one hitless at-bat in the 1971 Series, Clemente, who batted .310 against the Yankees in 1960 and had garnered at least one hit in all 10 World Series games he had played in thus far, was emerging as the star of this interleague clash.

Pittsburgh's past glories meant nothing to the Orioles, the defending champions, who were playing in their third consecutive World Series and had captured the title over the Dodgers in 1966. The Orioles put the wood to Walker as soon as home-plate umpire Ed Vargo finished yelling, "Play Ball!" Paul Blair, Mark Belanger, and Merv Rettenmund all singled to load the bases for Frank Robinson. The two-time MVP (1961 for the National League's Cincinnati Reds and 1966 for the Orioles in the American League) never got a chance to hit as Pirates catcher Manny Sanguillen let one of Walker's offerings get by him and was charged with a passed ball on a play on which Blair scored the first run of the game while Belanger and Rettenmund each advanced one base.

After the passed ball, Pirates skipper Danny Murtaugh had Walker issue an intentional walk to Robinson. Third baseman Brooks Robinson, another former league MVP (1964) and the 1970 World Series MVP, now stepped to the plate. Both Brooks and Boog Powell, Baltimore's third MVP (1970, AL) who batted next, were perhaps overeager at the sight of runners on base, but each managed to hit a sacrifice fly that scored Belanger and Rettenmund respectively.

With Baltimore already leading 3-0 and threatening to add another run, Murtaugh pulled Walker and sent Kison to the mound. The 21-year-old rookie, a 6-foot-4 string bean who was listed at a generous 178 pounds, had posted a 6-5 record with a 3.40 ERA in 18 games (13 starts) during the regular season. Exactly how much Murtaugh expected of Kison is unknown, but the gangly righty delivered far more than anyone had a right to anticipate. For starters, he induced an inning-ending grounder from Davey Johnson that ended Baltimore's onslaught.

When Dave Cash led off the home half of the inning by drawing a walk from Orioles starter Pat Dobson, Pittsburgh fans hoped their team could score quickly as well. Things looked bleak, though, after Richie Hebner lofted a pop fly to shortstop and Clemente struck out, one of only two times he would whiff in 29 at-bats in this World Series. However, Pittsburgh had plenty of big boppers. Willie Stargell doubled to drive in Cash for the Pirates' first run, and Al Oliver followed with another double that scored Stargell. Bob Robertson's grounder to Dobson ended the rally, but the Pirates had closed the gap to 3-2.

Kison and Dobson both settled down after the first inning and runs became much harder to come by for the remainder of the game. Kison worked around Blair's two-out double in the top of the second, while Dobson set the Pirates down in order in the bottom of the frame. After Kison responded in kind in the top of the third, there was excitement in the Pirates' half of the inning.

Hebner hit a one-out single to bring up Clemente for the second time. Clemente smashed a slicing shot to right field that, from some angles, looked as though it might have been fair when it went over the wall, but right-field umpire John Rice called it a foul ball. Pirates first-base coach Don Leppert, Clemente, and Murtaugh argued with Rice to no avail. The problem did not have to do with Rice's eyesight, or that of any players or coaches, but concerned a facet of Three Rivers Stadium's "unusual architecture."[2] In the case of Clemente's shot, the issue involved the fact that "[t]here [were] no orthodox foul poles, but concrete facades on which [were] painted wide white stripes. Flat against the stripes, flanked on each side by three feet of green concrete, [were] the foul screens, held in place by thin rods."[3]

Clemente's slicing drive "hit the green concrete to the foul side of the screen," which was "about 20 inches in front of the concrete façade."[4] Thus, the illusion was created, for some, that the ball had only gone foul after clearing the wall. Frank Robinson, who was often blunt, averred, "I don't give a damn where the white line is. ... There's no way the ball could have gone over the fence fair, hit the wall foul and the umpire could've called it fair. That's it."[5]

Indeed, that was it, and Clemente's at-bat continued. The Great One calmed down and lashed a single to right field that advanced Hebner to second base. After Stargell flied out, Oliver garnered his second RBI of the day with a base hit that drove in Hebner with the tying run. Robertson again ended the Pirates' rally with his second comebacker to Dobson on the mound, but he was to play a key role later in the game.

The Pirates failed to capitalize on two opportunities to blow the game open when they left the bases loaded in both the fifth and sixth innings. In the fifth, Clemente and Stargell banged out consecutive one-out singles, and Baltimore manager Earl Weaver had Dobson issue an intentional pass to Oliver to load the bags. This time, Robertson popped out to Belanger at shortstop and Sanguillen's grounder ended the Pirates' threat.

Jackie Hernandez led off the bottom of the sixth with a single and stole second base as Kison swung at strike three. He advanced to third when Cash beat out an infield single in Dobson's direction that heralded the end of the Baltimore right-hander's day. Lefty Grant Jackson took the mound and induced a liner to third from Hebner. He then walked Clemente (unintentionally) to load the bases, but Stargell's grounder to second quashed the latest opportunity for Pittsburgh to take the lead.

Baltimore could only wish for scoring opportunities, whether they were to cash them in or blow them as Pittsburgh was doing. After Blair's second-inning double, the Orioles failed to get a hit or draw a walk from either Kison or Dave Giusti, who followed him. The only Baltimore traffic on the basepaths was due to the amped-up Kison hitting a World Series-record three batters: Johnson in the fourth, Frank Robinson in the sixth, and Andy Etchebarren in the seventh.[6]

The Pirates finally broke through in the bottom of the seventh with relief ace Eddie Watt on the mound for Baltimore. After Oliver's leadoff strikeout, Robertson and Sanguillen swatted singles to set up an RBI opportunity for pinch-hitter Vic Davalillo, who was batting for Hernandez. Davalillo lofted a fly ball to far right field that Blair ran after but then uncharacteristically dropped for an error. Sanguillen overran second base and was tagged out, but Robertson was at third and Davalillo on first when Milt May stepped up to pinch-hit for Kison.[7] May lashed a single to right field that drove in Robertson and finally gave Pittsburgh the lead.

Cash flied out to end the seventh, but the 4-3 margin held up as the final score. Giusti, who had earned 30 saves in the regular season, set the Orioles down in order in the final two innings to earn his third save of the postseason. Thanks to stellar relief pitching and May's timely single, the Pirates overcame the fact that they had stranded 13 batters (and 41 in four games thus far) to pull even with the Orioles in the 1971 World Series. Thanks to his three-hit performance in four at-bats, the eventual World Series MVP Clemente was 8-for-17 through the first four games.

SOURCES

The author consulted baseball-reference.com and retrosheet.org for the box score and play-by-play of the game.

NOTES

1   Lou Hatter, "Bucs Even Series with 4-3 Victory," *Baltimore Sun*, October 14, 1971: 1.

2   Phil Musick, "Clemente Gets a Foul Ruling," *Pittsburgh Press*, October 14, 1971: 33.

3   Musick.

4   Musick.

5   Musick.

6   Charley Feeney, "Kison Holds O's, Bucs Even Set," *Pittsburgh Post-Gazette*, October 14, 1971: 26.

7   Milt May happened to be the son of Pinky May, a Phillies third baseman who had played alongside current Pirates manager Danny Murtaugh from 1941 to 1943 in Philadelphia. Pinky May had managed numerous minor-league teams, and his son Milt had served as a batboy in stops at Keokuk, Dubuque, Tampa, Rock Hill, and Reading. See Bill Christine, "Orioles Feel Pinch (by May); Pirates Get Even in Series," *Pittsburgh Press*, October 14, 1971: 34.

PIRATES WISH FOR CLEMENTE CLONES AFTER ORIOLES EXTEND WORLD SERIES TO GAME SEVEN

OCTOBER 16, 1971
BALTIMORE ORIOLES 3, PITTSBURGH PIRATES 2 (10 INNINGS)
GAME SIX OF THE 1971 WORLD SERIES,
AT MEMORIAL STADIUM, BALTIMORE

BY FREDERICK C. BUSH

After winning three straight games at home, including Nelson Briles' masterful two-hit, 4-0 shutout in Game Five, the Pirates returned to Baltimore's Memorial Stadium with the hope of clinching their fourth World Series championship in Game Six. A win in Baltimore was a tall order, 6-feet-3 to be exact, which was Orioles starter and 20-game winner Jim Palmer's height.[1] Palmer already had defeated the Pirates in Game Two, striking out 10 batters in the process, and owned a 6-1 record in the postseason to this point in his career, his lone defeat coming at the hands of the 1969 Miracle Mets. Still, the Bucs had Roberto Clemente, who was batting .385 in the postseason (including a .429 average through five World Series games), and who also was doing his usual stellar job at patrolling right field while appearing to be on a mission to will his team to victory.

A partisan crowd of 44,174 fans was on hand, and they may have become nervous quickly when Clemente stroked a triple to left field after Palmer had retired Dave Cash and Richie Hebner in the top of the first. However, Willie Stargell, who had led the major leagues with 48 homers and had knocked in 125 runs during the regular season, struck out to end the inning. The Pirates' slugger was slumping badly as he was batting only .133 in the postseason (.250 through the first five World Series games). Pirates righty Bob Moose allowed a leadoff single to Don Buford in the Orioles' half of the inning, but he escaped unscathed when Davey Johnson hit into a double play and Boog Powell flied out.

In the top of the second, Pittsburgh went to work on Palmer. Al Oliver led off with a double and scored the game's first run when Bob Robertson, the next batter, lashed a single to left field. Catcher Manny Sanguillen registered the Pirates' third consecutive hit with a single, but Palmer managed to extricate himself from his jam without allowing another run. The lack of production was a running theme for the Pirates in this World Series as they had stranded 50 runners on base through the first five games. Moose worked another one-two-three inning to preserve Pittsburgh's 1-0 lead.

Clemente came to bat for the second time in the top of the third and smashed a one-out solo homer to deep right field that extended the margin to two runs in favor of the visitors. After the game, Clemente said, "Lots of people think home runs is the whole thing. ... To me, having a great year and helping the ball club is more than to hit homers. I can hit homers, no question in my mind, but the only things [sic] is I don't particularly care to hit homers."[2] Considering how much trouble the Pirates were having at bringing runners home, Clemente apparently thought differently in this instance, and his round-tripper accounted for the Bucs' only run of the inning.

Palmer and Moose now registered zeroes on the scoreboard with neither hurler encountering any serious trouble through the Pirates' half of the sixth inning. The next run to be scored belonged to Baltimore when Buford led off the bottom of the sixth with a home run. Johnson then reached base on an error by Hebner at the hot corner, and he advanced to third on Powell's single. With runners on the corners and no outs, Pirates skipper Danny Murtaugh pulled the plug on Moose and sent Bob Johnson to the mound. Johnson, who had started 27 games and pitched to a 3.45 ERA during the regular season, bailed out his team by setting the next three batters – including former MVPs Frank Robinson and Brooks Robinson – down in order and kept the game at 2-1.

Unfortunately for the Pirates, Johnson's magical touch did not extend into the seventh inning. Initially, no difficulties appeared to be looming. Mark Belanger hit a one-out single, but Johnson struck out Palmer for the second out of the inning. Then, with Buford batting, Belanger stole second base. After Johnson fell behind in the count to Buford, Murtaugh replaced him in mid-at-bat with Dave Giusti. Buford still worked a walk (charged to Johnson) that extended the inning. The Orioles took advantage of the opportunity and tied the game, 2-2, on Davey Johnson's single. Giusti did not allow Baltimore to take the lead;

however, given Pittsburgh's lack of clutch hitting with men on base, the road to a Series-clinching win had just become much rockier.

The Pirates were so desperate for runs that Sanguillen tried to stretch his ninth-inning one-out single into a double and ended up being tagged out at second. Palmer finished out the ninth without any additional blemish to his pitching line.

Baltimore had a chance to win the game in the bottom of the ninth, but Clemente came to the Pirates' rescue once more. Giusti issued a one-out walk to Belanger and, after Tom Shopay (batting for Palmer) flied out, Buford smashed a double off the right-field wall. Clemente "played the carom perfectly on Buford's shot, then threw a one-hop strike to the plate from deep in the corner to keep Belanger nailed at third."[3] Giusti induced an inning-ending grounder from Davey Johnson, and it was time for what turned out to be only one extra inning.

Pat Dobson went to the hill for Baltimore in the top of the 10th. Cash lined a one-out single to right field and stole second base as Hebner struck out. Orioles manager Earl Weaver had Dobson issue an intentional walk to Clemente, a decision that Weaver later told the press was "one thing you guys aren't going to second-guess me about."[4] Weaver then replaced Dobson with Dave McNally, who walked Stargell unintentionally to load the bases. Once again the Pirates failed to capitalize on a scoring opportunity as Oliver lofted a fly ball to center field for the third out.

Bob Miller, the third Pirates pitcher of the day named Bob, opposed the Orioles in the bottom of the 10th. He was destined to follow in the footsteps of the previous two Bobs by allowing the Orioles to score one run. Vic Davalillo, who had pinch-hit for Giusti in the top of the inning, remained in the game, replacing Oliver in center field.

Miller retired Powell on a grounder to second but then walked the second batter he faced, Frank Robinson. Merv Rettenmund stroked a base hit to center field, and the Orioles had runners at the corners with only one out. Brooks Robinson sent a fly ball to Davalillo in center field on which Frank Robinson attempted to score. Sanguillen had to leap up the third-base line for Davalillo's throw and was unable even to attempt a tag on Robinson as he crossed the plate with the decisive run in a 3-2 Baltimore triumph.

After the game, a crestfallen Davalillo explained, "It was supposed to be a two-hop throw, but the ball took off instead of sinking. It only took one hop, and it was a high one."[5] There was, of course plenty of second-guessing of Murtaugh's decision to put Davalillo in center in the final frame. Oliver had been caught by surprise, saying, "I started to go to my position. I heard someone call and when I turned around, Vic was trotting out. It was a funny feeling going back in. I don't know why I was taken out. I always expect to play."[6] When Murtaugh was asked if he had considered sending Gene Clines to center instead of Davalillo, he responded, "No. As far as I'm concerned, Davalillo's arm is as good as Clines's."[7]

It was common knowledge that one Pirates outfielder had a golden arm that was better than all others. A reporter asked Frank Robinson, "Would you have tried to score if Clemente had caught the ball?" Robinson answered, "Clemente is a helluva outfielder, but I don't think he can cover two positions," leading the *Pittsburgh Press*'s sports editor to lament, "If Clemente were twins, the Pirates would have won it in four straight."[8]

There was, of course, only one Roberto Clemente. In the next day's Game Seven, he homered in the fourth inning for the game's first run, and the Pirates rode Steve Blass's stellar pitching effort to a 2-1 victory and a World Series championship. Clemente, who had batted .414 (12-for-29), had run like a gazelle on the basepaths, and had intimidated Baltimore baserunners with his arm, was named the MVP.

Photograph by Duane Rieder.

SOURCES

The author consulted baseball-reference.com and retrosheet.org for the box score and play-by-play of the game.

NOTES

1   Palmer (20-9) was not the only 20-game winner on the Baltimore staff; he was joined by Dave McNally (21-5), Pat Dobson (20-8), and Mike Cuellar (20-9). The 1971 Orioles were only the second team to have four 20-game winners in a single season, after the 1920 Chicago White Sox. Considering how pitchers are used in the twenty-first century, the odds that a third team ever will accomplish this feat are infinitesimally high.

2   Roy McHugh, "If Clemente Were Only Twins," *Pittsburgh Press*, October 17, 1971: 82.

3   Bob Maisel, "The Morning After," *Baltimore Sun*, October 17, 1971: 21.

4   McHugh.

5   Bill Christine, "Pirates Lose in 10th, 3-2; Blass in Final [sic]," *Pittsburgh Press*, October 17, 1971: 81.

6   Ken Nigro, "Bucs Blame Bounce of Ball," *Baltimore Sun*, October 17, 1971: 21.

7   Christine.

8   McHugh.

BLASS, CLEMENTE LEAD PIRATES TO VICTORY IN WORLD SERIES GAME SEVEN

OCTOBER 17, 1971
PITTSBURGH PIRATES 2, BALTIMORE ORIOLES 1
AT MEMORIAL STADIUM, BALTIMORE
GAME SEVEN OF THE 1971 WORLD SERIES

BY WAYNE STRUMPFER

It was the culmination of the 1971 baseball season. Game Seven of the World Series pitted the defending world champion Baltimore Orioles vs. the upstart Pittsburgh Pirates. For the Orioles, it was their third consecutive World Series appearance, losing to the New York "Miracle" Mets in 1969 and defeating the Cincinnati Reds in 1970. It was the first World Series appearance for the Pirates since Bill Mazeroski's dramatic walk-off home run against the New York Yankees in 1960.

In 1971, the Orioles were 101-57, winning the American League East Division by 12 games over their nearest rivals, the Detroit Tigers. Baltimore was led by a strong pitching staff that included a record four 20-game winners. Mike Cuellar (20-9), Pat Dobson (20-8), Jim Palmer (20-9), and Dave McNally (21-5) made up the starting rotation for manager Earl Weaver. The Orioles also had a formidable and balanced lineup with five players hitting at least 18 home runs and four players stealing at least 10 bases. Baltimore's defense had a well-built reputation of excellence with Gold Glove winners Mark Belanger at

shortstop and Brooks Robinson at third base. Between these two players, they would win 24 Gold Glove awards in their career. The Orioles had swept the Oakland A's in the American League Championship Series, 3-0, to return to the Fall Classic.

The Pittsburgh Pirates won the National League East Division with a 97-65 record, besting second-place St. Louis by seven games. It was the Pirates second consecutive division title. The Pirates were led by veteran manager Danny Murtaugh, 31-year-old slugger Willie Stargell's 48 home runs and 125 runs batted in, and by 36-year-old Roberto Clemente, who batted .341 and recorded 11 outfield assists. Pittsburgh's pitching staff was led by Dock Ellis, who won 19 games, and Steve Blass, who was 15-8 with a 2.85 ERA. Dave Giusti led a deep bullpen with 30 saves. Pittsburgh beat the San Francisco Giants in the National League Championship Series, three games to one, to gain entrance to the World Series and a matchup against the heavily-favored Orioles.

The first six games of the 1971 World Series were won by the home team. In Baltimore, the Orioles took the first two games, 5-3 and 11-3. When the Series shifted back to Pittsburgh, the Pirates won three in a row, 5-1, 4-3, and 4-0. Back in Baltimore for Game Six, the Orioles staved off elimination with a come-from-behind 10-inning 3-2 victory. Game Seven was played at Baltimore's Memorial Stadium on October 17.

The visiting Pirates sent Steve Blass to the mound. Baltimore countered with Mike Cuellar. It was a rematch of Game Three when Blass pitched a three-hitter to beat Cuellar and the Orioles, 5-1, in Pittsburgh. NBC announcer Curt Gowdy joked before the game, "Poor Earl Weaver, he's down to his last 20-game winner."[1] Cuellar, who was considered by many to be the best screwball pitcher in the majors at the time, was only two years removed from winning the AL Cy Young Award in 1969. Brooks Robinson, in a pre-game interview, commented that he "could really feel it inside" before the game and that a World Series going seven games was "the way it's supposed to be."[2]

The United States Army played the National Anthem and Secretary of State William Rogers, sitting with Baseball Commissioner Bowie Kuhn, threw out the first pitch to Orioles catcher Elrod Hendricks. There was a 15-mile-per-hour wind blowing in from right field and there were high-scattered clouds on the Autumn Maryland day.[3]

Cuellar set the Pirates down in order in the first three innings. Blass started the game shakily by walking leadoff hitter Don Buford. After Blass retired Davey Johnson, Earl Weaver came out of the dugout to complain to the home plate umpire about the Pirates hurler not keeping his foot on the pitching rubber. Curt Gowdy noted he thought the complaint was a "needling tactic" by the Orioles manager. "If he thought of anything to upset Blass or the Pirates, he'll do it," the announcer said.[4] And at first, it seemed to work, as Blass threw three straight balls to slugger Boog

Powell. But then Blass regained his composure and retired both Powell and Frank Robinson to end the first inning. Blass later said, "I thank Earl Weaver every time I see him. In the first inning, I was all over the place until Earl came out and it calmed me down with his nonsense."[5]

In the second inning, Blass walked Brooks Robinson and then Pirate first baseman Bob Robertson booted Elrod Hendricks' ground ball to put runners at first and second with one out. But the Pirate hurler induced Mark Belanger to hit into a double play to end the threat. In the third inning, Buford again reached base, this time with a single to right field. However, Blass picked Buford off first base and the Orioles went down quietly.

In the fourth inning, after the first 11 Pirate hitters had been set down by Cuellar, Roberto Clemente hit a home run to left-center field to give Pittsburgh a 1-0 lead. Steve Blass settled down over the next four innings, allowing only one base runner — Elrod Hendricks with a one-out double in the fifth inning — during that stretch. Cuellar matched Blass through seven innings, giving up only a leadoff single to Manny Sanguillen in the fifth inning.

In the top of the eighth, with a 1-0 lead, the Pirates struck again. Willie Stargell led off with a single to left field. Third baseman Jose Pagan then rapped a double off Cuellar scoring Stargell. The Pirates took a 2-0 lead into the bottom of the eighth inning with Blass looking unbeatable. But in the bottom of the eighth, the Orioles bats came to life. Hendricks singled to lead off the inning and he went to second on a single by Belanger. Tom Shopay pinch hit for Cuellar and sacrificed the runners over a base. With runners in scoring position and just one out, Blass was able to get Orioles leadoff hitter Don Buford to ground out to Robertson at first base. Hendricks scored on the play, but Belanger was left stranded at third base when Davey Johnson grounded out to shortstop for the third out.

In the ninth inning, Earl Weaver brought in 20-game winner Pat Dobson to shut down the Pirates. After Dobson retired the first two batters, he gave up consecutive singles to Robertson and Sanguillen. Weaver then brought in another 20-game winner, Dave McNally, from the bullpen to retire Willie Stargell on a groundout to second base.

In the bottom of the ninth, Steve Blass was once again masterful, retiring Boog Powell, Frank Robinson, and Merv Rettenmund in order. Rettenmund hit a bouncer straight up the middle and shortstop Jackie Hernandez fielded it and threw to Robertson at first, and the celebration began. The Pirates were world champions for the fourth time in their franchise history.

Steve Blass, who would be out of baseball by 1974 due to control problems, pitched two complete-game victories in leading Pittsburgh to the championship. Roberto Clemente, playing in his last World Series before his tragic death on December 31, 1972, was named MVP. Clemente, who rarely received national attention due to being overshadowed by the likes of Willie Mays and Henry Aaron, made a statement in the Fall Classic. He collected 12 hits in 29 at-bats and hit two home runs, including the shot in the fourth inning to give the Pirates the lead in Game Seven. Roger Angell wrote that Clemente was "at last the recipient of the kind of national attention he always deserved but was rarely given for his years of brilliant play."[6]

SOURCES

In addition to the sources cited in the Notes, the author consulted Baseball-Reference.com.

This article originally appeared in *Moments of Joy and Heartbreak: 66 Significant Episodes in the History of the Pittsburgh Pirates* (SABR, 2018), edited by Jorge Iber and Bill Nowlin.

https://www.baseball-reference.com/boxes/BAL/BAL197110170.shtml

https://www.retrosheet.org/boxesetc/1971/B10170BAL1971.htm

NOTES

1   NBC broadcast, October 17, 1971. https://www.youtube.com/watch?v=1zBhRvQIqW0.

2   NBC broadcast, October 17, 1971.

3   NBC broadcast, October 17, 1971.

4   NBC broadcast, October 17, 1971.

5   Bob Hurte, "Steve Blass," SABR Baseball Biography Project, http://sabr.org/bioproj/person/27a6a54d.

6   Hurte.

CLEMENTE'S TWO ASSISTS HELP THE PIRATES WIN AGAIN

JUNE 25, 1972
PITTSBURGH PIRATES 9, CHICAGO CUBS 2
AT WRIGLEY FIELD, CHICAGO

BY BILL NOWLIN

Over the course of his career, there were 14 games in which Roberto Clemente earned two outfield assists in the game. The Pirates lost the first 12 games. On September 14, 1971, he recorded two assists in a game the team won.

In 1972, which proved to be his last season, Clemente added another game during which he had two assists – and the Pirates won. They beat the Chicago Cubs at Wrigley Field, 9-2, on June 25.

Neither assist was on a deep throw from right field to home or to third base. But Clemente still earned two assists. And his team won. The assists were in the sixth and eighth innings.

The Pirates were in first place coming into the game, 1½ games ahead of the New York Mets. The Cubs were in third place but only four games behind Pittsburgh. Leo Durocher was managing the Cubs. After winning seven in a row, they had lost their last three games. Durocher's starter was 22-year-old Burt Hooton (6-4). Starting for Bill Virdon's Pirates was Dock Ellis (6-3).

The Cubs scored once in the first on a Don Kessinger double and a two-out single by Jim Hickman. They added another run in the bottom of the fifth after José Cardenal singled and Billy Williams tripled "high off the vines," hitting maybe six or seven inches from the top of the center-field wall.[1]

The Pirates got their first run in the top of the sixth. With one out, Clemente singled to right field. He went to third base on a ground-rule double by Willie Stargell, a weird wind-blown hit of which Cubs left fielder Williams said, "The wind had it. It landed about a foot and a half fair, took one bounce, and spun into the clubhouse door."[2] The Associated Press said it "caromed off the left field wall and into the open door of the Cub clubhouse in foul territory."[3] Al Oliver grounded to short, but Clemente scored on the play.

In the bottom of the sixth, Ron Santo singled to left field with one out. Second baseman Paul Popovich popped up to second baseman Dave Cash. Santo was thrown out on the basepaths, in the books as Cash to Clemente to shortstop Gene

Alley. Inning over. The 4-9-6 play sounds like a confusing one. The "wind blew" the popup "all over the place" with Cash "finally making a diving catch and throwing to second, where a confused runner, Ron Santo, was tagged to complete a double play."[4] The *Chicago Tribune*'s Bob Logan quoted Santo: "It was a hit-and-run play. I hurried back to first and then I saw Clemente trying to pick the ball out of Cash's glove, so I thought he had dropped it. That's why I went to second."[5]

Neither team got the ball out of the infield in the seventh, three groundouts for the Pirates and two groundouts and a strikeout for the Cubs.

The Pirates scored four runs in the top of the eighth. Cash made the first out, but Hooton gave up a single to Richie Hebner, who was thrown out trying to stretch it to a double, an assist to right fielder Cardenal. "It was a big play, but the Bucs shook it off," wrote Charley Feeney.[6] Clemente singled to right, and so did Stargell, who took second base on Cardenal's throw to third base hoping to get Clemente. Durocher replaced Hooton with left-hander Dan McGinn, who walked Al Oliver. He then replaced McGinn with Tom Phoebus, a right-hander, to pitch to catcher Manny Sanguillen, who hit a 1-and-1 pitch for a grand slam "into the wind in left center field."[7] It was the first grand slam of Sanguillen's career. He came up with the bases loaded the day before, also in the eighth inning, and drove in two runs, breaking a 1-1 tie and producing a 3-1 Pirates win. The grand slam took him to 12-for-25 against the Cubs through this game. Having grown up in Panama, where there was no night baseball, Sanguillen said he liked playing at Wrigley. "When I come to Chicago, I feel like I'm in my home town. I like to play in the daylight. ... The grass is beautiful here."[8]

The Pirates were now sitting on a 5-2 lead, with Virdon giving the ball to Ramón Hernández. Kessinger popped up to second base. Billy Williams singled to right. Hickman came up and he hit the ball to right fielder Clemente, who decoyed Williams into thinking he was going to

catch the ball, then let it bounce and fired it to shortstop Alley for a force out at second base, removing Williams – by far a faster baserunner than Hickman. Pittsburgh sportswriter Smizik credited the play to "the guile of Roberto Clemente."[9] It was Clemente's second outfield assist in the game.

Rick Monday reached on an infield single. Dave Giusti relieved Hernández, and the inning ended as it had begun, with a popup to second base, off the bat of Santo.

The Pirates scored another four runs in the top of the ninth. Alley began the rally by drawing a walk. Giusti laid down a bunt and made it safely to first base. Cash singled to left, scoring Alley. Giusti was out trying to go first to third. Hebner singled to right; Cash advanced to third. Jack Aker took over pitching for Phoebus. Clemente reached on a fielding error by shortstop Kessinger; Cash scored while Hebner took third and Clemente took second. Vic Davalillo grounded out, Hebner scoring. Oliver singled back to the pitcher, and Clemente scored. Sanguillen struck out to end the top of the ninth.

In the bottom half, Giusti got Popovich to hit the ball back to him and then struck out the final two batters. He earned his 10th save of the season; he'd earned a save in each of the three games against the Cubs.

In the final standings, the Pirates (96-59) finished first in the National League East and considerably ahead of the second-place Cubs, who at 85-70 were 11 games behind. After the first 91 games, with the Cubs at 46-44-1, Whitey Lockman was brought in to replace Durocher as manager. Under Lockman, the team went 39-26.

The Pirates played the best-of-five National League Championship Series against the Cincinnati Reds, but lost the final game, 4-3, when the Reds overcame a 3-2 deficit in the bottom of the ninth inning. Johnny Bench led off the inning with a home run, tying the score. With two outs and runners on first and third, a wild pitch by

Pittsburgh's Bob Moose allowed George Foster to score from third base with the winning run.

In all, Clemente had 14 games in which he had two outfield assists. Working with Retrosheet data, SABR member Vinay Kumar compiled a list of all players from 1947 through 2020 showing the number of games in which a given outfielder had eight or more two-assist games.

MOST TWO-ASSIST GAMES, 1947–2020

Player	Num	First	Last
Roberto Clemente	14	1958-04-17	1972-06-25
Hank Aaron	11	1956-04-20	1967-06-17
Carl Yaztremski	11	1964-09-01	1977-04-20
Larry Walker	10	1991-04-26	2002-06-07
Chili Davis	9	1982-04-19	1989-09-03
Rusty Staub	9	1966-06-23	1982-09-07
Tony Gwynn	9	1983-08-23	1992-07-14
Jesse Barfield	9	1982-04-22	1991-06-15
Amos Otis	8	1970-04-25	1984-04-07
Andre Dawson	8	1980-08-20	1995-05-16
Bob Bailor	8	1977-04-25	1980-05-20
Gerardo Parra	8	2011-05-18	2019-03-31
Carl Furillo	8	1947-05-08	1952-05-03

SOURCES

In addition to the sources cited in the Notes, the author consulted Baseball-Reference.com and Retrosheet.org. Thanks to Gregory H. Wolf for supplying Pittsburgh newspaper accounts for this game. Thanks to Chris Dial and Vinay Kumar.

https://www.baseball-reference.com/boxes/CHN/CHN197206250.shtml

https://www.retrosheet.org/boxesetc/1972/B06250CHN1972.htm

NOTES

1   Richard Dozer, "Pirates' Late Rallies Slam Door in Cubs 9-2," ???? "on Cubs"???? *Chicago Tribune*, June 26, 1972: C1.

2   Bob Logan, "Monday Cites 'Pride' of Cubs, 'A Good Team,'" *Chicago Tribune*, June 26, 1972: C3.

3   Associated Press, "Pirates Whip Cubs, 9-2 on Sanguillen's Homer," *Hartford Courant*, June 26, 1972: 31.

4   Logan.

5   Logan. Cash made the putout, with Clemente apparently taking the ball from him and throwing to get another out.

6   Charley Feeney, "Sangy/Giusti Duo Clinches Sweep of Cubs," *Pittsburgh Post-Gazette*, June 26, 1972: 16.

7   "It was not a crushing wind," wrote Feeney, "about six miles an hour. It couldn't stop Sangy's drive from carrying over the wall."

8   Bob Smizik, "Manny Right at Home as Bucs Rout Cards," *Pittsburgh Press*, June 26, 1972: 25. Clemente said, "He should have been the All-Star catcher last year. Nobody deserved it more. ... But no matter what he does, he'll never be the All-American kid. He'll always be a black Panamanian." Associated Press, "Sanguillen Loves to Play Day Ball," *Bloomington* (Illinois) *Pantagraph*, June 26, 1972. B-1. The AP story noted that Clemente "always has held the black and Latin players never get due recognition."

9   Smizik.

CLEMENTE'S SECOND HOMER IS A WALK-OFF TO KEEP PIRATES ATOP EAST DIVISION

JULY 1, 1972
PITTSBURGH PIRATES 4, CHICAGO CUBS 3
AT THREE RIVERS STADIUM, PITTSBURGH

BY ANDREW HARNER

Ferguson Jenkins was not intimidated by many major-league hitters.

Jenkins, the reigning National League Cy Young Award winner, respected every man who came to bat, but as one of the best pitchers in baseball in the early 1970s, he was confident in his ability to get outs. Still, there were a couple of players the Chicago Cubs ace did not like seeing come to the plate, and one of them resided in the Pittsburgh lineup.

Roberto Clemente in the on-deck circle "would scare the hell out of me," Jenkins said of the Pirates right fielder. "I never liked seeing him there. Didn't I just pitch to him? The lineup always seemed to come around to him too quickly."[1]

That surely made for a tough spot on July 1, 1972, when Clemente was the second man due up in the bottom of the ninth inning as the Pirates looked to rally and erase Chicago's one-run lead in a midseason game between a pair of playoff hopefuls. With one home run already to his credit that afternoon,[2] Clemente strode to the plate with a man on first to put a buzz into the 16,102 weekenders who came to Three Rivers Stadium.

"He came to the plate and he [always] had an idea of how he was going to hit the ball. He hit the ball up the middle a lot, right-center, and if you pitched him hard in, he would pull the ball," Jenkins recalled decades after his career. "He wasn't an individual you learned to pitch to one way."[3]

And on that warm Saturday, when Jenkins tried to zig, Clemente – unsurprisingly – zagged.

After Milt May singled to center to open the bottom of the ninth, Clemente slugged a Jenkins fastball into the center-field seats to send the Pirates to a 4-3 victory and polish off his triumphant return from a four-game absence caused by a knee injury and viral infection.

"[T]here was something about his Saturday homerics that make you appreciate the greatness of this 37-year-old superstar all the more," *Pittsburgh Post-Gazette* sports editor Al Abrams wrote in his weekly column after Clemente's walk-off homer kept the Pirates .003 points ahead of the New York Mets in the East Division standings.[4]

Little did Abrams know that the time to appreciate Clemente was running out. After helping the Pirates get two more wins over the Cubs, he played in five of the seven games on the ensuing road trip before a recurrence of the virus knocked him out until July 23. After a single start, Clemente missed the next 10 games and made only four pinch-hit appearances in the 16 games from August 4-20 while he also dealt with troublesome Achilles tendons.

Throughout the season, the Pirates were noticeably better when Clemente started (59-29, .670) than when he didn't (37-30, .552). So even with an 11-game lead going into September, there was no doubt the club was pleased that Clemente was healthy for the 32-game stretch run, and he delivered with a .333 average in 26 games as Pittsburgh went 18-11 in September to claim a third straight division crown.

But before that, there came one of the finest performances of Clemente's final season.

In the series opener against the Cubs, a 4-3 loss on June 30, Clemente hit his 164th career triple to move into a tie with Pie Traynor for third place on the franchise's all-time list.[5] Despite that fourth loss in five games, the Pirates rebounded to win on Clemente's walk-off home run, and then took the division lead for good on July 2 with a 7-4 win. The next day, *Sports Illustrated* released its latest edition with a cover story about the Pirates, who secured another walk-off win – this time a 3-2 victory on Willie Stargell's home run.[6]

The three straight wins to open July were reminiscent of July 1971, when the Pirates went 18-10 and gained 6½ games in the standings to firmly grasp control of the East Division on the way to a World Series championship. In July 1972 Pittsburgh went 20-10 and built a seven-game lead in the division.

But the Cubs didn't make it easy for the Pirates to secure their third straight July-opening victory.[7]

Chicago struck first on a two-out RBI double by Billy Williams in the third, but Pirates starter Bob Moose wouldn't allow another hit until the eighth. In the meantime, Jenkins was also cruising. He retired the first 15 batters, but the Pirates threatened in the sixth. Bob Robertson led off with a single, but Gene Alley grounded into a double play. Jenkins nearly fell off-track, allowing two more singles to Moose and Dave Cash, but with Clemente in the on-deck circle, Jenkins got Jose Pagan to ground into a fielder's choice, keeping Clemente from potentially hitting with runners on base.

"Baseball's hard to figure sometimes," said Robertson, who was hitting a paltry .143 coming into the game and got his hit on a curveball when he was anticipating an outside slider. "I was completely fooled on the pitch, yet I hit it and things started to happen."[8]

Though Jenkins escaped that scoring opportunity, he couldn't stop Clemente from tying the game when he led off the seventh. Clemente tore into a Jenkins curveball and sent it over the 385-foot marker in left field for a homer that tied the game at 1-1. Stargell followed with a single. Pinch-runner Gene Clines stole second, moved to third on Al Oliver's fly out and scored on Manny Sanguillen's sacrifice for a 2-1 lead.

"He had the best stuff I've seen him have in a long time," Clemente said of the right-handed Jenkins, who held Clemente to a .111 average over five games in 1971. "It was one of those things. We just started hitting him."[9]

Undeterred, Jenkins started an offensive rally in the top of the inning, leading off with a single and scoring on Williams's two-out home run off reliever Ramon Hernandez that gave Chicago a 3-2 lead.

Jenkins retired the Pirates in order in the eighth but knew the pesky Clemente would be on deck to open the bottom of the ninth. After May's pinch-hit single, Jenkins and Clemente met for the 98th time in their classic rivalry. Clemente was left to enjoy the 13th and final multi-home-run game of his career,[10] while Jenkins was left to ponder the "what-ifs" of his third loss to Pittsburgh in 1972,[11] though he could rest easier knowing he was beaten by one of the best in the game.

"I cannot despise any man who comes to bat wearing a major-league uniform. No man would be at bat unless he could hit," Jenkins wrote in 1973. "But you have to respect some hitters more than others. The two best hitters in my first seven years in the National League were the late Roberto Clemente and Hank Aaron."[12]

SOURCES

In addition to the sources cited in the Notes, the author consulted Baseball-Reference.com and Retrosheet.org.

https://www.baseball-reference.com/boxes/PIT/PIT197207010.shtml

https://www.retrosheet.org/boxesetc/1972/B07010PIT1972.htm

NOTES

1. David Maraniss, *Clemente: The Passion and Grace of Baseball's Last Hero* (New York: Simon and Schuster, 2006), 225.

2. It was Clemente's first home run against Jenkins since August 21, 1967, a span of 70 plate appearances.

3. Wes McElroy, "Catching Up with baseball Hall of Famer Ferguson Jenkins," July 13, 2018, Richmond.com, accessed November 12, 2021. (https://richmond.com/sports/wes-mcelroy/catching-up-with-baseball-hall-of-famer-ferguson-jenkins/article_1a0bc633-4e9e-59ec-b032-0e22e8757f20.html).

4. Al Abrams, "Sidelights on Sports," *Pittsburgh Post-Gazette*, July 3, 1972: 12.

5. Clemente would surpass Traynor on September 6 and had earlier passed him in career RBIs on June 19.

6. Clemente almost played the role of the hero in that game, too, having popped out to second before Stargell's home run.

7. On July 1, 1971, the Pirates beat the New York Mets, 3-0, and on July 1, 1970, Pittsburgh was a 4-3 winner over the Mets.

8. Dan Donovan, "Clemente Lowers the Boom, 4-3," *Pittsburgh Press*, July 2, 1972: D-1.

9. Donovan.

10. Clemente's last previous multi-home-run game came on July 4, 1970, the second of back-to-back two-homer games.

11. Jenkins also lost to the Pirates on June 23 and April 20.

12. Ferguson Jenkins, as told to George Vass, *Like Nobody Else: The Ferguson Jenkins Story* (Chicago: Henry Regnery Company, 1973), 210.

CLEMENTE'S TORMENT OF FERGIE JENKINS CONTINUES WITH FINAL CAREER HOME RUN

SEPTEMBER 13, 1972
PITTSBURGH PIRATES 6, CHICAGO CUBS 4
AT WRIGLEY FIELD, CHICAGO

BY ANDREW HARNER

When Roberto Clemente watched a Ferguson Jenkins pitch on the inside corner of the plate pass for a strike on September 13, 1972, young teammate Fernando Gonzalez didn't understand.

The pitch was in Clemente's wheelhouse, and when Gonzalez questioned his mentor about why he held up on such a pitch, Clemente, an 18-year veteran, told the rookie and fellow Puerto Rican countryman he would get his answer later in the game.

In the seventh inning, Jenkins placed another pitch at the same location in an effort to fool Clemente again, but the "ageless marvel"[1] won the mental chessmatch by blasting a two-run home run to center field that broke a 3-3 tie on the way to Pittsburgh's 6-4 victory at Wrigley Field in front of a scant weekday crowd of 4,418.[2]

"When he came to the bench, he said, 'That's why I gave him that pitch in the first at-bat,'" Gonzalez recalled years later. "He was doing things by that time that I never saw anyone do and I haven't seen anyone do since. He was like a computer. He

was set to play baseball. He always knew what he had to do."[3]

Jenkins – who five days earlier had declared he was "in a class by myself" after earning his sixth straight season with at least 20 victories[4] – often had trouble figuring out Clemente throughout his first seven full major-league seasons.

The tiebreaking homer was the 240th and last of Clemente's career. In 95 at-bats against Jenkins, Clemente hit .274 and hammered six home runs,[5] but he was especially strong in '72, going 7-for-12 with three homers and two triples when facing the reigning National League Cy Young Award winner.

"I think Clemente is the only superstar in our league," Jenkins said after Clemente reached base four times in their final meeting. "Well, he and [Henry] Aaron. ... Today, he just hit everything I had."[6]

With his second straight three-hit showing, Clemente's career hit total moved to 2,984, and it was expected he would become the 11th player to reach 3,000 hits before the season was through – considering there were 19 games left on the schedule.

"He won't need to play in 19 more games to reach that goal," said first-year Pittsburgh manager Bill Virdon of Clemente's late-season hot streak,[7] "if he keeps belting the way he has."[8]

But despite all of Clemente's Wednesday afternoon heroics, the Cubs nearly saved Jenkins from a loss in the bottom of the ninth.

With one out, Carmen Fanzone reached on an error and Randy Hundley followed with a single to chase reliever Bob Miller from the game and bring the go-ahead run to the plate in pinch-hitter Glenn Beckert, who was 3-for-10 in pinch-hit situations in his career. Beckert poked a grounder up the middle, but second baseman Rennie Stennett fielded the ball, stepped on second, and threw to first to complete the double play, giving new reliever Ramon Hernandez his 12th save after just a handful of pitches.

"If I had looked at Stinnett earlier, I would have figured outfield was his best position," Virdon said. "But the more I see him play second base, I think that might be his best position."[9]

Virdon liked Stennett's play at second base so much that after Clemente's untimely death on December 31, 1972, Stennett didn't become one of the primary players used in 1973 to replace the void in right field – despite having spelled Clemente there for 53 innings during the 1972 campaign. Instead, Stennett remained a staple in Pittsburgh's infield for the rest of the decade.

Clemente's afternoon in Chicago started with a harmless single in the top of the first, but his two-out triple to left in the third helped put the Pirates on the scoreboard.[10] Willie Stargell followed with a grounder into the hole at first, but while first baseman Jim Hickman made a nice defensive play to stop the ball, Jenkins failed to cover the base. By the time Hickman recovered to his feet, he lost a foot race to the bag, allowing Clemente to score and Stargell to pick up an infield single.[11]

"I started to first then stopped, thinking Hick could handle it. I didn't realize he was that deep," Jenkins said. "When I tried to start again I couldn't. It was just a lapse of memory by me."[12]

To open the sixth, Clemente drew a walk and moved to third when Stargell's high chopper went over Hickman's head and into right field for a double. Richie Hebner lifted a sacrifice fly to bring home Clemente, and Manny Sanguillen's grounder went through Don Kessinger's legs for an error, allowing Stargell to cross the plate.

A two-run double by Chicago's Jose Cardenal and an RBI single by Hickman tied the game in the bottom of the sixth. Pittsburgh starting pitcher Nelson Briles singled to open the seventh, and after two quick outs, Clemente again strolled to the plate to face Jenkins.

"I should have walked Clemente," Jenkins said after the game.[13]

Instead, Jenkins tried to fool him on the inside corner but paid the price. Clemente's home run sealed what became Jenkins' fourth loss of the season to the Pirates.[14]

"He hit a slider for the single, a fastball for the triple, and another slider for the home run," said Jenkins, who fell to 20-11 for the season and didn't win another decision until his third start of 1973. "He's something."[15]

Briles recorded 13 straight outs to open the game[16] and was credited with the victory, moving his season ledger to 14-7.[17]

In addition to the ninth-inning comeback try, Chicago worked to regain the lead in the eighth. Billy Williams had an RBI double to move the Cubs within a run, but Stennett pushed across another run for Pittsburgh with a single in the top of the ninth.

Clemente was instrumental in completing the series sweep the next day, helping spark a two-run rally in the seventh inning that extended Pittsburgh's one-run lead on the way to a 5-2 victory.[18] He had two hits to complete his best single-series showing of the year,[19] which marked the first time he had posted at least eight hits in a three-game series since he recorded 11 against the Los Angeles Dodgers on August 21-23, 1970.[20]

"I always play better in this ballpark. I always seem to do better against the tougher teams like Chicago," Clemente said after the series opener. "I always say I would not play for any other team except Pittsburgh. But I would like to play with Chicago. I like the park. I like day baseball and the crowds here are very good."[21]

Clemente hit 23 home runs at Wrigley Field throughout his career. None were more famous than the one he slugged in the second game of a doubleheader on May 17, 1959, which sailed out of the ballpark. With an estimated distance of more than 500 feet, it is among the longest ever hit at the park.

One fellow slugger – Cubs legend Ernie Banks, who hit 512 career home runs – said Clemente would have flashed more power had he called Chicago home and wasn't surprised that Clemente found a way to take advantage of Wrigley Field in his limited opportunities.

"Had he been a Cub, I'm sure he would have adopted a power style of swinging," Banks wrote in 1969. "... Only the great hitters can alter their batting styles to fit certain parks."[22]

By sweeping the Cubs, the Pirates moved a season-best 15 games ahead of Chicago in the standings[23] and knocked down to three their magic number to clinch the East Division crown. Pittsburgh locked up its third straight division title on September 21, but despite holding the best record in the major leagues, the defending World Series champion Pirates lost to the Cincinnati Reds in the NL Championship Series.

"I know people get tired of hearing it, but those guys are just having a helluva year," Cubs manager Whitey Lockman said of the Pirates. "And Clemente is one of the three best hitters I've seen among those I've had a chance to watch on a regular basis. The others were Stan Musial and Aaron. I never had a chance to see much of Ted Williams."[24]

SOURCES

In addition to the sources cited in the Notes, the author consulted Baseball-Reference.com and Retrosheet.org.

https://www.baseball-reference.com/boxes/CHN/CHN197209130.shtml

https://www.retrosheet.org/boxesetc/1972/B09130CHN1972.htm

NOTES

1   Jerry Liska (Associated Press), "Clemente's HR Beats Cubs" *Clearfield* (Pennsylvania) *Progress*, September 14, 1972: 17.

2   That was Wrigley Field's second-smallest crowd of the season after just 4,153 showed up to the series opener. Down the stretch, seven more games at Wrigley Field would feature smaller crowds, including a low mark of 1,362 against the Montreal Expos on September 19.

3   David Maraniss, *Clemente: The Passion and Grace of Baseball's Last Hero* (New York: Simon and Schuster, 2006), 277.

4   George Langford, "Jenkins Captures No. 20; 'I'm in a Class by Myself,'" *Chicago Tribune*, September 9, 1972: 2, 2.

5   Hall of Famer Sandy Koufax also surrendered six home runs to Clemente.

6   George Langford, "Pirate Guns Scuttle Cubs, Fergie 6-4," *Chicago Tribune*, September 14, 1972: 3, 1.

7   Clemente hit .400 over his first 12 games of September. He hit .291 in 14 games the rest of the month, but got his 3,000th hit in his final at-bat of the season.

8   Liska.

9   Bob Smizik, "Stennett Cashes In on Second Chance," *Pittsburgh Press*, September 14, 1972: 42.

10 The triple was the 166th and last of Clemente's career, and through 2021, no player has matched his mark, which stands in a tie for 27th all-time.

11 Langford, "Pirate Guns Scuttle Cubs, Fergie 6-4."

12 Langford, "Pirate Guns Scuttle Cubs, Fergie 6-4."

13 Liska.

14 It was the first decision Jenkins had lost since August 4.

15 Langford, "Pirate Guns Scuttle Cubs, Fergie 6-4.".

16 Briles also took a perfect game into at least the fifth inning two other times in 1972. On June 24 he retired the first 14 batters during a 3-1 victory over the Cubs, and on August 22 he retired 20 straight before allowing the only hit in his 14th career shutout, a 1-0 victory over the Giants.

17 Briles was forced from the game in the bottom of the seventh with a bleeding blister on the middle finger of his right hand.

18 The Pirates became the first road team since the 1894 New York Giants to win every game in Chicago in a season. Pittsburgh won the opening game of the series, 7-0, and also swept three games from June 23-25. The 1972 Pirates played only six games at Wrigley Field due to the players' strike early in the season, which wiped out three games scheduled between the teams in Chicago.

19 Clemente's second-best effort of the season came May 5-7 when he had seven hits at Cincinnati.

20 Clemente had back-to-back five-hit games in the series, though that included a 16-inning game. He also had 11 hits in a four-game series from August 23 to 25, 1971, at Atlanta.

21 Joe Mooshil (Associated Press), "Bucs Cut Magic Number" *Clearfield* (Pennsylvania) *Progress*, September 13, 1972: 17.

22 Ernie Banks, "Clemente Toughest, in Banks' Opinion," *Chicago Tribune*, July 6, 1969: B1.

23 This was a stark difference from the NL West Division, which saw the Cincinnati Reds leading the Houston Astros by seven games. By the end of the season, however, the division leads were separated by just a half-game (the Pirates winning by 11 games and the Reds winning by 10½ games).

24 Langford "Pirate Guns Scuttle Cubs, Fergie 6-4."

REDS' 9TH-INNING RALLY DETHRONES THE PIRATES IN CLEMENTE'S LAST GAME

OCTOBER 11, 1972
CINCINNATI REDS 4, PITTSBURGH PIRATES 3
AT RIVERFRONT STADIUM, CINCINNATI

BY TIM OTTO

The Pittsburgh Pirates and Cincinnati Reds split the first four games in the best-of-five 1972 National League Championship Series. The defending World Series champion Pirates had cruised to the Eastern Division title with a regular-season record of 96-59, 11 games ahead of the second-place Cubs. The Reds (95-59), who had defeated the Pirates in the 1970 NLCS, were just as dominant in the Western Division, finishing 10½ games ahead of the Los Angeles Dodgers and Houston Astros.

The Pirates had not made any significant changes to their roster heading into the 1972 season. However, they started the campaign with a new manager. Danny Murtaugh moved from the dugout to the front office as farm director after Pittsburgh's 1971 World Series win over the Baltimore Orioles. He was replaced by Bill Virdon, the starting center fielder for Pittsburgh's 1960 championship team and a coach for the Pirates since 1968.

Cincinnati, after losing the 1970 World Series to the Orioles in Sparky Anderson's first year as manager, finished a disappointing fourth in 1971. In the offseason, the Reds traded first baseman Lee May, second baseman Tommy Helms, and infielder Jimmy Stewart to the Astros. In return, Cincinnati received second baseman Joe Morgan, starting pitcher Jack Billingham, outfielder César Gerónimo, infielder Dennis Menke, and outfielder Ed Armbrister. The addition of Morgan and catcher Johnny Bench's return to his 1970 MVP form were key factors contributing to the team's first-place finish.

A crowd of 41,887 attended the decisive fifth game on a soggy, overcast afternoon in Cincinnati. Rain had delayed the 3 P.M. start by an hour and 28 minutes.[1] Don Gullett, the losing pitcher in Game One, was matched against the Pirates' Game One winner, Steve Blass. Gullett (9-10 with a 3.94 ERA) allowed five runs over six innings in that game. Blass (19-8, 2.49 ERA) gave up only one run during his 8⅓ innings of work in Pittsburgh's 5-1 victory.

Roberto Clemente's two-out single accounted for the only baserunner either team managed in a scoreless first inning. Manny Sanguillen led off the second for the Pirates with a single. Richie Hebner hit a line drive into the right-field corner. César Gérónimo made an accurate throw to second, attempting to catch Hebner before he reached the base, but shortstop Darrell Chaney wasn't covering the bag and the ball rolled past him into foul territory.[2] Sanguillen scored and Hebner advanced to third on the play. Dave Cash's single scored Hebner, giving Pittsburgh the lead, 2-0.

Chaney singled to start the Reds' half of the third inning with the score still 2-0. He advanced to second on Gullett's sacrifice. Pete Rose hit a bouncer toward first. The ball skipped high off the AstroTurf, over the glove of a leaping Willie Stargell, and into right field for a double,[3] driving in Chaney and cutting the Pirates' lead in half.

Sanguillen and Hebner each singled to center to begin the Pirates' half of the fourth inning. With runners at first and second, Pedro Borbon relieved Gullett. Cash singled to center, and Sanguillen scored to put Pittsburgh back up by two runs, 3-1. A fly out to right and a groundball double play ended the rally.

Leading off the bottom of the fifth, Gérónimo hit a home run to cut the Reds' deficit to one run, 3-2. "I adjusted to César Gérónimo in the first game of the playoffs," Blass said after the game. "He had hit a good fastball for a homer off me during the season, so I adjusted to slow curves in the playoffs. Well, he adjusted back and hit a slow curve out today. It is to his credit."[4]

Tom Hall relieved for the Reds and did not allow a baserunner in the sixth and seventh. Bench, who singled with two outs in the sixth, was the only Cincinnati batter to reach base against Blass in the two innings.

Rennie Stennett singled to start the top of the eighth, the first Pirate hit since Cash's RBI single in the fourth. He advanced to second on Al Oliver's sacrifice. Hall intentionally walked Clemente and struck out Stargell looking. Sanguillen grounded to Morgan at second, who backed up on the ball but threw out Sanguillen in a close play at first.[5]

Joe Hague pinch-hit for Hall and walked to start the Reds' half of the eighth. Dave Concepción ran for Hague and advanced to second on Rose's sacrifice. With the next two hitters batting left-handed, southpaw Ramon Hernandez relieved. Second baseman Cash bobbled Morgan's grounder but threw him out on another close play at first.[6] With Concepción at third, Hernandez struck out Bobby Tolan.

Clay Carroll retired the Pirates in order in the top of the ninth. Virdon called on right-handed closer Dave Giusti (22 saves, 1.93 ERA) to face Bench, the Reds' leadoff batter in the bottom of the inning. Bench, whose 40 home runs topped both leagues, hit a high outside palm ball into the right-field seats, tying the game at 3-3. "It's only the second homer I've hit that way and both of them were against the Pirates," he said after the game.[7]

Tony Pérez followed Bench's home run with a single to center. George Foster ran for Pérez. After two failed bunt attempts,[8] Denis Menke singled to left, with Foster stopping at second. Guisti's first two pitches to the next batter, Gerónimo, were balls. Bob Moose relieved and, after another failed bunt attempt, Gérónimo hit a fly ball to Clemente in deep right that advanced Foster to third.[9]

Chaney popped up to the shortstop in shallow left, and the runners at first and third held. Hal McRae batted for the pitcher, Carroll. McRae swung and missed on the first pitch from Moose. The next pitch was a ball. The third pitch landed in the dirt, wide of the plate. Catcher Sanguillen was unable to make a backhanded play on the ball as it bounced past him,[10] and Foster dashed home with the winning run.

"It looked like it hit something, I don't know what," said Sanguillen, describing the wild pitch that allowed Foster to score. "I jumped to the ball.

Les Banos photograph courtesy of The Clemente Museum.

The ball hit me on my hand and bounced on by. No, I didn't get my glove on it."[11]

Moose said, "It was a slider. It hit in front and wide of the plate and bounced straight up – I don't know why. I didn't want to throw it for a strike anyway. How many do you see bounce straight up?" Answering his own question, he continued, "Oh, I don't know. It happened."[12]

During the Reds' clubhouse celebration, Bench discussed coming to bat in the ninth. "I knew I was going to hit it," he said. "Sometimes you get a funny feeling about that, and I had it. I just felt I was going to hit it." Recounting his opposite-field home run, he said, "I knew it was gone as soon as I hit it."[13]

Rose tried to describe the crowd's reaction to Bench's ninth-inning blast. "I've never heard people that emotional," he said. "It was the greatest homer I've ever seen, and I've seen a lot."[14]

Sparky Anderson had high praise for the Pirates. "This series proves that neither team is better than the other," he said. "There are two number 1 teams in the National League"[15]

Virdon kept the Pirates clubhouse door closed long enough to talk to his players individually. Clemente summed up the emotions of his teammates. "We accept the loss as we accepted the win," he said, "not saying we are worse because of one inning or that we are better because we think so. We have won and we have lost and we remain the same."[16]

This was the last game Clemente ever played.

POSTSCRIPT

Exhilarated by Cincinnati's hard-fought play-off win, Reds center fielder Bobby Tolan declared, "As far as I'm concerned the World Series is over. The two best teams have played."[?] However, the Oakland A's defeated Cincinnati in seven games, winning the first of three straight World Series championships.

On December 31, 1972, 69 days after Oakland defeated the Reds, a DC-7 cargo plane carrying supplies to earthquake survivors in Nicaragua crashed after taking off from San Juan, Puerto Rico. None of the five passengers survived. Clemente, who organized a committee to collect the relief materials, was one of the crash victims.[?]

SOURCES

The author accessed Baseball-Reference.com and Retrosheet.org. for box scores/play-by-play information, player, team, and season pages, pitching and batting game logs, and other data.

https://www.baseball-reference.com/boxes/CIN/CIN197210110.shtml

https://www.retrosheet.org/boxesetc/1972/B10110CIN1972.htm

NOTES

1   Al Abrams, "Sidelights on Sports," *Pittsburgh Post-Gazette*, October 12, 1972: 20.

2   Charles Feeney, "Reds Dethrone Bucks, 4-3, with Heroics in 9th," *Pittsburgh Post-Gazette*, October 12, 1972: 20, 22.

3   Feeney: 20.

4   Tom Callahan, "The Pirates Showed Class," *Cincinnati Enquirer*, October 12, 1972: 73.

5   Feeney: 22.

6   Feeney: 22.

7   Bob Hertzel, "Foster, Who Scored 'The' Run, Enjoys Quiet," *Cincinnati Enquirer*, October 12, 1972: 73.

8   Earl Lawson, "Wild Pitch Sets Off Reds' NL Pennant Party," *The Sporting News*, October 28, 1972: 9.

9   Feeney: 1.

10 Feeney: 1.

11 "The Strike That Bounced," *Pittsburgh Post-Gazette*, October 12, 1972: 20.

12 Callahan, "The Pirates Showed Class."

13 "Reds Bench Erupts with Johnny," *Pittsburgh Post-Gazette*, October 12, 1972: 20.

14 "Reds Bench Erupts with Johnny."

15 "Reds Bench Erupts with Johnny."

16 Callahan.

CONTRIBUTORS

MALCOLM ALLEN lives in Brooklyn, New York, with his wife, Sara, and daughters, Ruth and Martina. He manages the warehouse for Crossfire Sound Productions. Reading Phil Musick's *Who Was Roberto?* when he was a high-school freshman changed his perspective on baseball and life. Originally from Baltimore, he used to work at Memorial Stadium, where Roberto Clemente capped his MVP performance in the 1971 World Series.

JEFF BARTO left Pittsburgh in 1992 to teach at UNC Charlotte. In 2005 he began teaching the History of Baseball and Baseball Through Critical Thinking at UNCC. As an avid Pirates fan, he focuses on the Bucs for his Game-and-BioProject contributions. He especially enjoyed interviewing his boyhood heroes for their biographies, Richie Hebner and Freddie Patek. Rick Monday serves as his current biography subject. He spotlights the Pirates for the Games Project. These include Forbes Field's final Opening Day and its last two games, which he attended. For a non-Pirate game, he picked Germany Schaefer's Called Shot in 1906 and recently worked on Rick Monday's Flag-Saving game during 1976's Bicentennial.

GARY BELLEVILLE is a retired information technology professional living in Victoria, British Columbia. He has written articles for SABR's *Baseball Research Journal*, Games Project, and Baseball Biography Project, in addition to contributing to several SABR books. Gary grew up in Ottawa, Ontario, and graduated from the University of Waterloo with a bachelor of mathematics (computer science) degree.

JOHN BLANKSTEIN is a senior advisor with Econsult Solutions, Inc., in Philadelphia and an assistant baseball coach at Haverford College.

STEVE BRATKOVICH hails from Pennsylvania. As a youth he rooted for the Pittsburgh Pirates and enjoyed watching Roberto Clemente patrol right field at Forbes Field. He has been a member of SABR since 2015. Steve has authored two baseball books: *Bob Oldis – A Life in Baseball* and *The Baseball Bat*. He lives with his wife in Medina, Minnesota, and cheers for the Twins.

THOMAS J. BROWN JR. is a lifelong Mets fan who became a Durham Bulls fan after moving to North Carolina in the early 1980s. He was a national-board-certified high-school science teacher for 34 years before retiring in 2016. Tom taught science to ELL students in the last eight years of his career and still mentors many of them. He has been a member of SABR. since 1995, when he learned about the organization during a visit to Cooperstown on his honeymoon. Tom became active in SABR after his retirement, writing biographies and game stories, mostly about the New York Mets. He loves to travel with his wife, always visiting major-league and minor-league baseball parks whenever possible. Tom also loves to cook and writes about the diverse recipes that he makes on his blog, Cooking and My Family.

FREDERICK C. (RICK) BUSH has written articles for over two dozen SABR books and, together with Bill Nowlin, has co-edited five SABR books about the Negro Leagues, including *When the Monarchs Reigned: Kansas City's 1942 Negro League Champions* (2021), which received the 2022 Robert Peterson Recognition Award, and *The First Negro League Champion: The 1920 Chicago American Giants* (2022). Rick lives with his wife, Michelle, their three sons – Michael, Andrew, and Daniel – and their Border Collie mix, Bailey, in the Houston metro area. He has been an educator for over 25 years, the past 18 of which have been spent teaching English at Wharton County Junior College's satellite campus in Sugar Land, which is home to the Astros' Triple-A franchise.

RICHARD CUICCHI joined SABR in 1983 and is an active member of the Schott-Pelican Chapter. After his retirement as an information-technology executive, Richard authored Family Ties: A Comprehensive Collection of Facts and Trivia about Baseball's Relatives. He has contributed to numerous SABR BioProject and Games publications. He does freelance writing and blogging about a variety of baseball topics on his website, TheTenthInning.com, and is a regular contributor to CrescentCitySports.com. Richard lives in New Orleans with his wife, Mary.

Born and raised in Newfoundland, **MARK DAVIS** developed a passion for baseball and the Toronto Blue Jays in his youth that continues to this day. A lifelong learner, he holds an undergraduate and master's degrees in economics, as well as a PhD in public policy. Mark is a published academic author and a relatively new SABR member. He enjoys researching baseball history and has contributed three articles to the SABR book commemorating the 30th anniversary of the Toronto Blue Jays' 1992 World Series championship. He currently resides in Ottawa with his wife, Melissa, and their young daughter, Felicity.

PETER DREIER is the E.P. Clapp Distinguished Professor of Politics at Occidental College. He earned his BA in journalism from Syracuse University and his PhD in sociology from the University of Chicago, and has also worked as a newspaper reporter, community organizer, and senior policy deputy to Boston Mayor Ray Flynn. He is coauthor (with Robert Elias) of two new books, *Baseball Rebels: The Players, People and Social Movements That Shook Up the Game and Changed America* (University of Nebraska Press) and *Major League Rebels: Baseball Battles Over Workers' Rights and American Empire* (Rowman & Littlefield). His other books include *The 100 Greatest Americans of the 20th Century: A Social Justice Hall of Fame* (Nation Books), *Place Matters: Metropolitics for the 21st Century* (University Press of Kansas), *The Next Los Angeles: The Struggle for* a Livable City (University of California Press), and We Own the Future: Democratic Socialism, American Style (The New Press). His articles have appeared in Baseball Research Journal and NINE as well as in the New York Times, Los Angeles Times, Washington Post, The Nation, American Prospect, Harvard Business Review, Perspectives on Politics, the Journal of the American Planning Association, Urban Affairs Review, New Republic, and other publications. He wrote the SABR profiles of Sam Nahem and Joe Black. He coauthored a 2018 report on working conditions at Disneyland, Working for the Mouse, and a 2022 study of working conditions among America's grocery workers during the COVID pandemic, Hungry at the Table, both of which generated significant media attention.

ROBERT ELIAS is a professor of law and politics at the University of San Francisco. A longtime SABR member, he's published many baseball essays, including the Octavius Catto bio for the SABR Biography Project. His dozen published books include five on baseball: The Empire Strikes Out, The Deadly Tools of Ignorance, Baseball and the American Dream, Major League Rebels, and Baseball Rebels. He's now writing a baseball biography for the University of Pennsylvania Press entitled Danny Gardella: Post-War America and the Neglected Working-Class Hero to Today's Millionaire Athletes. He recently joined in the Century Committee's work on baseball and the Supreme Court.

HOWARD ELSON is a longtime SABR member, actor, and semi-retired pediatric dentist. He wrote "Mickey Mantle Returns in a Pinch" for SABR's Games Project, was "Professor Baseball" for four MLB All-Star Game FanFests, and traveled throughout North America performing his one-man show for dental conventions, "Ladies and Gentlemen, Dr. Howard Elson!" His "Sports Family" includes son Phil, "the baseball voice

of the Arkansas Razorbacks," and son-in-law Dan, the athletic director at Western Michigan University. At age 74, Howard still pitches competitive baseball in both the Men's Senior Baseball League and he plans to be Roy Hobbs. He planned to be in Phoenix in October helping defend his USA Volkers team's Over 73 National Championship. He and his wife, Robin, a CPA who worked with Richard Kantrowitz and helped prepare the Clemente tax returns, are native New Yorkers, saw Roberto play at Shea Stadium, have lived in Pittsburgh for over 40 years and revel in the exploits of their four grandchildren.

JAMES FORR is a recovering Pirates fan in the heart of Cardinals country. His book Pie Traynor: A Baseball Biography, co-authored with David Proctor, was a finalist for the 2010 CASEY Award. He is a winner of the McFarland-SABR Baseball Research Award and has spoken at the Frederick Ivor-Campbell 19th Century Base Ball Conference and the Jerry Malloy Negro League Conference.

JOHN FREDLAND, an attorney and retired Air Force officer, grew up in a suburb of Pittsburgh. As an undergraduate at Rice University, he covered Rice's nationally ranked baseball teams for the school newspaper, the Rice Thresher. John received his law degree at Vanderbilt University, then served as an active-duty attorney in the Air Force's Judge Advocate General's Corps for 20 years. He currently lives in San Antonio, Texas, and chairs SABR's Baseball Games Project Research Committee. John has a batting-practice pitcher in common with Roberto Clemente: his father, also named John, who spent the summer of 1968 as a left-handed batting-practice pitcher for the Pirates while playing on the University of Pittsburgh baseball team.

STEVE GINADER is a retired logistics manager residing in Green Valley, Arizona, with his wife, Julie. His love of baseball ignited as a child in his hometown of Reading, Pennsylvania, where he received his first baseball publication, a 1963 Phillies yearbook sent by his grandfather. Steve joined SABR in the late 1980s and became an active member of the Halsey Hall Chapter in Minnesota during the All-Star Game festivities in 2014. After retiring, he started writing game stories for the Games Project, including several articles for SABR published books. Steve plans to continue his research and writing in Arizona using the many platforms of the SABR Research Collection.

DUKE GOLDMAN is a longtime SABR member who specializes in the Negro Leagues and the process of baseball integration. Duke began to idolize Roberto Clemente as a 9-year-old watching Clemente dominate the 1971 World Series with his unbelievable arm and all-around dazzling performance.

VINCE GUERRIERI saw his first major-league game at Three Rivers Stadium in Pittsburgh. A native of Youngstown, Ohio, he spent his salad days as a young reporter for the *Pittsburgh Tribune-Review* and spent every day he could at the newly opened PNC Park. He's an award-winning journalist and author in the Cleveland area, and secretary/treasurer of the Jack Graney SABR chapter there.

A love of baseball was instilled in **ANDREW HARNER** from childhood, but since he had next to no athletic skills, he instead dove into the game's history and pored over box scores as often as he could. And because baseball history wasn't offered as a college major, he settled for the next best thing – a bachelor's degree in sports journalism with a minor in history. He graduated from Bowling Green State University in 2010 and spent nearly seven years as a sports editor before leaving the newspaper industry to pursue a career

in hospitality. Andrew has also published online content for *Sports Illustrated*. He has been married to his wife, Elizabeth, since 2011, and they have two daughters. They reside in north central Ohio.

JANE S. HEWITT is a longtime SABR member and a lifetime baseball fanatic. Before she was born, her father, a shortstop, and three of his 14 siblings, played semipro ball at all levels. One of them earned his way through Loyola Medical School in Chicago playing with Hall of Fame catcher Gabby Hartnett's All-Stars. As a child living in Kansas, she met and watched Satchel Paige play with the Kansas City Monarchs in the waning years of the Negro Leagues. When not teaching, she worked seven summers for the Northern League's Fargo-Moorhead RedHawks (now in the American Association), where Maury Wills was the color commentator for the local radio station. She loves everything about baseball, but these days is especially interested in the World Baseball Classic and how the love of the game has encircled the globe.

THOMAS E. KERN was born and raised in Southwest Pennsylvania. Listening to the mellifluous voices of Bob Prince and Jim Woods in his youth, how could one not become a lifelong Pirates fan? Ariba Roberto! He now lives in Silver Spring, Maryland, and sees the Nationals and Orioles as often as possible. He is a SABR member dating back to the mid-1980s. With a love and appreciation for Negro League baseball, he has written SABR bios for Leon Day, John Henry Lloyd, Willie Foster, Judy Johnson, Turkey Stearnes, Hilton Smith, Louis Santop, Andy Cooper, and Buck Ewing. Tom's day job is in the field of transportation technology.

JUSTIN KRUEGER is an assistant professor of social studies education at Delta State University in Cleveland, Mississippi, and was a 2021 recipient of the Woody Guthrie Fellowship awarded by the BMI Foundation. Recently he came across a letter that baseball coaching great Billy Disch wrote to his great-grandfather in 1908. It made him smile.

ALEX KUKURA fell in love with baseball while watching Cleveland's 2016 playoff run with his father, a lifelong baseball fan. When not watching, reading, or writing about baseball, he is an undergraduate researcher at Indiana University Bloomington studying cybersecurity and US diplomatic history. He has been a SABR member since 2020. This is his first contribution to a SABR publication.

For over 20 years, **KEVIN LARKIN** patrolled the highways and byways in his hometown of Great Barrington, Massachusetts. When not at work keeping the town's citizens safe, inevitably Larkin was listening to a baseball game on the radio. He has been going to baseball games since he was 5 years old. His baseball life is the only thing he loves more than his children and grandchildren. One day while he was browsing at the local bookstore, the owner of the bookstore asked him if he was interested in writing a book about baseball. Larkin's first effort was *Baseball in the Bay State: A History of Baseball in Massachusetts*. He then took quite an interest in the history of the game, authoring a book on one of his heroes, Lou Gehrig, called, *Gehrig: Game by Game*, a look at every game the Iron Horse played during his major-league career. He has since written a number of other books and articles on the sport and has a number of others ready for future publication. His latest book, *Big Time Baseball in a Small Berkshire County Town*, led to his heading an effort to erect a historical marker in the town where this semipro team played a number of major-league teams, Black baseball teams and the House of David touring team, with the plaque being dedicated July 6, 2022. He writes and fact-checks for SABR, an experience he considers the

best decision he has ever made. He also hosts a baseball history show on a local radio station. He believes writing about baseball is a great way to keep the memory of the sport alive and he will continue to delve into sports history with more to come

One of **JOE LEISEK**'s favorite early baseball memories is watching the final out of the 1969 World Series on television in the multipurpose room of his Northern California elementary school. When he moved overseas for high school, he took his APBA game – flat box, 1974 season cards, homemade scoresheets, and all. Joe lives with his wife, Tracy, and their Irish setter, Liam, in Sonoma County, California, where he works in corporate communications for a technology company.

LEN LEVIN is a longtime newspaper editor in New England, now retired. He lives in Providence with his wife, Linda, and an overachieving orange cat. He now (Len, not the cat) is the grammarian for the Rhode Island Supreme Court and edits its decisions. He also copy-edits many SABR books, including this one. He is just down the interstate from Fenway Park, where he has spent many happy hours.

NORMAN L. MACHT has been a SABR member for about 37 years and has written about 37 books, including a 1991 biography of Roberto Clemente for ages 12 and up published by Chelsea House.

MICHAEL MARSH is a freelance writer based in Chicago. A former staff writer for the *Chicago Reader*, he has also covered high-school sports for the *Chicago Sun-Times* and *Chicago Tribune*.

EMMANUEL MEHR is a public historian and researcher based in Washington, D.C. He works to illuminate and share US migration stories from the past and present. He also specializes in baseball's role in growing or constraining individual and group identities. Emmanuel's passion for exploring the life of Roberto Clemente began with the ¡Pleibol! *In the Barrios and the Big Leagues / En los barrios y las grandes ligas* exhibition at the Smithsonian National Museum of American History, where he worked as a young professional. His favorite artifact from this Latinx baseball history exhibition is Clemente's game-worn batting helmet, dated to around 1960. In 2021 Emmanuel received his master's degree in global, international, and comparative history from Georgetown University. In his free time, he can usually be found taking in the sights and sounds at either Nationals Park or Oriole Park at Camden Yards.

KELLEN NIELSON was born in Price, Utah, and was raised in Blanding, Utah, where he now resides with his wife, Lydia, and their five children, Madison, Austin, Charlotte, Bodil, and Gretchen. He graduated from Utah State University with a BA in history. He is a lifelong fan of the Atlanta Braves and the game of baseball.

BILL NOWLIN sadly never saw Roberto Clemente play, having grown up in an American League city (Boston) in the days before interleague play. (But he remembers his Topps baseball cards.) A lifelong Red Sox fan, he was a professor of political science and co-founder of Rounder Records, and has over the past 20 years become more active in writing and editing about baseball, primarily for SABR but also for a few other entities.

TONY S. OLIVER is a native of Puerto Rico currently living in Sacramento, California, with his wife and daughter. While he works as a Six Sigma professional and teaches at several University of California extension campuses, his true love is baseball and he cheers for both the Red Sox and whoever happens to be playing the Yankees.

He is fascinated by baseball cards and is currently researching the evolution of baseball tickets. He believes there is no prettier color than the vibrant green of freshly mown grass on a baseball field.

TIM OTTO grew up in northeast Ohio, 35 miles from Cleveland's Municipal Stadium. He attended his first major-league game during the summer of 1960. His first memory of the World Series was getting off the school bus that fall and running into his house to discover he had just missed Bill Mazeroski's home run that won the Series. He is a lifelong Cleveland fan, but the Pirates have been one of his favorite NL teams ever since that homer. One of his first baseball cards was Roberto Clemente's 1960 Topps card, so he was excited to have the opportunity to write about the deciding contest of the 1972 NLCS, Clemente's final game before his tragic death.

ZAC PETRILLO has a BA from Hunter College and an MFA from Chapman University's Dodge College of Film and Media Arts. He has directed multiple short films and produced shows for *Comedy Central* and *TruTV*. In 2016 he was instrumental in launching Vice Media's 24/7 cable network, *Vice TV*. As a Society for American Baseball Research member, he focuses his work on post-1980s baseball and the intersection between the game and the media industry. He is currently the director of post-production at A+E Networks and teaches television studies at Marymount Manhattan College.

RICHARD J. PUERZER is the chairperson of the Department of Engineering at Hofstra University. His writing on baseball has appeared in several SABR books, including *Moments of Joy and Heartbreak: 66 Significant Episodes in the History of the Pittsburgh Pirates* (2018) and *Pride of Smoketown: The 1935 Pittsburgh Crawfords* (2020), as well as in *Nine: A Journal of Baseball History and Culture; Black Ball; The National Pastime; The*

Cooperstown Symposium on Baseball and American Culture proceedings; Zisk; and Spitball. He and his wife, Clare, have four children, Casey, Aaron, Josh, and Addie.

CARL RIECHERS retired from United Parcel Service in 2012 after 35 years of service. With more free time, he became a SABR member that same year. Born and raised in the suburbs of St. Louis, he became a big fan of the Cardinals. He and his wife, Janet, have three children and he is the proud grandpa of two.

JUAN JOSE RODRIGUEZ is a senior consultant with EY's Business Transformation practice. He graduated from the University of Notre Dame's Mendoza College of Business in 2019 with a degree in business analytics, along with a second major in film, television and theatre and a minor in journalism. While on campus, Rodriguez worked for Fighting Irish Media as a play-by-play announcer and color commentator for more than 200 live events on ESPN's and NBC's digital platforms. He also served on the editorial staff of *Scholastic* Magazine, the nation's oldest continuously running collegiate publication, where he published 11 award-winning articles and led the staff as editor-in-chief during his senior year.

BENJAMIN SABIN is a baseball writer and editor for *Last Word on Sports*, editor-in-chief of *Cheap Seats Press*, and a baseball card artist. He enjoys keeping score at ballgames and prefers sauerkraut on his dogs. He is a proud SABR member since 2017.

MARK SIMON is a writer, editor and podcaster for Sports Info Solutions, and a longtime SABR member. He regularly interviews baseball players about their defensive excellence, so he purposely asked for an essay for this book that touched on Clemente's defense. Mark currently lives in Bethlehem, Pennsylvania.

GLEN SPARKS has a bachelor's degree in journalism from the University of Missouri and worked in community journalism for many years. He has coedited books for SABR and written several articles for BioProject and the Games Project. He and his wife, Pam, live in St. Louis with their cats, Lucy, Buster, and Kasper. His work on this book is dedicated to the memory of past felines Alfred, Sammy, Bob, and Teddy. They all watched him type.

WAYNE STRUMPFER has been a Giants fan since his dad took him to Candlestick Park to see a Dodgers-Giants game in May 1971. As a SABR member, he has combined his love of history and baseball to write about the 1970 All-Star Game, the seventh game of the 1971 World Series, and biographies of Mike Paul and Dave Dravecky. To support his baseball habit, Wayne is the general counsel for the Imperial Irrigation District, one of the largest water and power suppliers in California.

STEW THORNLEY is a baseball historian and author and a SABR member since 1979. Thornley's article, "Clemente's Entry into Organized Baseball: Hidden in Montreal?," appeared in *SABR 50 at 50: The Society for American Baseball Research's Fifty Essential Contributions to the Game.* His most recent book edited for SABR is *Metropolitan Stadium: Memorable Games at Minnesota's Diamond on the Prairie*

THOMAS E. VAN HYNING was born in Washington, D.C., and grew up in Santurce, Puerto Rico. He was fascinated by Winter League baseball. As a 12-year-old, he attended a December 1966 Roberto Clemente baseball clinic at Hiram Bithorn Stadium, where Clemente played and managed between October 1963 and January 1971. Tom served as stateside correspondent for the Puerto Rico Professional Baseball Hall of Fame, 1991-1996, and authored *Puerto Rico's*

Winter League, The Santurce Crabbers, chapters on Caribbean baseball, blogs for beisbol101.com, and negroleaguerspuertorico.com. He has written SABR bios and articles for *The National Pastime* and *Baseball Research Journal.* A charter member of SABR's Cool Papa Bell (Mississippi) Chapter, Tom was tourism economist/data analyst, Mississippi Development Authority.

STEVEN C. WEINER, a SABR member since 2015, is a retired chemical engineer and a lifelong baseball fan starting with the Brooklyn Dodgers of the 1950s. During his undergraduate years at Rutgers University, Steven worked in the sports information office and broadcast baseball and basketball play-by-play on WRSU radio. Steven obtained his doctoral degree in engineering and applied science from Yale University and has been a contributor to the technical literature on hydrogen and fuel-cell safety. Steven currently serves as assignments editor for the SABR Games Project with essay contributions in six SABR books, the *Baseball Research Journal,* and *Jackie Robinson 75: Baseball's Re-Integration.* He volunteers as an in-classroom teacher at local schools.

GREGORY H. WOLF was born in Pittsburgh, but now resides in the Chicagoland area with his wife, Margaret, and daughter, Gabriela. A professor of German studies and holder of the Dennis and Jean Bauman Endowed Chair in the Humanities at North Central College in Naperville, Illinois, he has edited more than a dozen books for SABR. Since January 2017 he has been co-director of SABR's BioProject, which you can follow on Facebook and Twitter.

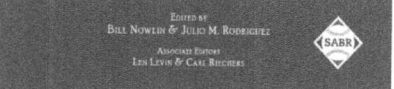

More from SABR

Available in paperback and ebook (Disponible en español y ingles)

Puerto Rico and Baseball: 60 Biographies

edited by Bill Nowlin and Edwin Fernandez

Puerto Rico and Baseball: 60 Biographies contains 60 biographies of players—but it also has two "ballpark bios" and an article on major-league games played in Puerto Rico, both spring training exhibition games and regular-season games from the time when "Los Expos" included San Juan as their home base.

This book highlights pioneers who played in the Negro Leagues, right up through Ivan Rodriguez, elected in 2017 to the National Baseball Hall of Fame. In reading this book you will get to know Perucho, who was compared with Ty Cobb and called the Babe Ruth of Puerto Rico; why Pancho Coimbre was considered one of the best hitters; the story of the great Roberto Clemente; who was "el Divino Loco," the first pitcher to win a major-league game on the Pacific Coast; who was "El Jibaro"; and even the great achievements of the man who was possibly the most complete catcher who ever stepped on a diamond.

Cuban Baseball Legends

edited by Peter C. Bjarkman and Bill Nowlin

Minnie Miñoso. Martín Dihigo. Luis Tiant. Orlando "El Duque" and Liván Hernández. These are some of the stars profiles in Cuban Baseball Legends. Out of the legions of memorable figures from the isle of Cuba who have made their mark on the game of baseball, 47 are included in this volume. For over a century and a half, Cuba has been a nation with an immense love for baseball, making it not a national pastime, but a national passion. These biographies were researched and written by members of SABR and was the first SABR book to be translated and published in Spanish.

Dominicans in the Major Leagues

edited by Bill Nowlin and Julio M. Rodriguez

Any fan of present-day Major League Baseball recognizes that the Dominican Republic is well-represented by many key players throughout the sport. Around 800 natives of the Dominican Republic have played in the majors—a full 300 more than any country outside of the United States. The first was Pedro Alejandro San, who pitched in the Eastern Colored League in 1926 for the Cuban Stars East. Later came Tetelo Vargas and Horacio "Rabbit" Martinez to the Negro Leagues. Osvaldo "Ozzie" Virgil was the first in the National League in 1956 with the New York Giants. In 1983, Juan Marichal became the first Dominican inducted into the National Baseball Hall of Fame in Cooperstown. He has since been joined by Pedro Martinez, Vladimir Guerrero, and David Ortiz, and no one doubts that many more will follow, as Dominican stars continue to shine in the major leagues. Also included: biographies Felipe, Jesús, and Matty Alou, Sammy Sosa, Raul Mondesi, and Fernando Tatis, as well as a recap of the Dominican team's passionate, action-packed sweep of the 2013 World Baseball Classic.

Visit SABR.org for more information

SABR Books on the Negro Leagues and Black Baseball

From Rube to Robinson: SABR's Best Articles on Black Baseball

From Rube to Robinson brings together the best Negro League baseball scholarship that the Society of American Baseball Research (SABR) has ever produced, culled from its journals, Biography Project, and award-winning essays. The book includes a star-studded list of scholars and historians, from the late Jerry Malloy and Jules Tygiel, to award winners Larry Lester, Geri Strecker, and Jeremy Beer, and a host of other talented writers. The essays cover topics ranging over nearly a century, from 1866 and the earliest known Black baseball championship, to 1962 and the end of the Negro American League.

Edited by John Graf; Associate Editors Duke Goldman and Larry Lester
$24.95 paperback (ISBN 978-1-970159-41-7)
$9.99 ebook (ISBN 978-1-970159-40-0)
8.5"X11", 220 pages

Pride of Smoketown: The 1935 Pittsburgh Crawfords

The 1935 Pittsburgh Crawfords team, one of the dominant teams in Negro League history, is often compared to the legendary 1927 "Murderer's Row" New York Yankees. The squad from "Smoketown"—a nickname that the *Pittsburgh Courier* often applied to the metropolis better-known as "Steel City"—boasted four Hall-of-Fame players in outfielder James "Cool Papa" Bell, first baseman/manager Oscar Charleston, catcher Josh Gibson, and third baseman William "Judy" Johnson. This volume contains exhaustively-researched articles about the players, front office personnel, Greenlee Field, and the exciting games and history of the team that were written and edited by 25 SABR members. The inclusion of historical photos about every subject in the book helps to shine a spotlight on the 1935 Pittsburgh Crawfords, who truly were the Pride of Smoketown.

Edited by Frederick C. Bush and Bill Nowlin
$29.95 paperback (ISBN 978-1-970159-25-7)
$9.99 ebook (ISBN 978-1-970159-24-0)
8.5"X11", 340 pages, over 60 photos

The Newark Eagles Take Flight: The Story of the 1946 Negro League Champions

The Newark Eagles won only one Negro National League pennant during the franchise's 15-year tenure in the Garden State, but the 1946 squad that ran away with the NNL and then triumphed over the Kansas City Monarchs in a seven-game World Series was a team for the ages. The returning WWII veterans composed a veritable "Who's Who in the Negro Leagues" and included Leon Day, Larry Doby, Monte Irvin, and Max Manning, as well as numerous role players. Four of the Eagles' stars—Day, Doby, Irvin, and player/manager Raleigh "Biz" Mackey, as well as co-owner Effa Manley—have been enshrined in the National Baseball Hall of Fame in Cooperstown. In addition to biographies of the players, co-owners, and P.A. announcer, there are also articles about Newark's Ruppert Stadium, Leon Day's Opening Day no-hitter, a sensational midseason game, the season's two East-West All-Star Games, and the 1946 Negro League World Series between the Eagles and the renowned Kansas City Monarchs.

Edited by Frederick C. Bush and Bill Nowlin
$24.95 paperback (ISBN 978-1-970159-07-3)
$9.99 ebook (ISBN 978-1-970159-06-6)
8.5"X11", 228 pages, over 60 photos

Bittersweet Goodbye: The Black Barons, The Grays, and the 1948 Negro League World Series

This book was inspired by the last Negro League World Series ever played and presents biographies of the players on the two contending teams in 1948—the Birmingham Black Barons and the Homestead Grays—as well as the managers, the owners, and articles on the ballparks the teams called home. Also included are articles that recap the season's two East-West All-Star Games, the Negro National League and Negro American League playoff series, and the World Series itself. Additional context is provided in essays about the effects of baseball's integration on the Negro Leagues, the exodus of Negro League players to Canada, and the signing away of top Negro League players, specifically Willie Mays. Many of the players' lives and careers have been presented to a much greater extent than previously possible.

Edited by Frederick C. Bush and Bill Nowlin
$21.95 paperback (ISBN 978-1-943816-55-2)
$9.99 ebook (ISBN 978-1-943816-54-5)
8.5"X11", 442 pages, over 100 photos and images